THE JOHN HARVARD LIBRARY

A FOOL'S ERRAND

By
ALBION W. TOURGEE

Edited by John Hope Franklin

THE BELKNAP PRESS OF
HARVARD UNIVERSITY PRESS
Cambridge, Massachusetts
London, England

10   9   8   7

Library of Congress Catalog Card Number 61-13744
ISBN 0-674-30751-8

Printed in the United States of America

CONTENTS

CONTENTS

ALBION TOURGEE, SOCIAL CRITIC

I<small>N</small> July 1877, Albion Winegar Tourgée, late of the 105th Ohio Volunteers and more recently of the Superior Court of North Carolina, spent a sleepless Saturday night in Raleigh, North Carolina. He was reviewing the exciting events that had occurred since he settled in the state in 1865. Early the following morning he aroused his wife and exclaimed, "I am going to write a book and call it 'A Fool's Errand.'"[1] His sojourn in the South was coming to a close. At the time, he was serving as pension agent, a position to which he had been appointed by President Grant. Tourgée was reluctantly reaching the conclusion that the venture begun on a note of high hope at the close of the war was now an utter, abject failure. The final admission would come with his return to the North in 1879 and the writing of *A Fool's Errand: By One of The Fools*.[2]

Tourgée's life, not merely the Reconstruction years, had been full of excitement. Perhaps high adventure was a family tradition. His paternal ancestors had become exiles when the revocation of the Edict of Nantes in 1685 made it unsafe for Huguenots to remain in France. They made their way across the Atlantic, going successively to Rhode Island, Massachusetts, and Ohio. Some of his maternal forebears were from the German Palatinate, others came from England on the *Mayflower* and finally made their way to the Western Reserve. There, Tourgée's mother and father met and married. Of the

[1] Roy F. Dibble, *Albion W. Tourgée* (New York, 1921), p. 60. I am grateful to Otto H. Olsen for sharing with me the findings in his "A Carpetbagger: Albion W. Tourgée and Reconstruction in North Carolina," unpublished Ph.D. dissertation (Johns Hopkins University, 1959), and "Albion W. Tourgée and the Controversial Carpetbagger," read at the Southern Historical Association, November 1959.

[2] New York, 1879.

three children born to Valentine and Louisa Winegar Tourgée, Albion, born in 1838, was the only one to survive infancy. The family moved frequently, before and after the mother's death in 1843. At fourteen Albion left his home in Kingsfield, Ohio, and went to live for two years with an uncle in Lee, Massachusetts. Upon returning he enrolled in the Kingsfield Academy.

At some point, perhaps while living with his uncle, Albion developed a love for books. By the time he entered the academy he was an avid reader and had begun to write. In 1857 he put together a group of poems and essays and called the unpublished volume "Sense and Nonsense." Two years later he was admitted to the sophomore class of the University of Rochester. Albion was restless, however, and in 1861 he withdrew from the university and took a teaching position in a school in Wilson, New York. In 1862 he received the degree of Bachelor of Arts in keeping with the practice of granting degrees to men who entered the service before completing the requirements for the degree. In Tourgée's case this was a most liberal concession, for he had withdrawn from the university *before* the outbreak of hostilities. Perhaps his promptness in entering the service after the war began had something to do with the university's granting him the degree the following year.[3]

In the first week of the war Tourgée enlisted in the 27th New York Volunteers and was soon off to the battle front. On July 4, 1861, he received a serious spinal injury at the first battle of Bull Run. He later claimed that he lost an eye in the battle, but his intimates insist that he had suffered this misfortune in a childhood accident.[4] The spinal injury was so severe that he was discharged from the army in August

[3] In 1880 the University of Rochester awarded Tourgée the degree of Doctor of Laws. In 1883 he received the honorary degree of Doctor of Philosophy from the University of Copenhagen. Dibble, *Tourgée*, p. 21.

[4] Olsen, "Tourgée and the Controversial Carpetbagger," p. 5.

1861. He never fully recovered, but by July 1862 he had sufficiently regained his health to re-enter the army as a lieutenant with Company G of the 105th Ohio Volunteers. In October he saw action at the battle of Perryville in Kentucky, where once again he received a spinal injury which hospitalized him for several weeks.[5]

Meanwhile, Tourgée was having other difficulties. In September 1862 he was arrested for insubordination. His offense was in refusing to obey orders to surrender a Negro who had saved his company. Apparently, Tourgée was not detained long, for he was out of the hospital in time to join his company for action in Tennessee early in 1863. In January he was captured by the enemy. He was a restless, perhaps an incorrigible prisioner. On one occasion he attempted to run away but was recaptured. In May he was exchanged. He promptly went to Ohio, where he married his Kingsfield Academy sweetheart, Emma Lodoiska Kilbourne, before returning to his comrades in arms.

Between May 1863 and January 1864, when he resigned from the army, Tourgée saw action on many fronts. He was in the battles of Tullohoma, Chickamauga, Lookout Mountain, and Missionary Ridge. When he left the army he returned to Ohio where he resumed his intermittent preparation for the bar, to which he was admitted in May 1864. He did not engage in the practice of the law with any regularity, for within a few months he was teaching at the Erie Academy. But this seemed not to satisfy him.[6]

Tourgée continued to suffer from the injuries he received in the war. He had, moreover, begun to entertain the notion that in the South, which was soon to begin a gigantic program of economic and political recovery, he would have an oppor-

[5] Tourgée has written the full history of the 105th Ohio Volunteers in *The Story of A Thousand* (Buffalo, 1896).

[6] Dibble, *Tourgée*, p. 31.

tunity not only to recover his health but to build a fortune and a life of constructive service. Therefore he went south in July 1865 to look for a place to settle. In Raleigh, North Carolina, he worked for several weeks as counsel in a court martial. Then he went to Georgia, where he visited several places. Upon returning to North Carolina he decided to remain in Greensboro, to which he moved with his wife in October.

The North Carolina into which Tourgée moved had not been a decisive battleground in the struggle with the North. There were suffering and privation, of course, but no real devastation except that which Sherman's men committed when they were en route to their encampment and demobilization in Alexandria, Virginia. It was an attractive area for settlers from less fortunate Confederate states and for carpetbaggers from the North. While Tourgée may be classified as a carpetbagger, it is improper to group him with those settlers from the North who have been opprobriously described as impecunious "soldiers of fortune" and who expected to get something for nothing in the South. After all, when Tourgée arrived with his wife in Greensboro in October 1865, he brought $5,000, which he immediately invested in a nursery business that unfortunately was not successful. By that time, however, Tourgée was deeply immersed in the political controversies of a state in the throes of Reconstruction.

North Carolina was not among the former Confederate states with which President Lincoln sought to resume normal relations before his assassination in mid-April 1865. Congress summarily rejected his efforts to bring Louisiana, Tennessee, Arkansas, and Virginia back into the Union.[7] They were hostile to his lenient ten-per-cent plan and apparently hoped to force him to be more severe or, better still, they would take the matter into their own hands. When Andrew Johnson

[7] John H. Franklin, *Reconstruction after the Civil War* (Chicago, 1961).

assumed the presidency on April 15, 1865, no Confederate state had returned to the Union. Johnson, attempting to assume Lincoln's role, adopted a similar plan for Reconstruction and issued a proclamation of amnesty similar to the one that Lincoln had issued late in 1863. He then turned to the task of reconstructing North Carolina. He appointed W. W. Holden provisional governor and called on the loyal people of the state to meet in a convention to make the constitutional changes that would facilitate their return to the Union. A convention then repealed the Ordinance of Secession, declared slavery abolished, repudiated the state war debt, and provided for the election of new state officials and of members of Congress.

It was during the course of these developments that Albion Tourgée settled in Greensboro. He witnessed the defeat of Holden and the election of Jonathan Worth, the state treasurer under the Confederacy, as governor of the state, and the refusal of Congress to seat the representatives and senators who were elected in November.[8] Negroes, already apprehensive about what the new government might do, had met in convention in October and had asked for protection and an opportunity for education. They also called for an end to legal discriminations against them.[9] While they did not make a formal request that the suffrage be extended to them, several leaders were already openly advocating that Negroes be permitted to vote. While the new legislature declared that Negroes were entitled to the same privileges as whites in suits at law and in equity, such privileges were clear only in cases where the rights and property of persons of color were involved. In the apprenticeship system that was established, former masters were to have preference over all other persons

[8] J. G. de Roulhac Hamilton, *Reconstruction in North Carolina* (New York, 1914), p. 134.
[9] *Ibid.*, p. 150.

in making selections of apprentices. There were other similar distinctions against which the Negroes had pleaded.[10]

Tourgée observed with interest the dramatic events that occurred during his first year of residence in North Carolina. He became convinced that the policies adopted by the state government would not only prevent the resumption of normal relations with the federal government but make peace and justice impossible. Soon he was expressing his views openly and, in the opinion of some, indiscreetly. At a meeting in August 1866 he came out for Negro suffrage. At the Philadelphia Convention of Loyalists in the following month, Tourgée, as a delegate, spoke with feeling on the subject and called for national support of his proposal. He described some alleged atrocities against North Carolina Negroes and insisted that neither Negroes nor Union whites were safe from attacks by the former Confederates. At least 1,200 Union soldiers, Tourgée asserted, had been forced to sacrifice their property and flee the state to save their lives.

The news of Tourgée's Philadelphia performance reached North Carolina before his return, and the adverse reaction and comment were immediate. Governor Worth was especially outraged. He called the speech "a tissue of lies from beginning to end." He called on the people of North Carolina to repudiate this "vile wretch." "If the truth were known, all good men at the North would respect and honor us but Tourgée and other like villians [sic], by a continual stream of slander, lead many to think where there is so much smoke there must be some fire." [11] Some North Carolinians began to write threatening letters to Tourgée. One declared that he would give him a coat of tar and feathers if his "lying tung"

[10] *Ibid.*, pp. 153–154.

[11] Jonathan Worth to Nerens Mendenhall, September 6, 1866, and Jonathan Worth to B. S. Hedrick, September 18, 1866, in J. G. de Roulhac Hamilton (ed.), *The Correspondence of Jonathan Worth* (Raleigh, 1909), II, 772–773 and 786.

was not stopped.[12] Tourgée would not stop, and the only cognizance he took of the threats was to obtain permission to carry firearms for personal protection.

By 1867 Tourgée was so immersed in the political life of the state that he gave up most of his other activities. Already he had organized the Union League in Guilford County and had become the first president of the state council. In January he began publishing *The Union Register*. Although it vigorously espoused the cause of Radical Reconstruction at a time when it was in the ascendancy, the newspaper suspended publication at the end of six months. Later in the year General E. R. S. Canby was inclined to appoint Tourgée to a judgeship made vacant by the resignation of Daniel G. Fowle, but he learned that Worth had asserted that Tourgée was of bad moral character. Upon inquiry, Canby received from the governor the declaration that Tourgée was a man "of most detestable character." Worth listed more than a score of prominent citizens who agreed with his appraisal of Tourgée, and he was gleeful upon learning that the hated carpetbagger from Ohio failed to secure the appointment.[13]

Tourgée was not daunted by this defeat. The former Confederates in North Carolina had already suffered a setback, as Congress took over the program of Reconstruction and laid down conditions that placed the advantage in the hands of the group of which Tourgée was a member. Among those who were elected delegates to the new constitutional convention early in 1868, Tourgée was prominent. He was active and influential in shaping the new constitution. In his unsuccessful advocacy of the repudiation of the entire state debt, he said that one would be a fool to migrate to North Carolina "if the new State is to be saddled with the debts of the old." [14]

[12] Dibble, *Tourgée*, p. 36.
[13] Jonathan Worth to E. R. S. Canby, January 9, 1868, in Hamilton, *Correspondence of Jonathan Worth*, II, 1124.
[14] Hamilton, *Reconstruction in North Carolina*, p. 263.

He was more successful in getting the convention to authorize the codification of all the laws of the state. Tourgée, Victor
C. Barringer, and W. B. Rodman were appointed commis-
sioners, at $200 per month, to undertake the task, which they
completed before the end of the year.[15]

In the elections of 1868 Tourgée hoped to go to Congress,
but he failed to secure his party's nomination. He seemed
content, however, with his nomination to the Superior Court,
with jurisdiction over eight counties. His enemies fought him,
but to no avail. Governor Worth incorrectly asserted that
Tourgée was not a member of the North Carolina bar. Others
claimed that he had served a prison term of more than four
years in Ohio for burglary. This Tourgée indignantly denied,
offering a reward of $1000 to any person who could establish
this as a fact. His election by a majority of 25,000 caused
Governor Worth to remark that this was "a very striking exhibit of the workings of Reconstruction." [16]

During his six years on the bench Tourgée displayed
abilities that surprised his enemies. He came to be regarded as
one of the best judges in the state, and even one of his most
unfriendly critics conceded that he was "a most capable judge
in all cases where politics could not enter." [17] He was utterly
fearless; and from the bench he excoriated white North Carolinians, especially the Klan, for their mistreatment of the
Negro. Frequently he received threatening letters from his
enemies, some of whom were gracious enough to notify him
that he was to be assassinated at a particular time. In the summer of 1870 the Klan was greatly incensed when a letter
from Tourgée to Governor Holden was published. In it
Tourgée renewed his attack on the Klan, citing several specific
cases of outrage against the Negroes. Soon, even the fearless

[15] Victor C. Barringer, Will B. Rodman, and Albion W. Tourgée, *The
Code of Civil Procedure, to Special Pleadings* (Raleigh, 1868).

[16] Jonathan Worth to the Editors of the *Wilmington Journal*, Febru-
ary 3, 1869, in Hamilton, *The Correspondence of Jonathan Worth*, II, 1276.

[17] Hamilton, *Reconstruction in North Carolina*, p. 414.

Tourgée began to be anxious for the safety of his family, including his infant daughter. For the first time he entertained serious thoughts of leaving the state.[18]

Tourgée attempted to "lose" himself in ill-fated business ventures, in writing articles and novels, and in his judicial duties. His enemies continued to harass him. In 1873 they made an unsuccessful attempt to remove him from office. When his term was up in 1876 President Grant appointed him to the position of pension agent in Raleigh, and Tourgée seemed relieved to be off the bench. He had not escaped his traducers, however; and he took his final fling at them in the "C" letters, published in Greensboro in the spring of 1878. In these he attacked the Klan, defended Negroes, and sneered at Democrats who presumed that they were qualified to fill offices of public trust. These were his valedictory. Within a year he was closing his business affairs and preparing to leave. In the summer of 1879 he and his family headed north. The fool's errand had come to an end.[19]

Tourgée's residence of fourteen years in North Carolina had provided him with abundant materials for the literary efforts in which he engaged even before he returned to the North. He had doubtless reached the conclusion that the South was beyond his powers to save. He said as much in an interview granted a reporter of the New York *Tribune* in September 1879. The South was still a most attractive source of materials for the writer. Even before he returned to the North he had predicted that Southern life would furnish the future American novelist with his richest and most striking material. Later he was to assert, not without some bitter memories, that the romantic possibilities of the South appealed to him "even more vividly than its political difficulty." [20]

[18] Dibble, *Tourgée*, pp. 44–45.
[19] *Ibid.*, pp. 57–58.
[20] Albion W. Tourgée, "The South as A Field for Fiction," *Forum*, VI (1888), 404.

Certainly in his last years in North Carolina he devoted an increasing amount of time to writing. There were political articles published in newspapers under the nom de plume, "Wenckar." Others were signed, "God's Anynted Phue." [21]

The most important work of the North Carolina years was *Toinette*, written in 1868–1869 and published in 1874 under the nom de plume, Henry Churton. It was republished under Tourgée's own name in 1881 as *The Royal Gentleman*. The novel was written at the height of Tourgée's intense feeling that slavery debased the master as much as the slave and that the Civil War had scarcely affected the attitudes of the Southern whites toward Negroes. Thus, after the war the royal gentleman, Geoffrey Hunter, was outraged when his former slave, Toinette, would not resume her pre-war intimacy with him unless he married her and made legitimate his child, born before the war. Replete with melodramatic episodes, *The Royal Gentleman* gave Tourgée many opportunities to denounce slavery, praise Lincoln and the Union cause, and to illustrate the corrosive effect of slavery on the character of the Southern whites.

On that Sunday morning in July 1877 when Tourgée told his wife that he would write a novel and call it *A Fool's Errand*, he proceeded immediately to work on the book. At the time, however, he wrote only three chapters, and did not take up the project again until shortly before he left the state in 1879. He must have worked diligently and rapidly. On October 4, 1879, his *Figs and Thistles*, a success story of the rise of a young man of humble origins to wealth and political power in the North, was published. Some believed that this was a thinly veiled biography of James A. Garfield, who was already a candidate for the Republican presidential nomination the following year. Six weeks later *A Fool's Errand* appeared, and almost immediately the author, one of the

[21] Dibble, *Tourgée*, p. 47.

fools, was being widely acclaimed as one of the most successful novelists of recent years.

While *A Fool's Errand* cannot be regarded as autobi-
ographical, many of the incidents in it are remarkably similar
to ones that had happened to Tourgée himself during his
North Carolina sojourn. Some were based on the experiences
of other people. All the issues and principal circumstances
were, as in his other works, "pictures . . . from life." [22]
Comfort Servosse, the fool, was an educated Northerner of
French ancestry, as was Tourgée. His main reasons for taking up residence were the same as Tourgée's: to live in a mild
climate that would be congenial to his afflictions and to build
a fortune with the capital he had already accumulated. Metta
Servosse is obviously modeled on Tourgée's wife, while his
mentor, the Reverend Enos Martin, is reminiscent of Tourgée's close friend, President M. B. Anderson of the University
of Rochester.

The threats against the life of Servosse are similar to those
frequently directed against Tourgée, especially while he
served as judge of the Superior Court. The exciting chapter,
"A Race Against Time," in which Lily Servosse foils a Klan
plot against her father's life, is perhaps inspired by Tourgée's
discovery of a Klan plot to murder him one day as he left his
courtroom.[23] The numerous other activities of the Klan in
A Fool's Errand are similar to those compiled by Tourgée
during his term of office as judge and published as an appendix
entitled "The Invisible Empire" in later editions of the novel.

There was also in *A Fool's Errand* Tourgée's view that the
North and South did not understand each other. This was
illustrated in their conflicting views of the carpetbagger. "To
the Southern mind it meant a scion of the North, a son of an

---

[22] *A Fool's Errand, By One of the Fools* (New York, 1879), "Letter to
the Publishers."
[23] *Ibid.*, chap. xxxvi.

'abolitionist,' a creature of the conqueror, a witness to their defeat, a mark of their degradation: to them he was hateful, because he recalled all of evil or shame they had ever known. . . . To the Northern mind, however, the word had no vicarious significance. To their apprehension, the hatred was purely personal, and without regard to race or nativity." [24]

In this work, as in many of Tourgée's other writings, there is the recurring theme that slavery debased the moral character of the slaveholder. In a very frank discussion between Servosse and his neighbor, Squire Hyman, a former slaveholder, Servosse speaks of the vehement intolerance of the average Southerner and his refusal to discuss on its merits even the very fundamental problem of the place of the Negro in the post-war South. " 'It is just such intolerance as this, Squire, which makes it next to impossible for the South to accept its present situation. You all want to shoot, whip, hang, and burn those who do not agree with you. It is all the fruit and outcome of two hundred years of slavery: in fact, it is part and parcel of it,' said Servosse." [25]

Another strong conviction that Tourgée held was that the Negro's survival required he be granted a measure of political equality. Servosse airs these views in a speech he is called upon to make before a hostile audience during the early months of his "Errand." In part, he says, "The practical question for you to consider is, How far and how fast shall the freedmen be enfranchised? . . . If you of your own volition will enfranchise a part of them, marked by some definite classification, — of intelligence, property, or what not, — and the others as they reach that development, it will suffice at this time. Wait, hesitate, refuse, and all will be enfranchised at the same time by the General Government." [26]

[24] *Ibid.*, chap. xxvi.
[25] *Ibid.*, chap. xv.
[26] *Ibid.*, chap. xii.

Thus there are numerous occasions and incidents in the novel that give Tourgée the opportunity to express with feeling the views he held on the problems of the South. It was only natural that he should make a general appraisal of the post-war period. "Reconstruction was a failure," he says, "so far as it attempted to unify the nation, to make one people in fact of what had been one only in name before the convulsion of war. It was a failure, too, so far as it attempted to fix and secure the position and rights of the colored race. They were fixed, it is true, on paper, and security of a certain sort taken to prevent the abrogation of that formal declaration. No guaranty whatever was provided against their practical subversion, which was accomplished with an ease and impunity that amazed those who instituted the movement." [27]

Tourgée was of the opinion that the South abounded in romantic possibilities for the writer of fiction, and he made full use of them in this and many other works. The novel has its share of contrivances and coincidences. It has its love affair and its melodramatic situations. But it also has its moments of pathos, suffering, and even stark tragedy. Above all, it has a message about sectional and racial problems that is never subordinated to less important matters.

Critical reaction to *A Fool's Errand* was varied, but everywhere there was immediately great interest in the work upon publication. The reviewer in *Harper's* asserted that "whoever takes up the volume . . . with the expectation that it is a novel of the stereotyped stripe will not remain under such a delusion." He then characterized it as an "earnest and at times passionate philippic . . . against the wisdom of the reconstruction policy that was adopted at the close of the late war." [28] The *Atlantic* said that the work was "not fiction, but history, and the weight with which it lies on the mind

[27] *Ibid.*, chap. xlv.
[28] *Harper's New Monthly Magazine*, LX (1880), 472.

of the reader is not the weight of imaginary woes. . . . It
is rare to find an author, with wrongs before him like those
which are portrayed in A Fool's Errand, who has the courage
and the conscience to turn, so clearly as he does, the best side
of the wrong-doer before one, and it is because this best side
is in part the explanation of the wrong that the historical honesty of the book is forced upon the reader." [29]

Although most reviewers gave some attention to the melodramatic aspects of the book, they were concerned primarily
with the major problems with which the book dealt. "The
story is given only to float the political and social study
which the book really is," the *Nation* declared. The author
had pursued his study with "great candor and no small dis-
crimination," the writer concluded.[30] In the South the Raleigh
Observer was rather generous in conceding that it "is a powerfully written work and destined, we fear, to do as much harm
in the world as 'Uncle Tom's Cabin,' to which it is, indeed, a
companion piece." [31] In one of the printings in 1880 the
publishers included in the front matter excerpts from more
than fifty very favorable reviews in the daily press. They
ranged from the influential papers of New York City and
Boston to small sheets in Okolona, Mississippi, and Troy,
New York.[32]

The interest of the general public in the work was manifested in a very tangible way. In its first six weeks of publication the book sold 5,281 copies. By the middle of 1880 it
had sold more than 43,000 copies. During that summer the
sales were so lively that the publishers made duplicate plates
and printed the work simultaneously in New York and Boston.
In early December the New York *Tribune* said, "No book
on the shop counter sells better and the fame of it has been

[29] *Atlantic Monthly*, XLVI (1880), 422-424.
[30] *The Nation*, XXIX (1879), 444.
[31] Press notice in one of the 1880 printings of *A Fool's Errand*, p. 2.
[32] *Ibid.*, pp. 1-4.

carried on the wings of newspapers into every state if not county in the land." By the end of the year approximately 90,000 copies had been sold.[33]

During its second year the success of *A Fool's Errand* was not as marked as during its first year, although a significant addition doubtless stimulated the sales. This was Tourgée's "The Invisible Empire," which was not available except as Part Two of *A Fool's Errand*. It has been estimated that the total sales may have finally reached 200,000, if one includes several pirated editions in England as well as in the United States.[34] This would be a good record for a novel of this type in any period. For the 1880's it was remarkable.

From the date of publication there was lively speculation over the identity of the author of *A Fool's Errand*. The publishers apparently enjoyed teasing the public by recounting some of these speculations in later printings of the book. The Chicago *Tribune* said, "One reasonable guess is, that the writer is Edmund Kirke, well known for his picture of the South in 'Among the Pines.' But since the book has been compared, and properly so, to 'Uncle Tom's Cabin,' why not make the parallel complete by attributing it to the same author?" The Boston *Daily Advertiser* did not attempt to name the author. "Who the author is we do not know. . . . It is evident that he possesses in an uncommon degree the traits of a strong and accomplished writer, and the power of constructing and narrating a story which is at once intensely interesting and profoundly thoughtful." The New York *Tribune* mentioned the governor of South Carolina, General Adelbert Ames of Mississippi, Tourgée, and several others. The speculation finally ceased when "The Invisible Empire" appeared in the same volume with *A Fool's Errand*, with Tourgée's name on the title page as the author of both works.[35]

[33] Dibble, *Tourgée*, p. 69.
[34] *Ibid*.
[35] *Ibid*.

"The Invisible Empire" was added to *A Fool's Errand* as an irrefutable documentation of the claims made in the novel. The greater portion of the incidents in the novel were actual occurrences, Tourgée insisted, "of which the author had either personal cognizance or authentic information." Many of these "occurrences" and, indeed, many more are recounted in this elaborate appendix. In it Tourgée carefully traced the rise, scope, purpose, and activities of the Ku Klux Klan, relying heavily on the Report of the Joint Congressional Committee on the Ku Klux conspiracy. This was a most difficult task, Tourgée asserted, "because of the superabundance of material from which selection must be made to bring the result within proper bounds. . . ." [36]

A Fool's Errand won for Tourgée a prominent place in political and literary circles. When the author visited the Republican National Convention in Chicago in 1880 he met James A. Garfield, who had read and enjoyed the book. After Garfield was nominated, he invited Tourgée to assist him in placing before the public some of the basic issues in the campaign. Tourgée accepted with alacrity and worked diligently throughout the campaign. When Garfield won the election, Tourgée sent a telegram to the President-elect saying," The family of fools send greeting." Garfield replied, "I thank you for your kind greeting from the 'Family of Fools,' and in return express the hope that the day may come when our country will be a paradise for all such fools." Later, Tourgée urged Garfield to support a program of federal aid to education as the only way to solve the South's major problems. Garfield agreed, but before he could institute such a program he was dead from an assassin's bullet.[37]

In the spring of 1881 *A Fool's Errand* was presented in dra-

[36] Albion W. Tourgée, *A Fool's Errand By One of The Fools* and *The Invisible Empire* (New York, 1880), pp. 385–386.
[37] Albion W. Tourgée, *An Appeal to Caesar* (New York, 1884), pp. 9, 17.

matic form, without the author's permission, in the West. The slight success of the presentation moved Tourgée to warn literary pirates that they would be prosecuted if they did not desist. He then decided to undertake such a dramatization himself. After one of Tourgée's lectures in New York, he met Steele MacKaye, the actor-producer, and they agreed to collaborate in the dramatization of Tourgée's novel. They planned to complete that task in time for the presentation of the play during the autumn tour of the MacKaye company. MacKaye was troubled not only by lack of funds (these Tourgée promised to raise), but also by Tourgée's insistence that MacKaye follow his suggestions in writing the script. On September 11, he wrote, "I send you herewith material which defines the position of Southern young men upon the Ku Klux question. It *must* be used . . . as its elements are *indispensable* to the success of the play." [38]

As late as a week before the opening, the fourth act was not yet written and several actors for leading parts had not been engaged. On October 26, 1881, the play opened at the Arch Street Theater in Philadelphia and, according to MacKaye, "was received with great enthusiasm by the audience." The performance would have done credit to any theater in New York, MacKaye wrote. The Philadelphia *North American* seemed to agree, when it praised the acting as well as the adaptation that had not destroyed the message of the novel. This, from MacKaye's point of view, was because he had cut out the "political verbiage of Judge Tourgée" and brought it down to his own dramatic action. "I have obtained laughter — applause — silence — tears, precisely where I calculated upon doing so. The money success is, of course, very moderate." This was apparently an understatement. Two weeks later, while playing in St. Louis, the show closed. The col-

[38] Percy MacKaye, *Epoch; The Life of Steele MacKaye* (New York, 1927), I, 416–417.

lapse was tersely summarized by MacKaye: "Business bad, company mutinous, body used up with fatigue." [39]

One Southerner was so outraged by Tourgée's strictures against the South that he decided to do something about it. William L. Royall was a Virginian who had fought in the Confederacy, studied law and practiced in Richmond until 1880, and then moved to New York, where he continued the practice of law. In the spring of 1881 he published *A Reply to "A Fool's Errand by One of the Fools."* He began by asserting that he was attempting to speak "for a race of whom the males are men, as I believe these men would have their race spoken for." Then followed a lengthy "Reply." In the first chapter, "A Pretender Unmasked," Royall said that Tourgée's book was small, "but it would be difficult to find more malice in a large one." To Royall *A Fool's Errand* was a "systematic and well-considered libel upon the people of the Southern States of this Union, and is very well calculated to do them a most foul injury and wrong."

Royall's criticism of Tourgée ranged from his improper and inaccurate use of Negro dialect to his analysis of North Carolina's political and economic problems. In a chapter entitled, "The Real Situation at the South," Royall attributed the principal difficulties in the Reconstruction period to the carpetbaggers of whom Tourgée was typical. He described the Reconstruction legislature of North Carolina as the "Carpetbag-Negro legislature" without bothering to discover that a majority of the members were native whites. He sought to impugn the integrity of Tourgée by pointing out that he had received more than $3,500 from the Swepson-Littlefield railroad ring, presumably to assist the ring in getting favors from the state.[40] Tourgée later replied that this was a business

[39] *Ibid.*, 419–429.
[40] William L. Royall, *A Reply To "A Fool's Errand, By One of the Fools* (New York, 1881). For another work inspired by Tourgée, see Rev.

transaction, a loan, that he had been unable to pay because of his losses in the panic of 1873. Far from assisting the ring in getting favors from the state, Tourgée had promoted the restriction of state aid to railroads.[41] It is to be doubted that Royall's work had any significant effect on the standing of Tourgée or his writings.

Tourgée later claimed that, many years earlier, he had conceived a series of works that would canvass the problems of the North and South. It would seem, however, that the pressure of his publishers to provide more of the same accounts for his continued efforts following the success of *A Fool's Errand*. By October 1880 he had completed *Bricks Without Straw*. Amid the story of the love and marriage of a Southern planter and a New England schoolmistress, Tourgée vigorously advances the idea that education will solve the principal problems created by Civil War and emancipation. By the end of the year more than 41,000 copies had been sold.

In the following year *Toinette* was reissued as *A Royal Gentleman*. In succeeding years there were other works, *John Eax* in 1882 and *Hot Plowshares* in 1883. The latter first ran serially in the short-lived magazine Tourgée published in Philadelphia in 1882–1883. It is concerned with the period before the Civil War and deals with the anti-slavery struggle "by tracing its growth and the influences of the sentiment upon contrasted characters." [42] It was neither a literary nor a financial success. It was well that Tourgée had concluded with *Hot Plowshares* his "historical novels" of the middle period.

Although Tourgée continued to write, he produced no other successes like *A Fool's Errand*. For a dozen years he was a regular contributor to the Chicago *Daily Inter-Ocean*,

J. H. Ingraham, *Not "A Fool's Errand"; Life And Experience of A Northern Governess in the Sunny South* (New York, 1880).

[41] Olsen, "Tourgée and the Controversial Carpetbagger," p. 8, and Jonathan Daniels, *Prince of Carpetbaggers* (Philadelphia, 1958), p. 145.

[42] See the preface.

and he published more novels and books, including two in 1887, *Black Ice* and *Button's Inn*, and, in 1888, *Eighty-Nine; or The Grand Master's Secret*, a thinly veiled attack on Standard Oil. None of his efforts brought financial success, and he continued to struggle against the bankruptcy that had stalked him as a result of several unsuccessful business ventures. In 1897 he was happy to accept from President McKinley an appointment as consul at Bordeaux, a post that he held until his death in 1905.[43]

With all their idealization and their polemics' *A Fool's Errand* and Tourgée's other novels of the middle period are important documents for a time in the nation's history that abounds in documentation but is strangely lacking in a constructive appraisal of it, even to this day. The value of *A Fool's Errand* lies in its fearless criticism not merely of the South for its post-war attitudes and policies but of the national government for its utter failure to come to grips with the fundamental problems raised by the war and its aftermath. At a time when public sentiment tended to frown on anything that might exacerbate the intersectional difficulties, Tourgée insisted on discussing the problem, because he was convinced that it had not been solved satisfactorily or, indeed, at all.

As a carpetbagger Tourgée was at once a confirmation and a refutation of contemporary and later views regarding this hated group. He was in the thick of the struggle to reconstitute the political life of his community. To this end he advocated Negro enfranchisement and supported programs that looked toward the economic independence of the Negro. But he was no mere adventurer in the South, and he disliked the self-seeking Northerner as much as he disliked the intransigent former Confederate. If he hated blind race prejudice and Klan violence, he was no equalitarian; and he distrusted blanket, unqualified enfranchisement of the Negro as much as he

---

[43] Dibble, *Tourgée*, pp. 124–131.

frowned on the wholesale disfranchisement of the rebel class. His political influence as a carpetbagger was by no means unlimited. His ambition to represent his district in Congress, for example, remained unfulfilled. In North Carolina, as in many other Southern states, carpetbeggers were in the minority and were unable to wield decisive influence. "The Fool" early discovered what would take others several generations to learn: that carpetbaggers, frequently few in number and with many aspirations that were at times in conflict with each other, could not always have their way.

In his understanding and interpretation of Reconstruction Tourgée would even today be regarded as radical. Over and over again he emphasized the fact that in the years immediately following the Civil War the former Confederates had control of their own state governments. It was during this period, he argued, that they clearly demonstrated their unwillingness or inability to face up to the implications of the surrender at Appomattox. In "The Invisible Empire" he made it clear that lawlessness and violence on the part of the former Confederates antedated the Ku Klux Klan and that it was not provoked by Radical Reconstruction but by the refusal of the former Confederates to change their ways of thinking and acting in 1865.

As an intelligent observer and participant in Southern Reconstruction, Tourgée was in an excellent position to provide his contemporaries and posterity with an important commentary and criticism of what he witnessed and experienced. He was a pioneer post-war social critic.[44] *A Fool's Errand* followed Mark Twain's *Gilded Age* by only a few years, and does for Southern Reconstruction what Twain's work does for political machinations in Washington and speculative activities in the West. In the case of Tourgée there is doubt-

[44] George J. Becker, "Albion W. Tourgée: Pioneer in Social Criticism," *American Literature*, XIX (1947), 59–72.

less more personal involvement and, thus, more passion and a
greater sense of urgency. But there was also greater optimism,
a deeper faith in the ultimate solution of the nation's problems.[45]

The man who regarded himself as a fool for having gone
into the post-war South confidently believing that he could
have a happy and constructive life there, left after more than
a decade, utterly disillusioned. He was convinced that education, and more education, was the only thing that could save
the South. Twenty years later, he was not so certain. Writing
to President Roosevelt to congratulate him for inviting
Booker T. Washington to dine at the White House, Tourgée expressed doubt that national education was the remedy
for the race problem. "It was a genuine fool's notion. I sincerely believed at the time that education and Christianity
were infallible solvents of all the evils which have resulted
from the white man's claim of individual superiority. Today
I am ashamed to have been that sort of a fool." [46]

John Hope Franklin

Brooklyn College
January 16, 1961

[45] Russel B. Nye, "Judge Tourgée and Reconstruction," *Ohio State
Archaeological and Historical Quarterly*, L (1941), 101–114.
[46] Dibble, *Tourgée*, p. 126. For Roosevelt's reply, see Joseph Bucklin
Bishop, *Theodore Roosevelt And His Time* (New York, 1920), 166.

EDITOR'S NOTE

There were numerous printings of *A Fool's Errand* in the year that followed its initial publication late in 1879. The John Harvard Library edition is based on an 1880 printing which incorporates changes Tourgée made after the book's first printing. A few typographical errors have been silently corrected, but with these exceptions, the text is now reissued exactly as it then appeared. The facsimile title page (see below, p. 1) is reproduced from the first edition of 1879.

A

FOOL'S ERRAND.

BY

ONE OF THE FOOLS.

VARR. SERV.   Thou art not altogether a fool.
FOOL.   Nor thou altogether a wise man: as much foolery
As I have, so much wit thou lackest.
Timon of Athens.

———◆———

NEW YORK:
FORDS, HOWARD, & HULBERT.
1879.

TO THE

ANCIENT AND HONORABLE FAMILY OF

FOOLS

THIS BOOK IS RESPECTFULLY AND LOVINGLY

DEDICATED

BY ONE OF THEIR NUMBER

LETTER TO THE PUBLISHERS

GENTLEMEN, — Your demand that I should write a "Preface" to the book you have printed seems to me utterly preposterous. It is like a man introducing himself, — always an awkward, and generally a useless piece of business. What is the use of the "prologue to the epic coming on," anyhow, unless it be a sort of advertisement? and in that case you ought to write it. Whoever does that should be

> "Wise enough to *play* the fool;
> And to do that well craves a sort of wit."

That is not the kind of Fool I am. All such work I delegate to you, and hereby authorize and empower you to say what you please of what I have written, only begging you keep in mind one clear distinction. There are two kinds of Fools. The real Fool is the most sincere of mortals: the Court Fool and his kind — the trifling, jesting buffoon — but simulate the family virtue, and steal the family name, for sordid purposes.

The life of the Fool proper is full of the poetry of faith. He may run after a will-o'-the-wisp, while the Wise deride; but to him it is a veritable star of hope. He differs from his fellow-mortals chiefly in this, that he sees or believes what they do not, and consequently undertakes what they never attempt. If he succeed in his endeavor, the world stops laughing, and calls him a Genius: if he fail, it laughs the more, and derides his undertaking as A FOOL'S ERRAND.

So the same individual is often both fool and genius, — a

fool all his life and a genius after his death, or a fool to one century and a genius to the next, or a fool at home and a prodigy abroad. Watt was a fool while he watched the tea-kettle, but a genius when he had caught the imp that tilted the lid. The gentle Genoese who wrested half the world from darkness was a fool to the age which sought for the Fountain of Youth; yet every succeeding one but multiplies his praises. These are but types. The poet has incorporated the recognized principle in the lines, —

"Great wits to madness, sure, are near allied,
And thin partitions do their walls divide."

It is, however, only in the element of simple, undoubting *faith*, that the kinship of genius and folly consists. One may be an unquestioned Fool without any chance of being taken for a Seer. This is, indeed, the case with most of the tribe. It is success alone that transforms the credulity of folly into acknowledged prophetic prevision.

Noah was one of the earliest of the Fools thus vindicated. The Wise Men of his day sat around on the dry-goods boxes, and whittled and whistled, and quizzed the queer craft on which he kept his sons and sons-in-law at work, till the keel was as old as the frigate "Constitution" before he was ready to lay her upper decks. If the rain had not come at last, they would never have got over laughing at his folly. The Deluge saved his reputation, and made his Ark a success. But it is not often that a Fool has a heavenly voice to guide him, or a flood to help him out.

This little tale is the narrative of one of Folly's failures. The hero can lay no claim to greatness. A believing Noah there is in it, a well-built ark, and an indubitable flood. But the waters prevailed, and the Fool went down, and many of the family with him. The Wise Men looked on and laughed.

The one merit which the story claims is that of honest, uncompromising truthfulness of portraiture. Its pictures are from life. And even in this which he boasts as a virtue may be found, perhaps, the greatest folly yet committed by

ONE OF THE FOOLS.

SEPTEMBER, 1879.

A FOOL'S ERRAND

CHAPTER I

THE GENESIS OF FOLLY

The Fool's patronymic was Servosse; his Christian name, Comfort. His father was descended from one of those Gallic families who abandoned the luxuries of *la belle France* for an Arcadia which in these later days has become synonymous with bleakness, if not sterility. It is supposable that his ancestors, before they adventured on the delights of Canadian winters in exchange for the coast of Normandy or the plains of Bordeaux, may have belonged to some noble family, who drew their blood, clear and blue, from the veins of a Martelian progenitor.

It is, perhaps, but fair to presume that the exchange of skies was made only for the glory of our gallant and good King Louis, and the advancement of the holy Catholic faith in the New World, rather than for the peace and quiet of the immediate vicinage in which the ancestor dwelt. However this may be, a later ancestor was among those, who, with that mixture of courage and suavity which enabled the *voyageurs* of that day so successfully to secure and hold the good will of the unsophisticated red-skin, pushed westward along the Great Lakes until they came to the Straits, where so many advantages of a trading-post were combined, that Detroit was there located and christened.

The mutations of government, the lapse of time, and the anglicization of their surroundings had robbed the descendants of the original Servosse of every trace of their Gallic ancestry except the name; and it is only mentioned here for the benefit

of some curious student of mental phenomena with credence
in hereditary traits, who may believe that an ancestor who
could voluntarily abandon the champagnes of Burgundy for
the Heights of Abraham, by whatever enticing name the same
might be called, was quite capable of transmitting to his descendants such an *accès de la folie* as was manifested by our
particular Fool.

Certainly, no such defect can be attributed to his maternal
line: they knew on which side their bread was buttered. Of
the truest of Puritan stock, the mother's family had found a
lodgment on a little hillside farm carved out of the Hop-Brook
Grant in Berkshire, which seemed almost as precarious in its
rocky ruggedness and inaccessibility as the barn-swallow's
nest, clinging in some mysterious way to the steep slope under
the eaves of the old hip-roofed barn against which it was
built. Yet, like the nest, the little hillside home had sufficed
for the raising of many a sturdy brood, who had flown away
to the constantly receding West almost before they had
grown to full-fledged man- and womanhood. Brave-hearted,
strong-limbed, and clear-headed, or, as they would now be
called, *level-headed*, were these children of the Berkshire hills.
There was no trace of mental unsoundness about any of them.
Especially free from such imputation was Eliza Hall, the
golden-haired, brown-eyed, youngest of nine, who, with her
saucily upturning nose, a few freckles on her round cheeks,
which made their peach-bloom all the more noticeable, —
despite the entreaties of friends, the prayers of lovers, and the
protest of parents, — would away to the West in her eight-
eenth year to become a Yankee schoolma'am in Michigan.

That the young lumberman, Michael Servosse, — rich in
the limitless possibilities of a future cast in the way which had
been marked out by nature as the path of advancing empire,
a brave heart and unquenchable energy, to whom thousands
of acres of unrivaled pine-lands yielded tribute, and whose

fleet of snug schooners was every year growing larger, —
that he should capture and mate with the fair bird from the
New-England home-nest was as fitting as the most enthusiastic
advocate of natural selection could desire. They were the fairest types of remote stocks of kindred races, invigorated by
the fresh life of a new continent.

The first fruit of such a union was the Fool, born on the
first day of the month of flowers, in the year of grace one
thousand eight hundred and thirty-four, on the very spot
where the Iroquois met in council with the great chief Pontiac
when the cunning plan was devised to gain entrance to the
fort by playing a game of lacrosse on the parade-ground for
the amusement of the garrison. The wife of a year, as the perils
of maternity drew nigh in the absence of her husband, who
was up the lake attending to his spring shipments, began to
sigh for her far-away mountain home, and so named the new
life, which brought consolation to her loneliness, *Comfort*.

During his babyhood, boyhood, and youth, our hero manifested none of those characteristics from which he afterwards
received the name by which he is known in these pages. He
was reared with care. Though his father died while he was
yet young, he left sufficient estate to enable the mother to give
to her children every advantage of education, and divide a
small surplus between them as each arrived at man's estate.
The young Servosse, therefore, ate, drank, and slept, studied,
played, and quarreled, like other boys. Like others who enter
college, and have constitutions sufficiently robust to avoid
dyspepsia arising from sedentary habits and the frying-pan,
he left it at the end of four years, with a diploma properly
signed and sealed, as well as very prettily printed on mock
parchment, which was quite as good as veritable sheepskin
for such a purpose. He studied law, as so many sensible men
have done before his day, and with his first mustache was
admitted under all the legal forms to sign himself "Attorney

and Counselor at Law," and allowed to practice his art upon such clients as he could decoy into any of the courts of the Commonwealth of Michigan. Thereupon, putting in force the *"Circumspice"* which appeared upon the seal attached to his license, he cast about for a place in which to set snares for the unwary, and pitched upon the town of Peru; hung out his shingle; obtained a fair business; married the pretty Metta Ward; and, in the summer of his twenty-seventh year, manifested the first symptoms of that mental weakness which led him to perform the task of unwisdom hereinafter narrated.

CHAPTER II

LE PREMIER ACCÈS

I T was the 23d of July in his twenty-seventh year. He had been for several days in a very depressed state of mind, nervous and irritable, beset by gloomy forebodings, wakeful, and, when he did sleep, moaning as if in anguish of mind, talking in his sleep, or waking suddenly and crying out, as if in danger or distress. There was nothing in his social or business relations to justify any such state of mind. He was very warmly regarded by the little community in which he was settled, — a leader in its social life, an active member of the church in which he had been reared, and superintendent of its sabbath school. He had a good home, undistinguished by mortgage or incumbrance of any sort; a wife, whose energy and activity kept this home in the neatest possible condition, almost as it seemed without exertion, and certainly without the tyranny of servants; an office in the very center of the town, where it could not escape the search of the most unwilling or unobservant seeker; and a practice which yielded him more than he had any call to spend. All this should have made him the most contented and happy of men.

Yet, in spite of all these comforting surroundings, he had for a considerable time neglected his business to a marked degree, and seemed to have little interest in those things which ought most nearly to have concerned him. For the last few days he seemed to have had no heart or interest in any thing save the results of a battle, which was said to have been fought half a thousand miles away, in which neither he nor any one of his clients had an interest which could have been measured by the American unit of value or any fraction thereof. Yet this young attorney was refusing to eat or drink, because he did not know the results of said battle, or perhaps because he feared that it might not turn out to his notion.

Metta, his young wife, was surprised and alarmed. Never before had there been any thing like trouble in the breast of her spouse, that he did not lighten his heart of at least half its load by at once revealing to her the cause of his annoyance. The difficulties of each puzzling case were talked over with her; and not unfrequently her pure unbiased heart had pointed out to him equities which his grosser nature had failed to perceive. Had he been cast in an action, he was sure to come home at night, perhaps dragging and weary with the story of his discomfiture, to receive consolation and encouragement from her lips; but this new trouble he had studiously concealed from her. At least he had refrained from all conversation in regard to it, and revealed its existence only by the involuntary symptoms which we have set forth. But who could conceal such symptoms from the eye of love? She had seen them, and wept and trembled at the evil that portended. She was no skilled student of mental phenomena; but, if she had been, she would have known that all these indications — insomnia, causeless apprehension, anxiety in regard to matters of no personal moment to him, moodiness, and studious concealment of the cause of his disquietude — were most infallible indicators of mental disorder. Yet, although she did not know this as a scientific fact, her heart had diagnosed the symptoms; and the prescience of love had taught her with unerring accuracy to apprehend the evil which impended. With the self-forgetfulness of womanly devotion, she had concealed her sorrow from the purblind eyes of the dull mole whose heart was occupied only with the morbid fancies which were eating their relentless way into his soul. She wept in secret over what she foresaw, and pressed her hands with tearful beseeching to her troubled heart, while her white lips uttered the prayer, which she felt could not be answered, "I pray Thee, let this cup pass from me!"

Yet she met him, through whom she knew this affliction must come, ever with smiles and gladness. At morn she kissed him farewell, as he stood on the vine-covered porch of their little cottage, when he started for his office, while the balmy breath of the summer morning blew over them, and the bees hummed from flower to flower, sipping the honeyed dew from the throats of the unclosed morning-glories. At noon, when he came for the mid-day meal, the door flew open before his hand had touched the knob, and she stood before him in the little hall, draped in the neat, cool muslin which became her so well, a smile upon her lips, and inextinguishable love-light in her eyes. And when he would sit in moody silence after their pleasant tea, while the evening shadows fell around, — brooding, ever brooding, over the evil which he would persist in making his own, — she would steal into his lap, and her soft arms would clasp his neck, while her lips would not rest from prattle or song until bribed into silence by kisses or laughter. Never had his home been so sweet. Never *could* home be sweeter. Yet all this seemed only to increase his melancholy, and make him even more moody and disconsolate.

On the previous day he had come home before the tea-table had been set, — an hour before his usual time; but somehow she had expected that he would do so. She had peeped through the blinds of her little chamber, and seen him coming; so that, as he climbed wearily up the steps, he found her standing on the lower stair in the hall, her lips wreathed in smiles, and her head crowned with roses, as she waited to spring into his arms.

"O Metta!" he said in an agonized voice, as he clasped her to his breast, and then put her away, and looked into her blushing face and into the eyes which were crowding back the tears she was determined should not flow, — "O Metta, we are beaten!"

"In what case?" she asked, at once pretending to misunderstand the purport of his words.

He saw the pretty little trick; but he was too sad, and melancholy had taken too firm a hold upon him, to allow him to reward it with a smile.

"Alas!" he sighed, "this can be laughed away no longer. Blood has been shed. Not a few lives, but a thousand, have been lost. Our army has fought at a place called Bull Run, and been terribly defeated."

CHAPTER III

SORROW COMETH WITH KNOWLEDGE

T HERE were no more smiles in the cozy home after that announcement. He had brought with him a newspaper, whose horrible details absorbed his attention, and from which he read aloud to her, as with noiseless step and white lips and ashen cheeks she went about preparing the evening meal, of which they had partaken together for the last time alone. Another presence — grim and terrible — sat at the board with them that night, and imbittered all the sweet viands which her pretty hands had prepared with such loving care. The name of this presence was *War*. It sat opposite the wife, and over against the husband. Its shadows blighted his brain, and paralyzed her heart. She could not eat; and the Fool noticed dully, when he could lift his eyes from the paper beside his plate, that there were great black circles about her eyes, which were not there when he had first met her in the hall that morning.

After supper he went out, which was another sign of mental alienation; since he had never before known a time when he would willingly leave his pretty home and gentle wife for the society of men. He stayed late, and she pretended to be asleep when he came in. She had been weeping in her loneliness; and her heart was so sore that she could not venture to give him the good-night kiss, which she had never before omitted. In the morning there was the same heaviness; and the same Shadow sat with them at the breakfast-table and mocked at the Fool, as he read the morning's paper, and did not see the tears that rolled down the wife's cheeks.

He did not come home to dine, but sent word that he was too busy to leave his office; and it was late when he came to supper. His melancholy seemed to have departed; and he was strangely, unnaturally cheerful and tender to his young wife. He came up the steps with a bound, took her lovingly from the lower stair, where she generally awaited him, and, when he had kissed her a dozen times or so, bore her in his arms to the dining-room, where the tea-table was already spread. Through the whole meal he rattled on of every thing except the fearful Shadow which sat opposite, and which *he* pretended not to see. When the meal was over, he led his wife into the sitting-room; and taking a seat by the window, over which clambered a rose-tree, some blossoms from which were in her hair, he seated her upon his lap, kissed her again and again, and finally said in tremulous tones, —

"Metta, the governor has called for more troops."

There was no response, except that the bowed head upon his breast nestled closer, and there was a sound as of a sob choked down in the white throat.

"Don't you think, Metta, that I — that is — we — ought to do something — for the country?"

Then came a little wailing cry.

"Didn't I pick lint for two whole days, and sew bandages, and roll them; and [a burst of tears] I'm sure I'm willing to do it every day — if — if — if it will do any good."

Then the tears flowed in a torrent, and the slender form shook with successive sobs, as if a great deep had been suddenly broken up.

"Oh, I didn't mean that!" said the Fool. "Don't you think *I* ought to do something? — that I ought to — to — go?"

"Go! where?" came the response in assumed wonder; for she would not understand.

"To the war, dear," he answered gently.

"What!" she cried. "You! you! my husband! Oh, it is not, it can not be so! Surely there is no need of that. Can we not do enough — our share — without that? O darling, I should die!"

She sobbed as if about to make good her words, and clung about his neck with kisses and tears mingled in distracted confusion.

"Oh, if I should lose you! Darling, darling! think of our pretty home! your bright future, and — and," she whispered something in his ear. "Surely some must stay at home; and why not you?"

"Nay, nay, darling," he said, "do not tempt me! I know it is hard; but I could not look you in the face, and know that I had shirked the call. Nay more, my darling! I could not gaze without a blush into the innocent face of that little child, if I should fail to take a man's part in the great struggle which the nation is waging with the wrong! I could not see your babe, and think that it might some time blush for its father's cowardice!"

As if it could make any possible difference to the little one who was expected, whether its father continued a thrifty and prosperous attorney, as he had hitherto been, or became a red-handed slayer of men! or, indeed, whether the said heir expectant would not be better pleased, and his interests better served, by his father taking the former course rather than the latter!

However, the young wife saw that it was useless to argue with a mind so evidently distorted in its apprehension of facts, and lay weeping and sobbing in his arms until he had fired her fancy with bright pictures of military glory and the sweets of the return home, when Peace should crown him with laurels, and spread a feast of all good things for the heroes who went forth to battle for the right.

So, in a few days, he marched forth clad in the foolish foppery of war, avoiding his wife's tearful gaze, and taking pride and credit to himself for so doing.

He was the captain of the "Peru Invincibles," which constituted Company B of an infantry regiment, that did an incredible amount of boasting at the outset, a marvelous amount of running soon after, and a reasonable amount of fighting still later in the Civil War, which had then just begun.

This species of mental alienation was then of such frequent occurrence that it might well be regarded as epidemic. It displayed itself chiefly in an irresistible inclination to the wearing of blue clothing and the carrying of dangerous weapons, together with a readiness to use them in a very unpleasant and reckless manner. There were many mild cases, in which the mania manifested itself in very loud and reckless talk about what ought to be done. These cases were not at all dangerous, as they never went beyond that point. The persons acutely affected received different names in different localities. In some they were called "Boys in Blue," "The Country's Hope," and "Our Brave Soldier-Boys;" while in others they were termed "Lincoln's Hirelings," "Abolition Hordes," and "Yankee Vandals." It may be observed, too, that the former methods of distinguishing them prevailed generally in the States lying to the north, and the latter in those lying to the south, of what used to be called "Mason and Dixon's line." Both meant the same thing. The difference was only in the form of expression peculiar to the respective regions. All these names, when properly translated, signified *Fools*.

CHAPTER IV

FROM BAD TO WORSE

Four years have elapsed, and our Fool is lying on the greensward, under the clustering maples, in front of the little cottage from which he marched away in stoical disregard of his young wife's tears.

A rollicking witch, whom he calls "Lil," is fighting a sham battle with the soldier-papa whom she has never seen until a week before, but whom she now tramples and punches and pelts with that sublime disregard for the feelings of the assaulted party which shows the confidence she has in his capacity to "endure hardness like a good soldier." Resting with her back against the tree-trunk, with a mass of fluffy white cloth overspreading the light dotted muslin which rises about her in cool profusion as she sits among the long grass, is Metta, the brave young wife, whose tears ceased to flow when she found they were powerless to detain the Fool away from war's alarms, and were all turned into smiles, and treasured up to await his return and restoration to his right mind.

Ah! many a thousand times her heart has stood still with fear for him; and now, as she playfully watches the struggle going on, we can see that there is an older look upon her brow than we had marked there before. The gray eyes have a soberer light, though brimming over with joy; the lips, a trick of closing sharply, as if they would shut back the sob of fear; and the hand wanders often to the side, as if it would hush by its presence the wild beatings of a sad heart. No wonder; for the Shadow that sat at their table four years before had breakfasted, dined, and supped with her ever since, until the Fool came back a week ago. She knows that she has grown old, — lived many a decade in those four years; but she has quite forgiven the unconscious cause of all her woe, and is busily engaged in preparing garments which shall carry no hint of his unfortunate malady. Indeed, it may be said that she has some pardonable pride in the *éclat* with which he returns. He has been promoted and gazetted for gallant conduct, and general orders and reports have contained his name; while the newspapers have teemed with glowing accounts of his gallantry. He is colonel now; has been breveted a brigadier-general, but despises the honor which comes as a thing of course, instead of being won by hard knocks. He is over thirty; and, as he romps with their first-born, she looks forward to how many ages of ecstasy in the sweet seclusion of their pretty home.

"There, there, Lily! go and play with Pedro," she says at length. "You will tire papa. He is not used to having such a sturdy little girl to romp with him."

She is half jealous of the child, who shares her husband's attention which she has hungered for so long. The child goes over to the old Newfoundland who is stretched at ease on the other side of the tree; and, when the parents look again, her golden curls are spread upon his shaggy coat, and both are asleep. The wife draws her husband's hand upon her knee, lets fall her needle, and forgets the world in the joy of his presence and of communion with him.

"Do you know, Metta," he said after a long silence, "that I have half a mind to go back?"

"Back! where?" she asked in surprise.

"Why, back to the South, whence I have just come," he answered.

"What! to live?" she asked, with wide, wondering eyes.

"Certainly: at least I hope so," he responded gayly.

"But you are not in earnest, Comfort, surely," with an undertone of pain in her voice.

"Indeed I am, dear!" he replied. "You see, this is the way I look at it. I have been gone four years. These other fellows, Gobard and Clarke, have come in, and got my practice all away. It could not be otherwise. If not they, it must have been some others. People must have lawyers as well as doctors. So I must start anew, even if I remain here."

"But it will not be difficult," she interrupted. "You do not know how many of your old clients have asked about you, and were only waiting for your return to give you their business again."

"Of course; but it will be slow work, and I have lost four years. Remember, I am over thirty now; and we have only our house and the surplus of my savings in the army, — not any thing like the competency I hoped to have secured by this time," he said somewhat gloomily.

"But surely there is no haste. We are yet young, and have only Lily. We can live very snugly, and you will soon have a much better business than ever before. I am sure of that," she hastened to say.

"But, darling, do you know I am half afraid to stay here? It is true I look brown and rugged from exposure, — as who that went to the sea with Sherman does not? — and my beard, which has grown long and full, no doubt gives me a look of sturdiness and strength; but for several months I have been far from well. I weigh much less than when I left here; and this old wound in my lungs has been troubling me a deal of late. Dr. Burns told me that my only chance for length of days was a long rest in a genial climate. He says I am worn out; and of course it shows at the weak point, just like a chain. I am afraid I shall never practice my profession again. It hardly seems as if I could stand it to sit at the desk, or address a jury."

"Is it so, darling?" she asked with trembling lips, while the happiness fled out of her face, and left the dull gray which had come to be its accustomed look during those long years of waiting.

"Yes," he answered tenderly; "but do not be alarmed. It is nothing serious, — at least not now. I was thinking, as we had to begin over after a fashion, whether, considering every thing, it would not be best to go South. We could buy a plantation, and settle down to country life for a few years; and I may get over all traces of this difficulty in that climate. This is what the doctor advises."

"But will it be safe there? Can we live there among the rebels?" she inquired anxiously.

"Oh," he responded promptly, "I have no fear of that! The war is over, and we who have been fighting each other are now the best of friends. I do not think there will be a particle of danger. For a few months there may be disorders in some sections; but they will be very rare, and will not last any time."

"Well, dear," she said thoughtfully, "you know that I will always say as Ruth did, and most cheerfully too, 'Whither thou goest, I will go.' You know better than I; and, if your health demands it, no consideration can be put beside that. Yet I must own that I have serious apprehensions in regard to it."

"Oh," he replied, "there must be great changes, of course! Slavery has been broken up, and things must turn into new grooves; but I think the country will settle up rapidly, now that slavery is out of the way. Manufactures will spring up, immigration will pour in, and it will be just the pleasantest part of the country. I believe one-fifth of our soldiers — and that the very best part of them too — will find homes in the South in less than two years, just as soon as they can clear out their old places, and find new ones there to their mind."

So he talked, forgetful of the fact that the social conditions of three hundred years are not to be overthrown in a moment, and that differences which have outlasted generations, and finally ripened into war, are never healed by simple victory, — that the broken link can not be securely joined by mere juxtaposition of the fragments, but must be fused and hammered before its fibers will really unite.

CHAPTER V

THE ORACLE IS CONSULTED

THE doubt which Metta had expressed led the Fool, a few days afterwards, to address a grave, wise man, in whose judgment he had always placed much reliance, in order to obtain his views upon the proposed change of domicile. So he wrote to his former college-president, the Rev. Enos Martin, D.D.: —

"MY DEAR OLD FRIEND, — The fact that I paid so little heed to your monitions when under your charge, is perhaps the reason why I prize your opinion upon any important matter now. I would like to have your views on the question following, promising to weigh them carefully, though I may not act upon them.

"I am considering the idea of removing my household gods to Dixie. So far as my personal characteristics are concerned, you know them better than any one else probably, except myself, and would not take my own estimate of what you do not know. I can muster a few thousand dollars, — from eight to ten perhaps. I have come out of the war a little the worse for what I have been through; having some trouble in or about one lung, no none seems to know just where, and some other mementoes of the affectionate regard of our rebel friends. I find my practice gone, of course, and am a bit afraid of our cold winters. As I desire your views, I will not give mine. Of course I must burn my bridges if I go. I am too old to face a future containing two upheavals.

"Yours ever,

"COMFORT SERVOSSE."

In a few days there came this answer: —

"MY DEAR COLONEL, — I am glad to hear you are considering the question stated in your letter. Of course I can not *advise* you, in the ordinary sense of that word; nor do I suppose you desire that I should. I can only give my general impressions in regard to the future of that part of the country to which you think of removing.

"It is too soon to speculate as to what will be the course of the government in regard to the rebellious sections. A thousand plans are proposed, all of them, as it seems to me, crude, incomplete, and weak. One thing is certain, I think: no one will be punished for rebellion. It is true, Davis and a few others may be invited to go abroad for a few years for the country's good, and perhaps at its expense; but it will end there. There will be no examples made, no reprisals, no confiscation. At the same time, if the results of the war are to be secured, and the nation protected against the recurrence of such a calamity, these States must be rebuilt from the very ground-sill. I am afraid this is not sufficiently realized by the country. I have no idea of any immediate trouble in the South. Such exhaustive revolutions as we have had do not break forth into new life readily. It is the smoldering embers which are to be feared, perhaps a score of years hence. And this can be prevented only by a thorough change in the tone and bent of the people. How much prospect there is of such change being wrought by the spontaneous action of the Southern people, I do not know: I fear, not much.

"It seems to me that the only way to effect it is by the influence of Northern immigration. Of course the old economies of the plantation and the negro-quarters will have to give way. The labor of that section must be organized, or rather taught to manage itself, to become automatic in its operations. The former master is not prepared to do this: First, because he does not know how; and, secondly, because the freedman has no confidence in his old master's desire to promote *his* interests. There will be exceptions; but this will be the rule. In this re-organization, I think men who have been acquainted with free labor will be able to give valuable aid, and accomplish good results. I look and hope for considerable movements of population, both from the North to the South, and *vice versa*; because I think it is only by such intermingling of the people of the two sections that they can ever become one, and the danger of future evil be averted. Should the present controversy be concluded, and new States erected in the recently rebellious sections, without a large increase of the Northern element in their populations, I am confident that the result will be but temporary, and the future peace of the country insecure.

"As to the social and financial prospects of persons removing there, I suppose it depends very much on the persons themselves, and the particular locality to which they go. I should say you were well fitted for such pioneer work; and, if you should conclude to go, I wish you all success and happiness in your new home, and trust that you may find there friends as devoted and sincere as you have hitherto secured by an upright and honorable life.

"May God bless you and yours!

"ENOS MARTIN."

By this letter, both the notions of the Fool and the fears of his wife were strengthened. Metta, seeing him grow more and more settled in his determination, did not think it worth while to offer any further opposition; but consoled herself with the reflection that her husband's health was the thing of prime importance, and smothered her fear with a blind, baseless hope, that, because what they purposed doing was a thing born of good motive and kindly feeling, it would be prospered. Some people call that "faith;" and it is no doubt a great consolation, perhaps the only one, when reason and common sense are squarely opposed to the course one is taking.

CHAPTER VI

ALL LOST BUT HONOR

WHILE the matter was in this unsettled state, the Fool received a letter from Colonel Ezekiel Vaughn of Pipersville, a town in which his command had been for some time quartered just before he had quitted the service, to which fact, among other things, he was indebted for the honor of Colonel Vaughn's acquaintance.

Some few days after the collapse of the Confederacy, a gentleman had presented himself at the headquarters of the Fool in Pipersville, and directed the orderly in attendance to announce that, —

"Colonel Ezekiel Vaughn desired to surrender, and take the oath of allegiance."

Thereupon he was ushered into the presence of our hero, and with considerable pomposity announced the fact again. Somehow he did not seem to the young soldier to have that air of one accustomed to camps and the usage of armies which was to be expected from a veteran of a four-years' war, who came in at the last moment to give up his sword, after all his comrades had been paroled and had departed. It is true, he had on the regulation gray suit of "the enemy;" and the marks of rank upon the collar might at one time have been intended for the grade he had announced. He wore a light slouch hat, which, though not of any prescribed pattern, had evidently seen much service of some kind. But the surrender brought to light some queer specimens of uniform and equipments, so that Colonel Servosse would not have been surprised at any thing that an officer might have worn. There was something, however, in the loud and somewhat effusive greeting, which, even allowing all that it was possible should be credited to laxity of discipline, showed that the man before him was not accustomed to association with military men. So he asked quietly, —

"Of what regiment, sir?"

"Colonel Vaughn, — Colonel Vaughn," said that worthy, depositing himself upon a camp-stool, as if in assertion of his familiarity with military surroundings. "Well, sir," he continued in a loud and somewhat assuming tone, "you've got us, overpowered us at last. It was the Irish and Germans that did it. I had no idea you could get so many of them. They just swarmed on your side. The Yankees never could have whipped us in the world by themselves, — never. But it's over. I surrender, — give up, — quit. I'm not one of those that want to keep up a fuss always. I've come in to give myself up, and go to work now to try and make bread and meat, sir, — bread and meat. You uns have freed all the niggers, so that we have nobody to work for us. Have to come to it ourselves. Haven't you got a mule you could let me have, Colonel? Hain't got no money; but Zek'le Vaughn's credit's tolerably good yet, I reckon. Lost forty odd niggers, — as likely ones, too, as ever stood 'twixt soil and sunshine, — and now have got to go to plowing — at *my* age. It's hard; but we've got to have bread and meat, — bread and meat, sir. Hard, but can't be helped. Did all I could agin ye; but here you are. Let me take the oath. I want to be sworn, and go to plowing before the sun gets too hot."

"What regiment did you say, sir?" repeated the officer.

"Oh, never mind the regiment!" said the other: "that's all over now. Just say Colonel Ezekiel Vaughn: that's enough. Everybody knows Colonel Vaughn, — Zeke Vaughn. I shouldn't wonder if you should find they knew me up at headquarters."

"It is necessary, sir, that I have the name and number of

your regiment before you can be paroled," said the officer sharply.

"Ah, yes! the regiment. Well, Colonel, you are mighty particular, it seems to me. What difference can it make now, I should like to know?" he asked.

"It is necessary to identify you," was the reply.

"Ah, yes! I see. You are afraid I might break my parole, and give you some trouble. I confess I have not been whipped; but I am overpowered, — overpowered, sir, — and I surrender in good faith. I give my honor, sir, — the honor of a Southern gentleman, — as well as my oath, sir!" he said, with a great show of offended dignity.

"That may be, Colonel," responded the officer; "but our orders require that you shall be fully identified."

"Well, well! that's very proper. Just say Colonel Vaughn of Pipersville: that will identify me. Everybody in the State knows me. No use of my trying to get away. I shall be right here, when you want to find me, ready to come up, and be hung, if that is to be the end of it. Oh, I meant it! I was one of the original 'Secesh,' — one of the immortal thirteen that voted for it in this county. I never would have stopped fightin' ye if I'd had my way. You'd never 'a' got here if I'd had my way! But that's all over now. I want my parole, so I can go home, and go to killin' grass!"

"When I learn your regiment and command, I will find out the blank," answered the officer decisively.

"Oh, yes! the regiment. Well, Colonel, the fact is, — ahem! — that I've, — ahem! I've done forgot what number it was."

"What! forgotten the number of your regiment?"

"Dog-goned if I hain't, — slick as you please. You see, I wasn't in one of the regular regiments."

"Well, what was your command? to what division or brigade were you attached?"

"Well, I wa'n't exactly attached to any."

"Did you have an independent command?"

"No: not exactly."

"Were you on staff duty?"

"Not exactly."

"Will you tell me what you were '*exactly*'?"

"Well, you see, Colonel, I was just sorter sloshin' around loose-like."

"Orderly!" said the officer.

A soldier entered the room, and, saluting his chief, stood waiting for orders.

"Take that man to the guard-house!"

"But — Colonel, — I," —

"Go on!" said the officer.

"But — I protest, Colonel, — I," —

"Not a word, sir! Take him out!"

The soldier took a gun which stood in the corner of the room, and motioned towards the door.

Colonel Ezekiel Vaughn took his way through it without more ado, and was marched to the guard-house at the point of the bayonet, and in constant apprehension lest the orderly's gun might explode.

CHAPTER VII

AN OLD "UNIONER"

In a little time another party was ushered into the colonel's quarters. He was a tall, lank countryman, clad in a suit of country jeans, which was at that time almost the exclusive wear. He had a long, scraggly beard, of a dull, sandy color, with streaks of gray; and, as he took off his hat and bowed deferentially, his head appeared quite bald. There was a shrewd look in his small gray eyes, and he seemed to approach the officer as one who had a right to speak freely with him. He coughed slightly, and put a hand to his gray beard with a pathetic gesture as he said, —

"Colonel Servosse, I reckon."

"Yes, sir. What can I do for you?" was the answer.

"Wal, I don't know ez any thin'. I jes' thought I'd drop in an' chat a little." He coughed again, and added apologetically, "I'll set down, ef you'll allow."

"Oh, certainly!" said the officer; but the stranger had seated himself without waiting for a reply.

"I reckon you don't know me, Colonel. No? Wal! my name's Brown, — Jayhu Brown."

"Jehu Brown! Not the man who piloted the boys that escaped from Salisbury prison through the mountains in eighteen sixty-four?"

"Yes," with another cough, "I'm that man. You weren't in the crowd; were ye, Colonel?"

"No; but I had a friend who was, and he gave me an explicit injunction, if ever I came into this section to find you out, remember him to you, and, if I could serve you in any manner, to do so for his sake."

"Thank ye. What might be his name?"

"Edgarton — Captain Edgarton — of the Michigan Battery!"

"Oh, yes! I mind him well now. A big-shouldered, likely man, with long hair curlin' in his neck. I cut it off, so that it shouldn't be a mark to foller us by. He's well, I hope." And the old man coughed again.

"In excellent health. Is a colonel of artillery now, and chief of that arm, on the staff of General Davis of the Fourteenth Corps. He would be overjoyed to see you."

"Thank ye, thank ye! So you'd heard of ole Jayhu before?" said he with another apologetic cough. "I thought I'd never seed ye. It's not often Jayhu Brown forgits a man he's once sot his eyes on, or his name either; an' I couldn't make out that I'd ever run across yours, though them prisoners was that thin an' wasted that the best man might forgit to make 'em out arter they'd hed a few months of full feed." He coughed again, a sort of chuckling hack, which seemed to take the place of laughter with him.

"You seem to be in bad health, Mr. Brown," remarked the colonel, alluding to his cough.

"Wal, not partickelar," answered Brown. "[Hack, hack.] I never was very stout, though I've managed to pull through as many close places as most men. That was a monstrous close time going with them ar fellows from Salisbury. [Hack, hack.]"

"Won't you have a little whiskey?" asked the colonel, mindful of what constituted hospitality in the region where he was.

"Wal, now, Colonel, it's mighty kind of you to think on't. I don't keer ef I du just drink the health of an old friend with ye. [Hack, hack.]"

The orderly was called, glasses set out, and liquor, sugar, and water placed before the old man.

"No, I thank ye!" said he: "none of them fixin's fer me.

I allers did like my liquor clar, — clar an' straight." And he poured out a brimming goblet of the fiery liquid. "I never drinks liquor, as some folks does, just for the fun of the thing; but I takes a full charge, an' means business. A man at my day hain't got no time to fool away mixin' drinks. [Hack, hack, hack.]"

He placed his hand over his mouth, as he coughed, with a pathetic expression of countenance that suggested visions of the churchyard.

"I don't often drink, — never, unless I need it, or feel a hankerin' fer it. Never was drunk in my life, and don't 'llow to be; but I've allers hearn that what was wuth doin' at all was wuth doin' well."

Again he pressed his hand to his breast with that peculiar, hacking cough, which seemed to be an apology, chuckle, or explanation, as served. His tall, slender form and solemnity of manner gave it a strange, almost ghastly, effect.

"You seem to have a very troublesome cough, Mr. Brown," said the colonel.

"Wal [Hack, hack], I reckon, now, it mout *seem* so to ye. [Hack, hack.] But do you know, Colonel, it's jest about the handiest thing I ever hed? I've seen the time I wouldn't take no money fer that cough, — no money! [Hack, hack.]"

"How is that? I don't understand you," said the colonel.

"No, I 'spect not. Wal, that ar cough's my exemption-papers. [Hack, hack, hack.]"

"Your 'exemption-papers!' I am still in the dark."

"Wal, you see [Hack, hack, hack, apologetically], the Confederates used to git a notion every now and then that nigh about everybody was fit fer duty in the army, ye know [Hack, hack]; an', among the rest, old Jayhu. [Hack, hack.] An' them on us that couldn't handily leave home, or, least-ways, them that thought they couldn't, was mighty hard put up for excuses. [Hack, hack.] An' I, — wal, you see, they couldn't never find a Board, no matter who they put on it, that wouldn't say 'twas|jest a waste of transportation tu send a man tu the front in my con-di-di-tion. [Hack, hack, hack.]"

And the old man coughed and groaned, and rolled his eyes as if the moment of dissolution could not be far off.

"I never made no complaint, ye see; but they never wanted to hear my cough, when it was right holler, more'n once or twice, before they sent me home. [Hack, hack.] 'Twas a wonder, they said *freq*uently, how I lived; an' so 'twas: but I've managed to pull through thus fer, tollable peart-like. [Hack, hack, hack, chucklingly.]"

The colonel laughed heartily at this recital; and the old man hacked approvingly at his mirth, but did not show a smile.

"Some on 'em," he continued, "hez laid aside ther exemption-papers now thet the war's over; but mine hez sarved me so well, I believe I'll hang on tu it. [Hack, hack.] It's been right handy, an' may come in play agin. They wasn't all ez handy ez mine. Thar's my neighbor Mastin, now: he hed a powerful good paper; but it was onhandy, — mighty so. He got it up in a hurry; but mine was home-made, an' no sort of inconvenience. Ye see, Mastin was stout as a b'ar, — didn't even look delicate, which is a great help in such a thing. But, the mornin' of the day that he was ordered tu report fer examination, he come tu town with his head tied up ez if he'd hed the mullygrubs fer a coon's age. [Hack, hack.] Everybody asked him what was the matter, an' he told 'em he'd come in tu git the government doctors tu tell him. He'd been mighty bad off, he said, fer a long time, an' was tu pore to git a doctor hisself, an' was mighty glad he'd been draw'd, 'cause he 'llowed he'd git some treatment now, 'thout payin' for it. So, when they asked him afore the Board what was the matter, he said, arter some fussin', ez ef he couldn't hear good, that 'twas his ear was a-troublin' him. An' one of the doctors pulled off the bandages, an' dug about half a bale o' cotting out; an', jest ez he pulled out the last plug, he turned away his head, an' hollered out, 'Git out o' here! yer head's rottener than Lazarus!' [Hack, hack.] Yer see, Mastin's wife hed dropped about half of a bad egg inter his ear that mornin'. [Hack, hack, hack.] 'Twas good papers enough, but onhandy. [Hack, hack.]" *

"I should think so," said the colonel, when he could subdue his laughter.

"But they wasn't all so," continued the old man. "That man you hed in here this mornin', an' sent off so unceremoni-ous, he had some mighty good papers; but I see he's laid 'em aside, an' that perhaps is the reason he's in the guard-house now."

"Whom do you mean? Not Colonel Vaughn!" said the colonel.

"Thet's what he calls himself; but we mostly calls him 'Zeke Vaughn,' or more ginerally jist 'Zeke,' or 'hollerin' Zeke.'"

"What did he want of exemption-papers?"

"Wal, — mostly for the same purpose we all on us did, I reckon!"

"Why, I thought he was an original Secesh, a regular fire-eater!"

"So he was at the start, an' in fact all the way through when it was a question of talkin' only; but when it come to fightin' he wa'n't fire-eater enough to want to deprive any one else of a fair show of the fire. [Hack, hack.] So he got on two sticks in the spring of sixty-two, an' hain't been off 'em sence, except to go to bed, till last week he went out on his legs into old Polly Richardson's field to keep the Yankees from gobblin' him up."

"He hasn't been in the army, then?"

"Been in the army! Why, bless yer soul! he hasn't seen a

* The questionable taste of this anecdote must be admitted; but the story is genuine and true, and is here given because so thoroughly characteristic of the time, place, and people.

Yankee, alive or dead, since the thing begun, till he seed you; an' ef you treat him ez you hev to-day he's not like tu die tu git a sight of ye agin."

"But isn't he a colonel?"

"Wal, — not much, tu hurt. [Hack, hack.]"

"Then how did he get the title?"

"That would be hard tellin', Mister!"

"A militia colonel, I suppose."

"I doubt it. Never heard on't, ef he was. I think he jest picked it up ez about ten thousand more in the State hez. Got it by registerin' hisself ez sech at hotels, an' givin' fellers a drink tu holler fer 'Colonel Vaughn' at perlitical meetin's, an' then answerin' tu the call."

"Well, what was his exemption-paper, as you call it?"

"Oh! he jest hobbled around on two sticks, pretendin' tu be the worst drawd-up man with rheumatiz you ever seed, till you uns come. You served him right, an' I was glad on't."

In the afternoon several of the leading citizens of the town dropped in, and confirmed indirectly the old Unioner's report in regard to the doughty colonel. They said he was loud-mouthed and imprudent; but there was not a bit of harm in him, and he was *very* much of a gentleman, and of a most respectable family.

So, towards night, he sent an order for the prisoner's release, accompanied by this note addressed to him: —

"SIR, — Having learned the origin of your title, I have ordered your release, and beg to say that the government of the United States does not consider any parole necessary in your case. You are therefore at liberty to go anywhere you choose.

"Respectfully,

"COMFORT SERVOSSE,
"*Colonel commanding Post.*"

The colonel supposed he had seen the last of "Colonel" Vaughn: but in this he reckoned without the "colonel;" for that worthy at once attached himself to his headquarters as a sort of supernumerary orderly and chief volunteer adviser of the young officer. He managed to get a fine team, and made himself indispensable in planning and executing the daily drives into the surrounding country, which the colonel and his officers so much enjoyed as a pleasing contrast to the restraints of a long and arduous campaign. He was a man of great local knowledge, and a sort of good-natured persistency, which induced the impression that he was nothing worse than a well-meaning bore, who was to be endured at all times for the sake of his occasional usefulness and universal cheerfulness.

Among other things talked of in these drives had been the subject of Northern immigration, the revival of business, and the re-organization of labor. On such occasions Vaughn had always clamorously contended that what the subjugated section most required was Northern capital, Northern energy, and Northern men to put it again on the high road to prosperity.

In one of their drives they had often passed a plantation known as the "Warrington Place," which had particularly attracted the attention of our Fool, and he had frequently expressed his admiration for it. Indeed, he had more than once ridden over the grounds, and examined the premises with that air of remonstrant anger at its neglected state which betrays the incipient interest of the would-be owner. This fact had not been unnoted by the observant Vaughn; and he had determined, if possible, to coin an honest penny out of the young colonel's admiration. He was a keen observer of human nature, and knew that it would not do to flush his game too quickly. He reasoned rightly, that, when the freshness of his return to old associations had worn away, the young man's mind would be sure to recur with something like longing to his recent surroundings. No active-minded man can settle down after four years of war to the every-day life of former years, without more than one twinge of restlessness and vague regret for the time when "boots and saddles" ushered in the ever-changing days.

The months passed; and, as recorded in Chapter VI., our Fool had returned to his home. One day he received a brief letter, under date of Sept. 1, 1865, which was as follows: —

"DEAR COLONEL, — The 'Warrington Place' is for sale, cheap as dirt. Five thousand dollars cash will take the whole place (six hundred acres); that is, five thousand dollars gold. Our folks haven't got to understand greenbacks much as yet. We have had paper money enough for four years. This is a grand chance for a gentleman of your stamp. We need just such. Northern men are crowding in here every day. One man is putting up a factory, and three have opened stores. Shall I tell Griswold, who has the property in charge, that you will take Warrington? I am very anxious you should have it. I know it will suit you so well. If you don't conclude to take it, let me know at once, as some other parties are offering.

"Yours truly,
"COLONEL EZEKIEL VAUGHN.

"P.S. — I can get it on better terms than anybody else, because of my relations with Griswold.

"E. V."

CHAPTER VIII

"THEIR EXITS AND THEIR ENTRANCES"

WARRINGTON had been the seat of an old family whose ancestor, many years before the Revolution, had erected the usual double log-house (or "two-decks-and-a-passage," as it is still called in that country), in the midst of a charming oak-grove, upon a gently sloping hill, which rose in the bend of as fair a stream as ever babbled over the rocks in foolish haste towards the far-away sea. This log-house had in time given way to a more pretentious structure of brick; the grove had been thinned and trimmed, and avenues laid out in it; and the years which had made the house old and damp, worn the mortar from the bricks, and covered the cypress roof with a carpet of moss, had added glory to the forest monarchs which stood around it, and stretched, year by year, their great arms closer and closer about it, as if to hide its imperfections, and screen its decrepitude from the beholder.

The Warringtons themselves were akin to some of the highest families in the State, and so prided themselves upon their opulence and position that they became chary of alliances with others. They intermarried until the vigor which had amassed great estates became weakened, and imbecility and vice succeeded. The estates were squandered, the revenues lessened, and one plantation after another absorbed, until finally Warrington itslf, the family-seat, went to satisfy the demands of importunate creditors half a score of years before our story. Fortunately (or unfortunately, rather, for our Fool) the plantation fell into the hands of an eccentric Frenchman, a bachelor with an abundant fortune, and a taste for horticulture and pomology. He was struck with the beauty of the situation, and the quality of the fruits produced there; and building a neat lodge on one side of the grounds,

almost over-hanging a little waterfall, which he had improved
until it became one of the chief attractions of the place, he
shut up the great house, and devoted himself to the culture of
fruits and flowers with a contented zeal which yielded marvelous results. All about the central grove of oak and hickory
were orchards and vineyards of the rarest and most luscious
fruits. Evergreens had been interspersed with deciduous va-
rieties in the grove, and trees of quaint habit and striking foliage were grouped here and there through the grounds.

Of the plantation beyond the immediate surroundings of
the house — the six hundred acres of alternate hill and bottom,
with woodland and old field interspersed — he had been less
careful, having left it in the hands of an overseer to be cultivated or left idle as the fancy or inclination of that worthy
might dictate. All he wanted from that portion of his property was, that it should pay the expense of its own cultivation,
and furnish enough corn, meat, and forage to subsist himself
and the two "boys" (slaves) whom he kept to help him in
his horticultural operations, together with the horses and
mules employed on the plantation. This was easy, without
cultivating more than one-half the arable land. The overseer
consequently reduced his cares, and accomplished all his employer required, by "turning out" from year to year portions
of the plantation, and failing to "take in" any new ground.
The consequence was that when Mr. Noyotte died, in the second year of the war, the bulk of the farming-lands had grown
up into pine and sassafras, with rank sedge-grass waving thick-
ly between, and great red gullies stretching across towards
every ravine and water-course. The lands which had been
under actual cultivation had become very much worn and
depreciated by slothful management, until the hillsides were
washed, and the bottoms filled with the *detritus*, to the great
detriment not only of the slopes above, but also of the rich
alluvium beneath.

The eccentric owner had died, so far as was known, without heirs. He had never been a favorite in the neighborhood, and very little was known of his affairs. His housekeeper, a quadroon woman, claimed his estate under a will duly executed; but as it was suggested that she was a slave and incapable of "taking" under it, and as she was unable to prove the contrary, the will was set aside, and an administrator appointed. It was found that the deceased had become indebted to an extent which his personal estate was insufficient to discharge, especially considering the very low prices which it brought at the sale which the administrator made for that purpose.

Nearly every thing was bought by Colonel Vaughn at figures which would have amazed one who knew nothing of how such matters may be arranged. It was given out and believed that Colonel Vaughn had been authorized, by a letter which had passed the blockade, to represent the heirs of the deceased, — nephews and nieces who lived in France, — and that he was buying in the property just to hold for them. Therefore, when likely negro slaves were bid off by Colonel Vaughn for fifty dollars apiece in Confederate money, every one said it was all right, and there was no counter-bidding. The administrator made his report of sales, and, there being a deficiency of assets, obtained an order to sell the lands, which he was authorized to do either at public or private sale.

Less than ten dollars an acre for such a plantation seemed to the Fool, who was accustomed to the high prices of land at the North, extravagantly cheap, — as perhaps it was in the abstract. He did not know that in its palmiest days the plantation would never have brought that price at a cash sale; while its condition had so deteriorated, that, by the same scale of prices, it would now hardly have been worth more than half that sum: besides which, the deleterious effects of the war upon the value of all property in that region were hardly to be estimated. Of all this he took no account. He answered at once that Colonel Vaughn might take the property at the price named, if he could get a good title. Of that he wished to be sure. Then there came an abstract of title from an attorney of the highest repute, as he well knew, and with it this note: —

"Griswold was anxious to sell: so I bought, knowing that you would be sure to take the place when satisfied of the title, as you will be when you read this. I got it a trifle below the price I named to you; and you can have it for what I paid, any time within two months.

"COLONEL EZEKIEL VAUGHN."

So the Fool sold his pretty home, packed up his household idols, took his wife and little daughter, and went to seek health, happiness, and fortune in Dixie. The trade which had been initiated by the persistent Vaughn was duly consummated, and Comfort Servosse became the owner in fee of the family-seat of the Warringtons. It took almost all of his little fortune to pay for it; but, when he had done so, he felt that he had accomplished a good work. He had made a fair bargain, and had now a basis for future happiness and prosperity; and for this he felt himself under some obligation to Colonel Vaughn, and came to the conclusion, that, if that worthy was not gifted with a stomach for fight, he was at all events a good-hearted, obliging fellow. It was not till afterwards that he found out how many prices he had paid; for, when the heirs of Mr. Noyotte — the nephews and nieces in France — sent over to reclaim the residue of the property in the hands of the administrator, it appeared from the record that the land had been sold privately to Colonel Vaughn in 1863, and that there had been received in payment thereof a certain amount of Confederate money, which was duly filed by the administrator, and reported by him as having been lost by the events of the war.

But these things were unknown to the Fool for several years; and Warrington came into his hands a new toy, unsmutched by any suspicion that he had paid too much for his whistle.

CHAPTER IX

THE NEW KINGDOM

WHY attempt to paint the delights of that first winter at Warrington?

Upon examining the place, it was found that the Frenchman's lodge had been used for purposes which prevented its present occupation as a dwelling, and they were forced to go into the old brick mansion. It needed much repairing, and at the best was worth more to look at than to occupy. Yet there was a certain charm about the great rooms, with their yawning fireplaces and dingy ceilings. Transportation was yet defective; and it was long before their furniture could arrive over railroads, worn and old, which had been the object of attack by both armies at different periods of the war.

It was the middle of October when they entered upon their new possession; and all was so new and so lovely to Metta and the little Lily, that no lack of creature-comforts could have checked their enthusiasm. The balmy air, the unfamiliar landscape, the strange sense of isolation which always marks the Southern plantation life, and, above all, the presence of the husband and father who had been absent so long, all united to make them superlatively happy.

Metta rode with her husband all over the country, whose strange irregularity became every day more pleasing to them, — through the thick woods along the bridle-path, where the ground was covered with autumn foliage which had fallen from ripeness rather than from the effects of frost; past the little country farm-houses and the seats of wealthy planters; fording rivers, and crossing rude ferries; every one whom they met, whether of high or low degree or of whatever race, having something about him which was new and strange to one of Northern birth and education.

A letter which Metta wrote to her sister shortly after they arrived will show the feelings of the young wife: —

"MY DEAR JULIA, — I do not know how I can better employ a few hours of Thanksgiving Day than in writing you the promised letter of our new home and our journey here. While you are shivering with cold, perhaps looking out upon ice and snow, I am sitting upon a little veranda, over which clambers a rose-vine still wreathed with buds and blossoms. There has been a slight frost; and those on the outside are withered, but those within are yet as fresh as if it were but June. The sun shines warmly in, and every thing without is touched with that delicious haziness which characterizes the few peculiar autumn days of the North that we call Indian summer. There is the same soft, dreamy languor, and the same sense of infinite distance around us.

"Every body and every thing is new to us; that is, to Lily and me. Comfort's four years of soldier-life made him very familiar with similar scenes; and, I doubt not, a large part of our enjoyment comes from having him to explain all these wonders to us.

"It did seem terribly lonely and desolate when we first arrived. You know Comfort had come before, and completed the purchase, and made some preparations for our reception; that is, he had engaged somebody to make the preparations, and then returned for us. We had a fearful journey, — rough seas and rickety boats, a rough country, and railroads which seemed to lack all that we have considered the essentials of such structures. The rails were worn and broken, the cross-ties sunken and decayed; while every now and then we would see where some raiding party had heated the rails, and twisted them around trees, and their places had been supplied with old rusty pieces taken from some less important track. Comfort said be believed they would run the train on 'the right of way' alone pretty soon. All through the country were the marks of war, — forts and earthworks and stockades. Army-wagons, ambulances, and mules are scattered everywhere, and seem to be about all the means of transportation that are left. The poor Confederacy must have been on its last legs when it gave up.

"The last twelve hours of the trip it rained, — rained as you never saw it, as I think it never can rain except in this climate. To say that it poured, would give you but a faint idea of it. It did not beat or blow: there was not a particle of *storm*, or any thing like excitement or exertion about it. It only *fell* — steadily, quietly, and uninterruptedly. It seemed as if the dull, heavy atmosphere were shut in by an impenetrable canopy of clouds, and laden with an exhaustless amount of water, just sufficiently condensed to fall. There was no patter, but one ceaseless sound of falling water, almost like the sheet of a cascade in its weight and monotony, on the roof of the old leaky car. In the midst of this rain, at midnight, we reached the station nearest to Warrington. It is, in fact, a pretty little town of two thousand or so inhabitants; but it was as dark as the catacombs, and as quiet, save for the rain falling, falling everywhere, without intermission. The conductor said there was a good hotel, if we could get to it; but there was no vehicle of any kind, and no light at the station except the conductor's lantern, and a tallow candle flickering in the little station-house.

"Comfort got our baggage off, and stored in the station-house, after a deal of trouble; and with bags and boxes on our arms, and muffled up to the chin to keep out the rain (which seemed to come through an umbrella as if it scorned such an attempt to divert it from its course), we started for the hotel under the pilotage of the conductor with his lantern. Such a walk! As Comfort helped me out of the car, he said, 'It's fearfully muddy.' He need not have said it. Already I was sinking, sinking, into the soft, tenacious mass. Rubbers were of no avail, nor yet the high shoes I had put on in order to be expressly prepared for whatever might await me. I began to fear quicksand; and, if you had seen my clothing the next morning, you would not have wondered. Luckily it was dark, and no one can ever more than guess what a drabbled procession we made that night.

"And then the hotel; but I spare you that! Lily cried herself to sleep, and I came very near it.

"The next morning the earth was as bright and smiling as if a deluge had not passed over it a few hours before. Comfort was all impatience to get out to Warrington, and we were as anxious to leave that horrible hotel. So he got an ambulance, and we started. He said he had no doubt our goods were already there, as they had been sent on three weeks before, and he had arranged with a party to take them out to the plantation. At least, he said, we could not be worse off than we were at that wretched hotel, in which I fully agreed with him; but he did not know what was in store for us!

"Warrington is only six miles from the station; but we were two mortal hours in getting there with our trunks and the boxes we had brought with us. Think of riding through mud almost as red as blood, as sticky as pitch, and "deeper than plummet ever told," for two hours, after an almost sleepless night and a weary journey of seven days, and you may faintly guess with what feelings I came to Warrington. As we drove up the avenue under the grand old oaks, just ripening into a staid and sober brown, interspersed with hickories which were one blaze of gold from the lowest to the topmost branch, and saw the gray squirrels (which the former owner would not allow to be killed, and no one had had time to kill since) playing about, and the great brick house standing in silent grandeur amid this mimic forest, I could have kissed the trees, the squirrels, the weather-beaten porch, the muddy earth itself, with joy. It was home, — rest. Comfort saw the tears in my eyes, the first which I had shed in it all, and said tenderly, —

" 'There, there! It's almost over!' as if I had been a tired baby.

"Lily was in rapture over the beauties of the old place, as indeed she had good right to be; but I was tired. I wanted rest. We drove to the house, and found it empty, — desolate. The doors were open; the water had run across the hall; and every thing was so barren, that I could only sit down and cry. After some trouble Comfort found the man who was to have made the repairs, and brought out the goods. He said the goods had not come, and he 'llowed there wa'n't no use fixin' things till they come.

"Comfort sent the ambulance which brought us out to go back and get some provisions, a few cooking utensils, and some other absolute necessities. A colored woman was found, who came in, and, with the many willing hands which she soon summoned to her aid, made the old house (or one room of it) quite cozy. Our things have been coming by piecemeal ever since, and we are now quite comfortable.

"Comfort has bought me a riding-horse, — a beautiful blooded bay mare; and he has his old war-horse, Lollard, which he had left in this vicinity with an old man named Jehu Brown, — who, by the way, is a 'character,' — having an impression that we might come here. So we ride a great deal. The roads are so rough that it is difficult to get about in any other way; and it is just delightful riding through the wood-paths, and the curious crooked country roads, by day or night.

"The people here seem very kind and attentive. A good many gentlemen have called to see Comfort. They are all colonels or squires, and very agreeable, pleasant men. A few ladies have called on me, — always with their husbands though; and I think they are inclined to be less gracious in their manner, and not so cordial in their welcome, as the gentlemen. I notice that none of them have been very pressing in their invitations for us to return their courtesy. Comfort says it is not at all to be wondered at, but that we ought rather to be surprised and pleased that they came at all; and I do not know but he is right.

"Two or three countrymen came to see Comfort a few days after our arrival. They were all 'misters,' not 'colonels' and 'squires.' They said they were Union men; and it was wonderfully interesting to hear them tell, in their quaint provincialisms, what happened to them during the war.

"We rode out to see one of them afterwards, and found him a thrifty farmer, with four or five hundred acres of good land, living in a log-house, with a strange mixture of plainness and plenty about him. Somehow I think I shall like this class of people better than the other, — though they are rough and plain, — they seem so very good-hearted and honest.

"We are going to have the teachers from the colored school at Verdenton here to dinner to-day to keep Thanksgiving. There are some half-dozen of them, — all Northern girls. I have not met them; but Comfort says they are very pleasant ladies. Of course they have no society except a few Northern people; and he has gone to bring them out to give them a treat as well as ourselves, I suppose.

"Yours ever, with love to all,

"METTA."

CHAPTER X

POOR TRAY

THE next letter was during the week which succeeded Christmas Day, and explains itself: —

"MY DEAR JULIA, — My last letter to you was written while I was waiting for the young ladies, who are teaching at Verdenton, to come and share our Thanksgiving dinner. That was a momentous day for us, and that dinner a most important affair. We were a little short of some things necessary for such an occasion; but we pieced and fitted, and, with the help of the willing hands of many colored girls (you must remember that all colored women are 'girls'), we made out to spread a very respectable table. Comfort had gone into town early with my little bridle-wise mare Jaca, in leading for one of the young ladies to ride; and the ambulance followed for the others. Just as my letter was finished, they all came up the avenue to the house; and a merrier crowd I am sure I never saw in my life. Six sweeter girls could not be found. They are employed by the Missionary Association to teach in the colored schools that have sprung up all over the South like magic, and are real 'missionaries' in the very best sense of the word. They are from six different States, and never saw each other until they met here at the school in Verdenton, and are all cultivated, refined ladies of the best class of our Northern people, who have come here simply to do good. It was really charming to see them, so fresh and girlish, just from loving homes and tender friends, coming away down here on a noble errand, where they are despised and insulted for the very good they perform. Only the few Northern people who are here will have any thing to do with them. They are as much missionaries, and have as much to undergo, as if they were in Turkey; indeed more, if our old friend who is teaching in Beirût tells the whole truth in regard to her difficulties. We had a delightful day; and towards night both of us returned with them, and sending back the ambulance, and keeping only our saddle-horses, staid at the Mission House, as their abode is called, until after nine o'clock; and then Comfort and I rode home in the moonlight. I don't think I was ever happier in my life, or felt that I had been the cause of more happiness to others, than on that day; and, when we knelt for our evening prayer, I did thank God with all my heart that he had directed our steps hitherward, for I believe we have a blessed work to do, and that our lives here will not be in vain.

"A few days afterward I went to call on some of the ladies who had visited me. It was so far that Comfort went with me, and I persuaded him to let me go on horseback; for it is so unpleasant to ride in an ambulance, which is the only alternative. This would not be quite *en règle* at home, I know; but here it is a very general thing, and it is a mode of traveling too delightful ever to be abandoned. We called at three houses, and were received at all of them with a very marked restraint of manner, and with positive rudeness in one case. I felt as if I could cry from disappointment and chagrin. We wanted to be friendly, and avoided every subject of conversation which could give pain; and it seemed too bad to be met with such coolness. Comfort tried to console me as we rode home; but I could see that he felt it as well as I.

"A day or two after this, Squire Hyman, who is one of our nearest neighbors, though he lives a mile away, came over to see us. He is a queer old gossip, who is so anxious to be on good terms with everybody that he has hard times to keep anybody on his side. During the war, it seems, he played fast and loose; and it is amusing enough to hear Colonel Vaughn and his Confederate friends caution us against him as a man who professed to be 'all right,' but was all the time encouraging deserters and harboring bushwhackers; and then to hear Jehu Brown, and other known and reliable Unionists, say, 'He won't du tu tie ter. He was always claimin' tu be a powerful good Union man, an' at the same time givin' information agin any o' the boys that was hidin' out.'

"I knew that he had something 'very particular,' as he says, to tell the moment he came into the room; but it was a long time before he could get to it. I think Comfort suspected what it was, and purposely led him away from the point he was striving to reach. At length he 'bounced it squarely,' as the country-people hereabout say, with the statement, —

" 'I hear they've got a powerful big school for the — the niggers as we call them, — in Verdenton.'

" 'Oh, yes!' I answered in all innocence. 'We had the young ladies who are teaching there out here to our Thanksgiving dinner, and liked them very much.'

" 'Indeed! I don't know any thing about them, good or bad. Of course I hear a good deal said; but that's neither here nor there. Some folks make a heap of fuss about every thing; but I'm one of them that lets other folks alone if they don't trouble me. That's right, ain't it, Colonel? He, he!'

" 'I don't see why there should be any thing said against these young ladies,' said I.

" 'Well,' he replied, 'you know how we Southern people are. We have our own notions.' And he winked, and chuckled to himself; and I said rather sharply, —

" 'I don't see what your notions have to do with these young ladies, who are certainly doing God's work in teaching these poor colored people, old and young.'

" 'Oh, certainly! it would look so; but' —

" 'But what?' said Comfort so markedly that the old man jumped in his seat.

" 'Oh — nothing — that is — nothing of account — only — you know, Colonel, we can't help thinking that any one that comes from the North down here, and associates with niggers — can't — well — can't be of much account at home.'

" 'And you call teaching colored people associating with them?' asked Comfort.

" 'Well, of course, in a manner,' answered the squire hesitatingly.

" 'And you doubtless think it disreputable to associate with such teachers?'

" 'Well, Colonel, I'm glad you mentioned it. I didn't want to broach it myself, being a delicate subject, you know; but it is so counted — by — the best society, you know.'

" 'So you came to warn us that if we continue to associate with these teachers we must forego the pleasure of good society hereabouts?'

" 'Well, I had heard remarks, you know. I name no names; but I thought it would be no more than neighborly, being as you were strangers as I may say, and not accustomed to our ways, to let you know, so that you might be careful in the future.'

" 'Thank you. We are certainly under many obligations to you for letting us know whom we are to be permitted to associate with, and whom not.'

" 'Oh, not at all! not at all! I'm sure it's no more than I would do for any neighbor,' said the squire with an air of gratified vanity.

" 'Certainly not, Squire,' said Comfort sarcastically, — and I knew from the flashing of his eyes that some one would get a shot, — 'certainly not; and it is my confidence in your neighborly inclination which makes me presume to ask a favor at your hands.'

" 'Any thing in the world that I can do, sir. I'm sure I shall be proud to serve you,' said the squire with marked enthusiasm.

" 'Then, Squire, I would be glad if you would say to these good people who have undertaken to regulate our associations, that I bought this property, paid for it cash down, and am quite capable of regulating my own affairs without their aid.'

" 'What do you mean, sir?' said the squire, starting from his seat, white with rage. 'Do you mean to insult me?'

" 'I mean,' said Comfort quietly, 'to say that the ladies who are teaching in the colored school at Verdenton are ladies of character and culture, fit associates for my wife, and fully the equals of any lady in the State. I desire to say further, that, regarding them as such, if it comes to a choice between ostracizing them simply because of the good work in which they are engaged, and losing the approval of the first families of Verdenton and vicinity, I shall certainly choose the latter.'

" 'Well — of course," said the squire, somewhat staggered by this view of the matter, 'of course you have a right to your own way. I mean no harm, not the least in the world. Good-evening, sir! Good-evening, Madam!' And he was gone to do the errand at Comfort's bidding.

"Colonel Vaughn came the next day upon the same errand. I did not hear the conversation he had with Comfort; but he talked very loud, and I suppose was answered much as the squire had been. I heard Comfort say to him, just as he was leaving, —

" 'I fought four years, sir, for the privilege of living under the flag of the United States with all the rights of a citizen in any part of the Union, and I do not intend to permit anybody to dictate my conduct towards anybody else.'

" 'If your family associates with nigger teachers, you can not expect respectable people to recognize them as associates.'

" 'We do not ask anybody to associate with us, sir. We are not suppliants for recognition. If people desire our friendship, we are frank and outspoken, pretending to nothing more than we are, and accepting others as we find them. If they do not wish to associate with us, we do not complain, and are not likely to mourn.'

"The colonel, as he calls himself, went away in high dudgeon; and the next week the paper published at Verdenton had a dirty little squib in regard to the matter, which I send you.

["It read as follows: —

" 'Our readers will regret to learn that the Canadian Yankee Servosse, who has bought the Warrington Place, is one of those fanatical abolitionists whose infamous doctrines were the real cause of all the suffering and bloodshed of the last four years. Our citizens had extended many favors to him, and our ladies had shown very marked courtesy to his family. Instead of appreciating these things, he has chosen to slander our first ladies by comparing them with the nigger schoolmarms who have come down here to teach social equality by example.

" 'We understand that Servosse had all these free-love nigger-missionaries of the female persuasion out at Warrington to celebrate the

new Yankee holiday, which has been added to the governmental
calendar since the first year of Lincoln's reign, called Thanksgiving
Day. The day itself is a relic of New-England Puritanical hypocrisy,
and, we understand, was fitly observed at Warrington, where they ate
and drank, and sung "John Brown," "We're coming, Father Abraham," and similar melodies. It is said that one of the "N. T.'s" became
so full of the good spirit of the occasion, that she kissed one of the
colored boys who waited at the table. Colonel Servosse cannot expect
his family to be recognized by respectable people if he chooses such
associates for them.']

"Did you ever see any thing so mean? Of course we don't care any
thing about it: only one likes to live peaceably with one's neighbors
if possible. Comfort was very much exasperated when he first saw
this, and went into town in a very angry mood. I don't know what he
did; but the next week there was a very abject apology in the paper.
It made a great excitement though, and even many of the colored
people advised us not to have the teachers here any more. ('N. T.,'
you know, is Southern euphemism for *Nigger Teacher*.) Of course
we paid no attention to it, and will have them here just as often as we
can, both to show that we are not moved by such things, and because
they enjoy coming so much.

"Some time ago Comfort concluded to establish a sabbath school
for colored people, as there are a great many in this neighborhood,
and no school of any kind for them nearer than Verdenton. So he
consulted with some of their leading men, and they fixed up an arbor
and some seats in a grove not far from the house; and you ought to
see what congregations gather there Sunday afternoons. Two or three
white men came in at first, as if to see what would be done. Comfort
asked them to take classes, and help us teach these poor people. One
old man with long, white hair, strange, dark eyes, and a mild, soft
voice, came forward, and said that it was a good work, and he thanked
God that he had put it into the mind of this new neighbor to do it;
and he for one would do all in his power to assist him.

"The others stood off, and did not seem to know what to do about
the matter. The old man's name is George D. Garnet. He is of
Huguenot descent, and belongs to a large family in the South, whose
name has been corrupted from its original orthography. He is very
proud of his descent, and was attracted to us by our name being also
French. He is a deacon of the Baptist church in Mayfield, about
twenty miles from here. He says he has been trying to get his church
to take hold of a colored sabbath school from the very day of the
surrender; but they will not hear him. He has often staid to tea with
us, and we find him very entertaining indeed. He is very eccentric,

as is evident from what he says, and the stories the colored people tell of him. He says he was a slaveholder who thought slavery wrong, — a 'Virginia abolitionist,' as he says. The colored people say that he used to buy slaves who were anxious to be free, and let them work out their freedom. He was not a rich man, only just a good 'common liver,' as they say; but in this way he bought and freed many slaves.

"The colored people flock around us as if they thought 'de Yankee kunnel' could do every thing, and hire them all. I think I could have a hundred housemaids if I would take all that come to me, and Lilian has nurses enough offered to take charge of all the children in your town.

"Comfort has decided to sell all of Warrington but a hundred acres. The rest lies along the creek, and is very well fitted to cut up into little farms of ten and twenty acres for colored men, giving them upland to live on, with a little timber, and a piece of good bottom to cultivate. He is going to put little log-houses on them, and sell them to colored people on six or ten years' time. It will make quite a little town.

"We hope to do some good, and trust that the foolish prejudice of the people will wear away. It is strange how credulous they are, though. An old country-woman, who came along with some things to sell the other day, said she had heard that the colonel had come down here to try and 'put the niggers over the white folks,' and wanted to know if it was true! She had a snuff-stick in her mouth, and neither she nor her two grown daughters could read or write! It is wonderful how many there are here who are so ignorant; and those who are not ignorant are full of strange prejudice against all who are not of their own particular set, and think and believe just as they do.

"There are some reports of difficulties experienced by Northern men in some parts of the South; but we hope they are exaggerated.

"Yours ever,

"METTA."

CHAPTER XI

A CAT IN A STRANGE GARRET

Servosse was very busy during the winter and spring which followed in building the houses referred to by Metta, and laying out and selling a large part of his plantation. He found the colored men of the best character and thrifty habits, anxious to buy lands, and no one else was willing to sell to them. He purchased some Confederate buildings which were sold by the government, tore them down, and, out of the materials, constructed a number of neat and substantial little houses on the lots which he sold. He also assisted many of them to buy horses, in some instances buying for them, and agreeing to take his pay in grain and forage out of the crops they were to raise. In the mean time he gave a great deal of attention to the improvement of Warrington, expecting to reap his reward from the thousands of fruit-trees which Mr. Noyotte had planted, and which had grown to be full-bearing, in spite of neglect since his death. These trees and vines were all carefully pruned and worked; and Warrington assumed the appearance of thrift and tidiness, instead of the neglect and decay which had before been its distinguishing features. There was some fault found with the sales which he made to colored men, on the ground that it had a tendency to promote "nigger equality;" but he was so good-natured and straight-forward in the matter that but little was said, and nothing done about it at that time, though he heard of organizations in some parts of the State instituted to prevent the colored people from buying land or owning horses.

The succeeding summer was well advanced when he went one day to attend a political meeting which was held in a little grove some seven miles from Warrington. It was a meeting purporting to be called for consultation in regard to the general interests of the county. Eminent speakers were advertised to attend; and Servosse felt no little curiosity, both to see such a gathering, and to hear what the speakers might have to say. He had never been any thing of a politician, and had no desire or expectation of being one. He rode to the meeting, which he found to be far greater than he expected, not less than a thousand people having assembled. Almost every man came on his horse or on foot; and the horses stood about, tied to the lower limbs of the trees in the grove where the meeting was held. There were many speeches of the kind peculiar to the Southern stump, full of strong, hard hits, overflowing with wit and humor, and strongly seasoned with bombast. Stories of questionable propriety were abundant, and personalities of the broadest kind were indulged in.

Servosse sat among the crowd, enjoying to the utmost this new experience, and wondering how people could relish contending so hotly over each other's records during and before the war. It all seemed to him very amusing. But, when they came to address themselves to the future, he became interested for another reason.

It will be noted by the reader who cares to trace back a few years of memory, or consult the records which have not yet become history, that this was in the primary period of what has since become memorable as the era of "reconstruction." The plan which was then sought to be put into operation by the Executive * was what has since been known as the "presidential plan," supplemented by the "Howard amendment," and dependent on the adoption of that by the different States recently in rebellion. The abolition of slavery by constitutional provision, the abjuration of the right of secession, and the repudiation of the Confederate state-debts were the conditions precedent. Of course the future status of the freedmen

* Andrew Johnson.

was a question of overwhelming interest, though that was left entirely to the decision of the various States.

It was for the discussion of questions thus arising that the meeting we have now in hand was called.

The great subject of contention between the opposing factions was as to whether the recently freed people ought to be allowed to testify in courts of justice.

"What!" said one of the speakers, "allow a nigger to testify! allow him to swear away your rights and mine! Never! We have been outraged and insulted! Our best men have been put under a ban; but we have not got so low as to submit to that yet. Our rights are too sacred to be put at the mercy of nigger perjurers!"

This sentiment seemed to meet with very general indorsement from the assembled suffragans, and more than one burst of applause greeted the speech of which it was a part.

When the meeting seemed to be drawing to a close, and Servosse was considering the question of going home, he was surprised at hearing from the rude stand the voice of this same orator addressing the assemblage for a second time, and evidently making allusion to himself.

"Mr. Chairman," he said, "I see there is a man on the ground who has lately come among us from one of the Northern States, who has been here all day listening to what we have said, whether as a spy or a citizen I do not know. It is currently reported that he has been sent down here by some body of men at the North to assist in overturning our institutions, and putting the bottom rail on top. I understand that he is in favor of social equality, nigger witnesses, nigger juries, and nigger voters. I don't know these things, but just hear them; and it may be that I am doing him injustice. I hope I am, and, if so, that an opportunity will now be given for him to come forward and deny them. If he has come among us as a *bona-fide* citizen, having the interest of our people at heart, now is a good time for him to let it be known. If he has come to de-grade and oppress us, we would like to know what reason he has for such a course. In any event we would all like to hear from Colonel Servosse; and I move that he be invited to ad-dress this meeting."

Had a bombshell fallen at the Fool's feet, it could not have amazed him more. He saw the purpose at once. Vaughn and several others, whom he had reason to suppose had no kindly feelings for him, were evidently the instigators of this speech. They were gathering around the orator; and no sooner had he ceased speaking than they began to shout, "Servosse! Servosse! Servosse!"

The chairman rose, and said something amid the din. Only a few words reach the ears of Servosse: —

"Moved 'nd sec'n'd — Servosse — 'dress — meeting. Those in favor — aye." There was a storm of ayes. "Opposed — no." Dead silence; and then a period of quiet, with only an occasional yell for "Servosse" from the party of malignants on the right of the stand.

Servosse shook his head to the chairman; but the shouts were redoubled, and there was a closing in of the crowd, who were evidently very curious as to the result of this call.

"Bring him on!" shouted Vaughn to those who stood around. "Bring him on! Let's hear from him! We haven't heard a speech from a Yankee in a long time."

"Servosse! Servosse! Servosse!" shouted the crowd. Those who stood about him began to crowd him towards the plat-form in spite of his protests. They were perfectly respectful and good-humored; but they were evidently determined to have a speech from their new neighbor, or else some fun at his expense.

"Oh, bring him along!" cried Vaughn from the stand. "Don't keep him all to yourselves, gentlemen. We can't hear a word here. Give us a chance!"

This sally was greeted with a shout; and Servosse, still expostulating and excusing himself, was picked up by a dozen strong arms, carried along between the rows of seats, — rough pine boards laid upon logs, — and hoisted upon the platform, amid a roar of laughter.

"We've got him now," he heard Vaughn say to his clique. "He's got to make a speech, and then Colonel Johnson can just give him hell."

There was another cry of "Speech! speech! speech!"

Then the chairman called for order; and there was silence, save here and there a dropping word of encouragement real or mock, — "Speech! Go on! Give it to 'em, Yank!" &c.

Servosse had noticed that the crowd were not all of one mind. It was true that there was an apparent unanimity, because those who dissented from the views which had been expressed were silent, and did not show their dissent by any remarks or clamor. He knew the county was one which had been termed a "Union county" when the war began; and there was still a considerable element whose inclinations were against the Rebellion, and who only looked back at it as an unmitigated evil. They had suffered severely in one form and another by its continuance and results, and smarted over the sort of compulsive trickery by which the nation was forced into the conflict. He had marked all these things as the meeting had progressed; and now that those whom he recognized as his enemies had succeeded in putting him in this position, he determined to face the music, and not allow them to gain any advantage if he could help it.

He shook himself together, therefore, and said good-naturedly, —

"Well, gentlemen, I have heard that —

     'One man may lead the pony to the brink,
     But twenty thousand can not make him drink!'

So, while you have shown yourselves able to pick me up, and put me on the platform, I defy you to elicit a speech, unless you'll make one for me. However, I am very much obliged to you for putting me up here, as those rough boards without backs were getting very hard, and I shall no doubt be much more comfortable in this chair."

Whereupon he took a seat which stood by the table near the chairman, and coolly sat down. The self-possession displayed by this movement struck the crowd favorably, and was greeted by cheers, laughter, and cries of "Good!" "That's so!" and other tokens of admiration. If it had been the purpose of those who had started the cry to press him to an impromptu speech before a crowd already excited by a discussion they knew to have been in direct conflict with the views he must reasonably entertain, in order that he might meet a rebuff, he was in a fair way to disappoint them. Instead of making an exasperating speech or an enjoyable failure, he had simply refused to be drawn into the net spread for him by coolly asserting his right to speak or keep silence as he chose. And the crowd unmistakably approved.

The chairman, an old gentleman of courtly manner, whose very appearance was a guaranty of his character, urbanity, and moderation, evidently felt that the new-comer had been treated with rudeness, and that he had been made the unwilling instrument of a malicious insult. It was apparent that the stranger so regarded it, and the chairman could not rest under the imputation of such impropriety. So he rose, and, addressing himself to the occupant of the other chair, said courteously, —

"I have not the honor of your acquaintance, sir; but I presume you are the gentleman who has been called Colonel Servosse."

The latter bowed affirmatively.

"I assure you, sir, I am happy to know you, having heard so much to your credit that I have promised myself great pleasure in your acquaintance."

Servosse blushed like a boy; for there is no class whose flattery is so overwhelming as that to which the chairman belonged, it being united in them with a dignity of manner which gives peculiar force to the lightest remark.

"I am sure, sir," the chairman continued, "nothing could afford me greater happiness than to hear your views in regard to our duty as citizens of a common country at this peculiarly trying period in our history; and I am confident that such is the earnest wish of this assemblage. [Cries of "Yes, yes!"] The manner in which you have been invited may seem to you somewhat rude, and was certainly inexcusable, considering the fact that you are a stranger. I hope, however, that it will not have the effect of preventing us from hearing your views. Seen from your stand-point, it is to be expected that present events will bear a different interpretation to what they have when viewed from ours; but we have met as neighbors, and it is to be hoped that an interchange of views will do us good. I hope, therefore, that you will permit me to introduce you to this audience, and that you will make some remarks, if for nothing else, to show that you bear no ill will for our unintended rudeness."

Cries of "Servosse! Servosse! Colonel Servosse!"

There was no possible answer to an apology and a request so deftly framed as this, except compliance. Servosse perceived this, and, rising, gave his hand to the chairman, and was by him formally introduced to the audience. The crowd gathered around the stand in expectant curiosity; and a little group of colored men who had hung on the outskirts of the audience all day, as if doubtful of their right to be present, edged one by one nearer to the speaker's platform. The short

terse sentences of the new-comer were in very marked contrast to the florid and somewhat labored style of those who
had preceded him. It was the earnest practicality and abundant
vitality of the North-West, compared with the impracticality
and disputatious dogmatism of the South.

CHAPTER XII

COMPELLED TO VOLUNTEER

Gentlemen," said he, "I did not come here to make a speech. I am neither a speech-maker nor a politician. Never made a political speech in my life, and certainly am not prepared to make a beginning to-day. I have bought a home among you, and cast my lot in with you in good faith, for good or for ill. Whether I have acted wisely, or have run on a fool's errand in so doing, is for the future to reveal. I must say, from what I have heard, and heard applauded to the echo, here to-day, I am inclined to think the latter will prove the true hypothesis. Your chairman has intimated that my opinions may differ from yours; and, as this fact seems to be apparent to all, it is probably best, in order that we should part good friends, that I should not tell you what my views are."

Cries of "Yes, yes! Go on!"

"Well, then, if you don't like my notions, remember that you would insist on my giving them. As I said, I am no politician, and never expect to be. I hope I have common sense, though, and I shall try to know something of what is going on in the world while I am in it. I don't want to discuss what has been done, nor who did it. I want to say one thing, however, about the immediate future. I have heard a good deal to-day about what the South wants, and must have; what you will do, and what you will not do. I think you have two simple questions to answer: First, What *can* you do? And, second, What *will* you do? There has been much discussion here to-day in regard to freedmen being allowed to testify in courts, the repudiation of the war-debt of these States, and one or two other kindred questions. Allow me to say that I think you are wasting your time in considering such matters. They are decided already. There may seem injustice in it; but the war-debt of these States can never be paid. Neither can the freedman be left without the privilege of testifying in his own right. It makes no difference whether you accept the terms now offered or not, in this respect — yes, it may make this difference: it is usually better to meet an unpleasant necessity half way, than wait till it forces itself on you.

"The logic of events has settled these things. The war-debt became worthless as paper when Lee surrendered, and nothing can revive it. The taint of illegal consideration attaches to it, and always will. So, too, in regard to the colored man being allowed to testify. This is settled. He was allowed to testify on the battle-field, and will be allowed to testify in courts of justice. When he took the oath of service, he acquired the right to take the oath of the witness. These, I say, are already *facts*.

"The practical question for you to consider is, How far and how fast shall the freedmen be enfranchised? You have to-day assented to the assertion repeatedly made, that the South would never submit to 'nigger suffrage.' But again I say, the South has nothing to do with that question either. The war settled that also."

"We will have another four years of it before we will submit," interrupted Vaughn in great excitement. There was an approving murmur from a good portion of the audience at this interruption. The speaker did not seem at all disconcerted, but, turning to Vaughn, said, —

"I hope not, Colonel. *I've* had enough; but, if *you* will have it, lend me your crutches, and let me join the cripple brigade this time, won't you?"

The roar of laughter which followed interrupted the speaker for several minutes, and left Vaughn the picture of amazement. That the stranger should venture upon such a retort as that to a Southern gentleman was quite beyond his comprehension.

"As I said," continued the Fool, "with the general question of colored suffrage you have nothing to do. It is a fact accomplished. It is not yet recorded in the statute-books; but it is in the book of fate. *This* question, however, you have still in your hands: Shall negro suffrage be established all at once, or gradually? If you of your own volition will enfranchise a part of them, marked by some definite classification, — of intelligence, property, or what not, — and the others as they reach that development, it will suffice at this time. Wait, hesitate, refuse, and all will be enfranchised at the same time by the General Government. You say it will be a great evil. Then you ought to lighten it as much as possible. If you will give the elective franchise to every colored man who owns a hundred dollars' worth of real estate, and every one who can read and write, the nation will be satisfied. Refuse, and all will be enfranchised without regard to your wishes or your fears.

"I have told you, not what I think ought to be, but what I believe *is*, the fact of the present situation. I can see that you do not all agree with me, perhaps none of you; but it will stand thinking over. Don't forget what I tell you, and, if you dislike my remarks, remember that you forced me to say what I have said, as well by your own urgent importunity as by the kindly compulsion of your chairman."

There was a dull, surprised silence when he had concluded. The very audacity of his speech seemed to have taken away all power, if not all inclination, to reply. Some of his audience regarded him with sullen, scowling amazement, and others just with dull wonder that any one should have the hardihood to make such a statement. A few seemed to regard him not unkindly, but made no manifestation of approval. The chairman rose, and stated that the views of the speaker were somewhat startling and entirely new, he presumed, to the audience, as they were to him. As Colonel Servosse said, they would stand thinking about; and on behalf of the audience he returned to Colonel Servosse their thanks for an exceedingly frank and clear statement of his views. If there was no farther business, the meeting would stand adjourned.

Thereupon the crowd separated; and, after a few moments' conversation with the chairman and one or two others, the Fool mounted his horse, and took his way homeward.

CHAPTER XIII

A TWO-HANDED GAME

H<small>E</small> had not proceeded far, when, in descending a hill towards a little branch, he overtook two men, who were evidently sauntering along the road, and waiting for some one to come up with them. He recognized them as men whom he had seen at the meeting. When he came up with them, they greeted him pleasantly, but with something like constraint in their manner. It was nearly sundown; and one of them, glancing at the west, remarked, —

"Goin' back to Warrin'ton to-night, Colonel?"

"Yes," was the reply. "It's just a pleasant hour's ride."

"It'll be right dark afore ye git there," said his interrogator cautiously.

"A little moonlight will make it all the pleasanter," he laughed.

"Ef ye'll take pore folks' fare," said the other man somewhat anxiously, "you're welcome to supper and a bed at my house. It's right near by," he continued, "not more'n a mile off your road at the farthest. You might ride by, and stay tu supper anyhow. 'Twouldn't hinder long, an' we'd be right glad tu chat with ye a bit."

"No, thank you," he replied: "my wife will be looking for me, and would be alarmed if I did not get home by dark, or a little after. Good-evening!"

He was about to spur on, when one of the men cried after him in their peculiar way, —

"*O* stranger! wait a minit. Don't stop, but jest walk along as if we was only passin' the time o' day. I don't want tu 'larm ye; but it's my notion it would be jest as well fer ye not to go home by the direct road, arter makin' that speech ye did to-day."

"Why not?"

"Wal, ye see, there was a crowd of rough fellers thar that was powerful mad at what ye said about the nigger, though I be cussed ef I don't believe it's gospel truth, every word on't, myself. However, they're mad about it; an' thar's a parcel of towns-folks hez been eggin' 'em on tu stop ye somewhar on the road home, an' they may make ye trouble. I don't think they mean tu hurt ye; but then ther's no tellin' what such a crowd 'll do."

"You say they intend to waylay me?" asked Servosse.

"Wal, no! we didn't say that: did we, Bill?" appealing to his comrade. "But we thought they mout stop ye, and treat ye rough, ye know."

"So you think they'll stop me. *Where* do you think they'll do it?" he asked.

"Oh, we don't *know* it! Mind ye, we don't say so; but they *mout*, an', *ef* they did, 'twould ez likely ez not be somewhar about the ford."

"All right, my friends. When I'm stopped, it will be a queer thing if some one's not hurt."

"Better stop with us now," said his new friends anxiously, "an' not git into trouble when ye can jest ez well go round it."

"No, thank you," he answered: "I'm going home; and no one will stop me either."

He spurred on, but had gone only a short distance, when a pebble fell in the road in front of him, and then another, evidently thrown from the bushes on his right. He drew rein, and was about to take a pistol from his belt, when he heard some one, evidently a colored man, say, —

"O Mars' Kunnel! don't shoot!" And at the same time he saw a black face, surrounded by gray hair and whiskers, peering out from behind a bush. "Jes' you git down off'n yer hoss, an' stan' h'yer one minit while I tells ye sumfin'."

"What do you want?" he asked impatiently. "It's getting towards sundown, and I don't want to be late home."

"Dar! jes' h'yer him now!" said the colored man reproachfully. "Ez ef ole Jerry ebber wanted tu keep him 'way from home!"

"Well, what is it, Jerry? Be in a hurry!" said Servosse, as he dismounted, and led his horse into the dense undergrowth where the man was. It was without misgiving that he did so. He did not know the man, and had never seen him before, except, as he thought, at the meeting that day. He had been warned of danger; but such was his confidence in the good will of every colored man, that he left the highway, and came into the thicket to meet him, without fear. The confidence which his service as a Federal soldier had inspired in the good faith, trustworthiness, and caution of the colored man, had not yet departed.

"Dey's waitin' fer ye, Mars' Kunnel," said the man almost in a whisper, as soon as he came near. "I'd sot down to rest my lame leg in de bushes jes' a little while ago, an' they come 'long, an' stopped nigh 'bout where I was; an' I heard em' lay de whole plan, — tu stop ye down by de fo'd, an' tie ye out into de woods, an' give ye a whippin' fur de speech ye made to-day."

The man came from behind his bush, and Servosse saw that he was strangely deformed, or rather crippled from disease. He walked almost bent double, supported by two staves, but had yet a very bright, intelligent countenance. He remembered then having seen him before. His name was Jerry Hunt, and he lived on a plantation adjoining Warrington.

"How did you come to be so far from home, Jerry?" he asked in surprise.

"Went to h'yer de speakin', sah. Can't tell what fer. Tought de Lor' hed sumfin' fer old Jerry tu du out h'yer; so started 'arly, an' come. I knowed de Lor' sent me, but didn't know what fer till I heerd 'em a-fixin' it up tu git ye, mars' Kunnel. Den I knowed, 'cause yu'se our fren'; *I* knows dat."

Then he told how, as he was lying in the bushes to rest, six

men came along; and he heard them arrange to waylay Colonel Servosse, "an' war' him out wid hick'ries. Dey said dey
wa'n't gwine to hurt him, but jes' tu let him know dat he
couldn't make sech infamous speeches as dat in dis region
widout gettin' his back striped, — dat's all."

"And where are they to be, Uncle Jerry?"

"Jes' on dis side de fo'd, sah, — jes' as ye goes down de hill
in de deep cut."

"But how are they to know which road I take? The road
forks three miles before I come to the creek, and I can as well
take one as the other."

"Yes, sah!" said Uncle Jerry. "Dey tought o' dat: so dey's
gwine to leabe one man at de fawks wid a good hoss to come
down whichever road you don't take, an' gib 'em warnin',
leastwise ef you takes de upper road, which dey don't 'spect,
cos you come de lower one. Dey's gwine to put a grape-vine
cross de cut to catch yer hoss."

"And who stops at the forks?"

"Mars' Savage, sah."

"What horse is he riding?"

"He'll not hev any at de cawner, but will claim to be waitin' for Mars' Vaughn's carryall to come; but de gray filly's hid
in de bushes."

"All right, Jerry. I'm much obliged. If I don't take care
of myself now, it's my own fault. Good-night!"

"God bless you, sah!"

Servosse rode on, revolving in his mind a plan by which he
should discomfit his enemies. To evade them after such
warning was a matter of no difficulty whatever; but he was
too angry to wish to do this. The idea that he should be waylaid upon the public highway, and maltreated, because, after
their own urgency, he had spoken his opinion frankly and
plainly about a public matter, was more than he could endure.
He determined to do something more than escape the threat-

ened attack, and give the parties to understand that he was
not to be trifled with.

On arriving at the forks of the road, he found Savage in
waiting, as he had been told, and, after some little chat with
him, started on the upper road. Savage called to him, and
assured him that the lower road was much better, and a nearer
way to Warrington.

"Well," was the reply, "my horse has chosen this, and I
always let him have his own way when we are going toward
home."

The horse of which he spoke was a bay Messenger, which
he had captured in battle, and afterwards ridden for nearly
two years in the service. In speed, endurance, and sagacity the
horse had few equals even among that famous stock. Hoof,
limb, and wind were sound; and his spirit did honor to his
illustrious parentage. Upon his steadiness and capacity his
rider could count with the utmost certainty. Horse and man
were well mated, each understanding with exactness the
temper and habits of the other.

"Now, Lollard," he said, as soon as he was well hidden from
the place where Savage was posted, "make the old 'Tabernacle Church' in the best time you can, and see if we do not
make these gentlemen repent the attempt to circumvent us."

"The Tabernacle" was the name of a church which stood
on the upper road, about two miles from the lower ford, from
which there was a bridle-path through the woods, coming out
on the lower road about half a mile above the ford. To reach
the latter road by this path before Savage should have time
to pass the point of intersection was now the immediate object.

Lollard covered the ground with mighty stretches, but
evenly and steadily, in a way that showed his staying qualities.
When they reached the church, his rider threw the reins on
his neck, and leaped to the ground. He was well acquainted

with every bush around the church, having frequently attended meeting there. After groping around for a few seconds, he bent over a small hickory, and cut it off with his knife. It made a goad about six feet long, and perhaps an inch and a half in diameter in the heaviest part. He trimmed off a few shoots, and then laid the top on the ground, and held it with his foot while he gave the butt a few turns, deftly twisting the fiber so that it would not snap from any sudden blow. This done, he had a weapon which in the hands of an expert might well be deemed formidable. He had a revolver in his belt; but this he determined not to use.

Mounting again, he dashed down the bridle-path until he came to the lower road. A little clump of pines stood in the angle made by this path and the road; and on the soft sward behind this he stopped, and, leaning forward, stroked his horse's face to prevent him from neighing upon the approach of the expected horseman. He had waited but a few moments when he heard Savage coming at a brisk gallop on his gray filly. The moon had now risen; and between the straggling pine-tops he caught occasional glimpses of the rider as he came along the stretch of white road, now distinctly seen in the moonlight, and now half hidden by the shadow. Holding his horse hard until the other had passed the opening of the path, he gave the gallant bay the spur, and in half a dozen bounds was on the filly's quarter. The long, lithe hickory hissed through the air, and again and again lashed across the mare's haunches. Stung with pain, and mad with fright, she bounded forward, and for a moment was beyond reach; while her rider, scarce less amazed than his horse at the unexpected onset, lost his self-control, and added unintentionally the prick of the spur to her incentives for flight. It was but a moment's respite, however; for the powerful horse was in an instant again at her side, and again and again the strong arm of his rider sent the tough hickory cutting through her hide or over the shoulders of her rider. Half-way to the cut in the road this race of pursuer and pursued kept up. Then Servosse with sudden effort drew in the bay, and subdued his excitement; and, taking the shady side of the road, he advanced at an easy gait to observe the result of his artifice. Meantime the party at the cut, hearing the swift clatter of horses' feet, concluded that the man for whom they were waiting had been warned of the ambush, and was pushing forward to avoid being stopped by them in the woods.

"By heavens!" said one, "it will kill him. Let's undo the grape-vine." And he sprang forward, knife in hand, to cut it loose.

"No," said another: "if he chooses to break his neck, it's none of our business."

"Yes," said a third: "let it alone, Sam. It's the easiest way to get rid of him."

An opening in the wood allowed the rising full moon to shine clear upon the upper part of the cut. Faster and faster came the footstrokes of the maddened filly, — nearer and nearer to the ambuscade which the rider's friends had laid for another. Her terrified rider, knowing the fate that was before him, had tried in vain to stop her, had broken his rein in so doing, and now clung in abject terror to the saddle.

"Good God! how he rides!" said one.

"Heavens! men, it will be murder!" cried another; and as by common impulse they sprang forward to cut the rope. It was too late. Just as the hand of the foremost touched the tough vine-rope, the gray filly bounded into the spot of clear moonlight at the head of the cut; and the pale face of their comrade, distorted with terror, flashed upon their sight.

"My God!" they all cried out together, "it's Tom Savage!"

The mare's knees struck the taut vine. There was a crash, a groan; and Tom Savage and his beautiful young mare were lying at the bottom of the rocky cut, crushed and broken, while on the bank stood his comrades, pallid and trembling with horror.

It needed not a moment's reflection to show even to their half-drunken minds what had been the result of their cowardly plan; and, smitten with the sudden consciousness of blood-guiltiness, they turned and fled without waiting to verify their apprehension by an investigation of the quivering wreck of mangled flesh upon the rocks below. Hastily mounting their horses, which were picketed near, they dashed through the ford; and he against whom this evil had been devised heard the sharp clatter of their horses' hoofs as they galloped up the rocky hill beyond. Then he dismounted, and went cautiously forward to the edge of the cut. A moment of listening told him there was none there except the man whom he had lashed on to his fate. His heart beat fast with sickening fear as he glanced at the mangled form below. A low groan fell upon his ear. He clambered down the steep side of the cut, and groped about in the shadow until he found the body of the man. He struck a match, and found that he was still living, though insensible.

At this moment he heard the sound of a rumbling vehicle on the road above.

"Dis way, boys! dis way!" cried the voice of old Jerry. " 'Twas right here dey was gwine to stop de Kunnel."

There were hasty footsteps, and a rattling one-horse cart drove into the moonlight with the white-framed face of old Jerry peering over the dashboard; while a half-dozen more colored men, each armed with a stout club, rode with him, or ran beside it.

"Stop!" cried a voice from below.

"Bress de Lor'!" shouted Jerry. "Dat's de Kunnel's voice. Dey hain't killed him yit. Hurry on, boys! hurry on!"

He scrambled from the cart, unmindful of his decrepitude, and in an instant willing hands were helping the "Kunnel" bear something limp and bleeding towards the light. Then one brought water in his hat, and another gathered something to make a blaze for closer examination of the body of Savage. Fortunately he had slipped from the saddle when his mare struck the rope, and before she took her final plunge upon the rocks where she now lay crushed and dying. He had been dashed against the clayey bank, and was battered and bleeding, but still alive. He was put carefully in the cart, and carried on to Warrington.

"Jes' arter ye passed me, Kunnel, the cart comed on, an' I tole 'em what was up, an' got 'em to drive on peart-like, so that we might help ye ef ther was any need on't, which, bress de Lor'! dey wa'n't," was uncle Jerry's explanation of their unexpected appearance.

CHAPTER XIV

MURDER MOST FOUL

T HE next day there was a great stir over the horse of Savage, which was found dead at the foot of the cut. The grapevine still remaining attached to a tree on each side of the road fully explained her condition. Savage himself could not be found; and his five companions had all fled, each fearing the others, and each believing the others had removed and hidden the body. That a murder had been committed was evident, every one said; and those who had been privy to the design, though not engaged in its execution, were hardly at fault to imagine how it occurred, at least the main features of it; and the flight of Savage's comrades confirmed them in this belief. The scheme to entrap the new-comer had evidently failed, and a greater evil than had been intended him had befallen one of the conspirators. Strangely enough no one associated Servosse in any way with this result. Public justice, however, and the safety of those who were thought to be the real though unintentional murderers, required that some one should be punished. A scape-goat was absolutely necessary to insure the peace and safety both of those who had fled and those who remained, as well as to satisfy the natural demands of public justice.

So three colored men were arrested on suspicion, and, after being maltreated and threatened to induce them to confess, were haled before Justice Hyman for examination. With hands bound with tightly knotted cords before their breasts, and elbows tied behind their backs, they were led each one by a man on horseback — a great crowd attending, all armed — along the big road which led by Warrington to the house of Squire Hyman. Old Jerry came to inform "de Kunnel" of the arrest. He immediately mounted his horse, and rode over to attend the examination.

The court was held in the grove before the squire's house, the magistrate sitting by a table in his shirt-sleeves, and smoking a long reed-stemmed pipe, the bowl of which was of that noted clay which the smokers of the Allegany slopes declare to be little inferior to the meerschaum, and which the *connoisseur* who looks for a "sweet smoke," rather than a highly colored bowl, will be apt to prefer even to that vaunted article.

The prisoners were charged with the murder of Thomas Savage. They had been arrested without a warrant, such formality not being considered important, as they were "only niggers." The gravity of the offence charged would have justified an arrest without a warrant; but no one thought of putting it on that ground. One was now filled out, however; affidavit being made by the ever-ready Colonel Vaughn, that he had reasonable ground to believe, and did believe, that the defendants, —— and —— and ——, being malicious and evil-disposed persons, moved and seduced by the instigation of the Devil, at and in the county of ——, one Thomas Savage, in the peace of God and the State then and there being, did kill and murder, contrary to the form of the statute, in such cases made and provided, by tying a grape-vine across the cut on the west side of Gray's Ford on Reedy Run in said county.

The constable made return thereon that he had the bodies of the accused before the court, and the examination proceeded.

The county-attorney, who had been sent for in hot haste to conduct the trial, arrived just as these formalities were concluded, and, after a brief consultation with Colonel Vaughn and one or two others, announced his readiness to proceed, and stated what he expected to prove at some length and with considerable vehemence of expression; after which he proceeded to introduce his evidence. This consisted of proof of the finding of the mare, evidently killed by her fall upon the rocks, the grape-vine drawn tightly across the road, the hat of Savage found in the cut, and traces of blood along the track in the same. These facts, he claimed, sufficiently established the death, without the production of the *corpus delicti*, — sufficiently, at least, to justify a binding over. He had no doubt but that the body would be found.

To connect the accused men with the crime, he relied upon the fact that they had reason to harbor malice towards the supposed defunct, having had, each of them, some difficulty with him a short time previous to the event. In addition to that, certain tracks were found about the ford in the moist earth, which must have been made by colored men; and those tracks were about the size and general appearance of those of the accused.

When the evidence was concluded, the magistrate remarked that he would have to commit the prisoners; and there was a murmur ran through the crowd to the effect that a better and cheaper way would be to string them up to a tree.

"If you send them to jail," said one, "the damned Bureau will turn them out!"

Then Servosse quietly stepped forward, and inquired if the prisoners had not a right to be heard and to introduce testimony in their own behalf.

A look of blank amazement, not unmixed with righteous indignation, ran through the crowd at this proposal. The magistrate said he supposed they had, — that is, if they had any testimony to offer.

Thereupon Servosse said he would be sworn, and, being asked what he knew about the killing of Thomas Savage by the accused, said he knew they did not kill him.

"Do you know this of your own personal knowledge, Colonel?" asked Justice Hyman.

"I do, sir."

"Will you please tell the court how you know this fact?" asked the county-attorney.

"Because, sir, Mr. Thomas Savage, the man supposed to be dead, is at this moment alive, and at my house."

Had a clap of thunder burst from the clear sky above the crowd, their surprise could not have been greater.

At length the county-attorney broke into a laugh, and, extending his hand to the witness, said, —

"Well, sir, you bring us very good news. What is his condition?"

"He is very much injured; but you had better ask him in regard to the cause of it. He will be able to tell you soon, or, if necessary, might do it now. I prefer not to say any thing about it myself, — at least, not unless in his presence. One thing I can say, however: these men you have under arrest had nothing to do with the accident which befell him."

"All right!" said the attorney. "We may as well discharge them, your worship. I am much obliged to you, Colonel, but wish you had told me before this farce begun. I believe you did it just to see me make a fool of myself."

"Not at all, sir," was the reply. "I never dreamed of a lawyer consenting to a conviction for murder without proof of the fact of death."

"Sh—!" said the attorney; then, putting his hand to his mouth, and leaning forward close to the ear of his interlocutor, he said in a whisper, —

"Don't you see this, Colonel? What would have become of the poor devils if they had been turned loose on this charge before your testimony?" He glanced around, and then said aloud very significantly, —

" 'There needs no ghost come from the dead to tell us that, my lord.' Eh?"

Then the squire wanted them all to take a little brandy with him. A decanter with glasses, and a sugar-bowl with a half-dozen spoons bristling from its mouth, were set on the table, and the whole crowd were invited to partake. A bucket of water and a gourd were brought, and each one helped himself to the apple-jack, sugar, and water. The late prisoners were not forgotten. When they had been unbound, the justice himself poured out a stiff dram for each, and congratulated them on their escape. The change from seemingly savage cruelty to sympathy and good will was instantaneous, and to Servosse inexplicable.

The sullen stoical apathy which had marked the defendants during the previous proceedings had been changed into profound astonishment by the introduction of "dat ar Yankee kunnel." They had listened with dilated eyes to his brief testimony, and when their cords were cut they had no memory of previous ill treatment in the joy of unexpected deliverance. So when the squire offered them a dram, and congratulated them in kind words on their release, each one tossed off his glass of apple-brandy with a grin and a shuffle, and a hearty, "Here's luck to ye, Mars'!"

The only unpleasant thing about it was that the wife of one of them who came rushing upon the ground at this time with loud cries of grief, upon being hastily informed of the facts, would persist in throwing herself upon her knees before the Fool, and thanking him in the name of her helpless babes for saving their father from being hanged without law or justice, "jes' because he was a nigger."

"The pore critter don't know any better," as the squire informed the Fool apologetically.

To which remark the Fool replied, —

"Evidently not." A reply which left the good justice in grave doubt as to what was intended by it.

Mr. Thomas Savage remained at Warrington until his bruises were healed. A great many of his friends came to see him, and were very anxious as to the cause of his injuries. He said but little while under the roof of his new neighbor, but after he left made no secret of the matter, and strangely enough was thenceforward the stanchest of friends to Servosse and his family.

CHAPTER XV

"WHO IS MY NEIGHBOR?"

O NE day their neighbor, shortly after the events narrated
in the last chapter, Squire Hyman, came over, ostensibly to see
Mr. Savage, but really, as Mrs. Servosse thought, to renew his
intimacy with them, which he broke off in a miff the year
before, because they would invite the teachers of the colored
schools to visit them. He seemed rather shy at first; and Mr.
Savage was absent, so that his excuse did not hold good. As
Colonel Servosse was away, Metta thought she should have
a hard time to bridge over his discomfiture. He evidently
remembered the last time he was there, and knew that she
had not forgotten it. However, as it happened, she had one
of the new novels of Victor Hugo upon her worktable; and
knowing him to be a somewhat bookish man in his queer,
rough way, having heard her husband say that he had read a
great deal, and had quaint and original views in regard to
what he read, she called the book to his attention, and soon
had him sitting *vis à vis* with her; his great stick and hat lying
by him on the floor, and his long-stemmed pipe in his mouth,
but hardly ever burning, though he lighted it every few
minutes. Of course he did not smoke in her sitting-room without her leave, nor even did he presume to ask such leave; but,
knowing what the old man's pipe must be to him by the
pertinacity with which he carried it about, she insisted on
his lighting it. It was but a short time before he was discours-
ing familiarly on books and events in a manner so quaint that
she was well repaid.

"Victor Hugo," said he meditatively. "Do you know, Madam, it seems almost a dream to me the way that name has
become familiar this side the water? He must be an old man

now, smartly older than I am, ma'am; and he has been a most prolific writer, I believe, from a very early age. Yet — would you believe it? — I never saw or read, to my present remembrance at least, any thing that he had written before the war. And I don't know anybody who had either. Not that I am any scholar, ma'am: but we Southern people had a good deal of time to read in those days; and, as I had not much education, I took to reading, so as not to feel behind my associates. I did not read every thing of course, and didn't have any particular end in view, I'm sorry to say; but I read what other folks read of novels and politics and religious controversies, and whatever fell in my way. But I didn't read any of Hugo's works, and hardly heard on 'em, till, some time along the last year of the war, a neighbor's son came back from the hospital, where he'd been lyin' sick for a good bit, and loaned me a book he called 'Lee's Miserables.' It was a shallow sort of pun, as I found out; but I reckon it was a most earnest one to the poor fellows in the trenches. Well, it's wonderful the run that book had here in the South, in spite of the blockade; and I was not a bit surprised to see it stated the other day that he had almost as many readers in America as at home. He's the most American Frenchman I ever read after."

Then he would dip into the new book for a while, or read aloud some little passage which struck him, until he had mastered the period treated of and the general drift of the book. He bespoke its loan as soon as she had finished it, but could not be induced to take it before.

After a time he asked to look into the book-case, and was soon engrossed in making new, and renewing old friends, as he said. There were some works which Servosse had put on an upper shelf, lest they should attract any one's attention, and be thought to have been displayed with any intent to offend. They were works upon slavery and kindred subjects.

She noticed that the old man was peculiarly attracted to this shelf. He seemed very soon to have forgotten all about Victor Hugo, and he presently asked if he might borrow some of these volumes. She hardly knew what to tell him. She did want to ask him to wait until Comfort came; for it seemed so absurd, in what was called a free and Christian land, to hesitate as to whether it would be safe to lend a simple book. He noticed her hesitation, and said, —

"I have a curiosity to read them. I have heard so much about them, and never saw them before. You may not be aware, madam, that they were regarded as 'seditious publications' before the war; so that one could only get to read them at considerable risk and trouble. This I never cared to take; but now that it is all over, and the doctrines of these books have come to prevail, I would like to read the books just to see what hurt us."

She remarked that her husband had put them on the top shelf in order that he might not seem either to obtrude them upon his neighbors' notice, or to deny their possession by concealment.

"No, he has no cause for that now," said he; "though I remember when a man was tried and convicted, and sentence of whipping and imprisonment passed on him too, just for having one of those in his possession."

"I did not know," she said, "that the law actually made it criminal, or, rather, I supposed it was never enforced."

"Oh, yes! it was," he answered. "The case I allude to was Mr. Wanzer, who belonged to a very well-known family here in the county, though he had just come in from Indiana, which was the way he come to have the book about him. There was a big trial and a powerful excitement over it. He was very ably defended, and his lawyers took a heap of points on the law, which it was thought might be declared unconstitutional. But 'twasn't no manner of use. The Supreme Court stood by the law in every particular."

"I thought it was only mobs that interfered with people for reading what they chose," said she; "at least since the good old days when they used to burn people for reading the Bible."

"Well," said he, "there used to be mobs about it too: at least we used to get very much excited at the idea of people bringing what were called 'abolition' books here, to stir up our slaves to insurrection; and probably did some things that had as well not have been done."

"But how could you, Squire?" she asked. "This claimed to be a free country; and how could you think you had any right to persecute one for reading, writing, or saying what he believed? I suppose in those days you would have hung my husband for expressing his opinions?"

"In those days," said he solemnly, "Colonel Servosse would never have expressed such opinions. I admit that he is a brave man; but no one would any more have uttered such sentiments as he puts out now than he would have carried a torch into a powder-magazine. The danger was so apparent, that no one could be found fool-hardy enough to attempt it. I think such a one would have been torn limb from limb, as by a wild beast, by any crowd in the South."

"But you could not have thought that right, Squire," she interposed.

"Well, now, I don't think you ought to say that, madam. You see, you are blaming a whole people whom we are bound to admit were, in the main, honest in what they did. If any one believed slavery to be a divinely appointed and ordained institution, I can not see how he could do otherwise."

"If!" she said hotly. "Do you suppose there were any such?"

"Undoubtedly," he answered seriously, — "many thousands of them, and are to-day. In fact, you may say that the bulk of the Southern people believed it then, and believe it now. They regard the abolition of slavery only as a temporary triumph of fanaticism over divine truth. They do not believe the negro intended or designed for any other sphere in life. They may think the relation was abused by bad masters and speculators and all that, and consequently God *permitted* its overthrow; but they have no idea that he will permit the permanent establishment of any system which does not retain the African in a subordinate and servile relation."

"But you do not believe any such horrible doctrine, Squire?" she could not help asking quickly.

"I beg your pardon, ma'am," he answered politely enough: "I don't know what I believe. I have been a slaveholder from my youth, and ever since I could remember have heard the institution of slavery referred to in the pulpit and in religious conversations, not so much as a thing that might be proved to be holy, but which was incontestably divine in its origin and character, just as much as marriage, or any other Christian institution. I don't think a minister who had a doubt upon that subject could have found any market for his religion here. Until the war was over, I think, if there was any one thing that I believed stronger and clearer and firmer than another, it was that niggers were made for slaves; and cotton, terbacker, sugar-cane, an' rice, were made for them to raise, and could not be raised in any other way. Now I'm most ready to say that I'll be dog-goned if I know what I *do* believe. I *know* the niggers are free, and, for all I can see, they are likely to stay so; but what's to come on't I don't know."

"My husband," said she, "thinks they will remain so, and become valuable citizens, and that the Southern people have actually gained by the war more than emancipation cost them."

"Yes, yes, I know," said he: "I've heard the colonel talk, and what he says looks mighty plausible too. I think it's that has had a heap to do with unsettlin' my faith. However, I do wish he would be more keerful. He don't seem to realize that he's among a people who ain't used to his free and easy ways of talking about every thing. I'm afraid he'll get into trouble. I know he means well, but he is so inconsiderate."

"He's not used to hiding his opinions," she said with something of pride.

"No," he answered; "nor are those he is among used to having their pet notions assailed in that manner. I'm afraid there'll be trouble. I was anxious to see him to-day, an' talk with him about it; but I shall have to come again. Meantime, if you'll let me take these books, I'll read 'em carefully, an' perhaps find some way out of my dilemma."

"Certainly," she said. "We have no books that our neighbors are not welcome to read, believe or disbelieve, accept or refute, as they may see fit. We practice what we preach, Squire."

"I believe that, madam," said he, as he stooped for his hat and stick; "an' I believe you're very much in earnest, both in preachin' an' practicin'. Oh! did I tell you?" he added suddenly, "my son Jesse, he's heard the colonel speak once or twice, an' he's clean carried away with him. Says he's got more sense than anybody he ever heard talk about such matters. He's quite took up that notion you spoke of a while ago, — that freein' the slaves is the best thing that's ever happened for the white folks of the South. Maybe he's right, but it sounds right queer to hear him talk so. He's like you say, though, — practicin' what he preaches, an' is going in to work as if he'd been raised to it all his life. It looks hard, and sounds queer; but maybe he's right. Good-evening, ma'am! Tell the colonel I'm right sorry he was not at home. I'll come again when I've read these through," — touching the books with his pipe, — "an' hope I may catch him then."

Servosse was not quite pleased when his wife told him that night of what she had done. He had been very careful not to give any *just* ground of offense, as he thought, to their neighbors. While he did not hesitate to avow his opinions upon any question of present interest, he did not think it well to open the controversies of the past, and had studiously avoided all reference to them, unless it became necessary in considering the present. He did not say much, however; and when, a few nights afterwards, the Squire came over to return the books, the Fool was rather glad she had loaned them.

The old man had evidently come for a chat. One could see that as he laid down his hat and stick, filled his pipe, and drew up his chair to the corner of the wide fireplace, in which the dry hickory and black-jack was blazing brightly, and coaxed their little golden-haired pet to sit beside him.

"Well, Colonel," he said, after he had chatted a while with the child, "I've brought back the books I borrowed of the madam the other day."

"So I see," laughed Servosse. "Well, I hope you enjoyed reading them?"

"That I did, Colonel," he answered, — "more, I suppose, than you would ever imagine that I could."

"Indeed!" said Servosse. "I was half afraid they would make you so angry that you would feel like visiting your displeasure on me."

"No, indeed!" said the old man with a sort of chuckle. "I had no notion of being angry; though, now I come to think on't, I can't imagine why I am not. There's certainly hard things enough in those books about me and my people to make any man mad. But the truth is, Colonel, it seems to be all about the past, — what is all over and done with now, — so that I seem to be reading of somebody else, and some other time than my own. Do you know, Colonel, that I never read any 'abolition' books before, only some of the milder sort? and I am of the notion now, that our folks made a mistake in keeping them out of the South. I was a little surprised when the madam here," — waving his hand gallantly towards Metta,

— "asked me if any one really believed in slavery. If it had been you, I should have asked if any one really believed in 'abolitionism.' But I am satisfied that the people who wrote those books believed what they were writing; and it does seem as if they had good reason to do so. It's a thousand pities we couldn't have talked these things over, and have come to the right understanding of them without this terrible war."

"That was quite impossible, Squire," said Servosse. "We could never have agreed. I have learned enough of the former state of affairs here already to see that. Each party distrusted the other's sincerity, and despised the other's knowledge. War was inevitable: sooner or later it must have come. Why, even now we can not agree in regard to the incidents flowing from emancipation, — the mere corollaries of the problem God has wrought out for us in the blood of our best."

"That's true, too true," sighed the old man. "And it's curious too. It's all common sense at the last. Why can't we agree to hunt together until we find it?"

"It seems to be human nature, Squire."

"That's it, Colonel; an' when you've said that you've said all. We can't go no further, nor learn any more. It's human nature, and there's no more use of asking questions of human nature than of an owl. 'What' and 'why' are things that don't concern human nature. It don't care no more for reason than a mule does for persuasion. Human nature is a sullen, obstinate, unreasonable brute; but it always has its own way with all on us. Ain't that so, Colonel?" he asked with a self-appreciative chuckle.

"Just so, Squire," replied Servosse. "And almost always disappointing too. Now, I can not see why the South should not have seen its own interest to have lain in the way of gradual emancipation long ago."

"The very idea I was going to advance as to the North," laughed the old man. "I never could make out what *interest* they had in the matter at all. Now, the people who wrote those books I can understand. With them it was a principle, a religious idea. They thought it was a wrong and a sin which they would do God's service to exterminate. They are what we call 'fanatics.' No one can blame them, only for not crediting us with like sincerity. They might have done that, I should suppose. They made too much, too, out of the abuses of slavery. It *was* abused, — no doubt of that, — and many bad things done by bad men under cover of it; but they might have credited us with honesty, at least. We were not all bad, nor all cruel and unjust. Some of us thought the master's relation one of divine duty; and others, who weren't quite so clear upon that point, or didn't care so much whether it was true or not, felt that the institution was on our hands, had come to be there lawfully, and we didn't see how we were to get rid of it without immense loss and sacrifice. So we just let it float along. But we were not hard masters, nor cruel owners. We did feel bound to protect the institution. Not only our interests, but the safety of society as we honestly thought, depended on its continuance, unimpaired and perfect, until something else should take its place, at least. As long as the nigger was *here*, we were all satisfied that he must be a slave. A good many of us thought it would not be any injury if they could all be removed somewhere else."

"No doubt you are right," said Servosse. "And it is not surprising, either, that you should have felt so, or that those who wrote these books should have misconceived your motive. Slavery did two things which naturally prevented such knowledge from being obtained: it excluded the stranger from its inner sanctuary with rigorous care, and persecuted with unsparing severity all who rejected its dogmas."

"Yes, yes, I see," laughed the Squire. "You and I are getting back to human nature again in our anxiety to excuse our respective sides. But do you know I have a still greater reason for being angry, after reading one of those books, on my own personal, individual account? — I, Nathaniel Hyman?"

"No, indeed, I did not," said Servosse. "You are not one of the characters, are you?"

"That's exactly what I am," was the reply, "and not cast in a very enviable *rôle*, either. Besides, the worst of it is, that the author takes pains to write a note about the matter, and tell everybody who was meant to be represented by the character. Hadn't you noticed it?"

"I had no idea of it," said Servosse, flushing. "I have never read the book since it first came out, and had then no personal interest in the individual characters."

"No, of course not," assented Hyman; "though I did think the madam's hesitation the other day might have sprung from that. I'd heard of the fact before, and was anxious to see if it were true. That's why I wanted to read the book."

Metta assured him that she had no knowledge of it, and he continued, —

"Well, I don't know as I mind it, though one hardly likes to go down to posterity as one of the black sheep of his day. The affair of which so much is made was a very trifling matter, and I had mighty little to do with it, at best."

Then he read aloud the passage and the note, and explained: "Now, the whole matter was this. There were a couple of Northern ministers, — Wesleyans, I believe they called themselves, — who couldn't make out to hold their tongues, but were a-spoutin' an' argyfyin' around here as if the Lord hadn't given them any instructions, only to abuse and denounce slaveholders and slavery. I went to hear 'em once or twice just to satisfy myself. They were very imprudent and very intemperate. I spoke to one of them after meeting was out that day, an' told him so. He wouldn't listen at all, but rattled off more Scripture at me than I ever heard in the same time from any body else on earth. I didn't quarrel with him (you know I never quarrel with anybody, Colonel), an' I presume I did tell him I was his friend. I'm everybody's friend, an' always have been. I didn't want him to get into no trouble, an' didn't want no harm to come to him. That's all true, an' I've no doubt I said so to him. But I did *not* approve his doctrine, nor sympathize with his sentiments; nor did I tell him so, though he says I did in the note. I never thought of such a thing. I probably told him I was a magistrate, which was true, and that I was afraid of trouble, which was equally true. Come to think of it, I am of the notion that I told him he had better not preach at the Level Cross. If I didn't, I ought to have done so; for, if they had gone into that neighborhood, they would have been strung up to a tree, certain. Anyhow, the appointment was changed to Shallow Ford meeting-house for the next Sunday. That is true, an' I presume it was on my warning. Now, I am represented as doing all this to get these men into my power. I swear to you, Colonel, it's false. I hadn't such an idea. I thought they were fools, and think so yet; but I hadn't any malice or harm against them in the world. But as it happened, without any knowledge or advisement of mine, directly or indirectly, the next Sunday morning, when the meeting was to be at Shallow Ford, there came by my house a party of gentlemen going on to Level Cross, to hear the Wesleyans, they said. I told them they were on the wrong road, just as a matter of politeness, you know; and they came on up to the fork of the road above your place here, and took over to Shallow Ford, sure enough. After they had been gone about an hour or so, it occurred to me that they might be bent on mischief. I don't say I might not have done just the same if I had known their errand; but as a fact I did not, and never suspected it till afterwards."

"Well," asked Servosse, "is the rest of the incident true, — that about dragging the ministers from the pulpit, bucking them across a log, and beating them?"

"Well, I heard afterwards that they did break up the meeting, and give the preachers a little brushing. They might have bucked 'em across a log; more'n likely they did: it's a powerful handy way to larrup a man. I don't allow, though, that it was any thing like so severe as it's represented in the book, though no doubt the preachers thought it pretty rough. I s'pose they weren't used to it — perhaps thought their cloth would save them. I understand they got away powerful quick after that, not waiting for any repetition of the dose, which was about the only sensible thing they did do."

The old man told it with twinkling eyes, and an evident relish of the whole proceeding.

"I have always had some doubt in regard to these incidents," said Servosse, "and am glad to have this confirmed by one who was an actor in it; but you don't pretend to justify such proceedings, Squire?"

"Well, now, Colonel, I don't really see what there is to make such a fuss about," said Hyman. "Here was a peaceable community, living under the protection of the Constitution and laws of the country; and these men, who had no business or interest here, came among us, and advocated doctrines, which, if adopted, would have destroyed the constitution of our society, and perhaps have endangered our lives and families. Such doctrines lead at once and naturally to insurrection among the blacks, and threatened us with all the horrors of San Domingo. I must say, Colonel, I think the gentlemen were very lenient and forbearing, when they only striped the preachers' backs a little, instead of stretching their necks, as would have been done in any less peaceable community under like provocation."

"It is just such intolerance as this, Squire, which makes it next to impossible for the South to accept its present situation. You all want to shoot, whip, hang, and burn those who do not agree with you. It is all the fruit and outcome of two hundred years of slavery: in fact, it is part and parcel of it," said Servosse.

"But you don't think those men had any right to come here, and preach such dangerous doctrines, do you?" asked his neighbor in surprise.

"Certainly," said Comfort: "why not?"

"Why not?" echoed the Squire. "Why, it seems to me the most evident thing on earth that every community has an undoubted right to protect itself. That is all we did, — protected ourselves and our institutions."

"Protected yourselves *against* your institutions, more properly," said Servosse. "That is the very strength of the abolitionists' position, Squire. No community has any right to have, cherish, or protect any institution which can not bear the light of reason and free discussion."

"But, suppose they do tolerate such an institution, does that give one a right to bring a firebrand among them? Are not they the proper judges of what is the correct thing for their own good, — the keepers of their own consciences?"

"It is useless to discuss the matter," said Servosse. "The arguments you use are the arguments of intolerance and bigotry in all ages. Even men who wish to be liberal-minded, like you, Squire, are blinded by them. You thought it was fair to whip those ministers for preaching what they deemed God's word, *because* the bulk of the community did not agree with them. That was the very argument which would have been used to justify Tom Savage and the others, if they had succeeded in giving me a flagellation a while ago, as they attempted to do. The principle is the same. I had disagreed with my neighbors, and advocated strange doctrines. By your reasoning they had a right to suppress me by violence, or even by murder if need be."

"Oh, not so bad as that, I hope, Colonel!" said the Squire.

"Yes, it is just as bad as that; and I tell you what it is,

neighbor Hyman," said Servosse, "the most dangerous and difficult element of the future, at the South, is this irrepressible intolerance of the opinions of others. You deem disagreement an insult, and opposition a crime, which justifies any enormity. It will bring bitter fruit, and you will see it."

"Oh, I hope not!" said the old man lightly. "I want to get along peaceably now, and I am sure our people want to do the same. We may be a little hot-blooded, and all that; but we are not mean. We are poor now, — have lost every thing but honor; and I hope we shall not lose that. But I must be going. By the way, if you should be writing to any of your friends at the North, and should think of mentioning Nathaniel Hyman, I wish you would just say that he never practiced any deception on the ministers, and was responsible for the licking they got, directly nor indirectly. Good-evening, ma'am."

He lighted his pipe, and went home, evidently thinking that his connection with this *ante bellum* barbarity had somehow increased his importance in the eyes of his new neighbors.

CHAPTER XVI

THE EDGE OF HOSPITALITY DULLED

From the day of his speech in the grove, the new proprietor of Warrington was a marked man in the community. He was regarded as an "abolitionist" and an incendiary. While his neighbors did not seem to have towards him any especial distrust in their personal intercourse, and generally met him with affability, yet he gradually became aware that a current of wonderful strength was setting against him. He became an object of remark at public assemblies; the newspaper at Verdenton had every now and then slighting allusions to him; and the idea was industriously circulated that he was somehow connected — identified — with "Yankee power," and had been sent to the South for some sinister motive. He was not one of them. He represented another civilization, another development, of which they were naturally suspicious, and especially so on account of the peculiar restrictions which slavery had put around them, and which had acted as an embargo on immigration for so many years before the war.

The intercourse between his family and those who constitute what was termed "good society" gradually dwindled, without actual rudeness or tangible neglect, until the few country-people who "neighbored with them," as it is termed there, comprised their only society, if we except the teachers of the colored school and the few Northern families in the town.

Now and then this feeling of hereditary aversion for the Yankee manifested itself unpleasantly; but it was usually only an undemonstrative, latent feeling, which was felt rather than seen in those with whom he associated in business or otherwise, until the first year had passed away, and the crops had been gathered.

Little attention had been paid to the manner in which he had chosen to build houses and sell lands to the colored people, — it being perhaps regarded as merely a visionary idea of the Yankee abolitionist. When, however, the crops were harvested, and some of these men became owners of horses and houses in their own right, it seemed all at once to awaken general attention. One night a gang of disguised ruffians burst upon the little settlement of colored men, beat and cruelly outraged some, took the horses of two, and cut and mangled those belonging to others.

When the Fool arose the next morning, he found the following attached to his door-knob, wrapped in a piece of black cloth on which was traced in white paint a death's-head and cross-bones above the figure of a coffin: —

"Colonel Comfort Servosse. *Sir*, — You hev got to leeve this country, and the quicker you do it the better; fer you ain't safe here, nor enny other miserable Yankee! You come here to put niggers over white folks, sayin ez how they should vote and set on juries and sware away white folkes rites as much as they damm please. You are backin up this notion by a sellin of em land and hosses and mules, till they are gittin so big in ther boots they cant rest. You've bin warned that sech things wont be born; but you jes go on ez if ther want nobody else on arth. Now, we've jes made up our minds not to stan it enny longer. We've been and larned yer damm niggers better manners than to be a ridin hossback when white folks is walkin. The Regulators hez met, and decided thet no nigger shant be allowed to own no hoss nor run no crop on his own account herearter. And no nigger-worshipin Yankee spy thet encourages them in their insolense shel live in the county. Now, sir, we gives you three days to git away. Ef your here when that time's over, the buzzards wil hev a bait thats been right scarce since the war was over. You may think wes foolin. Other people hez made thet mistake to ther sorrer. Ef you don't want to size a coffin jest yit you better git a ticket that will take you towards the North Star jes ez far ez the roads been cut out.

"By order of
"The Capting of the Regulators."

The Fool at once published this letter in "The Verdenton Gazette," with a short, sturdy answer, saying that he was minding his own business, and expected other people to mind theirs. He paid for it as an advertisement, — the only terms on which the editor would admit it to his columns. This proceeding, which in the North or in any other State of society would have awakened the liveliest indignation towards those who thus attempted to drive him away from his home, as well as a strong sympathy for him, had no such effect upon this community. Many openly approved the course of the mob; others faintly condemned; and no one took any steps to prevent the consummation of the outrage threatened. No one seemed to think that the Fool was entitled to any support or sympathy. That he should sell land to colored men, and assist them to purchase stock, was considered by nearly the entire community as an offense deserving the worst punishment; and that he should go farther, and publicly favor their enfranchisement, was such a gross outrage upon the feelings and prejudices of the whites, that many seemed much surprised that any warning at all had been given by the "Regulators."

The one most interested, however, was not idle. He procured arms and ammunition, and prepared for the defense of his life and property, and the protection of his tenants and those to whom he had sold. A stockade was built for the horses in a favorable position, a guard provided, and signals agreed on in case of an attack. The commandant of the troops at a neighboring station sent a small detachment, which remained for a few days, and was then withdrawn. They had not been required by the owner of Warrington; but the rumor went out that he had called for troops to protect him, and the feeling grew day by day more hostile towards him.

CHAPTER XVII

THE SECOND MILE POST

WHEN the second Christmas came, Metta wrote again to her sister: —

"DEAR JULIA, — It is more than a year since I wrote you my first letter from our Southern home. Alas! except for the improvements we have made in Warrington, and the increased sense of homeliness which we feel in our inanimate surroundings, it is hardly any more like home than it was then. Comfort has been very busy. He has put quite a new face on Warrington, which is more delightful than any description could convey to you. Almost every day he is out super-intending and directing the work, and, Yankee-like, 'doing right smart of it' himself, as they say here. This, with the delightful climate and my care, — for I must have some of the credit, — has transformed my invalid husband into a cheerful, stalwart man, who seems to be in constant enjoyment of life.

"Most of my time is occupied with teaching our little daughter, or rather coaxing her to learn, for she is the most strangely willful child in this respect you ever saw. I am taking much pains with her, and she is making wonderful progress in a peculiar sort of a way. She is out with her father on the plantation a great deal, and, as a result, knows the name of every tree and flower, wild or cultivated, which grows about Warrington. She has either inherited or acquired that wonderful power of observation which Comfort has, and is already better versed in some branches of knowledge than I am likely ever to be.

"This, with my few household cares, and the enjoyment of rides, walks, and all sorts of excursions, makes up my life. Mere existence here is a constant joy. The sunshine is brighter, the moonlight softer, the sky fairer, the earth more seductive, than in the old home. There is a sort of intoxication in it all, — the flowers, coming at odd times and with unwonted richness and profusion; the trees, of a strangely charming outline and foliage, making forest and grove, which have always some sort of weird charm, so different from what we ever knew at the North; and over all the balmy air.

"And yet we miss our friends, — ah! sadly enough, — for we have none here, and somehow can not make any. I am sure no one ever came to a new home with kindlier feelings for all who might surround us than we did. You know Comfort would not hear a word about trouble with the people here. He would insist that they were a brave, genial people; that the war was over; and that everybody would be better friends hereafter from its having occurred. He has found out his mistake. I am afraid we shall have no *real* friends here. There are some, perhaps, who think well of us, and, no doubt, wish us well in the main; but they are not friends. Somehow it seems that the old distrust and dislike of Northern people will not let them be friendly and confiding with us; or perhaps the fault may be with us. We are so different, have been reared under such different influences, and have such different thoughts, that it does not seem as if we should ever get nearer to them.

"You heard about our trouble with the 'Regulators.' Comfort got a lot of guns and ammunition for the colored men, and made preparations to fight in good earnest; but they have not disturbed us since. Mr. Savage sent them word that they could not hurt us until they had killed him, and came over and staid with us some weeks. I think it was his influence which saved us from further attack.

"The feeling is terribly bitter against Comfort on account of his course towards the colored people. There is quite a village of them on the lower end of the plantation. They have a church, a sabbath school, and are to have next year a school. You can not imagine how kind they have been to us, and how much they are attached to Comfort. They are having a 'tracted meeting,' as they call it, now I got Comfort to go with me to one of their prayer-meetings a few nights ago. I had heard a great deal about them, but had never attended one before. It was strangely weird. There were, perhaps, fifty present, mostly middle-aged men and women. They were singing in a soft, low monotone, interspersed with prolonged exclamatory notes, a sort of rude hymn, which I was surprised to know was one of their old songs in slave times. How the chorus came to be endured in those days I can not imagine. It was —

'Free! free! free, my Lord, free!
An' we walks de hebben-ly way!'

"A few looked around as we came in and seated ourselves; and Uncle Jerry, the saint of the settlement, came forward on his staves, and said, in his soft voice, —

"'Ev'nin', Kunnel! Sarvant, Missus! Will you walk up, an' hev seats in front?'

"We told him we had just looked in, and might go in a short time; so we would stay in the back part of the audience.

"Uncle Jerry can not read nor write; but he is a man of strange intelligence and power. Unable to do work of any account, he is the faithful friend, monitor, and director of others. He has a house and piece of land, all paid for, a good horse and cow, and, with the aid of his wife and two boys, made a fine crop this season. He is one of the most promising colored men in the settlement: so Comfort says, at least. Everybody seems to have great respect for his character. I don't know how many people I have heard speak of his religion. Mr. Savage used to say he had rather hear him pray than any other man on earth. He was much prized by his master, even after he was disabled, on account of his faithfulness and character.

"The meeting was led that night by a mulatto man named Robert, who was what is now called an 'old-issue free nigger' (freed before the war). He seemed very anxious to display the fact that he could read, and, with comical pride, blundered through 'de free hunner'n firty-fird hymn,' and a chapter of Scripture. Some of his comments on passages of the latter were ludicrously apt. 'I indeed baptize with water; but he that cometh after me shall baptize with the Holy Ghost and with fire,' he read with difficulty. 'Baptize wid water,' he repeated thoughtfully. 'We all know what dat is; an' baptizin' wid de Holy Ghos', dat's what we's come here arter tonight. ['Amen!' 'Bress God!' 'Dar now!'] But baptizin' wid fire! — 'clar, brudderin' an' sisters, it allers makes my har *stan' straight* tu think what dat ar *muss* mean! Baptize wid fire! I spec' dat's de tryin' ob de gold in de furnace, — de Lord's furnace, — dat clars out all de dross, but muss be powerful hot!'

"There was nothing special then for some time, until one man began weaving back and forth on his knees, and shouted, in a voice which might have been heard a mile, for fifteen or twenty minutes, only one sentence — 'Gather 'em in! O Lor', gather 'em in! Gather 'em in! O Lor', gather 'em in!' — in a strange, singing tone, the effect of which upon the nerves was something terrible. Men shouted, women screamed. Some sprang from their knees, and danced, shouting, and tossing their arms about in an unconscious manner, reminding me of what I had read of the dancing dervishes of the Orient. One woman fainted; and finally the see-sawing shouter himself fell over. Some water was poured on his head, a slow soothing hymn was sung, and in five minutes the assemblage was as quiet as any country prayer-meeting in Michigan. For me, I found myself clinging to Comfort's arm in almost hysterical fright. I begged him to take me away, but am very glad now that he did not.

"After a time Uncle Jerry raised his head, which had all the time been bowed upon his knees since the meeting began, and, lifting his thin hands towards the people, said, in a soft, clear voice, —

"'Let us all kneel down, an' pray, — one mo' short pra'r! short pra'r!'

"He knelt with his face towards us. The guttered candle on the rough pine table threw its flickering light over him, as, with upturned face and clasping hands, he 'talked with God,' oh, how simply and directly! And, as he prayed, a strange light seemed to come over his brown face, set in its white frame of snowy hair and beard. He prayed for all, except himself, and seemed to bring the cares and troubles of all before the throne of grace, as if he had the key to the heart of each.

"Then he came to pray for us, — 'the stranger fren' whom God has raised up an' led, in his myster'ous way, to do us good, — bless him, O Lord, in basket an' sto', heart an' home! He don't know what he's got afo' him! Stay his han', an' keep him strong an' brave!' But I can never reproduce the strange tenderness and faith of this prayer. I leaned my head on Comfort's shoulder, and the tears fell like rain as I listened. All at once there was silence. The voice of prayer had ceased; yet the prayer did not seem ended. I raised my eyes, and looked. Uncle Jerry still knelt at his chair, every worshiper still kneeling in his place; but every head was turned, and every eye was fastened on him. His eyes were fixed — on what? He was looking upward, as if he saw beyond the earth. His face was set in rigid lines, yet lighted up with a look of awful joy. His breath came slow and sobbingly; but, aside from that, not a muscle moved. Not a word was uttered; but every look was fastened on him with hushed and fearful expectancy.

" 'Hain't bin dat way but once afo' sence de surrender,' I heard one of the women whisper, under her breath, to another.

"Five minutes — perhaps ten minutes — elapsed, and he had not spoken or moved. It was fearful, the terrible silence, and that fixed, immovable face and stony figure! There was something preternatural about it.

"At length there came a quiver about the lips. The eyes lost their fixity. The hands which had rested on the chair were clasped together, and a look of divine rapture swept across the upturned face, as he exclaimed, in a tone fairly burdened with ecstatic joy, —

" 'I *sees* Him! I sees *Him!* Dar He *is!*' And he pointed, with a thin and trembling hand, towards the farther corner of the room. 'I sees Him wid de crown ob salvation on His head; de keys o' hebben a-hangin' in His girdle, — God's keys for de white pearl gates, — wid de bress-plate ob Holiness an' de mantle ob Righteousness. Dah He is a-walkin among de candlesticks *yit!* He's a-comin' nigh us, — bress His holy name! — a-lookin' arter His people, and a-gatherin' on 'em in!'

"I can not tell you what a strange rhapsody fell from his lips; but it ended as it began, — suddenly, and without warning. The glorified look faded from his face. The sentence died midway on his lips. His eyes regained their conscious look, and ran around the hushed circle of attent faces, while a knowledge of what had taken place seemed first to flash upon him. He covered his face with his hands, and sank down with a groan, exclaiming, in apologetic tones, —

" 'O Lor'! O Lor'! thou knowest de weakness ob dy sarvant! Spar' him! spar' him!' The meeting ended, and we went home. Somehow I can not get over the feeling that the little log-church is a place where one has indeed seen God.

"They told us afterwards that Uncle Jerry often had these 'spells,' as they call them, whenever there was a great battle pending or imminent during the war, and they could always tell which way the fight had gone, by what he said in these trances. They say he knows nothing of what he says at such times. I asked him about it one day. He simply said, 'I can't 'splain it, Missus. 'Pears like it's a cross I hez specially to carry. It's made me a heap o' trouble. Bin whipped fer it heaps o' times; an', 'sides dat, I allers feel ez if I'd lived 'bout ten years when I comes out o' one o' dem spells. Can't understan' it, Missus; but Uncle Jerry'll quit in some of dem spells yit!'

"We do not often go to church now. There is no positive incivility offered us; but there is a constant coldness, which says, plainer than words can, that we are not wanted. Comfort still has hope that these things will wear away as time passes; but I begin to think that we shall always be strangers in the land in which we dwell. I do not see any chance for it to be otherwise. The North and the South are two peoples, utterly dissimilar in all their characteristics; and I am afraid that more than one generation must pass before they will become one.

"Your loving sister,

"METTA."

CHAPTER XVIII

CONGRATULATION AND CONDOLENCE

Soon after the Fool's publication of the Regulators' warning and his own reply in "The Verdenton Gazette," he received many letters, some of which may be given as illustrative of the atmosphere in which he lived. The first of these came from a remote portion of the State, and from one of whom the Fool had never even heard: —

"Colonel Comfort Servosse. *Dear Sir*, — I saw your letter in 'The Verdenton Gazette,' and was so struck with the similarity of our positions, that I determined to write to you at once. Some of the worst of our people, as I believe, have formed themselves into a band of Regulators for the sake of attending to everybody's business but their own. I am a native of this State, and fought through the war in the Confederate army, from Bull Run to Appomattox, never missing a day's duty nor a fight. When it was over, I found myself with only a few hundred acres of land (which had been tramped over and burned and stripped by both armies), and no money, no crop, no stock, a large family, some debts, good health, and a constitution like white hickory. I made up my mind to go to work at once. I went to the nearest post, told my story, and got two horses. I did some hauling, and got some other things, — an army wagon and an ambulance. A friend who happened to have saved some cotton sold it, and loaned me a little money. I went to work, hired some niggers, told them I would feed them, and work with them, and, when the crop was sold, we would divide. They turned in, and worked with me. We made a splendid crop, and I divided right smart of money with them in the fall.

"This year some of them wanted to work crops on shares. I could trust them, as they had worked for me the year before. I knew they had enough to bread themselves, and were well able to run a 'one-horse crop.' This would allow me to use my means in putting in more land elsewhere, and so be decidedly to my advantage as well as theirs. I was thinking of my own profit, though, when I did it. Well, I sold some of them horses and mules, and helped others to get them elsewhere. The spring opened, and I had the busiest farm and finest prospect I have ever seen. I was running a big force, and every nigger on the plantation had a full crop about half pitched, when all at once I got a notice from the Regulators, just about like the one you publish, only they didn't require me to leave, only to stop selling horses to niggers and letting them crop on shares. They said they had made up their minds that no nigger should straddle his own horse, or ride in his own cart, in this county.

"I saw in a minute that it meant ruin to Exum Davis either way. If I gave in to them, I discouraged my hands, spoilt my crop, and would be swamped by my fertilizer account in the fall. If I didn't, the cussed fools would be deviling and worrying my hands, hamstringing their stock, and my crop would be short. It didn't take me long to decide. I made up my mind to fight.

"It wasn't an hour after I read that notice, before I had every horse and mule on the place hauling pine-logs for a stockade; though I didn't let anybody know what I had on hand. Then I went off to Gainsborough to see the post commander there, Colonel Ricker. He is a good fellow and a gentleman, if he is a Yankee. I told him square out what the matter was; and he let me have as many old guns as I wanted (part of them surrendered arms, and part extra guns of his command), and a couple boxes of ammunition. When I got back, I told the boys what was up, and distributed the arms. We put our horses in the woods that night, stood to our arms all night, put up the stockade next day, and sent word to the Regulators that they might go to hell. We've kept at work, being mighty careful not to be surprised, and have not been disturbed yet. I don't reckon we shall be; but there is no telling. I say, Stand your ground. They say you're a 'Yank;' but that don't make any difference. Law's law, and right's right; and I hope you will give anybody that comes to disturb you as warm a welcome as they would get here from

"Yours respectfully,

"EXUM DAVIS."

The next was from the old doctor, George D. Garnet: —

"MY DEAR COLONEL, — I was sorry to see that the feeling against you, because you are of Northern birth, which has been smoldering ever since you came among us, has at last burst into a flame. I have been expecting it all the time, and so can not say I am surprised; but it has been so long in showing itself, that I was truly in hopes that you would escape further molestation. I know that I had no reason to anticipate such a result, because you represent a development utterly antagonistic to that in the midst of which you are placed, and are so imbued with its spirit that you can not lay aside nor conceal its characteristics. That civilization by which you are surrounded has never been tolerant of opinions which do not harmonize with its ideas. Based and builded on slavery, the ideas which were a part of that institution, or which were necessary to its protection and development, have become ingrained, and essential to the existence of the community. It was this development which was even more dangerous and inimical to the nation than the institution itself. You must remember, dear Colonel, that neither the nature, habits of thought, nor prejudices of men, are changed by war or its results. The institution of slavery is abolished; but the prejudice, intolerance, and bitterness which it fostered and nourished, are still alive, and will live until those who were raised beneath its glare have moldered back to dust. A new generation — perhaps many new generations — must arise before the North and the South can be one people, or the prejudices, resentments, and ideas of slavery, intensified by unsuccessful war, can be obliterated.

"I hope you will not be discouraged. Your course is the right one, and by pursuing it steadily you will sow the seed of future good. You may not live to reap its advantages, or to see others gather its fair fruits; but, as God is the God of truth and right, he will send a husbandman who will some time gather full sheaves from your seeding, if you do not faint.

"To show you that not only you who are from the North are made to feel the weight of disapproval which our Southern society visits upon those who do not accord with all its sentiments, I inclose you a certificate which I received from the church at Mayfield the other day. I have been a member and a deacon of this church for almost quarter of a century. I was lately informed that my name had been dropped from the church-roll. Upon inquiry, I found that I had been expelled by vote of the church, without a trial. I demanded a certificate of the fact as a vindication of my character, and the inclosed is what was given me. It is neither more nor less than I had expected for some time; but it comes hard to a man who has reached his three-score years, and now sees his children pointed at in scorn, contemned and ostracized by the church of God, because their father does what he conceives to be his Christian duty.

"With warmest regards for yourself and wife, and the fair-haired child who fills the sad old house with sunshine, I remain,

"Yours very truly,
"GEORGE D. GARNET."

The inclosure to which he referred read as follows: —

"To WHOM IT MAY CONCERN, — This is to certify, that on the first day of April, 1867, the deacons and members of the Baptist Church, at Mayfield, in regular church meeting assembled, Brother R. Lawrence acting as moderator, did unanimously pass the following resolution: —

" 'Resolved, That brother Deacon George D. Garnet be dropped from the roll of this church, because he walketh not with us.' And subsequently, on the same day, at the request of brother George D. Garnet, and to show that it was not from his bad moral character that the said church refuses longer to fellowship with him, the following was added to said resolution as explanatory of it; to wit, 'but persists, after repeated warnings and advice, upon organizing, encouraging, and teaching in a negro sabbath school, by which he has made himself a stumbling-block and means of offense to many of the members of said church.'

(Signed)

"JOHN SENTER, Clerk.
"ROBERT LAWRENCE, Deacon and Moderator."

The next letter was from a Union man of considerable eminence, who occupied the important position of public prosecutor in the courts of the State. He wrote a letter which is significant in many ways of the public sentiment of the day: —

"COLONEL COMFORT SERVOSSE. Dear Sir, — I notice by your letter in 'The Gazette' that you are not only angry, but also surprised, at the outrageous demands of the Regulators. Your anger is but natural; but your surprise, you will allow me to say, shows 'an understanding simple and unschooled.' That you should be unable to measure the strength of prejudice in the Southern mind is not strange. You should remember that the war has rather intensified than diminished the pride, the arrogance, and the sectional rancor and malevolence of the Southern people. If you will consider it for a moment, you will see that this is the natural and unavoidable result of such a struggle. All that made the Southern slaveholder and rebel what he was, still characterizes him since the surrender. The dogma of State-sovereignty has been prevented from receiving practical development, but as a theory it is as vital and as sacred as ever. The fact of slavery is destroyed: the right to enslave is yet as devoutly held as ever. The right of a white man to certain political privileges is admitted: the right of a colored man to such, it will require generations to establish. It is not at you as an individual that the blow is struck; but these people feel that you, by the very fact of Northern birth, and service in the Federal army, represent a power which has deprived them of property, liberty, and a right to control their own, and that now, in sheer wantonness of insult, you are encouraging the colored people to do those two things which are more sacred than any other to the Southern mind; to wit, to *buy and hold land* and to *ride their own horses.* You can not understand why they should feel so, because you were never submitted to the same influences. You have a right to be angry; but your surprise is incredible to them, and pitiable to me.

"To show you to what extent prejudice will extend, permit me to relate an incident yet fresh in my mind. During a recent trial in the court at Martinsville I had occasion to challenge the jurors upon the trial of an indictment of a white man for killing a negro. The Court, after some hesitation, permitted me to ask each juror this question, 'Have you any feeling which would prevent you from convicting a white man for the murder of a negro, should the evidence show him to be guilty?' Strange and discreditable as it may appear to you, it became necessary, in addition to the regular panel, to order *three writs of venire, of fifty each, before twelve men could be found who could answer this simple question in the negative.* When prejudice goes so far that a hundred and fifty men acknowledge upon their oaths that they will not convict a white man for killing a negro, you must not be surprised that the *ante bellum* dislike and distrust of Northern men should show itself in the same manner. The South has been changed only in so far as the overwhelming power of the conqueror has rendered change imperative. In its old domain, prejudice is still as bitter and unreasoning as ever. Perhaps I ought not to reproach you for expressing surprise; since it was not clear even to me, a native, until I had carefully studied the cause and effect. While I sincerely regret the unfortunate folly of these men, and hope it may extend no farther, I must still beg you to consider that it is only what must always be expected under such circumstances as the recent past has witnessed.

"If you have any clew to the persons guilty of this act, or if I can be of any service in freeing you from annoyances, please to consider me, both personally and officially,

Yours to command,

"Thomas Denton."

The other two were directed to Metta. The first was from the wife of a Northern man who had settled in a neighboring State, and whom Metta had met at the house of a common friend some months before. It was edged with black, and told a sad story: —

"My dear Mrs. Servosse, — I have desired to write you for several days, but have been too overwhelmed with grief to do so. You have probably seen in the papers the account of my husband's death. You know he was appointed sheriff of this county a few months ago by the general commanding the district. There was a great deal of feeling about the matter, and I begged him not to accept. Somehow I had a presentiment of evil to come from it; but he laughed at my fears, said he should only to his duty, and there could be no cause of increased hostility against him. Indeed, I think he had an idea, that, when the people found out that his only purpose was to administer the office fairly, they would respect his motives, and be more friendly than they had been for the past few months. He never would believe that the hostility towards Northern men was any thing more than a temporary fever.

"After he entered upon the office, there were many threats made against him, and I begged him not to expose himself. But he did not know what fear was, and rode all over the county at all times, in the performance of his duties, coming home every night when it was possible, however, because he knew of my anxiety. One week ago to-day he was detained at the court-house later than usual. You know we live about five miles from the county-seat. As night came on I grew very anxious about him. I seemed to know that danger threatened him. Finally I became so uneasy that I had my mare saddled, and rode to meet him, as I frequently did. The road is almost directly westward, winding through an overhanging forest, with only here and there a plantation road leading off to a neighbor's house.

"It was almost sundown when I started. Would to God it had been earlier! Perhaps I might have saved him then. I had gone about a mile, when, rising a little eminence, I saw him coming down the slope beyond, and at a little branch at the foot of the hill I stopped to wait for him. He waved his hat as he saw me, and struck into a brisk canter. I wanted to give the mare the whip, and gallop to him; but I feared he would see my alarm, and count it childish: so I sat and waited. He had come half the distance, when suddenly there was a puff of smoke from the roadside. I did not wait even to hear the report, but with a cry of despair struck my horse, and rushed forward like the wind. I saw him fall from his horse, which rushed madly by me. Then I saw three miscreants steal away from a leafy blind, behind which they had been hidden; and then I had my poor murdered husband in my arms, heard his last struggling gasp, and felt his warm heart-blood gushing over my hands as I clasped him to my breast. I knew nothing more until I was at home with my dead.

"Oh, my dear friend, I can not picture to you my desolation! It is so horrible! If he had died in battle, I could have endured it; even accident, or swift disease, it seems to me, I could have borne: but this horrible, causeless murder fills me with rage and hate as well as grief. Why did we ever come to this accursed land! And oh, my friend, do not neglect my warning! Do not cease your entreaty until your husband hears your prayers. Do not risk the fate which has befallen me.

"Yours in hopeless sorrow,

"ALICE E. COLEMAN."

The other letter was in a neat, feminine hand, written on the coarse, dingy paper known as "Confederate paper," which was the only kind accessible during the blockade. It was evidently written by a woman of culture. It was not signed with any name, but only "Your true friend," and bore the postmark of Verdenton: —

"MY DEAR MRS. SERVOSSE, — Though you do not know who I am, I have seen you, and am sure you are not only a lady, but a sensible, true-hearted woman. Though a stranger, I would not have you suffer grief, or incur trouble, if in my power to prevent it. Please, then, dear madam, listen to the advice of a sincere well-wisher, and do all in your power to persuade your husband to leave this part of the country. I am sure he can not be a bad man, or you would not love him so well. But you must know that his ideas are very obnoxious to us Southern people; and if he stays here, and continues to express them as he has hitherto, I feel that there will be trouble. You know our Southern gentlemen can not endure any reflections upon their conduct or motives; and the hopes and aspirations which gathered around the Confederacy are all the dearer from the fate of our 'Lost Cause.' I know whereof I write." [The next sentence had been commenced with the words "My husband," which had been so nearly erased that they could only be read with difficulty.] "Several gentlemen were speaking of the matter in my hearing only last night, and I tremble to think what may occur if you do not heed my warning."

"O dear lady! let me beg you, as a Christian woman, to implore your husband to go away. You do not know what sorrow you will save, not only yourself, but others who would mourn almost as deeply as you, and perhaps more bitterly. The war is over; and oh! if you have mourned as much as I over its havoc, you will be willing to do and suffer any thing in order to avoid further bloodshed, violence, evil, and sorrow. May God guide you!

"I can only sign myself

"YOUR TRUE FRIEND."

Metta took these letters to the Fool, and laid them silently before him. Her face looked gray and wan, and there was the shadow of a great fear in her eyes, as she did so. He read them over carefully, laid them down, and looked up into her face as he said, —

"Well?"

"I thought I ought to show them to you, dear husband," she said with quivering lip; and then the pent-up tears overflowed the swollen lids, as she buried her head on his breast, and, clasped in his arms, wept long and convulsively. When her grief was somewhat soothed, he said, —

"What do you wish me to do, Metta?"

"Whatever you think to be your duty, my dear husband," she replied, the sunshine of wifely devotion showing through the last drops of the shower.

He kissed her forehead and lips, — kissed away the briny tears from her eyes.

"We will stay," said the Fool.

The subject of removal from their adopted home was never again mooted between them.

CHAPTER XIX

CITIZENS IN EMBRYO

"WHAT you tink ob de League, Kunnel?" said a sturdy, intelligent colored man, who, under direction of Comfort Servosse, was pruning the grape-vines that were scattered about in all manner of unexpected places, as well as in the staid and orderly rows of the vineyard at Warrington. It was a bright day in winter; and the stricken soldier was gathering strength and vitality by the unconscious medicament of the soft sunshine and balmy breezes, and that light labor which the care of trees and vines encouraged. He stood now critically surveying a long-neglected "Diana," on which he was about to commence operations, his pruning-knife in his hand, and his shears sticking out from a side-pocket of his overalls. At the next vine was working his interlocutor, who glanced slyly towards him as he asked the question.

"The 'League,' Andy?" said Servosse, looking at his co-laborer with an amused smile, while he tried the edge of his knife with his thumb. "What league do you mean?"

"De Union League, ob co'se. Didn't know dar was any udder. Is dah?" said Andy, as he finished tying up the vine at which he had been at work, and started to the next.

"Oh, yes! there are various kinds of leagues. But why do you inquire about the Union League? How did you ever hear of it?"

"Wal, putty much de same way you did, I 'spects," answered Andy with a grin.

"Pretty much as I did?" said Servosse. "What do you mean?"

"Why, I 'llow you b'longs to it," said Andy. "Dey tells me every Union soldier b'longs to it. 'Sides dat, I made de

knocks de udder day on de work-bench, when you was work-
in' at de wisteria in front o' de winder, an' I seed you look up
kinder sudden-like, an' den smile to youself as if you thought
you'd heerd from an ole friend, an' woke up to find ye'd been
a-dreamin'."

"So I did, Andy," answered the Caucasian. "Some time during the war I heard of an organization known as the Union
League. It strikes me that I first heard of it in the mountains
of East Tennessee, as instituted for self-protection and mutual
support among the sturdy Unioners there in those trying times.
However that may be, I first came in contact with its workings in the fall of 1864. It was the very darkest period of the
war for us. The struggle had lasted so long that everybody was
tired out. The party in the North who were opposed to the
war" —

"Wasn't they called 'Copperheads'?" interrupted Andy.

"Yes, we called them 'Copperheads,'" answered the Fool.
"These men seemed to think that it would be a good time to
stop the war, on the idea that both sides were tired of it, and
would rather end it on any terms than keep it up on uncertain-
ties. So they were making great efforts to elect a president
who would let up on the Rebellion, and enable the rebels of
the South to accomplish their secession. At this time I escaped from a Confederate prison, and after a time arrived in
Philadelphia. While I waited there for orders, a friend asked
me one night if I didn't want to join the Union League. Upon
asking what it was, I found that it was a society of men who
were determined never to give up the Union under any hazard, but to uphold and sustain it with property and life if
need be. It was a secret association; and its chief purpose was
said to be to enable the loyal people of any city or neighborhood to muster at the shortest possible notice, to resist inva-
sion, put down riot, or enforce the law, — to protect themselves and families, or aid the government in extremities."

"Was it any good?" asked Andy.

"Well, indeed," responded his employer musingly, "I do not know. A soldier who was on duty at the front the greater part of the war had very little opportunity for knowing what went on in his rear. I have heard that when 'Lee marched over the mountain-wall' into Maryland and Pennsylvania, and threatened Philadelphia and Baltimore, the bells of Philadelphia struck the signals of the League, and thousands rallied at their places of assembly in an instant; and that regiment after regiment of resolute minute men were organized and equipped almost without an hour's delay. I know nothing about it."

"Do you want dis 'Concord' cut back to two eyes, like de rest, Kunnel? It's made a powerful strong growth, an' it seems a clar waste to cut it back so close," asked the hireling, as he held up for his employer's inspection a rank-grown cane of the previous year, which had run along the ground until it had appropriated the stake of a weakling neighbor, and clambered over it, smothering in its sturdy coils the growth of the rightful owner.

"Yes," said Servosse hesitatingly, "cut it down. It seems a pity, as you say, to destroy that beautiful growth; but, when vines have run wild for a time, the only way to bring them back to sober, profitable bearing, is to cut them back without scruple. Cut them down to two eyes, if they are as big as your wrist, Andy. It's wasting the past, but saving the future. And it's my notion that the same thing is true of peoples and nations, Andy. For instance, when a part of a country rebels, and runs wild for a time, it ought to have the rank wood, the wild growth, cut away without mercy. They ought to be held down, and pruned and shaped, until they are content to bear 'the peaceable fruits of righteousness,' instead of clambering about, 'cumbering the ground' with a useless growth."

"You was sayin' what de League had done, a while ago," said Andy, after there had been a period of silence, while they each cut away at their respective vines.

"Yes," said Servosse. "I have heard, too, that the order was very useful as a sort of reserve force in the rear, in putting down such terrible riots as were gotten up in New York in the dark days of the war, by emissaries of the enemy, acting with the Copperheads of the North."

"Was dar many of 'em — de Leaguers I mean?" asked Andy.

"I understand," was the reply, "that it spread pretty much all through the North in the later years of the war, and embraced a very large portion of the Union men in those states."

"Did all de Yankee soldiers belong to it?" queried the listener.

"Really, I don't know," said Servosse. "I don't suppose I have ever heard more than a dozen or two say any thing about it in the army. I suppose most of the veterans who went home on leave of absence in 1864 may have joined it while at home, and the new levies may have belonged to it. Of course, we had no need for such an organization in the army."

"Well, is der any harm in it, Kunnel? Any reason why anybody shouldn't jine it?" asked Andy earnestly.

"None in the world, that I can see," answered Servosse. "Indeed, I do not see why it should not be a good thing for the colored people to do. It would teach them to organize and work together, and they would learn in it something about those public duties which are sure very soon to be cast upon them. Besides, it is by no means sure that they may not need it as a means of self-protection. I had not thought of it before; but I believe it might be a good thing."

"Dat's my notion, Mars' Kunnel. We's got a little league down h'yer to Verdenton at de schoolhouse fer de culled folks, an' we'd be mighty proud tu hev ye come down some Chuseday night. Dat we would!" said Andy.

"What! you have got a chapter of the Union League there?"

"Yes: it's jes' like what you's been a-tellin' 'bout."

"How did you get it?"

"Wal, I don't jes' 'zactly know. Dar's some culled men belongs to it as was soldiers in de Union army, an' I 'llowed dey might hev fotch it wid 'em when dey come h'yer. Dat's what made me ax you so close 'bout dat."

"Who belong to it? Are they all colored members?"

"Wal, de heft ob 'em is culled, ob co'se; but der's a right smart sprinklin' ob white folks, arter all. Dar's all de Ufford boys: dey wuz Unioners, an' was hidin' out all de wah; an' dey say dey hed somefin' monstrous nigh like it in de bushes, an' 'long de lines, — what dey call de 'Red Stringems,' er somethin' like dat. Den dar's Mr. Murry: he was jes' de rantankerousest Union man dat ever was, all tru de wah. I'se heerd him cuss de Kinfederacy right out when de soldiers was marchin' long de street fo' his do'. He'll du tu tie tu, *he* will. He says it does him good tu hear us sing 'Rally roun' de Flag,' an' de 'Battle-Cry o' Freedom,' an' sech like songs, kase he says it's *his* flag, an' he's only 'sprised dat everybody don't rally roun' it. I reckon der's ez much ez a dozen white folks in all. Some ez you wouldn't 'spect on't, tu. You'd du us proud ef you'd come down, Mars' Kunnel."

"Who's your president, Andy?"

"Wal, sometimes one, an' sometimes anudder, jes' accordin' tu who's scholard enuff tu take de lead," answered Andy, with ready pride in his new toy.

The idea was very amusing to the Fool; and, the more he thought of it, the more he was convinced that it might be a valuable training-school to the inchoate citizens of the lately rebellious States. Even while he was discussing the facts which surrounded him, he could not realize them; and he quite forgot, in giving his assent to this idea, the fact that he was living at the South, among a people who did not kindly brook differences of opinion among equals, and who would be sure to resent with an implacable hostility any society which not only recognized the political autonomy of the recently subject race, but also encouraged that race to look up to the government their masters had failed to destroy as *their* government, *their* guardian, *their* protector; which not only promoted ideas not in harmony with those of the former rulers of this section, but promoted the elevation of the freedman, prepared him for civil life, and gave him confidence in himself as a political integer. Had he thought of this, it is certain that he would not have consented so readily to go and see Andy's society; for what he most feared was a conflict or permanent antagonism between the freedmen and their former masters; and he thought that any sacrifice, not going to the substance of their liberties, ought to be made rather than that such a conflict should be risked.

However, stumbling over these apparent facts, he went on the next Tuesday night to the schoolhouse in the suburbs of Verdenton. It was just beyond the line of Warrington; and the little village which had grown up on his own estate was but a continuation of the suburb, which, as in all Southern cities, had been tacitly given up to the blacks since the close of the war. It was a long, low building, made for service, — one of that numerous array of buildings which was mainly furnished to the recently emancipated seeker after knowledge by the systematic bounty of that much abused institution, the Freedmen's Bureau. Acting in conjunction with various religious and benevolent societies of the North, it furnished a class of buildings better adapted to the needs of those for whom they were designed, and affording greater results, than was ever done in all history with like means. In every village of the South was erected one or more of these rough wooden buildings, consisting only of roof, rafter, walls and floor of undressed plank. The minimum of cost and the maximum of space were the objects kept constantly in view, and usually attained beyond all question. These houses became to the colored people what the court of the temple was to the Jews, — the place of assembly and worship, as well as of instruction. They were usually unsectarian; and it was no unusual spectacle to see two or three denominations worshiping in the same house, while the school was under the management and control of still another.

To them thronged with wondrous eagerness the old and young alike of the recently emancipated race. The building to which Comfort Servosse went that night was an imposing structure in its dimensions. In it seven ladies who had come from far Northern homes, filled with the genuine spirit of the missionary, and no doubt thinking themselves endowed with the spirit of that Redeemer who taught publicans in the market or in the desert, despite the frowns of the Pharisees, held sway. These seven fair, pure-hearted Northern girls taught within its walls each day, and oftentimes at night, six hundred and more of the race which had just now its first chance at the tree of knowledge since our common mother persisted in eating the mystic apple. They, no doubt, thought they were doing God's service, and wondered why the earnest Christians who dwelt about them should regard the inhabitants of the Mission House with such open aversion and apparent hate. It must have seemed strange to these fresh young believers to see the seats of the churches in the town, in front and rear of where they sat, upon the sabbath, vacated by the most devout of God's people in Verdenton. They wondered at it for a time, and then blamed the good people of Verdenton, and thought ill of their religion; when it was not the good people who were at fault, nor their religion, but only the civilization of which they were the outcome. There was never a kindlier, more hospitable, or more religious people on the footstool, than those of Verdenton; only they were kind according to *their notion*, as everybody else is; hospitable according to custom,

like the rest of the world; and religious according to education
and tradition, as are other people; and the disjointure of opinion between them and the Yankee schoolmarms was all because the latter wanted to measure them by Northern ideas of
these virtues, instead of accepting those they found there.
Sometimes they wrote indignant letters to their friends at
home; but it was fortunate that the greater part of the evil
things which were said of them by the neighboring Christians
never came to their knowledge, and that their hearts were too
pure to comprehend the foul innuendoes which floated by
them. So they went on teaching, as they had been taught, those
who had been all their lives thitherto untaught; and the
others went on hating and defaming them because such a
course was counter to their traditions, and those who did it
were their hereditary enemies. And both, no doubt, felt that
they were doing God's service with their might.

Servosse found a cordon of watchers about the schoolhouse,
by one of whom he was challenged, and, after learning who
he was, taken to the house, where he was carefully examined
to ascertain whether he were a member or not; after which
he was admitted into the room where the meeting was held.
It was a large classroom in the second story, capable of seat-
ing, perhaps, two hundred people. It was about half full when
he arrived, as the meeting had not yet been called to order; and
constant arrivals were fast increasing the number. The great
bulk of those who were present were colored men; but in a
little group at the right of the platform were perhaps a dozen
white men.

The Fool found himself well known to all those present,
though he had not yet acquired the power readily to distin-
guish and retain the countenances of colored people. As he advanced into the room, he was met with numerous and delight-
ed greetings, to which he responded pleasantly, without, in
most instances, recognizing those who gave them. Near the

center of the room, however, he was met by Uncle Jerry, who, bowing ceremoniously, waved his hand toward the knot of white men, as he exclaimed, —

"Evenin', Mars Kunnel. Sarvant, sah! We's glad to see ye wid us, — powerful glad! Ye knows dese gentlemen, I s'pose. Mr. Durfee, Kunnel 'Vosse; Mr. Morgin, Kunnel 'Vosse. But you knows 'em all, Kunnel; I sees dat," said the old man, as Comfort clasped the hand of one after another, some of whom he was prepared to meet, and others of whom he was surprised to see there. Among the former was Durfee, a young man who belonged to a family of the strongest Union proclivities, who had faced far more danger in resisting and avoiding conscription than he would have been required to meet in the field.

"Ah!" said he warmly, as he clasped the hand of the Union colonel, "I'm glad to see you. I've a friend here to-night that I want to introduce to you. Mr. Walters, Colonel Servosse," he said, as he turned toward a slender, wiry-looking man, with sloping shoulders, a long neck, and arms which seemed to twine about, regardless of the usual articulations. His brown hair was cut short, and rose in a sort of bristling row above his narrow, reddish face. The mouth was pinched, the nose somewhat prominent, and the aspect of the countenance somewhat sharp. The eyes were keen, but rather sunken and close, and of a light gray. His age seemed to be about thirty-five.

"Mr. Walters," said Durfee, "was one of our stanchest Union men. I knew him all through the war. Strangely enough, he did not hide out, nor hold an office, nor take a contract."

"How in the world did you keep out of the army?" asked Servosse.

"I hardly know," answered Walters pleasantly. "I think it was my health mainly."

"Ha, ha, ha!" broke in Durfee. "Your health, did you say?

I vow I b'leve you're right. — He had better health, and more
of it, during the war, than any man I know of, Colonel."

"I don't understand how he kept out, then," said Servosse.

"There ain't anybody that I ever met that does understand
it," said Durfee. "He was living in Rockford when the war
began, in business, making money, and a member of the
Methodist Church. He wanted to go away at the first; but his
wife said she didn't want to leave her people: so John Walters
staid right where he was, and went on trading, and minding
his own business, the same as before. After a while, when
things begun to get hot, there was some talk among the town
loafers about his going to the army. Then he spoke out, and
said that he was a Union man, and didn't never calculate to
be any thing else. He shouldn't do any fighting against the
government willingly, and they'd better not try to make him
do it unwillingly. Things kep' gittin' hotter an' hotter; the conscript laws kep' growing closer an' closer: but John Walters
was right there in Rockford, a tradin' an' 'tendin' to his own
business, the same as ever. A good deal was said about it; because he was just the same Union man as ever, never saying
any thing about the matter unless tackled on it, and then giving
as good as was sent. It got noised around somehow that he had
said, that, if he was compelled to go, the man whom he thought
at the bottom of it would be in some danger. He wasn't no man
conscript officer came to the town, and talked pretty loud
about what he would do. Some things he said came to Walters's ears; and he went over to see him, carryin' a walking-
stick in his hand. They met on the porch. I never knew what
passed; but a man who saw it told me that the officer drew his
pistol, an' another man caught Walters's right arm. I don't
reckon anybody knows just how it was done, — not even
Walters himself. They were all there in a crowd; but when it
broke up Walters had the pistol, the officer had a bullet somewhere through his jaw, another man had a broken arm, and

another had somehow tumbled off the porch and sprained his foot, so that he could not walk for a month. Walters was the only one unhurt. He reported here next day; was examined by a medical board, and somehow pronounced unfit for duty. He went home a few days afterwards with his exemption-papers all in due form, and in fact they never did get him. Of course, he was prosecuted and bedeviled; but when the war was over there was John Walters, — just where he was when it begun."

"That is a very unusual experience, Mr. Walters," said the colonel, turning towards him as Durfee concluded.

"Yes," said Walters modestly: "I was very fortunate. I looked poorly, as I always have, and I did not push myself into difficulty. They knew if I went that I would desert, and go into the Union lines the first chance I got: so there was no use of sending me to the front. But I had a much easier time than Durfee or a half-dozen others here. Why, there is a man, Colonel, who lived in an excavation under his house for eighteen months. There is another who staid for five months under a cedar-tree which grew all alone on the top of a hill within two hundred yards of the big road. There's two others who were of a party of seven who hid from the conscript hunters in a cave on Martin Holbrook's land, which they dug out of the side of a creek, and up into the bank above, when the water was out of the pond. When the gate was shut down, and the water rose, they had to dive like otters to get into their hole."

"That's good enough material for a Union League, isn't it, Colonel?" asked Durfee.

"I should think so, indeed, if they are all like that," answered Servosse.

"That's the trouble," said Walters quickly, but without any change in his countenance, except to turn, and glance at one who had stepped upon the platform, and was preparing to open the meeting as its president.

"Never could trust *him* during the war," continued Walters in the same tone. "We had a sort of society, or rather a set of signals, which every one gave to his friend if he thought he could be trusted. If you served along the Tennessee or Georgia lines, you probably heard of it."

"Often, both before and since the surrender," said Servosse. "You mean the 'Red Strings,' I suppose."

"Yes, that's what I mean. People talk of them as if they were a society, a league, an order; but they were not. It was only a carefully devised set of signals of different kinds, which one Union man gave to another. There was no organization, no head, no official direction. All there was about it was, that it enabled persons of a common purpose to recognize each other. A bit of red string in the hat or in a buttonhole was the most ordinary symbol. This was adopted from the account given in the Book of Joshua of the red cord that Rahab let down from the wall, by direction of the spies whom she had succored, in order that her household might be saved from spoliation when the city was captured."

"I suppose there were a good many of them," said Servosse, "from what I have heard."

"The meetin' will come to order," commanded the president in a thin, stridulous voice, as he rapped upon the rough deal table with one of the teacher's rulers instead of a gavel. The room was crowded by this time, and an instantaneous hush fell upon the dusky crowd at this command. Every one sank into his seat, and those who had no other seats ranged themselves in front and along the aisles upon the floor. About the little group of white men was an open space; and immediately in front of the president was a small table, draped with a Union flag, and surmounted by a Bible and the Constitution of the United States.

"The officers will take their appointed stations," said the president.

Then the ceremonies of opening the meeting went on. Each officer was instructed as to his duty; and the general principles of the order were recapitulated in easy dialogue between them and the president.

"Will Colonel Servosse conduct the religious exercises?" asked the president.

Thus called upon, the ex-Union soldier arose, and approached the altar. Remembering the allusion made to the Book of Joshua in his conversation with Walters, he opened the Bible, and read the second chapter of that book, and called upon Uncle Jerry to pray. All stood reverentially silent during prayer, and then the business of the meeting went on. Names were proposed for membership, committees reported on former propositions, and the usual business of a secret order was disposed of. There was much awkwardness, no little bad grammar, but the most attent interest, and an evident pride and desire to improve, on the part of all. Resuming his seat by Walters, Servosse watched the proceedings with interest, while he continued in a low tone the conversation begun with him before the opening.

"You were asking if there were a good many of the 'Red Strings,'" said Walters. "I am sure I don't know. I traveled a good deal about the Confederacy, and I didn't find no place where there weren't some. I've met 'em in the streets of Richmond, and seen 'em standing guard on the wall of a military prison. The number, however, is merely a matter of estimate, as there was no head nor organization, no system of reports, and no means of knowing how many were initiated. It was slightly different in some sections from others, but sufficiently alike to convince me that it all came from a common source. Sometimes a fellow would tell what he knew; but he never knew much. He could only say that he knew a few men, and suspected more. Then we would change the signs and words, and go right on again. There being no lodges, nor lists of members, one man could do but little harm."

"Is the League organized to any great extent in the South?" asked Comfort.

"I don't know," responded Walters. "Just before the close of the war, I went up into East Tennessee on a little business that took me through the lines, and I joined it there. I don't like it."

"Why not?"

"It's too cumbrous. Our people ain't educated enough to run it well. Besides that, I don't like these big meetings."

"But is it not an educator for the colored men?"

"I've thought of that, and it's the great redeeming feature of the institution. I'm thinking we shall need something more practical, and that don't make so much show, before we have done with the matters rising out of the war."

"You do not take a hopeful view of the future, then?"

"Well, that depends altogether on the view of the present that the government and the Northern people take. If they get the notion that rebellion has transformed those engaged in it into sanctified and glorified saints, as they seem in a way to do, why, the war will not amount to any certain sum, so far as liberty and progress are concerned. Then Union men an' niggers will have to hunt their holes, and will be worse off in fact than they were during the war. I'm 'fraid it's going to be so, Colonel; and I feel as if I ought to go to the West, where I and my children can be free and safe."

"I hope you will not think of that, Mr. Walters," said the Fool.

"Well, I *have* thought of it strongly; but I have decided to stay," was the reply, "chiefly because so many of you Northern men have come down here. I think, that, if you can stand it, I can. At least, I don't think we native Unionists ought to run away, and leave you."

"You were speaking about the president," said Comfort suggestively.

"Well," laughed Walters, "I didn't mean that there was

any danger in him. He was every thing to all men during the war, and will be any thing to anybody until the end of time, if it will butter bread for Tommy Sanderson."

A dozen dusky candidates were instructed in the semi-public secrets of the order; one or two songs were sung with great enthusiasm; a few addresses were made; and the meeting adjourned. As he rode back through the moonlit woods to Warrington, the Fool recounted what he had seen to Metta, — who had come with him, and stopped at the Mission-House, visiting with the teachers while the meeting was in progress, — and told her that it gave him more hope for a peaceful and prosperous future than any thing he had yet seen. The enthusiasm of a soldier for his colors had not yet died out in his breast; and he could not conceive that any organization which cultivated only an unbounded devotion for the flag in the breasts of the embryotic citizens, and kept alive the fire of patriotism in the hearts of the old Union element, should be a source of evil to any one. If he could have seen what an affront such a meeting in itself was to his neighbors, what an insult it was to them to flaunt the flag of the Union in their faces while that of the Confederacy, equally dear to them, was yet unforgotten, he would have thought differently. If he had realized how the touch of those dusky hands fouled that gay banner in the thought of so many of his white neighbors, if he had but known what tears they would be called to shed for having sung those patriotic songs, his heart would have been sad indeed. But he saw no grim portents, and heeded no omen of evil.

CHAPTER XX

OUT OF DUE SEASON

WHAT is called the period of "Reconstruction" came at last; and in tracing our Fool's story it will be necessary to give some brief attention to this era of our nation's history. It is a short story as one reads it now. Its facts are few and plain. There is no escape from them. They were graven on the hearts of millions with a burning stylus. Short as is the story, it is full of folly and of shame. Regarded with whatever charity, folly and cowardice appear as its chief elements; and it has already borne too bitter a harvest of crime to believe that the future holds enough of good springing from its gloom to make it ever tolerable to the historian. Let us as briefly as possible retrace its essential features.

At the close of the great war of the Rebellion these conditions presented themselves to the statesmen of the land: — the hostile army was dispersed; the opposing governmental forms were disrupted; the Confederacy had set in a night which was declared to be eternal, and its component elements — the subordinate governments or states of which it had been composed — were dissolved.

The North, that portion of the country which for four years had constituted alone the United States of America, was full of rejoicing and gladness, which even the death of its martyr President could not long repress. Sorrow for the dead was lost in joy for the living. Banners waved; drums beat; and the quick step of homeward-marching columns echoed through every corner of the land. The clamor of rejoicing drowned the sighs of those who wept for their unreturning dead. All was light and joy, and happy, peaceful anticipation. The soldier had no need to beat his spear into a plowshare,

or his sword into a pruning-hook. He found the plow waiting for him in the furrow. Smiling, peaceful homes, full of
plenty and comfort, invited him to new exertion; and the
prospect of rich returns for his labor enabled him all the more
easily to forgive and forget, to let bygones be bygones, and
throwing away the laurels, and forgetting the struggles and
lessons of the past, contentedly grow fat on the abundance of
the present and the glowing promise of the future.

At the South it was far different. Sadness and gloom
covered the face of the land. The returning braves brought
no joy to the loving hearts who had sent them forth. Nay,
their very presence kept alive the chagrin of defeat. Instead of
banners and music and gay greeting, silence and tears were
their welcome home. Not only for the dead were these lam-
entations, but also for the living. If the past was sorrowful,
the future was scarcely less so. If that which went before
was imbittered by disappointment and the memory of vain
sacrifice, that which was to come was darkened with uncer-
tainty and apprehension. The good things of the past were
apples of Sodom in the hand of the present. The miser's
money was as dust of the highway in value; the obligor, in
his indefinite promise to pay, had vanished, and the hoarder
only had a gray piece of paper stamped with the fair pledge of
a ghostly nation. The planter's slaves had become freedmen
while he was growing into a hero, and no longer owed fealty
or service to him or his family. The home where he had lived
in luxury was almost barren of necessities: even the ordinary
comforts of life were wanting at his fireside. A piece of corn-
bread, with a glass of milk, and bit of bacon, was, perhaps, the
richest welcome-feast that wifely love could devise for the returning hero. Time and the scath of war had wrought ruin in
his home. The hedgerows were upgrown, and the ditches
stopped. Those whom he had been wont to see in delicate
array were clad in homespun. His loved ones who had been

reared in luxury were living in poverty. While he had fought, interest had run. War had not extinguished debt. What was a mere bagatelle when slaves and stocks were at their highest was a terrible *incubus* when slaves were no more, and banks were broken. The army of creditors was even more terrible than the army with banners, to whom he had surrendered. If the past was dark, the future was Cimmerian. Shame and defeat were behind, gloom and apprehension before.

Here and there throughout the subjugated land were detachments and posts of the victorious army, gradually growing smaller and fewer as the months slipped by. The forerunners of trade appeared before the smoke of battle had fairly cleared away. After a little, groups of Northern men settled, to engage in commerce, or to till the soil. The cotton and tobacco which remained of the slender crops of the years of war brought fabulous prices. The hope of their continuance was the one bright spot in the future.

The freedmen, dazed with new-found liberty, crowded the towns and camps, or wandered aimlessly here and there. Hardly poorer than their late masters, they were better prepared for poverty. They had been indurated to want, exposure, and toil. Slavery had been a hard school; but in it they had learned more than one lesson which was valuable to them now. They could endure the present better than their old masters' families, and had never learned to dread the future.

So a part of the re-united country was in light, and the other part in darkness, and between the two was a zone of bloody graves.

The question for the wise was: How shall this be made light, without darkening that? Not an easy question for the wisest and bravest; one which was sure of no solution, or only the ill one of chance or mischance, as the Fates might direct, at the hands of vanity, folly, and ambition.

For two years there were indecision and bickering and cross-purposes and false promises. The South waited sullenly; the North wonderingly.

There were *four plans* proposed: —

The *first* was, that the State machinery of the *ante bellum* days in the lately denationalized sections should be set in motion, and the re-organized communities restored to their former positions without change, except as to individuals; just as you renew a wheel in a worn-out clock, and, starting the pendulum, set it again to its work.

This, without unnecessary verbiage, was the President's plan. It would have done no harm if he had been content to suggest it merely; but he tried to carry it into execution, and thereby not only endangered himself, but raised hopes which he could not satisfy, and sowed the seeds of discontent with whatsoever might be done afterwards.

The *second* scheme was a makeshift, inspired by fright at what had been done, and a desire to avoid what must be done. Emancipation had left four millions of people in most anomalous relations to the other five or six millions under whom they had been enslaved. They were a new and troublesome element. They must be taken care of by their liberators, or abandoned. This plan was devised in the hope of finding a way to escape doing either. It was, in short, to allow the vagrant States to come back into the national fold, shorn of such strength as they might lose by deducting from their representation the ratio of representative power formerly allowed to the non-voting colored race, unless the same should be enfranchised by their organic law.

The South, which had been led by the foolish usurpative acts of the President to expect an unconditional restoration, rejected this proposition with scorn. They regarded it as an attempt to bribe them into the acceptance of the results of

emancipation by the offer of power as a reward for their con-
currence. Such a view can not be claimed to have been
illogical.

The *third* plan, which remains to be considered, was of a
different character. It neither shirked nor temporized. It
accepted the past, and sought to guarantee the future. It did
not regard immediate re-organization of the recently rebellious communities upon a Federal basis, as necessary or desirable. Without seeking vengeance, it took warning from
what had been, and sought to prevent a recurrence of evil. It
recognized the fact that a doctrine which had been known as
State Sovereignty was at the root of the evil, and that the
nation had taken a race from bondage which it was morally
bound to prepare for freedom. So it proposed that the States
which had been in the infected region should be quietly left to
molder in the grave of rebellion, — the bed they had themselves prepared; that the region they once embraced should be
divided up into Territories without regard to former statal
lines, and so remain for a score of years under national control, but without power to mold or fashion the national
legislation — until time should naturally and thoroughly have
healed the breaches of the past, till commerce had become
re-established, and the crude ideas of the present had been
clarified by the light of experience. It recognized as an undeniable fact the idea that men who had gazed into each other's
faces over gleaming gun-barrels, by the fateful blaze of
battle, were not so fit to adjust the questions arising out of the
conflict as those yet unborn. It was based upon the fact, too,
that the slave was not made fit for unrestrained political power
by the simple fact of freedom. Slavery might be ended as a
legal status by proclamation, but as a living fact it could not.
The hands could be unshackled by a constitutional amendment; but heart and brain must have an opportunity to expand,
before the freedman could be capable of automatic liberty.

To this doctrine the Fool subscribed all the more readily, because he thought he saw the exemplification of its principles about him day by day. Besides that, he thought it only fair and honest that the government which had cut the freedman loose from slavery should watch over him until he could walk erect in his new estate.

The second Christmas in his new home had come before any thing was done; then a plan was adopted which was a compromise among all these ideas. This was the *fourth* plan. It was not selected because those who chose it deemed it the best manner for settling the ills with which the body politic had been afflicted; not at all. No one can be so simple-minded as to believe that. The *far* future was very dim to the legislators' eyes when they adopted it: the *near* future was what they dreaded. A great election was at hand. The President and his supporters were going to the country on his plan of reconstruction. When the Congress threatened impeachment, he sought for justification at the ballot-box. Some plan must be devised with which to meet him. What should it be? The logic which carries elections answered, "One on which all who are opposed to the presidential plan in the North can be induced to unite." From this womb of party necessity and political insincerity came forth this abortion, or, rather, this monster, doomed to parricide in the hour of its birth.

Like all compromises, it had the evils of all the plans from which its pieces came, and the merits of none of them. The coward, who, running with his conscience and holding with his fear, makes a compromise by taking the head of one thought and the tail of another, is sure to get the wrong ends of both.

Added to this was the very remarkable fact that this plan, in common with two of the discarded ones, took no account of that strange and mysterious influence which ranges all the way from a religious principle to a baseless prejudice, accord-

ing to the stand-point of the observer, but always remains a
most unaccountable yet still stubborn fact in all that pertains
to the governmental organisms of the South, — the popular
feeling in regard to the African population of that section.
That a servile race, isolated from the dominant one by the
fact of color and the universally accepted dogma of inherent
inferiority, to say nothing of a very general belief of its utter
incapacity for the civilization to which the Caucasian has attained, should be looked on with distrust and aversion, if not
with positive hatred, as a co-ordinate political power, by their
former masters, would seem so natural, that one could hardly
expect men of ordinary intelligence to overlook it. That this
should arouse a feeling of very intense bitterness when it
came as the result of conquest, and the freedom enjoyed by
the subject-race was inseparably linked with the memory of
loss and humiliation in the mind of the master, would seem
equally apparent. But when to these facts was added the
knowledge that whoever should advocate such an elevation
of the blacks, in that section, was certain to be regarded as
putting himself upon their social level in a community where
the offender against caste becomes an outlaw in fact, it seems
impossible that the wise men of that day should have been so
blind as not to have seen that they were doing the utmost
possible injury to the colored race, the country, and themselves, by propounding a plan of re-organization which depended for its success upon the effective and prosperous administration of state governments by this class, in connection
with the few of the dominant race, who, from whatever motives, might be willing to put themselves on the same level
with them in the estimation of their white neighbors. Of these
there could be but the following classes: martyrs, who were
willing to endure ostracism and obloquy for the sake of principle; self-seekers, who were willing to do or be any thing and
every thing for the sake of power, place, and gain; and fools,

who hoped that in some inscrutable way the laws of human nature would be suspended, or that the state of affairs at first presenting itself would be but temporary. The former class, it might have been known, would naturally be small. Martyrs do not constitute any large proportion of any form or state of society. Especially were they not to be looked for in a section where public opinion had been dominated by an active and potent minority, until independent thought upon certain subjects had been utterly strangled. Self-seekers, on the contrary, those who can be swayed by motives of interest or ambition, regardless alike of principle and the approbation of those by whom they are surrounded, are to be found in all ranks and classes; while fools who have stamina enough to swim for any great time against a strong popular current are not to be looked for in any great numbers in any ordinary community.

CHAPTER XXI

HOW THE WISE MEN BUILDED

So it must have been well understood by the wise men who devised this short-sighted plan of electing a President beyond a peradventure of defeat, that they were giving the power of the re-organized, subordinate republics, into the hands of a race unskilled in public affairs, poor to a degree hardly to be matched in the civilized world, and so ignorant that not five out of a hundred of its voters could read their own ballots, joined with such Adullamites among the native whites as might be willing to face a proscription which would shut the house of God in the face of their families, together with the few men of Northern birth, resident in that section since the close of the war, — either knaves or fools, or partaking of the nature of both, — who might elect to become permanent citizens, and join in the movement.

Against them was to be pitted the wealth, the intelligence, the organizing skill, the pride, and the hate of a people whom it had taken four years to conquer in open fight when their enemies outnumbered them three to one, who were animated chiefly by the apprehension of what seemed now about to be forced upon them by this miscalled measure of "Reconstruction;" to wit, the equality of the negro race.

It was done, too, in the face of the fact that within the preceding twelvemonth the white people of the South, by their representatives in the various Legislatures of the Johnsonian period, had absolutely refused to recognize this equality, even in the slightest matters, by *refusing to allow the colored people to testify in courts of justice* against white men, or to protect their rights of person and property in any manner from the avarice, lust, or brutality of their white neighbors. It was done in the very face of the "Black Codes," which were the first enactments of Provisional Legislatures, and which would have established a serfdom more complete than that of the Russian steppes before the *ukase* of Alexander.

And the men who devised this plan called themselves honest and wise statesmen. More than one of them has since then hugged himself in gratulation under the belief, that, by his co-operation therein, he had cheaply achieved an immortality of praise from the liberty-lovers of the earth! After having forced a proud people to yield what they had for more than two centuries considered a right, — the right to hold the African race in bondage, — they proceeded to outrage a feeling as deep and fervent as the zeal of Islam or the exclusiveness of Hindoo caste, by giving to the ignorant, unskilled, and dependent race — a race who could not have lived a week without the support or charity of the dominant one — equality of political right! Not content with this, they went farther, and, by erecting the rebellious territory into self-regulating and sovereign States, they abandoned these parties like cocks in a pit, to fight out the question of predominance without the possibility of national interference. They said to the colored man, in the language of one of the pseudo-philosophers of that day, "Root, hog, or die!"

It was cheap patriotism, cheap philanthropy, cheap success!

Yet it had its excuse, which we are bound to set forth. The North and the South had been two households in one house — two nations under one name. The intellectual, moral, and social life of each had been utterly distinct and separate from that of the other. They no more understood or appreciated each other's feelings or development than John Chinaman comprehends the civilization of John Bull. It is true they spoke the same language, used the same governmental forms, and, most unfortunately, thought they comprehended each other's ideas. Each thought they knew the thought and purpose of the other better than the thinker knew his own. The Northern man despised his Southern fellow-citizen in bulk, as a good-natured *braggadocio*, mindful of his own ease, fond of power and display, and with no animating principle which could in any manner interfere with his interest. The Southern man despised his Northern compeer as cold-blooded, selfish, hypocritical, cowardly, and envious.

This is how they played at cross-purposes, each thinking that he knew the other's heart far better than he sought to know his own.

ANTE BELLUM.

NORTHERN IDEA OF SLAVERY.

Slavery is wrong morally, politically, and economically. It is tolerated only for the sake of peace and quiet. The negro is a man, and has equal inherent rights with the white race.

SOUTHERN IDEA OF SLAVERY.

The negro is fit only for slavery. It is sanctioned by the Bible, and it must be right; or, if not exactly right, is unavoidable, now that the race is among us. We can not live with them in any other condition.

NORTHERN IDEA OF THE SOUTHERN IDEA.

Those Southern fellows know that slavery is wrong, and incompatible with the theory of our government; but it is a good thing for them. They grow fat and rich, and have a good time, on account of it; and no one can blame them for not wanting to give it up.

SOUTHERN IDEA OF THE NORTHERN IDEA.

Those Yankees are jealous because we make slavery profitable, raising cotton and tobacco, and want to deprive us of our slaves from envy. They don't believe a word of what they say about its being wrong, except a few fanatics. The rest are all hypocrites.

POST BELLUM.

THE NORTHERN IDEA OF THE SITUATION.

The negroes are free now, and must have a fair chance to make themselves something. What is claimed about their inferiority may be true. It is not likely to approve itself; but, true or false, they have a right to equality before the law. That is what the war meant, and this must be secured to them. The rest they must get as they can, or do without, as they choose.

THE SOUTHERN IDEA OF THE SITUATION.

We have lost our slaves, our bank stock, every thing, by the war. We have been beaten, and have honestly surrendered: slavery is gone, of course. The slave is now free, but he is not white. We have no ill will towards the colored man as such and in his place; but he is not our equal, can not be made our equal, and we will not be ruled by him, or admit him as a co-ordinate with the white race in power. We have no objection to his voting, so long as he votes as his old master, or the man for whom he labors, advises him; but, when he chooses to vote differently, he must take the consequences.

THE NORTHERN IDEA OF THE SOUTHERN IDEA.

Now that the negro is a voter, the Southern people will have to treat him well, because they will need his vote. The negro will remain true to the government and party which gave him liberty, and in order to secure its preservation. Enough of the Southern whites will go with them, for the sake of office and power, to enable them to retain permanent control of those States for an indefinite period. The negroes will go to work, and things will gradually adjust themselves. The South has no right to complain. They would have the negroes as slaves, kept the country in constant turmoil for the sake of them, brought on the war because we would not catch their runaways, killed a million of men; and now they can not complain if the very weapon by which they held power is turned against them, and is made the means of righting the wrongs which they have themselves created. It may be hard; but they will learn to do better hereafter.

THE SOUTHERN IDEA OF THE NORTHERN IDEA.

The negro is made a voter simply to degrade and disgrace the white people of the South. The North cares nothing about the negro as a man, but only enfranchises him in order to humiliate and enfeeble us. Of course, it makes no difference to the people of the North whether he is a voter or not. There are so few colored men there, that there is no fear of one of them being elected to office, going to the Legislature, or sitting on the bench. The whole purpose of the measure is to insult and degrade. But only wait until the States are restored and the "Blue Coats" are out of the way, and we will show them their mistake.

There was just enough of truth in each of these estimates of the other's characteristics to mislead. The South, as a mass, was honest in its belief of the righteousness of slavery, both morally and politically. The North, in like manner, was equally honest in its conviction with regard to the wickedness of slavery, and its inconsistency with republican institutions; yet neither credited the other with honesty. The South was right in believing that the North cared little or nothing for the negro *as a man*, but wrong in the idea that the theory of political equality and manhood suffrage was invented or imposed from any thought of malice, revenge, or envy toward the South. The wish to degrade did not enter into the Northern mind in this connection. The idea that "of one blood are all the nations of the earth," and that "race, color, or previous condition of servitude," can not be allowed to affect the legal or political rights of any, *was* a living principle in the Northern mind, as little capable of suppression as the sentiment of race-antagonism by which it was met, and whose intensity it persistently discredited.

There was another thing which the wise men who were rebuilding the citadel of Liberty in such hot haste quite forgot. In judging of the South, and predicting its future course, they pictured it to themselves as the North would be with an infusion, so to speak, of newly-enfranchised blacks amounting to one-third of its aggregate population: in other words, they accounted the result of emancipation as the only differential feature by which the South was distinguishable from the North. They did not estimate aright the effects, upon the white people of the South, of an essentially different civilization and development. They said, "The South has heretofore differed from the North *only* in the institution of slavery. That is now removed; only the freedmen remain as a sign of its existence: therefore, the South is as the North would be with this element added to its population." It was a strange mistake. The ideas of generations do not perish in an hour. Divergent civilizations can not be made instantly identical by uprooting a single institution.

Among the peculiarities which marked the difference between Northern and Southern society was one so distinct and evident, one which had been so often illustrated in our political history, that it seems almost impossible that shrewd observers of that history should for a moment have overlooked or underestimated it. This is the influence of family position, social rank, or political prominence. Leadership, in the sense of a blind, unquestioning following of a man, without his being the peculiar exponent of an idea, is a thing almost unknown at the North: at the South it is a power. Every family there has its clientelage, its followers, who rally to its lead as quickly, and with almost as unreasoning a faith, as the old Scottish clansmen, summoned by the burning cross. By means of this fact slavery had been perpetuated for fifty years. It was through this peculiarity that secession and rebellion became dominant there. This fact seems to have been dimly recognized, though not at all understood or appreciated, by those who originated what are known as the Reconstruction Acts. They seem to have supposed, that, if this class were deprived of actual political position, they would thereby be shorn of political influence: so it was provided that all who had any such prominence as to have been civil or military officers before the war, and had afterwards engaged in rebellion, should not be allowed to vote, or hold office, until relieved from such disability.

It was a fatal mistake. The dead leader has always more followers than his living peer. Every henchman of those lordlings at whom this blow was aimed felt it far more keenly than he would if it had lighted on his own cheek. The king of every village was dethroned; the magnate of every crossroads was degraded. Henceforward, each and every one of their satellites was bound to eternal hostility toward these measures and to all that might result therefrom.

So the line of demarkation was drawn. Upon the one side

were found only those who constituted what was termed *respectable people*, — the bulk of those of the white race who had ruled the South in *ante bellum* days, who had fostered slavery, and been fattened by it, who had made it the dominant power in the nation, together with the mass of those whose courage and capacity had organized rebellion, and led the South in that marvelous struggle for separation. On the other side were the pariahs of the land, to designate the different classes of which, three words were used: "Niggers," the newly-enfranchised African voters; "Scalawags," the native whites who were willing to accept the reconstruction measures; and "Carpet-baggers," all men of Northern birth, resident in the South, who should elect to speak or act in favor of such reconstruction.

The ban of proscription spared neither age nor sex, and was never relaxed. In business or pleasure, in friendship or religion, in the market or the church, it was omnipotent. Men were excluded from the Lord's Communion for establishing sabbath schools for colored people. Those who did not curse the measure, its authors, and the government by which it was administered, were henceforth shunned as moral and social lepers. The spirit of the dead Confederacy was stronger than the mandate of the nation to which it had succumbed in battle.

The "scalawags" were few. Those who could brave the torrent of proscription poured upon them by that society which had been their boast as the most excellent on earth were not many. For a time, the instincts of what was termed "Unionism" either held some of the former political leaders in the background, or led them to affiliate somewhat coolly with the party of reconstruction. The "Union" of 1861, was, however, a very different thing from that of a half-dozen years later. The advocacy of a simple coherence of the States under one formal government was all that distinguished the "Unionist" of 1861 from his "Secessionist" neighbor, who favored the

expurgation of "*E pluribus unum*," and would write instead,
"*Ex uno duo*." Their views on all other subjects were in thorough harmony. It was only on this point that they differed.
It was a stubborn and a radical difference, however, for which
thousands of them had laid down their lives, and others suffered untold miseries and persecutions; for the gentlemen of
the South were harsh masters, and did not permit dissent from
their political views to be entertained or expressed with impunity. Those Union men who really maintained their integrity
and devotion to the Federal Union through the war, and embraced the republican view at its close, were, consequently,
mostly of that class who are neither rich nor poor, who were
land-owners, but not slave-owners. The few who were of the
higher class had been so completely shut out from the intellectual movements of the North during those momentous years,
that, as a rule, they were utterly confounded at the result
which was before them. They had looked for the nation to
come back to them, when its power was re-established, absolutely unchanged and unmodified. It came back, instead, with
a new impetus, a new life, born of the stormy years that had
intervened, putting under its feet the old issues which had
divided parties, scornful of ancient statesmanship, and mock-
ing the graybeards who had been venerated as sages in "the
good old days of the Republic."

But for those Southern men, who, knowing and realizing all
these changes, facing all these dangers and discomforts, recognizing the inexorable logic of events, and believing in and
desiring to promote the ultimate good which must flow therefrom, in good faith accepted the arbitrament of war, and
staked their "lives, fortunes, and sacred honor," in support of
this new dispensation of liberty, words enough of praise can
not be found! Nor yet words enough of scorn for their associates and affiliates of the North, who not only refused them
the meed of due credit for their self-sacrifice and devotion,

but also made haste to visit them with coolness, indignity, and discrediting contempt, because they did not perform the impossible task which the Wise men had imposed upon them. Phariseeism is by no means admirable in its best estate; but the genuine article is far less despicable than the spurious.

Another peculiarity of this remarkable scheme was, that, while it professed to punish one class by excluding them from the ballot (a punishment which had only the effect to enrage), it made no offer of encouragement or reward to those who had stood the fast friends of the nation in the hour of its peril. The ingratitude of republics is the tritest of thoughts, but there never was a more striking illustration of its verity. Perhaps no nation ever before, after the suppression of a rebellion which threatened its life, quite forgot the claims of those who had been its friends in the disaffected region.

There were throughout the South thousands of men who were Unionists pure and simple. As a rule, they had no sympathy with the antislavery idea which had come to permeate the whole mental life of the North. Slavery was to them as much a matter of course as any event of their every-day life. Very many of them were hereditary slave-owners. The inferiority, inherent and fore-ordained, of the colored man, was as much an article of faith with them as any portion of the Sacred Word. Not only this, but they believed with equal sincerity that the normal and proper sphere of the inferior race was slavery. They might regret its abuses, that there should be cruel and ruthless masters and brutal overseers, just as they did when an up-country teamster abused his overloaded horses; but they were no more troubled with qualms of conscience in regard to the enslavement of the one than as to the driving of the other. Such a man was in favor of the Union from a profound conviction of its glory, a traditional patriotism, or a belief that secession and disunion would be ruinous and fatal; but he did not look for or desire the

abolition of slavery in bulk or as an institution. His attachment to the Union was an absorbing devotion to an abstract
idea. He had no hostility to the ultimate object of secession,
— the security and perpetuity of slavery, — but only to the
means by which it was accomplished. He worshiped the
Union; but it was the Union *with* slavery, except as the right
to hold slaves might be forfeited by rebellion; which forfeiture
he believed would be purely personal, and would affect only
those actually guilty of rebellious acts. Such was the position
of the Southern Unionist at the beginning of the war. Some
receded from it as the struggle progressed; but many thousands held to their faith in spite of every persuasion and persecution which could be brought against them. The heroism
of many of these men was fully equal to the highest courage
and devotion shown upon the field of battle. They dodged,
hid, fought, struggled, and in all ways evaded the service of
the Confederacy, and were true to the Union of their faith.
The close of the war found them just where they had been at
its beginning. They had neither gone backward nor forward.

They regarded the abolition of slavery as justifiable solely
upon the ground of the master having personally and individ-
ually engaged in rebellion, — a punishment for his treason.
Upon this ground, and this alone, they regarded it as possible
that this idea should be sustained; and with this doctrine they
held, as an unavoidable corollary, that *they* were entitled,
either to be excepted from its operation, or to be compensated
for such slaves as were taken from them by the Military
Proclamation.

When it comes to the application of logic, and the principles of equity on which all such questions of national polity
are said to be based, it is difficult to perceive what is the
fallacy in the reasoning of these Southern Unionists. It has
always been claimed that slavery was abolished as a military
necessity, and not because of its inherent wrong, or merely as

a humanitarian measure to benefit the enslaved. Almost any one of the wise men who made the laws, and regulated the course of political events at that time, would have affirmed this. Yet, if this were true, there should have been no interference with the slaves of the Southern Unionist, or, if there were, he should have been compensated for the same as well as for his cotton, his corn, his tobacco, his fences, his timber, and cattle, unwittingly destroyed, or needfully appropriated, by the national forces. This was not done, however. The wise men decided that it would not do to attempt it.

So the result was, that, while the open and avowed rebel lost his slave-property by the events of the war, the most ardent and devoted Unionist lost his also. It was hard, very hard, when a man had given the best years of his life to the honest acquisition of a species of property which was not only protected, but seemed to have been peculiarly favored and encouraged, by our laws; and when, the life of the nation being in peril, at the risk of his own he stood by her, espoused her cause against his neighbors, made himself an outcast in his own land, — it was hard indeed, when the struggle was over, to see that nation to which he had been so devotedly attached reaching out its hand, and stripping him of the competence thus acquired, and leaving him to suffer, not only the pangs of poverty, but the jeers of those whose treason he had opposed. That the love of these men should gradually grow cold for the country which measured out to friend and foe alike one even measure of punishment, our Fool thought not a matter to be wondered at; but the wise men of the National Capital were unable to believe that this could be. So time wore on, and wise men and fools played at crosspurposes; and the locks of Samson grew while he wrought at the mill.

CHAPTER XXII

COCK-CROW

AFTER the Fool's speech at the political meeting, and the events which succeeded it became generally known, he was much sought after by what were known as Union men among the people. His words seemed to have touched a deep chord in their hearts, not so much from what he had said perhaps, as from the fact that he had dared to say it. They came to him with wonderings and warnings upon their lips. How he dared to stand up and maintain ideas at variance with the accepted creed of that class of men who had always formulated and controlled public opinion, they could not understand. They hated secession, always had hated it; they had voted against it in 1861; some had been outspoken against it on the stump, in the street, everywhere, and at all times: but in the main the opposition had been a silent one. The terrible suppressive power which slavery had exercised over liberty of thought and speech had grown into a habit of mind. Men who for generations had been unable to express their thoughts above a whisper, as to one of the institutions by which they were surrounded, became cautious to the verge of timidity. Many a time did our Fool listen to the approval of men who would glance cautiously around before addressing him, and then say in a low, hushed tone, —

"That is what we want. I tell you it did me good to hear you; but you must look out! You don't know these people as I do. It don't do to speak out here as you do at the North."

"But why not?" he would query impatiently. "That was my honest conviction: why should I not speak it out?"

"Hush, hush!" his interviewer would say nervously. "Here, let's step aside a little while, and chat."

And then, perhaps, they would pass out of the public way,

into that refuge of free thought at the South, the woods (or "the bushes," as the scraggly growth is more generally termed); and he would listen to some tale of heroic endurance by which his companion had evaded conscription in the time of the war, or avoided prosecution in the ante-war era, which elicited his wonder both for the devotion then displayed for principle, and the caution which was born of it.

"Why do you not speak out?" he would ask.

"Oh, it won't do! I could not live here, or not in any peace at least, if I did; and then my family — they would be cut off from all society: nobody would have any thing to do with them. Why, as careful as I have been, my children are insulted every now and then as 'nigger-worshipers,' and — and" —

"And what?"

"Well — 'Yankee-lovers,'" apologetically. "You see, it's got out in my neighborhood that I came to see you a few weeks ago."

"Well, what of that? Haven't you a right to do so? Can't a man speak his opinions, and act his preferences?"

"You will find out that this old pro-slavery, aristocratic element don't allow people to differ from them peaceably and quietly. If I were you, I'd be mighty careful who I talked to. You don't know any thing about what trouble you may get into any day."

"Well, I shall not," the Fool would reply. "I don't care any thing particular about the matter. I am no politician, and don't want to be; but I am going to say just what I think, at all proper times and places, when the spirit moves me so to do."

"Of course, of course," would be the reply. "You know best; but you ought to recollect that you are not at the North, where they allow every man to have his own opinions, and rather despise him if he don't have them, as I take it they do."

So the two men would separate, each wondering at the

other; the Fool amazed that one could endure so much for the sake of his own opinion, think so well, apprehend so clearly the state of affairs, and yet be so timid about declaring his convictions. He could not call it cowardice; for many of these men had taken their lives in their hands to shelter men on their way to the Union lines. Others, in the ante-war era, had circulated books and pamphlets in regard to slavery, *to be found in possession of which was a capital crime*. Others had helped fugitive slaves to escape to freedom, with the terrors of Judge Lynch's rope and fagots before their eyes. Others still, upon being conscripted into the Confederate ranks, had refused to bear arms, even when put into the front rank and under the hottest fire of battle.

They could look at danger and death very calmly; but they could not stand forth openly, and face the glare of social proscription. The Fool could not understand it.

On the other hand, the Southern Unionists could not understand the heedless outspokenness of the Northern man. To them it seemed the very height of folly. It meant proscription, broils, mobs, and innumerable risks which might be avoided by a prudent silence.

These were the warnings of his friends. He received others shortly afterwards, which impressed him more. He had been accustomed to ride into Verdenton occasionally on business, and when he did so, frequently did not start for home until after sundown, especially if the nights were light; a ride in the Southern summer moonlight being an ever-enjoyable romance to an appreciative nature. One night as he was thus returning to Warrington, the low western moon shining full in his face, he was startled, as he passed through a piece of woodland road, by seeing a man ride out from under a low-growing oak which stood close by the roadside, and call his name. The denseness of the shadow had quite hidden both horse and rider, and the Fool was within a few steps of his

interlocutor when he emerged into the moonlight. To draw
rein, and take a pistol from his belt, was the work of an instant
to the ex-soldier, and entirely an instinctive act.

"All right, Colonel," said the horseman pleasantly. "I am
glad to see that you carry that useful article, and are handy
about getting it out; but it is not necessary now. You know
me, I reckon."

"Dr. Gates?" said the Fool inquiringly, as he peered into
the shaded face of the horseman, with a blush of shame at
having drawn his weapon upon an unknown and undemonstrative wayfarer. "I — ah — you startled me, Doctor, coming
from under the tree there; and I have been so long accustomed
to an appeal to arms in case of surprise, that I half fancied
I had a fight on my hands," he continued half jocosely.

"No excuses, Colonel: I don't blame you, and am, as I said,
glad to see it. One frequently avoids danger by being prepared for it. I want to speak to you a moment."

"Well?"

"Come under the tree here," he said, glancing up and down
the road. "There's no use standing out there in the moonlight."

When they were in the shade, the doctor said, —

"You may think it is none of my business, and so it is not,
in fact; but I have just thought that some one ought to tell
you, — and as no one else seems to have done so, I thought I
would make it my business to let you know, — that you are
acting very imprudently."

"Ah!"

"Yes: I have noticed, that, when you are in town, you frequently leave about the time you did to-night. Now, you
ought to know that your speech, and indeed what you have
to say whenever you speak at all in regard to public matters,
is very distasteful to our people, especially when they congre-
gate in the town, and get filled up and warmed up."

"So you think a man can not be allowed to have his own opinions, but must have them countersigned by a committee of his neighbors before he makes them the coin of current speech," said the Fool somewhat sternly.

"No: I didn't come here to quarrel with your opinions, nor even with your time and manner of declaring them," answered the other. "I am not at all sure that you are not right in your notions. They are certainly very plausible, and to your mind, I doubt not, are quite unanswerable. However, I do think that you might learn a little prudence from the men you associate with. I saw you talking with David Nelson to-day. He is one of those I mean. A better Union man never stood between soil and sunshine; and I'll wager something he advised you to be cautious, not only as to what you said, but when and where you said it."

"Of course he did!" said the Fool, laughing. "It seems as if all these Union men were afraid to say their souls were their own."

"If they had not been cautious, their souls would have been all that could be called their own," said the doctor hotly. "*I* was not a Union man," he continued. "I am half ashamed to say it; for I knew and felt that secession and the Confederacy were simply folly. But the truth is, I had not the nerve: I couldn't stand the pressure. But I practiced here among these Union people, and was also with the army part of the time. I was at Fredericksburg when your people tried to take it; and I tell you now, Colonel, I would rather have come with your fellows across that bare plateau to the foot of St. Marye's Hill than have faced what these Union people here did, day after day, during the whole war. I saw many a strange thing; but I learned to hold my tongue from very admiration of their pluck."

"No doubt," said the Fool; "but they seem to have been more thoroughly whipped than you rebels have been. I can not understand why they should not speak out, and show their colors openly, now. Why, only the other day, I was invited to a Union meeting; and, thinking it might be a pleasant thing, I took along a garrison flag which I happened to have, and festooned it over the platform above where the speakers were to stand. In a little while some of the leading men came to me, and asked if I would not have it taken down. They were glad to see it, and all that, they said; but they were afraid it might cause trouble."

"You did not take it down, of course," said the doctor.

"You may well say that! I would have died before it should have been lowered an inch. I fought for a right to *put* it there, and would fight to *keep* it there," said the Fool warmly.

"There is not a doubt about that, Colonel," rejoined the other; "and yet it does seem to me, with all respect, that you were foolish to put it there. I can no more understand you than you can understand the Union people about you. Did you ever think that the Union people here are vastly in a minority, and that the rest of us — I mean the mass of our people — regard this needless flaunting of that flag in our faces as an insult and an arrogance on your part? Even your wearing of that old uniform coat, though I am glad to see that you have sacrificed the buttons, is regarded as a taunt. You should remember that you are one of the conquerors, in the midst of the conquered."

"But I have no hatred, no ill-will, towards any one who wore the gray," said the Fool protestingly.

"I am sure of that, or I would not have ridden out here to do you a good turn to-night," said the doctor.

"I do not understand you."

"I suppose not. But you can understand, that, if I felt confident of meeting you here for a friendly purpose, one who had an unfriendly one might be equally sure of doing so?"

"Do you mean to say that I might be waylaid?"

"I mean to say," said the doctor significantly, "that, if I were you, I would not make a habit of traveling any particular road after dark."

"But" —

"I shall answer no questions, Colonel, and will bid you good-night." He turned his horse, and was about to ride off, when he drew rein, and said, —

"You need have no fear *to-night*, and I suppose I need not request you to say nothing of this meeting. Good-night."

He gave his horse the rein, and cantered away towards the town with that easy, swaying seat, characteristic of the leisurely, well-to-do Southern man, who has been in the saddle almost every day from his infancy, who rides, not so much for the sake of riding as for covering the ground with the least inconvenience to himself and his horse. When this easy lope had carried the doctor around a bend of the wood, and only the measured thud of the horse's hoofs came back to his ear, the Fool rode out from under the shadow of the water-oak, and made his way thoughtfully homeward. If he scanned the thickets closely, and started when a stray cow burst with considerable noise through the half-lighted under-growth, he may be pardoned, after the repeated warnings of the day.

CHAPTER XXIII

THE DIE IS CAST

W HEN the time for the election of delegates to a Constitutional Convention was near at hand, the Union men of the county held a meeting to nominate candidates. The colored people, as yet unused to political assemblages, but with an indistinct impression that their rights and interests were involved, attended in large numbers. The Union men were few, and not of that class who were accustomed to the lead and control of such meetings. The place of assembly selected was an old country schoolhouse some two miles from the county-seat, and situated in a beautiful grove. The Fool, partly from curiosity, and partly to give such aid and countenance as he might to a movement which was based upon a recognition and support of the Federal Union as contradistinguished from the idea of voluntary secession and disintegration, attended the meeting, though hardly half-convinced of the practicability and wisdom of the proposed plan of reconstruction. By this time he was well known in the county, and, quite unconsciously to himself, regarded as a leader in the movement. Accustomed to command for four years, and previous to that time imbued with the spirit of ready and hearty co-operation and participation in matters of public interest which is almost the birthright of the Northern citizen, he was vexed and troubled at the retiring hesitancy of the Union men by whom he was surrounded. Why a hundred or a thousand men should come together for a particular purpose, and then "hem and haw," and wait for some one to move first, he could not understand. When he came on the ground, the hour for which the meeting had been appointed had already arrived. The colored people had gathered in a dense mass on one side of the platform, waiting in earnest expectancy to take whatever part might be allotted to them in the performance of the new and untried duties of citizenship. The white men were squatted about in little groups, conversing in low, uneasy tones, and glancing suspiciously at every new-comer. A little at one side was Colonel Ezekiel Vaughn, with a few cronies, laughing and talking boisterously about the different men who were taking part in the movement. This seemed to have a wonderfully depressing effect upon the white Unionists, who evidently dreaded his clamorous ridicule, and feared that some disturbance might ensue, should they attempt to proceed.

"Well," said the Fool, as he approached a group of a dozen or more, seated in a circle under a giant oak, "why don't you begin?"

"Hist!" said one of those whom he addressed. "Don't you see those fellows?" at the same time nodding, and winking towards Vaughn and his crowd.

"See them?" he replied, as he glanced towards them. "Yes. Why?"

"They've come here for a row," answered the other.

"Pshaw!" said the Fool. "They don't want any row; but, if they do, let them have it."

"But we can't do any thing if they have made up their minds to break up the meeting," said the Unionist.

"Break up the meeting! Fudge! Are we not enough to take care of that squad of non-combatant fire-eaters?"

"Oh, yes! But then — they would make a heap of trouble," was the reply. "Don't you think we had better put it off, and have a private understanding with our people that they shall come here on a certain day, and be sure and not let Colonel Vaughn or any of his crowd know about it?"

"No, I don't!" answered the Fool promptly. "If we are going to be cowed and browbeaten out of doing our duty by a crowd of men who never did any thing but talk, we may as well give up and go home. If not, let us stay and do our duty as good citizens."

"Why don't you open your show, Servosse?" asked Vaughn, in a loud and taunting voice, as he approached the group. "I tell you we are getting mighty tired of waitin'; and them niggers is just bustin' for a chance to begin votin'."

"Hello, Vaughn!" said the Fool, in a voice equally loud, but more jovial. "Are you here? Then we will begin at once. We were just waiting for the monkey before the show began; but, if you are on hand, we are all ready."

There was a laugh, and Vaughn retired disconcerted. But one of those with whom the Fool had been conversing drew him aside, and said with great seriousness, —

"Now, Colonel, you will excuse me; but I'm afraid you will get yourself into trouble if you talk to these folks in that way. You see they are not used to it."

"Then let them get used to it," said the Fool carelessly. "If Vaughn did not want a sharp retort, he should not have made an insolent remark."

"That's so, Colonel; but you see they are used to doin' and sayin' any thing they choose in regard to people who happen to differ with them. Why, I remember when a man was prose-cuted here in this very county for havin' a seditious book — one about slavery, you know — in his possession, and lendin' it to a friend; and people were almost afraid to speak to him, or go bail for him. You Northern people don't know any thing about what we call public opinion here."

"I'm sure I don't want to know, if it means that a man shall not speak his opinion freely, and throw stones when another throws them at him," said the Fool determinedly.

"Yet," said the Union man, "it is folly to defy and provoke such a spirit unnecessarily."

"I agree with you there, my friend," was the Fool's answer.

"But, if one has principles which are worth supporting or fighting for, they ought also to be worth standing up for against ridicule and arrogance."

"It would seem so; but it won't do, — not in this country, anyhow," said the Unionist with a sigh.

At this point there were symptoms of excitement among the crowd; and a faint, straggling cheer broke out, as Colonel Rhenn rode up, and dismounted from his horse, which he tied to an overhanging bough, and came forward, holding his well-worn beaver in his left hand, bowing, and shaking hands with his neighbors, and returning with slight but grave courtesy the boisterous greeting of the colored people. This arrival at once seemed to give confidence to those who had before evidently regarded the movement as a disagreeable if not a dangerous duty. Nathan Rhenn was a gentleman of a type peculiarly Southern, and exceedingly rare. He was of an old but not now wealthy family. His connections were good, but not high. Before the war he had been in comfortable circumstances only: now he was actually poor. Yet at no time had he abated one jot of that innate gentility which had always marked his deportment. He was clad now in "butter-nut-gray" homespun, wore black woolen gloves on his hands, a high black stock on his neck, with a high, narrow-brimmed, and rather dingy beaver hat, and would have been a figure highly provocative of mirth, had it not been for his considerate, graceful, and self-respecting courtesy. Since the meeting at which he presided, when the Fool made his maiden speech upon a political question, Colonel Rhenn had rarely attended public meetings, and was known as one whose *status* (despite his former Unionism, which was unquestioned) was very doubtful. He was known to be one who would not have attended the meeting unless he intended to give in his adhesion to the cause which it had assembled to promote. He was considered, therefore, an accession of very great importance, by those who were present, to the cause of Reconstruction. Hardly had he greeted his many friends, when some one arose and said, —

"I nominate Nathan Rhenn as chairman of this meeting."

It was unanimously concurred in; and the new arrival, with many grave bows and protestations, permitted himself to be led to the platform. Upon taking his seat as chairman, he made a brief speech, in substance as follows: —

"FELLOW-CITIZENS, — I have come here to-day for the purpose of giving my support and countenance to a movement in support of what are known as the Reconstruction Acts, which I presume to be the reason that you have honored me by making me your chairman. As you are well aware, I have always been a Union man. I believe that under all circumstances, and by all persons and parties, I have been accorded that distinction. At the same time, I have never been, or been considered, an abolitionist. I was a slaveholder, and belonged to a race of slaveholders, and never felt any conscientious scruples at remaining such. I did not pass upon slavery, it is true, as a new or an abstract question, but considered it as I found it, solely in relation to myself. I did not buy nor sell, except when I bought a woman that she might not be sold away from her husband, and sold one man, at his own request, that he might go with his wife. The act of buying and selling human beings, I admit, was repulsive to me; but I accepted the institution as I found it, and did not feel called upon to attempt its overthrow. In the attempt which was made to disrupt the government, this institution has been destroyed; and it is the question in regard to the future political relations of those who were, as it were, but yesterday slaves, which produces the present differences of opinion among our people, and promises future conflict. If it were the simple question whether we should now be restored to the American Union, and take our place as one of the co-ordinate States, which we had to decide, there would be no difference of opinion. Only an insignificant minority of our people would oppose such restoration upon any terms which did not embrace the conferring of political power upon the freed people. Many think this an unwise and impracticable measure: others believe it to be imposed upon us by the conquerors, simply as an act of wanton and gross insult, for the purpose of adding to the degradation of an already humiliated foe. The fact, also, that every one who had been an officer of the old government, and then served the Confederacy in any voluntary capacity, is barred from the right of suffrage, while his recent slave is given the power to vote, occasions much ill feeling. While I deem the exclusion wise and necessary, though it must strike some who are undeserving, I confess that I have had my fears in regard to the latter measure. After mature and earnest reflection, however, I have become satisfied, that, at the least, the best thing we can do is to accept what is offered, show our willingness to submit to whatever may be deemed wise and proper, and trust that the future may establish the right. Therefore I have come here to-day to co-operate with you. And now, gentlemen, what is your pleasure?"

For once there was a scarcity of candidates. No one seemed to desire a position which promised to be onerous, without honor, and of little profit; which it was felt would cast odium upon the individual, and social and religious ostracism upon his family. The names of the chairman and another were submitted; but the chairman stated that, having been a member of the Legislature before the war, and a justice of the peace during the Confederacy, he believed himself disqualified. Then the Fool's name was substituted for that of the chairman, and the nomination was made.

According to custom, the candidates were called upon to make speeches in acceptance; and the Fool in so doing acknowledged himself quite unprepared to state the line of conduct he should propose in the convention, beyond the acceptance of the conditions prescribed in the Acts under which the election would be held, but promised to set it forth in a printed circular, that all might read and understand his position. The next week this document came out. It does not seem half so revolutionary as it really was. It read, —

"I shall, if elected, favor: —

"1. Equal civil and political rights to all men.

"2. The abolition of property qualifications for voters, officers, and jurors.

"3. Election by the people of all officers — legislative, executive, and judicial — in the state, the counties, the municipalities.

"4. Penal reform: the abolition of the whipping-post, the

stocks, and the branding-iron; and the reduction of capital felonies from *seventeen* to one, or at most two.

"5. Uniform and *ad valorem* taxation upon property, and a limitation of capitation tax to not more than three days' labor upon the public roads in each year, or an equivalent thereof.

"6. An effective system of public schools."

The Fool had no idea that he was committing an enormity; but from that day he became an outlaw in the land where he hoped to have made a home, and which he desired faithfully to serve.

There was a short, sharp canvass, a quiet election, and one day there came to the Fool's address an official document bearing the imprint of the "Headquarters of the Military District" in which he lived, certifying that "Comfort Servosse had been duly elected a delegate to the Constitutional Convention to be held pursuant to the acts of Congress." With him went as members of that body some old friends whom we have met in these pages; among them John Walters, who was the delegate-elect from his county.

CHAPTER XXIV

"WISDOM CRIETH IN THE STREETS"

IMMEDIATELY after the fact of his election became known, the Wise Men who had framed those laws under which the greatest political experiment of modern civilization was to be made, began to write letters to the Fool, all filled with kind and paternal advice as to what the body of which he had just been elected a member ought to do, and when and how it should all be done, as well as a thousand cautions and warnings as to what ought not to be done. The wisdom of these men was most wonderful, in that it not only served for their own purposes, but actually overflowed in superabundant advice to the rest of mankind. It is true that they knew less than nothing of the thoughts, feelings, situations, and surroundings of those people for whose moral and political ills they were prescribing remedies, because the facts which they had apprehended were so colored and modified by others which they could not comprehend, that their conclusions were more likely to be wrong than right. But they were not troubled by any reflection of this kind, because they were quite unconscious that any thing could exist without their knowledge, and never dreamed that careful investigation, study, and time were necessary to restore a nation which had just outlived the fever-fire of civil war; and certainly they were not responsible for not knowing that which they did not dream had any existence.

One of these letters lies before me now. It bears the autograph of one of the wisest of the Wise Men. It is a very great name, — a name that is found in the statesman's annals, and appears on the roll of the United-States Senate, year after year, for a period longer than most men's public lives are privileged to reach. He was a man of wonderful foresight and unerring judgment, so it was said. He knew his State from center to circumference, and never missed the temper of its people. It was said that he was never an hour too late, nor a day too early, in proclaiming his opinions upon any political question. Through a certain range of thought his convictions rose and fell with the flood of popular sentiment; and, could the wavering lines described by the sphygmograph which the physician sometimes laid upon his wrist, have been translated into articulate words, they would have told the precise story of public sentiment in her domains ever since he engaged in the service of the Commonwealth of ——. This sentiment was the divining-rod by which he traced his political footsteps; and so he wrote the following persuasive letter to the Fool: —

SENATE CHAMBER, WASHINGTON, D.C.
Dec. 16, 1867.

MY DEAR COLONEL, — I was very much gratified to know that you are one of the delegates selected to represent your county in the Constitutional Convention of your State. Your record as a Union soldier, and well-known and acknowledged ability, lead us to expect very much of you. And by "us" I do not mean the members of Congress and senators merely, but the party of the Union throughout the country. We are well aware that you did not in all respects approve the plan of Reconstruction which was finally adopted; neither did I: and yet, perhaps, we could have done no better. You see it was absolutely necessary to do *something*. Three years have almost elapsed since the war was over, and nothing has been done to establish any permanent system of restoration or plan of government for that part of the national domain. The usurpative acts of the President have done much to complicate the situation. He has gone over to the enemy, — or, rather, they have rallied to his support, — and will no doubt have, in the coming presidential contest, not only the vast patronage which he controls thrown in their favor, but also the hearty support of those dissatisfied of our party who think that every thing should have been done and settled, and the South restored to her Federal relations, long before this time. This will make the contest a very close and doubtful one, unless we can do two things: —

1. We must be able to point to an accomplished restoration, — the

South reconstructed, represented, or ready for representation, under the congressional plan.

2. We must have the support of these States in the presidential contest next fall.

3. In order to secure the adoption of the new Constitutional Amendments beyond question, we must have the votes of these States. If this is not secured, it is more than doubtful whether the courts will recognize those acts.

The President will undoubtedly do all in his power to delay, hinder, and frustrate these ends. Your convention will probably be put off as long as possible, and every effort made to delay its proceedings. It is of prime importance, therefore, that its action, when once assembled, should not be unnecessarily protracted a single instant. We are looking confidently to you to promote these ends. It is the opinion of our best men here, that all your convention should attempt to do is to adopt the former Constitution of the State, with a provision inserted against slavery, and another denouncing secession, prohibit the payment of Confederate debts, provide for impartial suffrage, and adjourn. This can be done in a week or ten days, at the farthest, and the proceedings forwarded here so as to prevent delay. If this is done, the Southern States can all be counted on in the presidential election; and, under a favorable administration, whatever further changes are necessary can be easily effected.

Unless we can secure the votes of these States, the election of a President by our party and the adoption of the Constitutional Amendments are very doubtful, perhaps impossible. Upon the accession of a President from the opposition party, with a majority in the House of Representatives, the representatives from these States under the Johnsonian plan would no doubt be admitted; and the colored people and white Unionists of the South would have no protection, and the nation no guaranties against future rebellion.

A —— and B —— and C —— of your State, who have written to me, quite concur in these views. We confidently expect your approval and co-operation. Dispatch is of the utmost importance. Let there be no delay. I would like to hear from you immediately. Copies of such amendments as are deemed necessary to be made will be forwarded to some delegate before the convention meets, and I earnestly recommend that nothing further be attempted to be done.

With the highest respect, my dear Colonel,

I remain your obedient servant,

—— ——.

Col. Comfort Servosse, *Warrington.*

We omit the great name which appears in scraggly characters on the now yellow and dingy scroll. How swiftly the tooth of Time gnaws away the inscriptions of fame! Only a decade has passed, and the restless brain and heart of vaulting ambition which dictated these lines, no doubt hoping thereby to smooth somewhat his pathway to the highest place in the nation, overwhelmed with the chagrin of repeated disappointment, has moldered into dust, and almost passed into forgetfulness.

The Fool answered this and other letters of like character with that lack of reverence for great names which the active participant in great events unconsciously acquires. Ten years before, he would have accepted this wise man's views upon any question of governmental policy, with the same undoubting faith that the humblest believer gives to the written and revealed Word. He would neither have questioned his position, doubted his motives, nor suspected his statesmanship. Now, alas! since his unfortunate *accès de la folie*, he had seen so many great reputations wither in the councils of the nation, in the freer and grander struggle of public opinion, and on the field of battle, — he had so often seen the much-vaunted Old give way to the bolder and stronger New, that he had lost that due veneration and regard for age and rank which mark the thoroughly sound and well-ordered mind. Experience of the fallibility of the few very wise men whom he had met had no doubt tended to increase the effects of his infirmity, and confirm an unfortunate delusion which he had, that even wise men are capable of error.

Just about this time, too, there occurred a most unfortunate circumstance, which had the melancholy effect to confirm this delusion. One of the wisest of these very wise men had long been impressed with a belief that a new revelation of the Gospel of Peace, especially adapted to that time and occasion, had been made to him alone, and that it needed but the inspiration of his presence, the deep sincerity of his sonorous sub-vocals, and the power of his imperious but most kindly countenance, to bring the most obdurate of the recent rebels back to sub-servient complacency. Now, unfortunately, instead of leaving this beautiful theory to remain unmarred by the rude test of practice, as most wise men do with their finest theories, he insisted on submitting it to that coarse ordeal. Accordingly, after being duly heralded by the newspapers of the country, he tremblingly took his life in his hand, and, with a body-guard of reporters and stenographers, made a raid into this border-land of civilization to proclaim political light and life. Some-thing in his speech there was which failed to please; and first angry words, and then the angrier bark of Derringer and re-volver, followed. The crowd scattered, the body-guard disap-peared; and that most amiable of controversies, a genteel Southern fight, took place under the eye of the Wise Man, or, rather, under his ear, as he crouched behind the desk from which he had a moment before been expounding "the law of love as co-equal and co-ordinate with the love of law; these being mutually interdependent upon and generative of the other." The Fool had chuckled again and again at this Wise Man's discomfiture, and was never tired of adducing it as an instance of the failure of wisdom at long-range when pitted against sense at short-taw. So, in response to the letter which has been given, he very foolishly wrote thus: —

WARRINGTON, DEC. 20, 1867.

To THE HONORABLE — —, SENATOR.

Sir, — Your letter of the 15th, advising me as to my duties as a delegate to the Constitutional Convention to be held at the call of the general commanding this military district, was duly received, and has been given the consideration which it merits by the personal eminence and official station of the writer. It is with regret that I find myself compelled to differ from one occupying your exalted station, both as a statesman, a patriot, and a Republican leader, upon a matter which you deem so vital in many respects. I can not say I regard the conven-tion as less important than you do, but rather as even more so, though in quite a different sense. From a purely partisan stand-point, I should be inclined to concur with your view, if I could believe present success to be the highest policy; but when we come to regard the ultimate interest, not only of this State and this people, but also of the entire country, it seems to me indubitable that it is of much more importance that the work of the reconstruction of State governments in the recently rebellious territory should be *well* done, than that it should be *speedily* done. You will also allow me to say that it seems to me that one who has been on the ground, and has studied the tone and temper of the people from the very hour of the surrender, has had a much better opportunity to decide upon what is necessary to be done than one who has had none of those opportunities, and who seems to have regarded the question of restoring the statal relations as a move in a political game. As you say, I was opposed to this plan of Reconstruction. I regarded it then, as I still do, as eminently hazardous in its character, very imperfect in its provisions, and lacking all the elements of cautious, deliberate, and far-seeing statesmanship. My objections to it were based upon the following considerations: —

1. The true object and purpose of Reconstruction should be (1) to secure the nation in the future from the perils of civil war, especially a war based upon the same underlying principles and causes as the one just concluded; (2) to secure a development homogeneous with that of the North, so as to render the country what it has never been heretofore, — a nation. As an essential element of this, the bestowal of equal civil and political rights upon all men, without regard to previous rank or station, becomes imperative. It seems to me the Reconstruction Acts have made this postulate of greater importance than the result to which it is auxiliary.

2. I do not think the passions evoked by that struggle, based as it was upon a radical difference of development, and the ill-concealed hostility of many generations, can by any means be put out of sight in such a movement. I do not believe that those who have looked into each other's faces by the lurid light of battle are the fittest persons to devise and execute such rehabilitation, nor do I believe that a lately subject-race is likely to prove an emollient or a neutralizing element in this peaceful adjustment.

3. From a party stand-point, you will allow me to say that I do not think that a party composed of the elements which must constitute the bulk of our party in the South under the present plan of Reconstruction can ever be permanently successful. At least two-thirds of it must not only be poor and ignorant, but also inexperienced and despised. They are just freed from servitude; and the badge of that servitude, the leprosy of slavery, still clings to them. Politically they are unclean; and the contamination of their association will drive away from us the bulk of the brain, character, and experience which

has hitherto ruled these States, and through them the nation. Not only this, but thousands of those who went with us in the late election will fall away when they find themselves and their families focused in the eye of public scorn and ridicule. You wise men who concocted these measures do not seem to have comprehended the fact that the brain and heart of the South — the pulpit, the bar, and the planters; a vast proportion of its best men, and almost every one of its women — cast in their lot with the late Confederacy with all the self-abandonment and devotion of a people who fought for what they believed to be right. You do not realize that this feeling was intensified a thousand-fold by a prolonged and desperate struggle, and final defeat. You do not seem to appreciate the fact, which all history teaches, that there is no feeling in the human breast more blind and desperate in its mani-festations, or so intense and ineradicable in its nature, as the bitter scorn of a long dominant race for one they have held in bondage. You deem this feeling insensate hate. You could not make a greater mis-take. Hate is a sentiment mild and trivial in comparison with it. This embraces no element of individual or personal dislike, but is simply utter and thorough disgust and scorn for the race, — except in what they consider its proper place, — a feeling more fatal to any thing like democratic recognition of their rights as citizens than the most undying hate could be. A party builded upon ignorance, inexperience, and poverty, and mainly composed of a race of pariahs, who are marked and distinguished by their color, can not stand against intelligence, wealth, the pride of a conquered nation, and race-prejudice whose in-tensity laughs to shame the exclusive haughtiness of the Brahmins.

I know your answer to these views: I have heard it a thousand times. But it is builded upon the sand. The very idea is an outgrowth of what we call our Northern development, and sometimes arrogantly style "American civilization." It is not true even of that, however, and would not be true of the North, *ceteris paribus*. You say that the *interest* of the Southern leading classes will compel them to accept and carry out in good faith your reconstructionary idea. You can not find in all history an instance in which the collective advantage of a people has ever yet counterbalanced their prejudices, until at least one gen-eration had grown up under the new phase which conquest had im-posed on their affairs. It is useless to attempt to cite examples, for there is not *one exception* in all history. Individuals may come over, either from conviction of the general good, or for personal advantage, or from both these motives; but races, nations, and classes must be born again, must see another generation, before that result is ever obtained. Mark the dispersion of the Tories of our Revolution as an instance, and think how few of those who remained ever ceased to execrate the nation of which they were unwillingly components.

But, you say, it is needless to consider these questions now; and that I admit, except as it becomes necessary to explain my position. After mature deliberation, I concluded that I could not put myself in opposition to those measures when submitted to the vote of the people here, because the only opposition there was, was based solely upon hostility to the government for which I had fought. It was the spirit of the Rebellion revived. I could not ally myself with this. I was forced to take these measures, and aid in the attempt to make them subserve the purpose of rehabilitation as nearly as possible. This accounts for my opposition to your view. The Rebellion was not the mere incident of an accident; it was the culmination of a long smoldering antagonism, — a divergence of thought and sentiment which was radical and irreconcilable: it was a conflict between two divergent civilizations, and those civilizations had left their marks upon the laws of each section.

The constitutions of the North had fostered individual independence, equal rights and power, and general intelligence among the masses. The township system had been the cause and consequence of this. Almost all offices were elective, and, except in rare instances, all men were electors. It developed democratic ideas and sentiments, and was a nursery of democratic freedom.

In the South the reverse was true. The ballot and the jury-box were jealously guarded from the intrusion of the poor. Wealth was a prerequisite of official eligibility. It was a republic in name, but an oligarchy in fact. Its laws were framed and construed to this end. The land-holdings were enormous, and the bulk of those who cultivated the soil were not freeholders, but either slaves or renters.

To my mind, the first great prerequisite of successful Reconstruction is to break down the legal barriers to a homogeneous development of the country; to so organize the new State governments that they will tend to encourage individual action, freedom of opinion, diversity of industry, and general education. The task before the coming convention is herculean, even if it is not impossible to accomplish. I have pledged myself to those who elected me, to attempt what I can in this direction, and shall redeem the pledge to the letter. I inclose you a copy of the Circular issued to our electors.

In conclusion, allow me to say that I do not believe that the interest or success of the Republican party demands or would be promoted by the course you suggest. If it does, I am sure that the ultimate interest of the country does not; and as I was a citizen before I was a Republican, and as I fought for the country and not for the party, you must excuse me if I follow my convictions rather than your counsel. I am, very respectfully,

Your obedient servant,

COMFORT SERVOSSE.

CHAPTER XXV

A GRUMBLER'S FORECAST

T HE transition period was over, so it was said. The conventions had met in the various States, and in a marvelously short time had submitted constitutions which had been ratified by vote of the people. Officers had been chosen under them, they had been approved by the Congress of the nation as required by law, Legislatures had met, senators and representatives in Congress been chosen, the presidential election had taken place, and the Republican party had achieved an overwhelming success. It was all over, — the war, reconstruction, the consideration of the old questions. Now all was peace and harmony. The South must take care of itself now. The nation had done its part: it had freed the slaves, given them the ballot, opened the courts to them, and put them in the way of self-protection and self-assertion. The "root-hog-or-die" policy of the great apostle of the instantaneous transformation era became generally prevalent. The nation heaved a sigh of relief. For three-quarters of a century the South had been the "Old Man of the Sea" to the young Republic: by a simple trick of political legerdemain he was now got rid of for ever. No wonder the Republic breathed freely! Yankee-land could now bend its undivided energies to its industries and commerce. The South would take care of itself, manage its own affairs, look after its own interests. The nation was safe. It had put down rebellion, disbanded its armies, patched up its torn map. The Republican party had accomplished a great mission. It had promised to put down rebellion, and had done so. It had guaranteed freedom to the slave, and had redeemed its promise. There was nothing more to be done until, in the fullness of time, new issues should arise, based on new thoughts, new ideas, and new interests.

This is what the wise men said. But the Fool looked on with anxious forebodings, and wrote to his old tutor gloomily of the future that seemed so bright to others: —

WARRINGTON, DEC. 10, 1868.

To DR. E. MARTIN.

My dear old Friend, — Your kind and welcome letter, so full of congratulations and bright anticipations, was duly received, and for it I render thanks. Must I confess it, however? it impresses me with a feeling of sadness. The state of affairs which you picture does not exist at the South; and the bright anticipations which you base upon mistaken premises have, in my opinion, little chance of fulfillment. The freedman is just as impotent now of all power of self-protection as he was before the ballot was given him, — nay, perhaps more so, as an unskilled person may injure himself with the finest of Damascus blades. Pray keep in your mind my former classification. Of every hundred of the blacks, ninety-five at least can not read or write, ninety-five are landless, and at least eighty have not sufficient to subsist themselves for thirty days without the aid of those who are opposed to them in political thought with an intensity of prejudice you can not begin to understand. These constitute three-fourths of the Republican party of the South. Of the remainder (the whites), twenty-four out of every hundred can not read their ballots; and fifty-five or sixty of the same number are landless, being mere day-laborers, or at least renters, "crappers" as they are called here.

So that of this party, to whom the wise men of the North have given power, from whom they expect all but impossible things, three-fourths can not read or write, five-sevenths are landless, two-thirds are utterly impoverished, and nearly the whole is inexperienced in the conduct of public affairs. Yet upon this party the nation has rolled the burden of restoration, reconstruction, re-organization! That it will fail is as certain as the morrow's sunrise. For three years the nation has had this problem on the heads and hearts of its legislators, and has not made one step towards its solution. The highest wisdom, the greatest gravity, the profoundest knowledge, and that skill which comes only from experience, are indispensably necessary to this task. It is given into the hands of weaklings; while the great country, whose interest, prosperity, and good faith, are all involved in securing the liberty conferred by the war, and in so organizing these new constituent elements that they shall hereafter be a source of strength, and not danger, — this country stands off, and says, "I will not touch one of the least of these burdens with my little finger. The South must take care of itself."

My dear old friend, it can not be done. The experiment must fail;

and, when it does fail, it will involve us all — us of the South, I mean — in ruin; but the North, and especially the Republican party of the North, will be responsible for this ruin, for its shame and its loss, for the wasted opportunity, and, it may be, for consequent peril. Of course I shall share it. The North would not see the fact that war did not mean regeneration, nor perform the duty laid upon it as a conqueror. The alternative placed before us at the South was a powerless acceptance of the plan of reconstruction, or opposition and hostility to the government. I, in common with others, chose the former. A loyal man could not do otherwise. Now we, and probably we alone, must share and bear the blame of its failure. I protest in advance against it. If, of a steamer's crew of a hundred men, fifty be deaf-and-dumb, and only five of them all have ever been afloat, her voyage even in the calmest sea is not likely to be a safe one; but when it is in a season of typhoons, off a dangerous coast of which no chart has ever been made, its destruction may be certainly foretold. And, when it perishes amid the breakers of a lee-shore, the despairing wretches, who call for aid which cometh not, will curse, not so much the incompetent captain and inefficient steersman, as the negligent owners who sent her to sea with such a crew.

It is so with us. We Republicans of the South will go down with the reconstruction movement. Some of us will make a good fight for the doomed craft; others will neither realize nor care for its danger: but on neither will justly rest the responsibility. That will rest now and for all time with the Republican party of the North, — a party the most cowardly, vacillating, and inconsistent in its management of these questions, that has ever been known in any government.

These are my convictions. I might get away, and avoid this result, so far as I am concerned; but I have cast in my lot with this people. I have advocated this measure, and I will abide with them its results.

In fact, my dear Doctor, I begin seriously to fear that the North lacks virility. This cowardly shirking of responsibility, this pandering to sentimental whimsicalities, this snuffling whine about peace and conciliation, is sheer weakness. The North is simply a conqueror; and, if the results she fought for are to be secured, she must rule as a conqueror. Suppose the South had been triumphant, and had overwhelmed and determined to hold the North? Before now, a thoroughly organized system of provincial government would have been securely established. There would have been no hesitation, no subterfuge, no pretence of restoration, because the people of the South are born rulers, — aggressives, who, having made up their minds to attain a certain end, adopt the means most likely to secure it. In this the North fails. She hesitates, palters, shirks.

There is another danger. Rebellion has ended without punishment. It is true the South has lost, — lost her men, her money, her slaves;

but that was only a gambler's stake, the hazard placed upon the dice. There was talk of "making treason odious." How that result should be accomplished was a serious question; but how to make it *honorable*, I fear we have found an easy matter to demonstrate.

As I have said, the party, if it may so be called, to whom the mighty task of rehabilitation has been assigned, must fail at the South. Already we hear the threat from the highest seats in the hostile camps, "Just wait until the Blue Coats are gone, and we will make Sodom and Gomorrah more tolerable than these States to Republicans!" They will do it, too. They have the power, the intellect, the organizing capacity, the determined will. Our numbers only make us a cumbrous rope of sand. Weak, incoherent particles are not made strong by mere multiplication. In the struggle against us, the most reckless and unworthy of those who led in the war will again come to the front. Their success will make them the heroes of the people, and they will win place and honor thereby. It will result that turbulent, ambitious men will hereafter say that the road to honor, renown, fame, and power, in our nation, lies through the "Traitor's Gate." Burr and his coadjutors won only shame by their attempt to destroy the nation. Davis, Lee, and their compatriots have already won a distinction and eminence they could not have hoped for had they remained peaceful citizens of the Republic. They are destined to achieve far greater honor. From this day the prestige of the Federal soldier will begin to wane throughout the land. In the course of another decade, one will almost be ashamed to confess that he wore the blue. On the other hand, the glory of the Confederate leader will hourly wax greater and brighter. The latter has a people devoted and steadfast, to whose pride, even in defeat, he can appeal with certainty of receiving an unshrinking response. The former has a country debauched by weak humanitarianisms, more anxious to avoid the appearance of offending its enemies than desirous of securing its own power or its own ends. These men who have led in the Rebellion will not be slow to perceive and take advantage of their opportunity; and other generations following them will note the fact that the sure, safe, and brilliant road to fame and success is an armed rebellion against existing powers. You may think me discouraged and morbid; but mark my words, old friend, we have sown to the wind, and shall reap the whirlwind.

Yours truly,

COMFORT SERVOSSE.

So, with foreboding, the Fool looked to the future, and awaited the event of that great experiment, from the preliminaries of which he was only able to presage danger and disaster.

CHAPTER XXVI

BALAK AND BALAAM

THE re-action from subjection to autonomy was so sudden and astounding, that even the people of the late rebellious States were unable to realize it for a considerable period. That a nation, after four years of war, the loss of a million of men and uncounted millions of treasure, should relax its grip upon the subjugated territory, relieve its people of all disabilities, or only bar from a useless privilege a few superannuated leaders, who only thus were susceptible of martyrdom, and without guaranties for the future, or without power of reversal or modification, should restore this territory, this people, these States, to the position of equal, independent, and co-ordinate sovereignties, was so incredible a proposition, that years were required for its complete comprehension.

During these years the public press of the South was a curious study. Immediately after the close of the war, and until about the period of the rehabilitation of the States, its utterances were cautious and guarded. While there was almost always an undertone which might be construed to mean either sullen hate or unconcealable chagrin, there was little of that vindictive bitterness toward the North which had immediately preceded the war, or attended its prosecution. It is true, that, in some instances, its bottles of unparalleled infamy were unstopped, and poured on the heads of unoffending citizens of Northern birth, or those natives who saw fit to affiliate with the conqueror, or to accept office at his hands. This, however, was not a universal rule. As soon as the reconstruction period had passed, this caution relaxed. More and more bitter, more and more loathsome, became the mass of Southern journalism.

Defiant hostility, bitter animosity, unrestricted libertinism in the assaults of private character, poured over the columns of the Southern press like froth upon the jaws of a rabid cur. Whatever or whoever was of the North or from the North was the subject of ridicule, denunciation, and immeasurable malignity of vituperation. Whoever had aided, assisted, or assented to the process of reconstruction, became a target for infamous assault. Rank, station, purity of life, uprightness of character, religious connection, age, sex, were no safeguard from these assaults. The accumulated malignity of the years of quietude and suppression burst its bounds, and poured over the whole country a disgusting flood of hideous, horrible, improbable, and baseless accusation and rabid vituperation. Men of the fairest lives were covered over with unutterable infamy; women of the highest purity were accused of unnamable enormities; and even children of tender years were branded with ineffaceable marks of shame. The previous training which the press of the South had received in the art of vilification, under the *régime* of slavery, became now of infinite service in this verbal crusade. The mass of their readers had long been accustomed to believe any thing absurd and horrible in regard to the North. To them it was already the land of thieves, adulterers, infidels, and cheats. There might be good men there; but they were counted rarer than in Sodom. For fifty years the necessities of slavery had rendered the cultivation of such a sentiment necessary in order to preserve the institution from the assaults of free labor and free thought. To turn this tide of public sentiment against the ideas, principles, and men who were engaged in the work of reconstruction, to intensify its bitterness, increase its credulity, and make thereby a seven-times heated furnace of infamy for those who saw fit to favor this movement, was the assigned work and mission of the Southern press, and right nobly was it executed. Never was such unanimity, never was such persistency, never such rivalry in malevolence, never such munificence in invective, never such fertility in falsehood.

It was but natural, and in a great measure fair, upon the principle that all in war is fair. So far as the official representatives of the government were concerned, they had nothing of which to complain. They represented the conqueror; and if their master was inherently or accidentally too weak to protect them, or disinclined to compel obedience and respect from the recently vanquished enemy, it was only the fault of their employer, whose service was purely voluntary. The fools who had removed to these States from motives of ease or profit, engaging in production, manufacture, or trade, ought not to have complained, because they came among a conquered people, being of the conqueror, well knowing (or at least they should have known) the generations of antagonism which war had fused into hate, and having, therefore, no right to look for or expect kindliness, favor, or even fair play. If they did so, it was their own folly.

Those who had most right, or perhaps the sole right, to complain, were those among the conquered people who had espoused the cause of the nation before or after the downfall of the Confederacy. They had a right to suppose that the conquering power would at least make itself respectable, and would not permit its supporters to be disgraced by the mere fact of allegiance to it. It must have been a matter of sincere astonishment to the Union man — who during the war, from its inception to its close, perhaps, had been an uncompromising opponent of those by whom it was waged, had perhaps fought and hidden and endured, with a rare faith in that government from which he was cut off, but to which he had adhered with marvelous fidelity — to find, after the war, at the first, his neighbors flocking to him in order to obtain the benefit of his good word, his intercession with the powers that were, in their behalf. It must indeed have been a proud day to such when those who had persecuted came to sue; and, let it be said to their credit, rarely was application made to them in vain. These Union men were a most forgiving people, and not unfrequently bestowed the divine favor of forgiveness without price upon the very men who had wrought them the sorest evil. But such surprise must have been as nothing compared with the astonishment with which the Union man must have witnessed, after the accomplishment of reconstruction, himself made an object of scorn, and his family visited with contumely and insult, because of his Union record.

As Jehu Brown said to the Fool in regard to it, —

"I can't understan' it, Colonel. They say our side whipped; that the Union won, an' the Confederacy lost: an' yit here they be a-puttin' it on tu me like all possessed day arter day, an' abusin' my wife an' children too bad for white folks to hear about, jes cos I was a Union man. There must be some mistake, Colonel, about the matter. Either 'twas the t'other folks that surrendered at Appomattox, or else you an' I was on t'other side, an' hev jes been a-dreamin' that we was Yank an' Union all this time!"

The most amazing thing connected with this matter, however, was the fact that the press of the North, almost without exception, echoed the clamor and invective of the Southern journals. In order to express their abhorrence for such as dared to go from the North, thinking to become residents of the South without an absolute surrender of all that they had hitherto accounted principle, one who was of more intense virulence than the others invented a new term, or rather reapplied one which he had already helped to make infamous. The origin of this new vehicle of malignity is said to have been this. In one of the North-western States, during the early days of "wild-cat money" as it was termed, a plan was devised for preventing the solvency of the State banks from being too readily tested. An organization was formed which secured its issues by the mortgage of land, which mortgage the State had power to enforce as upon forfeiture, on behalf of the creditors, whenever the notes of the organization (they called it a bank) "should go to protest." To avoid this contingency was then the prime object. As the law had neglected to provide that banks organized under it should have a permanent place of business, this object was for a considerable time attained by neglecting to open any office, or having any permanent place of doing business, and putting their notes in circulation by means of agents, who carried the bills about the country in *carpet-bags*, and were hence denominated, "Carpet-baggers." It is said that one of these veritable carpet-baggers, an editor, who during the war had exhausted all the expletives of which he was master, in denunciation of Lincoln and the officers and men of the Federal army, and had, in return, been branded with that term of ineffaceable shame "Copperhead," was therefore at a loss for some fresh epithet to bestow upon the new class whom he had honored with his hate, and suddenly bethought himself of his own nickname. Whereupon he shouted, "Carpet-baggers!" Instantly it spread through the press of the South; and, with its usual subserviency, that of the North followed in its lead, and re-echoed its maledictions.

The name itself was a stroke of genius. Whoever first bestowed it on the peripatetic Wisconsin cashier was undoubtedly akin to the heaven-descended. In all history there is perhaps no instance of so perfect and complete an epithet. *Sansculotes* is its nearest rival. "Abolitionist," its immediate predecessor, has the disadvantage of an etymological significance, which sometimes interfered with its perfect application. "Carpet-bagger" had, however, all the essentials of a denunciatory epithet in a superlative degree. It had a quaint and ludicrous sound, was utterly without defined significance, and was altogether unique. It was susceptible of one significance in one locality, and another in another, without being open to any etymological objection. This elasticity of signification is of prime importance in a disparaging epithet: there is almost always a necessity for it. "Abolitionist" meant only one who was in favor of the abolition of slavery. At the North it had this significance, and no more. At the South it meant also, one who was in favor of, and sought to promote, negro-equality, miscegenation, rape, murder, arson, and anarchy, with all the untold horrors which the people there believed would follow the uprising or liberation of a race of untaught savages, lustful as apes, bloodthirsty as cannibals, and artful as satyrs.

So that this formulated difference then prevailed: —

AT THE NORTH.

Abolitionist. — One who favors the emancipation of slaves.

AT THE SOUTH.

Abolitionist. — One who favors emancipation + infidel + murderer + thief + ravisher + incendiary + all hell's accumulated horrors, "not otherwise appropriated."

This epithet, as was said before, was liable to objection among a people who thought and defined. It was possible to show by ratiocination, as well as example, that an "abolitionist" was not, of necessity, an infidel, nor, *ex vi termini*, a murderer or thief. So when an unfortunate minister of the gospel happened to allow somewhat too much of the Master's truth to escape his lips, while tarrying south of Mason's and Dixon's Line, and was thereupon treated to hickory on his bare back, or hemp around his gullet, because he was an "abolitionist," the North was somewhat shocked at the disproportion between the offense and punishment; but the South heartily and honestly rejoiced, and thanked God with renewed devotion, because, to its apprehension, an inconceivably atrocious monster had been destroyed from off the face of the earth! And so the game of cross-purposes went on.

"Carpet-bagger," which was in some sense the lineal descendant of "abolitionist," was, as was very proper for a second edition, a considerable improvement on its immediate predecessor. It was undefined and undefinable. To the Southern mind it meant a scion of the North, a son of an "abolitionist," a creature of the conqueror, a witness of their defeat, a mark of their degradation: to them he was hateful, because he recalled all of evil or shame which they had ever known. They hissed the name through lips hot with hate, *because* his presence was hateful to that dear, dead Confederacy which they held in tender memory, and mourned for in widow's weeds, as was but natural that they should do. They hated the Northern man, who came among them as the representative and embodiment of that selfish, malign, and envious North, which had sent forth the "abolitionist" in *ante bellum* days, had crushed the fair South in her heroic struggle to establish a slave-sustained republic, and now had sent spies and harpies to prey upon, to mock and taunt and jeer them in their downfall and misfortune. To their minds the word expressed all that collective and accumulated hate which generations of antagonism had engendered, intensified and sublimated by the white-heat of a war of passionate intensity and undoubted righteousness to the hearts of its promoters. The Northern man who set up his family altar at the South stood, by natural and almost necessary synecdoche, for *the North*. He was to all that portion of the South which arrogates to itself the term Southern, not only an enemy, but the representative in miniature of all their enemies. And this he was of course, and by consequence of his Northern nativity. It is true, he might in part relieve himself from this imputation; but it rested upon him to do so. The presumption was against him; and, in order to rebut it, he must take the Gaelic oath to "love whom thou lovest, hate whom thou hatest, bless whom thou blessest, and curse whom thou dost anathematize."

To the Northern mind, however, the word had no vicarious significance. To their apprehension, the hatred it embodied was purely personal, and without regard to race or nativity. They *thought* (foolish creatures!) that it was meant to apply solely to those, who, without any visible means of support, lingering in the wake of a victorious army, preyed upon the conquered people.

So these formulated significations prevailed: —

AT THE NORTH.

Carpet-bagger. — A man without means, character, or occupation, an adventurer, a camp-follower, "a bummer."

AT THE SOUTH.

Carpet-bagger. — A man of Northern birth + an abolitionist (according to the Southern definition) + incarnation of Northern hate, envy, spleen, greed, hypocrisy, and all uncleanness.

So the South cursed "carpet-baggers," because they were of the North; and the North cursed them because the South set the example.

In nothing has the South shown its vast moral superiority over the North more than in this. "I pray thee curse me this people," it said to the North, first of the "abolitionists," and then of the "carpet-baggers;" and the North cursed, not knowing whom it denounced, and not pausing to inquire whether they were worthy of stripes or not. Perhaps there is no other instance in history in which the conquering power has discredited its own agents, denounced those of its own blood and faith, espoused the prejudices of its conquered foes, and poured the vials of its wrath and contempt upon the only class in the conquered territory who defended its acts, supported its policy, promoted its aim, or desired its preservation and continuance.

CHAPTER XXVII

A NEW INSTITUTION

There had been rumors in the air, for some months, of a strangely mysterious organization, said to be spreading over the Southern States, which added to the usual intangibility of the secret society an element of grotesque superstition unmatched in the history of any other.

It was at first regarded as farcical, and the newspapers of the North unwittingly accustomed their readers to regard it as a piece of the broadest and most ridiculous fun. Here and there throughout the South, by a sort of sporadic instinct, bands of ghostly horsemen, in quaint and horrible guise, appeared, and admonished the lazy and trifling of the African race, and threatened the vicious. They claimed to the affrighted negroes, it was said, to be the ghosts of departed Confederates who had come straight from the confines of hell to regulate affairs about their former homes.

All this was a matter of infinite jest and amusement to the good and wise people of the North. What could be funnier, or a more appropriate subject of mirth, than that the chivalric but humorous and jocose Southrons should organize a ghostly police to play upon the superstitious fears of the colored people, who were no doubt very trifling, and needed a good deal of regulation and restraint? So the Northern patriot sat back in his safe and quiet home, and laughed himself into tears and spasms at the grotesque delineations of ghostly K. K. K.'s and terrified darkies, for months before any idea of there being any impropriety therein dawned on his mind or on the minds of the wise men who controlled the affairs of the nation. That a few hundreds, a few thousands, or even millions, of the colored race, should be controlled and dominated by their superstitious fears, deprived of their volition, and compelled to follow the behests of others, was not regarded as at all dangerous in a republic, and as worthy of remark only from its irresistibly amusing character.

It was in the winter of 1868–69, therefore, when the wise men were jubilant over the success of the Great Experiment; when it was said that already Reconstruction had been an approved success, the traces of the war been blotted out, and the era of the millennium anticipated, — that a little company of colored men came to the Fool one day; and one of them, who acted as spokesman, said, —

"What's dis we hear, Mars Kunnel, bout de Klux?"

"The what?" he asked.

"De Klux — de Ku-Kluckers dey calls demselves."

"Oh! the Ku-Klux, Ku-Klux-Klan, K. K. K.'s, you mean."

"Yes: dem folks what rides about at night a-pesterin' pore colored people, an' a-pertendin' tu be jes from hell, or some of de battle-fields ob ole Virginny."

"Oh, that's all gammon! There is nothing in the world in it, — nothing at all. Probably a parcel of boys now and then take it into their heads to scare a few colored people; but that's all. It is mean and cowardly, but nothing more. You needn't have any trouble about it, boys."

"An' you tink dat's all, Kunnel?"

"All? Of course it is! What else should there be?"

"I dunno, Mars Kunnel," said one.

"You don't think dey's ghostses, nor nothin' ob dat sort?" asked another.

"Think! I know they are not."

"So do I," growled one of their number who had not spoken before, in a tone of such meaning that it drew the eyes of the Fool upon him at once.

"So your mind's made up on that point too, is it, Bob?" he asked laughingly.

"I know dey's not ghosts, Kunnel. I wish ter God dey was!" was the reply.

"Why, what do you mean, Bob?" asked the colonel in surprise.

"Will you jes help me take off my shirt, Jim?" said Bob meaningly, as he turned to one of those with him.

The speaker was taller than the average of his race, of a peculiarly jetty complexion, broad-shouldered, straight, of compact and powerful build. His countenance, despite its blackness, was sharply cut; his head well shaped; and his whole appearance and demeanor marked him as a superior specimen of his race. Servosse had seen him before, and knew him well as an industrious and thrifty blacksmith, living in a distant part of the county, who was noted as being one of the most independent and self-reliant of his people in all political as well as pecuniary matters, — Bob Martin by name.

When his clothing had been removed, he turned his back towards the Fool, and, glancing over his shoulder, said coolly, —

"What d'ye tink ob dat, Kunnel?"

"My God!" exclaimed the Fool, starting back in surprise and horror. "What does this mean, Bob?"

"Seen de Kluckers, sah," was the grimly-laconic answer.

The sight which presented itself to the Fool's eyes was truly terrible. The broad muscular back, from the nape down to and below the waist, was gashed and marked by repeated blows. Great furrows were plowed in the black integument, whose greenly-livid lips were drawn back, while the coagulated fibrine stretched across, and mercifully protected the lacerated flesh. The whole back was livid and swollen, bruised as if it had been brayed in a mortar. Apparently, after having cut the flesh with closely-laid welts and furrows, sloping downward from the left side towards the right, with the peculiar skill in castigation which could only be obtained through the abundant opportunity for severe and deliberate flagellation which prevailed under the benign auspices of slavery, the operator had changed his position, and scientifically cross-checked the whole. That he was an expert whose skill justified Bob's remark — "Nobody but an ole oberseer ebber dun dat, Kunnel" — was evident even on a casual inspection. The injury which the man had sustained, though extensive and severe, was not dangerous to one of his constitution and hardened physique. To the eye of the Northern man who gazed at it, however, unused as are all his compeers to witness the effects of severe whipping, it seemed horrible beyond the power of words to express. He did not reflect that the African could have had none of that sense of indignity and degradation with which the Caucasian instinctively regards the application of the emblem of servility, and that he was but fulfilling the end of his dusky being in submitting to such castigation. He was filled with anger, surprise, and horror.

"What? — Who? — How? — My God! Tell me all about it. Can't I do something for you, my man?"

"Thank ye, Kunnel, nothing," said Bob seriously. "It's been washed in salt an' water. Dat's de bes' ting dere is to take out de soreness; an' it's doin as well as can be expected, I s'pose. I don't know much 'bout sech matters, Boss. I'se bin a slave goin' on forty-three years, but never hed a lash on my back sence I was a waitin'-boy till las' night."

His face was working with passion, and his eyes had a wicked fire in them, which clearly showed that he did not take this visitation in such a subdued and grateful spirit as his position properly demanded that he should. When his clothing had been resumed, he sat down and poured into the wondering ears of the Fool this story: —

BOB'S EXPERIENCE.

"Yer see, I'se a blacksmith at Burke's Cross-Roads. I've been thar ever sence a few days arter I heer ob de surrender. I rented an ole house dar, an' put up a sort of shop, an' got to-gedder a few tools, an' went to work. It's a right good stan'. Never used ter be ob any count, coz all de big plantations roun' dar hed der own smifs. But now de smifs hez scattered off, an' dey hev ter pay fer der work, dey finds it cheaper ter come ter my shop dan ter hire a blacksmif when dey's only half work fer him to do. So I'se been doin' right well, an' hev bought de house an' lot, an' got it all paid fer, tu. I've allers tended to my own business. 'Arly an' late Bob's bin at his shop, an' allers at work. I 'llowed to get me a snug home fer myself an' de ole 'ooman afore we got tu old ter work; an' I wanted to give de boys an' gals a little eddication, an' let em hev a fa'r start in life wid de rest ob de worl', if I could. Dat's what Bob's bin wukkin' fer; an' der ain't no man ner woman, black ner white, can say he hain't wukked honestly and fa'rly, — honestly an' fa'rly, ebbery day sence he's bin his own master.

"Long a while back — p'raps five er six months — I refused ter du some work fer Michael Anson or his boy, 'cause they'd run up quite a score at de shop, an' allers put me off when I wanted pay. I couldn't work jes fer de fun ob scorin' it down: so I quit. It made smart ob talk. Folks said I waz gettin' too smart fer a nigger, an' sech like; but I kep right on; tole em I waz a free man, — not born free, but made free by a miracle, — an' I didn't propose ter do any man's work fer noffin'. Most everybody hed somefin' to say about it; but it didn't seem ter hurt my trade very much. I jes went on gittin' all I could do, an' sometimes moah. I s'pose I acted pretty inde-pendent: I felt so, anyhow. I staid at home, an' axed nobody any favors. I know'd der wa'n't a better blacksmif in de country, an' thought I hed things jes' ez good ez I wanted 'em. When ther come an election, I sed my say, did my own votin', an' tole de other colored people dey waz free, an' hed a right ter du de same. Thet's bad doctrine up in our country. De white folks don't like ter hear it, and 'specially don't like ter hear a nigger say it. Dey don't mind 'bout our gettin' on ef dey hev a mortgage, so't de 'arnin's goes into ther pockets; nor 'bout our votin', so long ez we votes ez dey tells us. Dat's dare idea uv liberty fer a nigger.

"Well, here a few weeks ago, I foun' a board stuck up on my shop one mornin', wid dese words on to it: —

" 'BOB MARTIN, — You're gettin' too dam smart! The white folks round Burke's Cross-Roads don't want any sech smart niggers round thar. You'd better git, er you'll hev a call from the

" 'K. K. K.'

"I'd heerd 'bout the Klux, an' 'llowed jes' ez you did, Kunnel, — dat dey waz some triflin' boys dat fixed up an' went round jes' ter scare pore ignorant niggers, an' it made me all the madder ter think dey should try dat ar game on me. So I sed boldly, an' afore everybody, thet ef the Kluckers wanted enny thin' uv Bob Martin, they'd better come an' git it; thet I didn't 'bleve any nonsense about ther comin' straight from hell, an' drinkin' the rivers dry, an' all that: but, ef they'd come ter meddle with me, I 'llowed some on 'em mout go to hell afore it was over.

"I worked mighty hard an' late yesterday, an', when I went into de house, I was so tired thet I jes' fell down on de trundle-bed dat hed bin pulled out in front ob de souf do'. When my ole 'ooman got supper ready, an' called me, I jes' turned over, an' was that beat out an' sleepy, that I tole her to let me alone. So I lay thar, an' slep'. She put away de supper-tings, an' tuk part ob de chillen into bed wid her; an' de rest crawled in wid me, I s'pose. I donno nothin' about it, fer I nebber woke up till some time in de night. I kinder remember hearin' de dog bark, but I didn't mind it; an', de fust ting I knew, de do' was bust in, an' fell off de hinges ober on de trundle-bed whar

I was lyin'. It's a mercy I was thar. I don't s'pose I've lain down on it fer a year afore, an', ef de chillen hed all been thar alone, it's mor'n likely they'd all been killed. They hed taken a house-log I hed got (tinkin' ter put up a kitchen arter Christmas), an' free or four of 'em hed run wid it endwise agin de do'. So, when I woke from de crash, I hed do' an' house-log bofe on me, an' de ole 'ooman an' chillen screamin', so't I couldn't make out fer a minnit what it was, er whar I was. De moon was a-shinin bright, an' I 'spect de rascals t'ought I'd run, an' dey would shoot me as I come out. But, as soon as dey saw me heavin' an' strugglin' under de do', two on 'em run in, an' got on top of it. It was no use fer me to struggle any more under dat load. Besides dat, I was feared dey'd kill de chillen. So I tole 'em ef dey'd get off, an spar' de chillen, I'd surrender. Dey wouldn't bleve me, dough, till dey'd tied my han's. Den dey got off de do', an' I riz up, an' kind o' pushed it an' de house-log off de trundle-bed. Den dey pulled me out o' do's. Dar was 'bout tirty of 'em standin' dar in de moonlight, all dressed in black gowns thet come down to ther boots, an' some sort of high hat on, dat come down ober der faces, jes' leavin' little holes ter see fru, an' all trimmed wid different colored cloth, but mos'ly white.

"I axed 'em what dey wanted o' me. Dey sed I was gittin tu dam smart, an' dey'd jes' come roun' ter teach me some little manners. Den dey tied me tu a tree, an' done what you've seen. Dey tuk my wife an' oldes' gal out ob de house, tore de close night about off 'em, an' abused 'em shockin' afore my eyes. After tarin' tings up a heap in de house, dey rode off, tellin' me dey reckoned I'd larn to be 'spectful to white folks herearter, an' not refuse to work unless I hed pay in advance, an' not be so anxious 'bout radical votes. Den my ole woman cut me loose, an' we went into de house ter see what devilment dey'd done dar. We called de chillen. Dar's five on 'em, — de oldes' a gal 'bout fifteen, an' de younges' only little better'n a year ole. We foun' 'em all but de baby. I don' tink he ebber breaved arter de do' fell on us."

The tears stood in the eyes of the poor man as he finished. The Fool looked at him in a glamour of amazement, pity, and shame. He could not help feeling humiliated, that, in his own Christian land, one should be so treated by such a cowardly-seeming combination, simply for having used the liberty which the law had given him to acquire competence and independence by his own labor.

"Why have you not complained of this outrage to the authorities?" he asked after a moment.

"I tole Squire Haskins an' Judge Thompson what I hev tole you," answered Bob.

"And what did they say?"

"Dat dey couldn't do noffin' unless I could sw'ar to de parties."

"Did you not recognize any of them?"

"Not to say recognize; dat is, not so dat I could tell you so dat you could know de persons as de ones I named. I'm nigh 'bout sartin, from a lot of little tings, who dey was; but I couldn't sw'ar."

"Did you not know the voices of any of them?"

"Yes, I did. But de judge says I would jes' be makin' trouble fer myself to no 'count; fer he says no jury would convict on sech evidence when unsupported."

"I suppose he is right," mused the Colonel. "And there does not seem to be any way for you to get redress for what has been done to you, unless you can identify those who did the injury so clearly that no jury can resist a conviction. I suppose the vast majority of jurymen will be disinclined even to do justice. Perhaps some of the very men who were engaged in the act may be on the jury, or their brothers, fathers, or friends. So it would be useless for you to attempt a prosecution unless you had the very strongest and clearest testimony. I doubt not the judge was right in the advice he gave you."

"And do you tink der is any chance o' my gittin' sech testimony?" asked Bob.

"I confess," answered the Fool, "that I see very little. Time and care might possibly enable you to get it."

"Der's no hope o' dat, — no hope at all," answered the freedman sadly.

There was a moment's silence. Then the colored man asked, —

"Isn't dere no one else, Kunnel, dat could do any ting? Can't de President or Congress do somefin'? De gov'ment sot us free, an' it 'pears like it oughtn't to let our old masters impose on us in no sech way now. I ain't no coward, Kunnel, an' I don't want to brag; but I ain't 'feared of no man. I don't min' sufferin' nor dyin' ef I could see any good to come from it. I'd be willin' ter fight fer my liberty, er fer de country dat give me liberty. But I don't tink liberty was any favor ef we are to be cut up an' murdered jes' de same as in slave times, an' wuss too. Bob'll take keer of himself, an' his wife an' chillen too, ef dey'll only give him a white man's chance. But ef men can come to his house in de middle ob de night, kill his baby, an' beat an' abuse him an' his family ez much ez dey please, jes' by puttin' a little black cloth ober der faces, I may ez well give up, an' be a slave agin."

"If it keeps on, and grows general," responded the Caucasian, "the government will have to interfere. The necessity will be such that they can not resist it. I don't quite see how it can be done, now that these States are restored; but the government *must* protect the lives of its citizens, and it *ought* to protect their liberties. I don't know how it may be done. It may declare such acts treasonable, and outlaw the offenders,

authorizing any man to kill them when engaged in such unlawful acts."

"If dey would only do dat, Kunnel, we'd soon put an end
to de Ku-Kluckers. We'd watch de roads, an', ebery time dey
rode frue de bushes, dere'd be some less murderin' Kluckers
dan when dey started out. Hav' 'em du dat, Kunnel, an' we's
all right. Jes' gib us a fa'r chance, an' de culled men'll tak'
keer o' dersel's. We ain't cowards. We showed dat in de wah.
I'se seen darkeys go whar de white troops wa'n't anxious to
foller 'em, mor'n once."

"Where was that, Bob?"

"Wal, at Fo't Wagner, for one."

"How did you know about that?"

"How did I know 'bout dat? Bress yer soul, Kunnel, I was
dar!"

"How did that happen? I thought you were raised in the
up country here?"

"So I was, Kunnel; but, when I heerd dat Abram Linkum
had gib us our freedom, I made up my mine I'd go an' git
my sheer, an', ef dar was any ting I could do to help de rest
of my folks to git dars, I was gwine ter du it. So I managed
to slip away, one wayer 'nother, an' got fru de lines down
'bout Charleston, an' jined de Fifty-fo' Massachusetts Culled,
Kunnel. Dat's how I come to be at Wagner."

"That explains, in part, the feeling against you, I suppose,"
said Servosse.

"It s'plains annudder ting tu, Kunnel," said the colored man
doggedly.

"What is that?" asked the white ex-soldier.

"It s'plains why, ef dere's any mo' Kluckers raidin' roun'
Burke's Corners, dar'll be some funerals tu," was the grim
reply.

"I can't blame you, Bob," said the white man, looking

frankly into his face as it worked with agony and rage. "A man has a right to protect himself and his family; and, if our government is too blind or too weak to put down this new rebellion, there are only three courses before us, — you and me, and those who stood with us: the one is to fight the devil with fire, — to kill those who kill, — guard the fords, and, whenever we see a man in disguise, shoot him down; another is to give up every thing else for the privilege of living here; and the third is to get away."

"It will come to dat, Kunnel. Ef de gubment won't take keer o' de darkeys y'her, an' gib 'em a white man's chance, dey'll run away, jes' ez dey did in slave times. Dat's my notion," said the freedman, who had fought to save the life of the nation, which would not lift a finger to save his in return.

"God only knows," answered the soldier, who had been branded as a "Carpet-bagger" throughout the land, because he was born at the North, had fought for the country, and thought he had a right to live where he chose.

A hearty dinner and a glass of liquor were the only substantial benefits which he could confer on the suffering fellow, who went away with his companions to consult with friends in the village which had grown up as the colored suburb of Verdenton, and was now known as Huntsville, being named from the owner of the plantation out of which it was principally carved. It had been sold at public sale, and bought up by the Fool, who had divided it up into lots, and sold it out in this manner, together with a part of Warrington.

It was a new and terrible revelation to the Fool. He saw at once how this potent instrumentality might be used so as to effectually destroy the liberty of the newly enfranchised citizen, and establish a serfdom more barbarous and horrible than any on earth, because it would be the creature of lawless insolence. He saw, too, that this might easily be effected without any tangible and punishable violation of the law. His heart was wrung in agony for his poor neighbors. For himself, it did not yet occur to him to fear.

There was much excitement in the little village of Huntsville that day. Betwixt fear and rage, the heart of every one was in a ferment at the outrage committed upon Bob Martin. For once, Uncle Jerry forgot his accustomed prudence, and moved by a very unreasonable anger at the impotency of the law, which could not punish those who could not be clearly identified, he openly and boldly declared the monstrous doctrine that the colored people ought to defend themselves and each other. That he should entertain such ideas was in itself a misfortune; that he should give expression to such incendiary notions was a fatal error.

CHAPTER XXVIII

A BUNDLE OF DRY STICKS

To show more clearly the surroundings of the Fool, we make a few extracts from his little book, and records which he had collected and preserved, apparently in illustration of this interesting era.

The first is from a friend in a distant county: —

"The Ku-Klux have appeared in our county. I have been warned to leave within twenty days. A coffin was put at my door last night. I don't know what to do. It would leave my family very badly off if any thing should happen to me. All I have is invested here, and I am afraid they will get me if I remain."

The next was from an adjoining county: —

"Three colored men were whipped by the K. K. K. a few miles from this place on Saturday night. One of them I do not know: the others were as good colored men as there ever were in the county. The reason *given* was, that they had been *sassy*: the true reason is believed to be that they were acquiring property, and becoming independent. Can nothing be done? Our people are becoming very much excited. I am afraid this thing will lead to trouble."

The next was from still another county: —

"It seems as if things were getting too bad to think of with us. Two white and three colored men were terribly beaten in this county on Wednesday night. On Friday night two colored men were hanged. They were accused of arson; but there was not a particle of evidence of their guilt: indeed, quite the contrary; and they were men of good character, industrious, and respectful."

Again from the same: —

"James Leroy was hanged by the Ku-Klux on Tuesday night, his tongue being first cut out, and put in his pocket. He was *accused* of having slandered a white woman. The truth is, he was an independent colored man (though nearly as white as you or I), who could read and write, and was consequently troublesome on election-day, by preventing fraud upon his fellows."

Another: —

"The K. K. K. paraded in this town last night. There were about two hundred of them, all disguised, as well as their horses. They fired six shots into my house. Fortunately no one was there. We had news of their coming a little before their arrival, and I had time to get my family out into the corn-field south of the house. My wife and the servants took the children along the corn-rows to the woods. I staid in the corn near the house with my gun, determined to kill some one if they attempted to fire the house, as I supposed they would. My family staid in the woods all night. They tried to get hold of some of our prominent colored friends, but they also had escaped. They went into Allen Gordon's house, and, finding him gone, beat and abused his wife and family shockingly, and took his bed-cord out of the bed, saying they were going to hang John Chavis, who fired at them when they were here before. They went to Chavis's house. He was seen to leave a little while before, and it is hoped they missed him; but nothing has been seen of him since. He may have gone clean off, but it is not like him to do so."

Here is one from our old friend, Dr. Garnett: —

"My dear Friend, — It seems that it is even worse to be a 'native' here, 'and to the manner born,' if one presumes to disagree with his neighbors, than to be a 'carpet-bagger,' such as you are called; for the evil of which I lately warned you has befallen me. Night before last the Ku-Klux came. I had never believed they would attack me; but I had not neglected making some simple and obvious precautions for such a contingency. You know my house is a perfect blockhouse anyhow. It was first made of hewed logs, closely chinked, and afterwards weather-boarded, and ceiled with inch lumber on the inside. Since the K. K. K. came in vogue, I had put heavy wooden bars across the doors, and added heavy inside shutters of inch boards to the windows, with little loop-holes at the side in case of attack. It was a bright night, not moonlight, but starry. I had been out late; and, after getting supper, we were having family prayers before retiring. We always lock every thing about the house at dark. My wife and daughter Louisa were all that were at home with me. During the prayer, my wife, who was kneeling nearest the front-door, came over, and, touching me on the shoulder, said, 'They have come!'

"I knew to whom she referred at once; and, adding one brief petition for help, I closed my prayer. There were evident sounds of footsteps crowding the little front-porch by that time. Then there came a rap on the door, and a demand that it be opened. This I refused to do, ordered them to leave my premises, and warned them that they remained at their peril. I gave my wife and daughter each a revolver.

They are both delicate women, as you know; but they have learned to handle fire-arms for just such an occasion, and they did not quail. By this time those outside were assailing both the front and back doors. I looked out at one of my little port-holes, and could see them standing about the porch. A good many shots were fired also at the doors and windows. I thought I ought not to wait any longer; and so, with a prayer for myself and for my enemies outside, I put my gun to the port-hole, glanced along it, and pulled the trigger. There was a shriek, a groan, and a hurrying of feet away from the door. When the smoke cleared away, I thought I could see one of those cloaked and hooded forms lying across the path before the house. I dared not go out to proffer aid or bring him in, lest the others should be in ambush, and fall upon me. My sight is not first-rate; but Louisa said she could see them lurking about the fence and bushes before the house. After this the attack seemed to cease. I was on the alert, however, believing them to be as ruthless and reckless as wild Indians on the war-path. Presently, watching towards the front, I saw two figures come softly and cautiously up the road, and after a time into the yard. They stole along from tree to shrub like murderous red-skins, and I was about to fire on them, when they stopped at the body lying across the path. They consulted a moment, evidently examining the body; then one went off, and led a horse up to the gate. They lifted up the body, taking it between them to the horse, and with no little difficulty placed it across the saddle, and lashed it around the horse; then they rode off, and, as they passed up the hill by the Widow Johnson's, we could hear that there were a good many. We kept watch until morning, but neither saw nor heard any thing more of them. As soon as it was good light, I went out and examined the path. There was a great pool of blood, which had also dripped along the path to the gate, and beyond that in the road. Getting on my horse, and taking my gun, I followed the trail of blood until it crossed the Little Rocky River, after which I lost it.

"I have strong suspicions as to who were in the party. To-day there was a funeral down in the Fork, of a man who was *kicked by a mule yesterday morning*. The undertaker who buried him said he was already laid out when he came to the house, and some men who were there insisted on putting him in the coffin. When the undertaker was putting the cover down, however, he got a chance to put his hand down on the head of the corpse. He says, if that man was killed by a mule, it must have been a remarkably *tall* one. It seems impossible; yet I can not but suspect that this man was the leader, and that he died by my hand. Strange as it seems now, I have often met him at the Lord's table. He was a very active member of the church, and was a superintendent of a sabbath school.

"I have even a stranger fact to record. You remember my daughter's hair was a soft light brown. It was so the night of the attack. In the morning it was streaked with gray, and now it is almost as silvery as mine. She is but twenty-three. Ah! these villains have a terrible sight of crime and agony to answer for. I hear they are raiding all about the country, whipping and mutilating without restraint. Can nothing be done? Is our government so weak that it can not protect its citizens at home?

"Yours,
"GEORGE D. GARNETT."

But why give extracts from letters showing the horror of that time? Here is a document which shows more conclusively than a thousand letters could its abounding terrors, because the testimony is unconscious and unwitting. It is a letter from the governor of the State, addressed to Colonel Comfort Servosse. It seems the latter had an appointment to visit the town of P——— in a neighboring county, perhaps on some public duty; and the chief Executive wrote thus to him: —

"DEAR SIR, — I must beg that you will not go to P——— on next Monday. Your life has been threatened in the most open and defiant manner. Our friends have been warned, and they implore me to induce you not to hazard your life by so doing. As you know, I can give you no protection, but feel it my duty to give you this warning, and hope it may not come too late.

"Yours truly,
"——— ———,
"*Governor.*"

The Fool was not one of those who could be advised: so he wrote, in answer to this letter, —

"To ——— ———, GOVERNOR.

"*My dear Sir,* — I have received very many warnings of a similar nature to yours in regard to going to P———. I have no doubt but that there is a settled purpose to execute the threat too; but, as my duty calls me there at that time, I shall go, and leave the result with Him who presides over our destinies.

"Yours gratefully,
COMFORT SERVOSSE."

So he went, and by some good fortune came safely home again, very greatly to his own amazement.

CHAPTER XXIX

FOOTING UP THE LEDGER

One morning in the early winter, Squire Hyman came to Warrington at a most unusual hour. Comfort and his family were just sitting down to their early breakfast when he was announced. The servant stated that he had declined to join in the meal, but had taken a seat by the sitting-room fire. Lily, who was a prime favorite with the old man, went at once to persuade him to come and breakfast with them. She returned with the unexpected visitor, but no persuasions could induce him to partake with them. He seemed very much disturbed, and said, as he sat down in the chimney-corner, —

"No, I thank you kindly. I just came over to have a little chat, and perhaps get a little neighborly advice, if so be the colonel would be good enough to give it."

"I hope there is nothing wrong with you at home," said Servosse, with real anxiety; for the old man seemed greatly disturbed.

"I'm afraid, Colonel," he replied, with a deep sigh, "that there's a good deal of wrong, a good deal, — a heap more and a heap worse than I had ever counted on."

"Why, no one sick, I hope?" said the colonel.

"No, not sick exactly," was the reply; "worse'n that. The truth is, Colonel, the Ku-Klux took out my boy Jesse last night, and beat him nigh about to death."

"Shocking! You don't say!" burst from his listeners. The meal was abandoned; and, gathering near the old man, they listened to his story.

"You see," he said, "Jesse had been into town yesterday, and came home late last night. So far as I can learn, it must have been nine o'clock or so when he started out: at least, 'twan't far from twelve o'clock when he came through the little piece of timber on the far side of my house (you know the place well, Colonel, and you too, Madam; for you have ridden by it often, — just in the hollow, this side the black-smith's shop), when all at once a crowd of men burst out of the woods and bushes, all hidden with masks and gowns, and after some parley took him into the woods, tied him to a tree, and beat him horribly with hickories. Jesse said he hadn't no chance to fight at all. They were all on him almost afore he knew it. He did kick about a little, and managed to pull the mask off from one fellow's face. This seemed to make them madder than ever, though they needn't have been; for he says he didn't know the man from Adam, even when he saw his face. However, that didn't make no difference. They took him out and whipped him, because they said he was a 'nigger-loving Radical.' "

"Poor fellow! Is he seriously injured?" asked Comfort in alarm.

"I don't know as to that, Colonel," answered Hyman, "and it don't much matter. He's been whipped, and it could not be worse if he were dead. Indeed," continued the old man as he gazed sadly into the fire, "I would rather know that he was dead. He'd better be dead than be so disgraced! Did you ever know, Colonel, that the Supreme Court of this State once decided that whipping was worse than hanging?"

"No," said Comfort, "I never heard of such a thing."

"They did, though," said the old squire. "I don't recollect the precise case; but you will find it in our reports, if you care to look for it. You see the Legislature had changed the pun-ishment for some crime from hanging to whipping, and had repealed the old law. The result was, that some fellow, who was afterwards convicted of an offense committed before the passage of the act, appealed on the ground that whipping was an aggravation of the death-penalty, and the Court held with him. They were right too, — just right. I'd a heap rather my poor Jesse was dead than to think of him lying there, and mourning and groaning in his shame. If it had been openly done, it would not have been so bad; then he could have killed the man who did it, or been killed in the attempt to get a gentleman's revenge. But to be whipped like a dog, and not even know who did it; to think that the very one who comes to sympathize as a friend may be one of the crowd that did it, — oh! it is too much, too much!"

"Indeed," said the Fool, with an awkward attempt at consolation, "it is too bad; but you must console yourself, Squire, with the reflection that your son has never done any thing to deserve such treatment at his neighbor's hands."

"That's the worst part on't, Colonel," said the old man hotly. "He's a good boy, Jesse is, an' he always has been a good boy. I don't say it 'cause he's mine, nor 'cause he's the only one that's left, but because it's true; and everybody knows it's true. He's never been wild nor dissipated, — not given to drinkin' nor frolickin'. He was nothin' but a boy when the war came on; but when my older boy, Phil, — the same as was killed at Gettysburg, — went away, Jesse took hold as steady and regular as an old man to help me on the plantation. You know I'm gittin' old, and hain't been able to git about much this many a year, so as to look after the hands, an' keep things a-goin' as they ought to be. Well, boy as he was, Jesse raised two as good crops as we've had on the plantation in a long time. Then when they called for the Junior Reserves, toward the last of the war, he went and 'listed in the regular army 'bout Richmond, and took his share of the fightin' from that on. An' when it was over, an' the niggers free, an' all that, he didn't stop to dawdle round, and cuss about it, but went right to work, hired our old niggers, — every one of whom would lay down his life for Jesse, — an' just said to me, 'Now, Dad, don't you have any trouble. You just sit quiet, an' smoke yer pipe, an' poke 'round occasionally to see that things is goin' right round the house an' barn-lot, an' keep Ma from grievin' about Phil, and I'll run the plantation.' An' when I told him how bad off I was, owin' for some of the niggers that was now free, and a right smart of security debts beside, and the State-script and bank-stock worth almost nothin', he didn't wince nor falter, but just said, 'You just be easy, Pa. I'll take care of them things. You just keep Ma's spirits up, and I'll look out for the rest.'

"You know how that boy's worked, Colonel, early and late, year after year, as if he had nothing to look forward to in life only payin' his old father's debts, and makin' of us comfortable. He never meddled with nobody else's business, but just stuck to his own all the time, — *all the time!* An' then to think he should be whipped, by our own folks too, just like a nigger! — and all because he was a Radical!

"S'pose he was a Radical, Colonel: hadn't he a right to be? You're a Radical, ain't ye? and a Carpet-bagger too? Have they any right to take *you* out an' whip you? I reckon you don't think so; but it's a heap worse to mistreat one of our own folks, — one that fought for the South, and not agin her. Don't ye think so, Colonel?

"Well, it's natural you shouldn't see the difference; but I do. S'pose he *was* a Radical? He didn't have nothing to say about it, — just went an' voted on 'lection-day, and come home again. Are they goin' to whip men, an' ruin them, for that? I declare, Colonel, I'm an old man, and a man of peace too, and a magistrate; but I swear to God, if I knew who it was that had done this business, I'd let him know I could send a load of buckshot home yet: damned if I wouldn't!

"Beg pardon, Madam," he continued, as he remembered Metta's presence; "but you must allow for the feelings of a father. I'm not often betrayed into such rudeness, Madam, — not often.

"But Colonel," he went on meditatively, "do you know I don't think that was more than half the reason the Ku-Klux beat Jesse?"

"No?" said the Fool. "What else had he done to awaken their animosity?"

"He's been your friend, Colonel, — always your friend; and he thinks, and I think too, that what he's been made to suffer has been more on your account than his own. You know they've been a-threatenin' and warnin' you for some time, and you haven't paid no heed to it. When they rode off last night, they told Jesse he might tell his 'damned Radical Yankee friend Servosse that they were comin' for him next time.'

"Jesse's mighty troubled about it, for he thinks a heap of you all; and he wanted me to come right over here, and let you know, so that, bein' forewarned, you might be fore-armed."

"Poor fellow!" said the Fool. "It was very kind and thoughtful of him. It is altogether too bad that any one should suffer merely for being my friend."

"Well, you know how our people are, Colonel," said the old man, with the impulses of a life still strong upon him to make excuse for that people whose thought he had always indorsed hitherto, and whose acts he had always excused, if he could not altogether approve, — "you know how they are. They can't stand nobody else meddlin' with their institutions; and your ideas are *so* radical! I shouldn't have wondered if it had been you, — candidly, Colonel, I shouldn't, — but that they should do so to my boy, one that's native here, of good family (if I do say it), and that never troubled nobody, — it's too bad, too bad!"

"Yes, indeed!" said the Fool. "And I must go and see him at once. I don't suppose I can do him any good, but I must let him know how I sympathize with him."

"That brings me around to the rest of my errand," said the old man. "I am so upsot by this thing, that I like to have clean forgotten it. He 'llowed you'd be comin' to see him as soon as you heard of it, and he wanted me to tell you that he couldn't see anybody now (not while he's in this condition, you know); but he — he wanted I should say to you — say to you," he repeated, with the tears running over his face, "that he was goin' to Injianny to-night, and he would be glad if you could give him some letters to any friends you may have in the West. You know he can't stay here any more (not after this); and he thought it might be well enough to have some introduction, so as not to be exactly goin' among strangers, you know."

"He will take the train at Verdenton, I suppose," said the Fool.

"Yes, I s'pose so," answered the old man. "He hain't made no arrangements yet, an' it'll be a hard thing for him to ride there in his condition."

"Has he any particular point to which he wishes to go?"

"None at all — just to get away, you know: that's all he goes for."

"Yes," said the Fool thoughtfully; then, after a moment, he continued decisively, "See here, Squire! You tell the boy not to trouble himself about the matter, but keep quiet, and I will arrange it for him. He must not think of going to-night, but you may give out that he has gone. I will come for him to-night, and bring him here; and after a time he can go West, and find himself among friends."

This arrangement was carried out, almost against the will of the one most concerned; and it was under the roof of the "carpet-bagger" that the outraged "native" found refuge before he fled from the savage displeasure of the people who could not suffer him to differ with them in opinion.

In his behalf the Fool wrote a letter to the Reverend Theophilus Jones, detailing to him the event which this chapter narrates, and the condition of the young man at that time. To this letter he received the following reply: —

WEDGEWORTH, KAN.

MY DEAR SIR, — Your very interesting letter has awakened strange memories. It is only twelve years ago that Brother James Stiles and myself were interrupted in the midst of a gospel service at a place called Flat Rock by a mob, which was said to have been put upon our track by your neighbor Nathaniel Hyman, because we preached the word of God as it had been delivered unto us, and denounced the sin of slavery according to the light that was given us.

We were sorely beaten with many stripes; but we continued instant in prayer for them who did despitefully use us, calling out to each other to be of good cheer, and, even in the midst of their scourging, praying, in the words of the blessed Saviour on the cross, —

"Father, forgive them; for they know not what they do."

When they loosed our bonds, we gave thanks that we were permitted to bear testimony to the truth, even with our blood, and went on our way rejoicing, tarrying not in those coasts, however, since we perceived that this people were joined to their idols, and given up to sin. We said unto our persecutors, in the words of the apostle, "The Lord reward thee *according to thy works*."

Verily, the Lord hath heard the cry of his servants, and hath not forgotten their stripes. My heart was hushed with holy awe when I read in your letter that the son of this man, who caused *us* to be scourged, had suffered a like chastisement at the hands of wicked men — perhaps the very hands by which we were smitten aforetime. Through all these years the God of Sabaoth hath not forgotten our cry, nor to reward the evil-doers according to their works." Well may we exclaim, as we look back at these intervening years of wonder-working events, "What hath God wrought!" As the war went on, and I saw the bulwarks of slavery crumbling away, until finally the light of freedom shone upon the slave, I rejoiced at the wonderful power of God, who wrought out the ends of his glory through the instrumentality of human passion and human greed. How it reproached our weak murmurings and want of faith! Who could have believed that all the evils which slavery was for so many years piling up as a sin-offering in mockery of the Most High and his mandates, — the blood, the tears, the groans, and the woes of God's stricken and crying people, — were so soon to become the forces which should destroy the oppressor, root and branch! Ah! if that grand old St. John of this new dispensation of liberty — John Brown — could have foreseen this in the hour of his ignominious death! But perhaps he did see it, and the sting of death was removed by the beatific vision.

Nothing of it all, however, has so humbled and terrified me as this immediate and fearful retribution visited on one of my persecutors. God knows I had never entertained feelings of malice or revenge towards them. I have never forgotten to pray for these, my enemies, as we are commanded to do in the canon of Holy Scripture; but I had never thought to see the hand of God thus visibly stretched forth to avenge my wrongs. The very thought has humbled me more than I can express, and I have been moved to ask myself whether this occasion does open to me a way of duty which is in strictest harmony with the dictates of our holy religion. The young man who has suffered for his father's sin, and of whom you speak so highly, you say desires to escape from what he considers his shame, though it ought to be deemed his glory. Why not let him come hither, my friend, — for as such I can not but esteem you henceforth, — and let me thank the good Father by succoring the son of him whe persecuted me? Gladly, humbly, will I perform this duty as an act of praise and thanksgiving to Him who ruleth and over-ruleth all things to his glory. Faithfully, as He was faithful to me, would I perform such trust, tenderly and humbly, so that the young man should never know whose hand was extended to do him kindness. Please to consider this suggestion, and, if it accord with your views, send him to me, assured that I will intermit no effort in his behalf.

I am in truth,

Thy servant and brother in the Lord
THEOPHILUS JONES.

The Fool knew that the fanatic was in serious earnest, and that, despite his ready assumption of the divine act as having been performed in his individual behalf, there was a sort of chivalric devotion to what he deemed duty and religion, which would make him untiring in the performance of his self-imposed trust. So the castigated son of the old squire went to the free West to begin life anew under the protection and patronage of the man whose back was striped at his father's instigation, in the good old days "befo' the wah."

CHAPTER XXX

A THRICE-TOLD TALE

I.

The newspapers told it first.

The Dunboro' Herald of May 17, 18—, said, —

"The good people of Rockford County met in convention at the court-house to-day, to nominate candidates for county offices, and to discuss the political situation. Since the military usurpation took away from the people the right of self-government, and made them subservient to the will of the degraded Radical niggers, and the infamous scalawags and Carpet-baggers who unite with and lead them, the honest people of Rockford have had no voice in her government. They have now concluded that the time has come when they will make one more effort to control their own affairs. They met to-day as one man, and listened to the burning words of such soul-stirring orators as General De Bang, Honorable John Snortout, and Colonel Whiteheat, until it was evident, from their wild enthusiasm, that the white people of Rockford intend to rule her affairs again. There was a rumor, just as our informant left, of some trouble or difficulty in connection with John Walters, the notorious Rockford Radical. We did not learn what it was, and do not care. The worst thing that could occur to him would be the best thing for the rest of the county."

The Moccason Gap Rattler (published the next day) said, —

"We learn, that, after the meeting at Rockford Court-House yesterday, there was considerable excitement among the colored population over the disappearance of their great leader, the infamous Walters. It seems that he had the cheek to attend the meeting, and sat taking notes of the speeches during the whole time. His presence caused considerable remark; for, although it was a public meeting, it was not supposed that he would have the impudence to show himself among decent white people, after joining the niggers to insult, oppress, and degrade them. It is said that the speakers, especially the Honorable John Snortout, alluded to him in terms which he richly deserves. It became noised through the meeting that he was taking notes of the speeches for the purpose of having troops sent to Rockford. It is even said that inquiry was made of him as to his object in taking notes; to which he impudently responded that his purpose was known to himself, which was quite sufficient. After the meeting adjourned, it seems he could not be found; and a great outcry was raised among the niggers on account of his disappearance. Search was immediately instituted; and all the niggers of the town, as well as hundreds from the adjoining country, came pouring in, surrounding the court-house, and clamoring for the keys. They were very much excited, and did not hesitate to declare that their leader had been murdered by the gentlemen at the meeting. This infamous charge against some four or five hundred of the best men of Rockford was borne with exemplary patience by that law-abiding people. The meeting quietly dispersed, and the niggers continued their search. It is believed that Walters has taken himself off at this time for the purpose of producing an impression that he has been murdered, and thereby having troops sent to that county to influence the coming election. No trace of him had been found at last accounts."

The Ringfield Swashbuckler (two days afterwards) said, —

"The niggers of Rockford are in tribulation, but the white people of the good old county will sleep easier. It appears, that, after the adjournment of the mass meeting held by the good people of that county at the court-house on the 17th inst., Walters, the infamous scalawag leader of the nigger Radicals, who have ruled the county since the military usurpation, could not be found. He was supposed to have been in attendance on the meeting as a spy upon its action; but several of the most respectable citizens say that he left a considerable time before its close. At once, upon its becoming known that he was missing, there was great excitement among the niggers; and when, towards morning, his body was found in one of the offices upon the lower floor of the court-house, there was great apprehension for a time that the town would be burned by the infuriated blacks. The manner of his death is a mystery. It is generally believed that some of the leading negroes, who have for some time been growing restive under his dictatorship, waylaid him as he came down from the meeting, killed him, put his body in this room, and then raised an alarm over his disappearance, hoping thereby at once to get rid of a troublesome leader, and produce the impression that he was murdered by his opponents, and for political effect. Of course such a claim is too ridiculous to be entertained for a moment. We learn that an inquest was held, but nothing was elicited to cast any light upon the mystery."

The Verdenton Gazette, in its next issue, remarked, —

"The death of that infamous Radical, Walters of Rockford County, is making a great excitement. The Radicals pretend to believe that he was killed by the Democrats, who had been holding a nominating convention in the court-house that afternoon. It is far more probable, indeed some circumstances which have since come to light, render it almost certain, that his death was procured by certain of his Radical associates. The Carpet-baggers and scalawags who run that party are fully aware of the fate which awaits them on election-day, unless something can be done to fire the negro heart, and bring troops into the State. It is therefore generally believed that this killing of Walters was a cold-blooded assassination planned by the Radicals at the Capital, and executed by their minions. It is even asserted that Morton was heard to declare, not many days ago, that we would 'hear h–ll from the South in less than a week.' In addition to this, it is said that a very reputable man, residing in the western part of that county, declares that he saw Colonel Tom Kelly, the chairman of the Radical committee for this district, driving rapidly away from Rockford very soon after four o'clock on that evening, — about the time the murder must have been committed. Perhaps Mr. Tom Kelly will now rise and explain what he was doing in Rockford at that time."

The Central Keynote (published a week afterwards) said, —

"Whether the Radical bummer Walters was killed by some of his nigger understrappers, by some of his Carpet-bag scalawag associates who were jealous of his power, by his own relatives, or by some paramour of his wife who was anxious that she should obtain the large amount of insurance which he had upon his life, we do not know. But one thing we do know, that the State is well rid of a miserable, unprincipled Radical and infamous scoundrel, who *ought* to have been a Carpet-bagger, but, we are sorry to admit, was a native. We sincerely trust that the State at large may share the good fortune of the county of Rockford very soon, and be equally well rid of his Radical associates."

The National Trumpet, which was the Radical organ for the State, very naturally gave a different version of the affair, denounced it as a most outrageous political murder, and inveighed most bitterly against what it termed the inhuman barbarity of the opposition journals, which, not content with the death of Walters, sought to slay his good name by slanderous imputation, and to blast the reputation of the stricken widow with baseless hints of complicity in his death. It pronounced him "a faithful husband, a tender father, and a stanch friend, — one who from obscure parentage had raised himself through poverty and ignorance to competence; had aided orphan brothers and sisters, supported a widowed mother, and maintained a good Christian character until expelled from his church on account of his political opinions. His courage and organizing ability were unquestioned, and under his lead it was well known that nothing could prevent the County of Rockford from continuing to give overwhelming Radical majorities. John Walters was guilty of this offence, no more! And for this he was killed! He gave up his life for the rights of the people — the right of equal manhood-suffrage — as clearly as any soldier who fell upon the battlefield died for liberty! The time will come when his name will be remembered by a grateful people as that of a martyr of their freedom."

So the act passed into current history; and the great journals of the North recorded with much minuteness, and with appropriate head-lines and display, the fact that John Walters, a man of infamous character, and a prominent politician, and leader of the negroes in Rockford County, was killed by stabbing and strangling. By whom the crime was committed was by no means clear, they said, nor yet the motive; but one thing seemed to be well established, — that it was not done from any political incentive whatever. It was true he was a leading politician in a county having a decided colored majority, which was made effective almost solely by his organizing power; but it was certain that only personal feeling of some sort or another was at the bottom of this murder.

Thus it first came to the Fool's ears. He had known the man, not intimately, but well, having seen him often since their meeting at the League, and had grown into a sincere regard for him. He knew of his energy and daring, knew of his own premonitions as to his fate, and the coolness with which he had prepared himself to meet it. But the Fool had only half believed that it would come, — at least not so soon or suddenly, nor in a form so horrible, nor with such ghastly accompaniment of *post mortem* barbarity. It was strange how unreasoning he was in his sorrowful anger. He would not hear a word as to any other hypothesis of his friend's death, except that it was a political murder, coolly planned, and executed with the assent of the entire meeting of respectable men who were passing patriotic resolutions above the scene of its perpetration. It was very unreasonable, but perhaps not unnatural, that he should do so.

II.

Upon the second day after this unfortunate occurrence, there came to the Fool's house one who had been an eye-and-ear witness of all that had occurred in Rockford on that occasion, except the tragic act which has been once already narrated. This man said, —

"I was with John Walters when he went to the meeting, and went up and sat with him for a short time. I had tried to dissuade him from going there at all. There had been a good deal of excitement in the county for some time. The Ku-Klux had been riding about, and his life had been threatened a good many times. Only a few days before, a crowd of them had come, and, after riding about the town, had left at his house a coffin, with a notice stuck on to it with a knife. He knew he was in great danger, and told me repeatedly that he thought they would get him before it was over. On this day he was heavily armed, and very foolishly carried with him a considerable sum of money, which he had received the day before, and intended to bring here and put in bank the next day. He had been very careful about showing himself upon the street for some time, especially after dark. I don't suppose he had been out after sundown in six months. He said that it was necessary for him to go to this meeting for two reasons, —

first, to let them know that he was not afraid to do so; and, second, that he might know what course the opposition intended to pursue in the coming campaign.

"There was a very full attendance at the meeting, and when Walters came in there were a heap of sour looks cast at him. He sat down, took out his book, and began taking notes. The speakers turned on him the worst abuse you ever heard, Colonel; but he just smiled that quiet, scornful smile of his, and went on taking his notes as if no one was near him. By and by it got so hot that I thought we had better get out of there. I told him so in a whisper: but he just looked up, and said I could go; he should stay till it was over. He wanted to see some parties there who had made some proposition to him about a compromise-ticket for county officers. He was greatly in favor of this; for, although we had a large majority in the county, we had really only one or two candidates competent to fill the county offices. It was by his advice, that, at the election before, our folks had supported the Democratic candidate for sheriff and other county-officers. He said it would never do to put ignorant and incompetent men in such places. He was greatly troubled about his own lack of education, and studied hard to make it up. I've often heard him mourn his lack of early advantages. I think it was the only thing that used to make him right-down mad. He used to say that was what every *poor* man owed to slavery; and he appeared to think that institution had done him as much harm, and he had as good a right to hate it, as if he had been a nigger. He could read pretty peart, but writing always come hard to him.

"I heard him one time talking about his little gal, who was just beginning to learn to read. He said he was determined she should have what he missed because he happened to be a poor man's son in a slave country; and that was an education. Oh! he was very bitter in his denunciation of the slave-holding aristocracy, and would persist in declaring that they had starved the souls of the poor people, and kept them from the tree of knowledge, just to promote their own selfish aims, and enhance their own wealth. It's the only thing I've ever heard John Walters grow eloquent upon (you know he was a man of few words); but I've heard him sometimes on the stump when he seemed to get out of himself, and be another man, in the wild eloquence with which he urged the need of education, and deplored the manner in which he had been robbed of its privileges and advantages. I remember he said once, that he never asked grace before meat at his own table, nor conducted family worship in his own house, as he did every day, without feeling ashamed of the ignorance which hung like a millstone about his neck. He thought that even his little eight-year-old must be ashamed of her papa's blunders.

"I thought of all these things while the speakers were abusing him, and the people were turning towards him with black looks and threatening gestures, and wondered what would come of it all. When it got too hot for me, I left, and went back to his house. His wife was taking on terribly. She is not a very strong woman, but she thought a heap of John. She asked me all about what he was doing at the meeting, and then took on worse than ever. She pointed to their two children who were playing on the lawn back of the house, and said, 'Poor things, poor things! They'll be fatherless and alone pretty soon. Why won't John quit this foolish fight for what will do him no good, get away from here, and go West, where he and his children can have "a white man's chance"? Why won't he listen to me?' She kept on crying and mourning, and begged me to speak to John about it *if* he ever came home.

"I tried to comfort her; and we sat by the door, the little children playing on the green slope before us, until the meeting was over, and the people began to pass by on their way homeward. I noticed that Mrs. Walters seemed very restless, and every now and then looked anxiously over toward the court-house. Finally she called to some colored men who were passing, and asked if the meeting was over. They told her it was; and she then asked if they had seen her husband since it closed; and, when they said they had not, she threw up her hands, and moaned, and cried, 'They've killed him! They've killed him! I knew it! Oh, my God!' and just kept taking on terribly.

"I went over into the town at once, and began to make inquiries. None of our friends had seen him; but, as soon as they found I was inquiring for him, several of the white people kindly volunteered information in regard to him. This one had seen him in this place, and another in that, and another remembered hearing a third man speak of having seen him in still a different direction; and all about the same time. This disagreement of the reports which were made, as well as the fact that none of the colored people had seen him (though there were many more of them, and each felt a peculiar interest in him, so that they would be more likely to notice and remark his presence than the others), strengthened a dim suspicion that had been growing in the minds of all; so that, instead of waiting to go to the points indicated to ascertain their truth, the report went out at once that he was missing — had been killed.

"I never knew before what a hold he had on the colored people. Every one seemed as distressed as if he had lost a brother. Men, women, and children crowded into the streets. Moans and imprecations were about equally mingled in the surging crowds who hurried toward the court-house. From the first moment there was no question as to his death. It was assumed as a fact; and the conclusion was at once arrived at, that his body was concealed somewhere about the court-house. Strangely enough the fragments of the crowd who had been in attendance on the meeting gathered quietly about one or two of the stores, talked with each other in low tones, offered neither remonstrance, aid, nor ridicule of the search that was going on, and finally broke away by twos and threes, silently and solemnly to their homes. Every moment the excitement grew more intense among the colored people. In an incredibly brief time the crowd had swelled from a couple of dozen to as many hundred; and, in an hour or two, more than a thousand were gathered. The white people of the town looked on gloomily and silently, but took no part in the search. The court-house was at once surrounded, and every room examined into which access could be obtained; for the keys of some of them were said to have been lost, and one especially, it was claimed, had not been opened for many months. All trace of the key of this room seemed to have been lost by the officials in whose custody the law presumed it to have been. Then some of the white people came with very positive reports that Walters had been seen going out of town towards Dunboro', where it was known that he intended to go on the morrow. Several of the leading citizens came out at this time, and endeavored to convince the colored people of the folly of their course. The Honorable John Snortout was especially active in this endeavor. They might as well have talked to the wind. The colored people clung to their hypothesis with a sort of blind instinctive conviction of its truth, which nothing could move. As it came on dark, fires were lighted, and a regular line of sentries put around the building. Meantime attempts were made to get a glimpse of the interior of the rooms of which they could obtain no keys, by peering through the closed windows. Clambering from one window-ledge to another, they flashed the light of blazing torches into them, but in vain. Nothing could be seen.

"And so the night dragged on, and the crowd grew hourly greater with accessions from the country, and the conviction grew stronger that in one of these rooms they would find the nameless horror which they sought, and which they yet would not behold.

"Yet this half-barbarous crowd were strangely regardful of law. They did not violate anybody's right. Neither locks nor windows were broken. They sought the keys far and near, but they did no violence. They were sure their lost leader was within — dying or dead, they knew not which. They called him by name, but knew he could not answer. None slept of the colored people: they waited, watched, and mourned.

"Just in the gray of the morning light, one of those who had been most active and assiduous in the search mounted on the shoulders of a friend, and peered into the window of the most suspected room on the first floor. Shading his eyes with his hand, he scanned the dim-lighted interior, and was about to give up the quest, when his eye fell upon something mysterious and appalling. On the inside of the window-ledge he saw — *a single drop of blood!* Another look, and he saw, or thought he saw, the well-known hat which their leader had been wont to wear.

" 'Here he is — in there!' he shouted, as he leaped down, and started for the corridor. They had no longer any need of key. The door flew apart as if made of pasteboard, before the brawny shoulders that pressed against it. In that room they found their worst fears confirmed. There, pressed down into a box, with a pile of firewood heaped upon him, a stab in his throat, and a hard cord drawn taut about his neck, stark and cold, was the body of John Walters — the Radical! There was very little blood in the room, only a few drops on the floor, and *one drop on the window-sill!* The stab in his throat had cut the artery. Where was the blood? The physician who examined the body said he must have bled internally."

From the foregoing narrative it was evident to the Fool that between three and five o'clock of the day before, while the meeting of respectable white citizens was in progress in the room above, John Walters had either been killed in that room, or murdered elsewhere, and brought thither. The manner of his death was evident. The motive was not doubtful, since, strangely enough, this "bad man" seems to have had no personal enemies. In some mysterious manner the universal sentiment of execration that prevailed against him in the community had found an instrument; and John Walters, the Radical leader of Rockford, had met the doom which he might reasonably have expected when he presumed to organize the colored voters of that county in opposition to the wish and desire of its white inhabitants.

The coroner's jury, after a tedious examination of every person that could be found who would be likely, on ordinary principles, to know nothing whatever of the matter, returned that the death was "caused by some person or persons unknown;" which verdict was, no doubt, in strict conformity with the evidence taken.

III.

"Kunnel, dar's a man h'yer dat wants ter tell you sumfin'. He says he won't tell nobody else but you, widout your positive orders."

The speaker was old Jerry. He stood at the door of the Fool's library or office, and had with him a colored man, whom he introduced as Nat Haskell. This man had one of those expressionless faces, which, however, bear a look of furtive observation, so characteristic of the colored man who has been reared under the influences of slavery.

"Well," said Comfort, "what is it?"

"Didn't you know Mars' John Walter?" asked the colored man cautiously.

"Yes, certainly!" answered Comfort.

"An' ain't you de gemman as come an' tried ter find out who 'twas dat killed him?"

"Yes."

"Wal, den, you's de one I want ter see, an dat's what I want ter see ye about."

"Why, what do you know about that?"

"I don't *know* nothin'; but I done heard somefin' that may lead you to fine out who 'tis. Dat's what I come fer."

"Where do you live?"

"I lives wid ole man Billy Barksdill, 'bout five miles below Rockford Court-House; that is, I did live dar. I hain't no notion o' goin' back dar any mo'."

"Were you in Rockford that day?"

"No, sah!"

"Then, how do you come to know any thing about the matter?"

"Wal, yer see, Kunnel, I was wukkin' fer Mr. Barksdill, ez I tole ye; an' dat night, jest arter I come in from de fiel', he called me ter come an' take care of a hoss. I know'd dat hoss right well. 'Twas a gray filly dat Mars' Marcus Thompson hed rid by our place dat mornin'. Arter I'd put the critter away, an' fed it, I went inter de kitchen ter git my supper. I sot down ter de table; an' de cook — dat's Mariar, my ole 'ooman — she brings me my supper, an' den goes back inter de dinin'-room ter wash up de dishes de white folks hed been usin'. Presen'ly she come back mighty still like, an' says, 'Nat, come h'yer, quick!' An' wid dat she starts back agin.

" 'Sh—! take off yer shoes,' she says, half whisperin', ez we git ter de dinin'-room do'.

"I slips outer my shoes, an' we goes in. Der wa'n't no light in de room; but she led me a-till we come nigh de do' a-twixt de dinin'-room an' de settin'-room. Dar we stopped an' listened, an' I could hear Mr. Barksdill an' Mr. Marcus Thompson talkin' togeder mighty plain. Cynthy Rouse — dat's anudder servant-gal — she was dar too, a-crouchin' down by de do', dat wasn't shet close; but dar wa'n't no light in de settin'-room, but de fire. When I come, Cynthy puts her hand on her lips, shakes her head, an' says, 'H'sh!' an' put her head down to listen agin. The fust words *I* heard was ole Mr. Barksdill, — he's sorter half-def, yer knows, — a-sayin', right peart, —

" 'It must a' been a good day's work, in fact, if we've got rid o' John Walters finally. How was it done? I did hear der was some notion o' sendin' a committee from de meetin' ter tell him he must leave; but I hadn't no notion he'd du it. He's pluck to de back-bone, John Walters is. Whatever else he may be, we must allow, Thompson, dat he ain't nobody's fool nor coward; an' I 'llowed, dat, ef de meetin' should do dat, jest ez likely's not some o' dat committee mout git hurt. Ye didn't try dat, I reckon?'

" 'No,' answered Mars' Thompson, 'we didn't hev no need ter du dat. De brazen-faced cuss hed the impudence ter come ter the meetin' hisself!'

" 'Dar now, you don't tell me!' sed old man Barksdill. 'Wal, now, what was I sayin'? — he's pluck.'

" 'Yes; and he sot dar as cool as a cucumber, a-takin' notes ob all dat went on,' says Mr. Thompson.

" 'You don't! Wal, I declar!' sez the ole man.

" 'Yes: de damned fool hadn't a bit more sense dan to show his head dar, when we'd met most a-purpose to fine a way to get rid of him. He mout 'a' knowed what would come on't.'

" 'Wal, what did? I s'pose de people was pretty hot, an' perhaps dar was smart of a row.'

" 'Not a bit, Mr. Barksdill! Jest de quietest affair you ever heard on. De fac' is, some one on us hed made an appintment wid Walters, ter see him' bout what we called a fusion ticket we purtended ez we wanted ter git up. So some on' em signified to him dat we wanted ter see him, an' we got him down inter the old County Clerk's office, an' shet de do'. Dar was ten on us, an' he seed de game we was up to in a second; but he didn't even wince.

" ' "Well, gentlemen," sez he, ez cool ez if he'd been settin' over on his own porch, which we could see ez plain ez day from de winder, "what d'ye want o' me? Der seems tu be enough on ye ter du ez you've a mine ter: so I mout ez well ask yer will an' pleasure." '

" 'Law sakes!' sez de ole man; 'but dat wuz monstrous cool.'

" 'Cool? I should tink it was, ez cool es hell," sez t'oder one. 'Den some on 'em took out a paper dat hed been drawed up aforehand fer him ter sign, an' handed it over tu him. He read it over kinder slow like, an', when he got frough, handed it back, an' sed, "I can't sign dat paper, gentlemen." '

" 'What was de paper?'

" 'Noffin, only jest a statement dat he, as leader ob de Radical party in dis county, hed been de gitter-up ob all de devilment done here in de last two or free years, includin' de burnin' o' Hunt's barn; an' dat he done dese tings under de direction ob de Radical leaders at de capital. We tole him, ef he'd sign dis, an' agree tu leab de State in ten days, we'd let him off safe an' sound.'

" 'An' he wouldn't do it?' bust in de ole man.

" 'Do it? Hell! He sed we mout kill him, but we couldn't make him sign no sech paper ez dat. Dat made de boys mad. You know, we didn't want ter kill him, dough we hed no notion ob backin' out after goin' dat far: in fac', we couldn't.'

" 'No mo' you couldn't, I should say,' put in Mars' Barksdill.

" 'Ob course not! an' I fought fer a minit de boys would jest hack an' tear him to pieces, dey was so mad. I tried ter pacify 'em, an' persuade him to sign de paper, an' not force us to sech extremes; but he wouldn't hear tu me, an' fust I know'd, he hed jumped back an' pulled out a pistol. De low-down, ornary cuss! Ef it hadn't been fer Buck Hoyt, who caught his arm, an' Jim Bradshaw, dat whipped a slip-noose over his neck, an' pulled him back, der's no knowin' what he might 'a' done wid dat ten-shooter o' his.'

" 'He's a nasty hand wid shootin'-irons,' sed the ole man.

" 'Wal,' says Thompson, 'dey got him down, an' frottled him, an' tuk de pistol away from him, an' every ting he had in the weepon line. Den dey let him up, an' all agreed dat sech a pestiferous, lyin', deceitful cuss ought ter be killed. We told him so, an' dat he could hev jest five minutes ter git ready in. He didn't never flinch, but jest sed, "I s'pose I ken be allowed ter pray." An', widout waitin' fer an answer, he jes' kneeled down, an' prayed fer all his frien's an' neighbors, an' fer each one ob us too. Dis prayin' fer *us* wuz gittin' a little tu damn pussonal: so Jim Bradshaw, dat held de cord, gin it a jerk, an' tole him we didn't want no more o' dat. Den he got up, an' I axed him ef der wuz any ting else he wanted ter do or say afore he died. You see, I fought he might like ter make some 'rangement 'bout his property or his family, an' I wanted to gib him a white man's chance.'

" 'Ob co'se, ob co'se,' said Mars' Barksdill, 'an' very proper an' considerate of ye, tu.'

" 'I fought so, certain,' said Thompson. 'Wal, he axed us to let him look out o' de winder, at his childern playin' on de slope o' de hill over by his house. Dar was some o' de boys didn't want to do dat, but I persuaded 'em to let him. His hands was tied, an' de cord was 'roun' his neck, so't he couldn't git away nohow. De lower sash hed been raised; but we had some two or three fellows standin' outside anyhow. So we led him to de winder, an' he looked at his two gals a smart while. I declar' it come hard to see de tears a-standin' in his eyes, an' know what was waitin' fer him; but it couldn't be helped den. An', jest while I was tinkin' ub dis, he made a spring, and, wid all dat agin him, managed to git his left leg ober de winder-sill, an' I'm not at all sure't he wouldn't 'a' wriggled hisself out entirely, ef Jack Cannon hadn't 'a' gathered a stick of wood, an' dropped it over his leg till it straightened out ez limp ez a rag. We pulled him back in, an' frew him on de long table dat's in de room. He jest give one groan when he seed all was over. It was de fust an' last. Der wasn't no use tryin' ter hold de boys back no longer. Jim Brad he drew de cord till it fairly cut inter de flesh. Den dey turned him half over, all on us holdin' his arms an' legs, an' Jack Cannon stuck a knife inter his throat.[1] He bled like a hog; but we caught de blood in a bucket, an' arterwards let it down out o' de winder in a bag to de fellers outside; so't der wa'n't a drop o' blood, nor any mark ub the squabble, in de room. We stowed him away in de wood-box, an', arter it comes on good an' dark, de boys are goin' to take him ober, an' stow him away under dat damned nigger schoolhouse o' his; an' den you see we'll claim de niggers done it, an' perhaps hev some on 'em up, an' try 'em for it.'

" 'Good Lord!' sed ole man Barksdill arter a minit. 'So he's dead!'

" 'Dead!' said Thompson wid a queer laugh. 'You may count on dat, — ez dead ez Julius Cæsar! De county's well rid o' de wust man dat was ebber in it.'

" 'Yes, yes!' said de ole man, 'a bad fellow, no doubt, mighty bad; dough I dunno ez he ever done any ting so *very* bad, except hold political meetin's wid de niggers, an' put all sorts o' crazy notions in der heads, makin' 'em lazy, an' no 'count, an' impudent to white folks.'

" 'An' ain't dat 'nough?' said Thompson.

" 'Oh, ob co'se!' Mars' Barksdill said: 'dat's mighty bad, — but arter all' —

[1] This account of an incredible barbarity is based on the sworn statement of a colored person who overheard just such an account, given of just such a performance, by one of the actors in it. It is too horrid to print, but too true to omit.

" 'Well, what?' said Mars' Thompson, kinder hot like.

" 'Oh, well, noffin'! — dat is, noffin' to speak of. I was no friend o' John Walters; but I would 'a' felt better ef he'd been killed in a fa'r fight, an' not shut up like a wolf in a trap, an' killed in — in' —

" 'In cold blood, I s'pose you mean,' put in Thompson quick and husky; fer he was a-gittin' mad.

" 'Wal, yes, it does look so,' said ole Mars', kinder 'pologizin' like.

" 'Ob co'se,' said Thompson, 'it'll do fer you ter set dar an' fine fault wid what's done. Here de whole county's been wishin' somebody would rid 'em ub John Walters fer two years an' mo. Everybody's been a-cussin' an' bilin', an' tellin' what ought ter be done; an', now dat some on us hez hed the pluck ter go in an' *du* the very ting ye've all been talkin' on, ye stan' back, an' draw on an affidavy face, an' say yer sorry it's done. It's damned encouragin' to dem dat takes de risk! Perhaps de next fing you do'll be tu go an' tell on us.'

"De ole man wouldn't stan' dat. We heard him rise up, an' say, mighty grand like, —

" 'Mr. Thompson!'

"Jest then, Cynthy, who's a mighty excitable gal, an', besides dat, used ter live with Mrs. Walters, an' so knew de one dey'd been talkin' on right well, bust out a-sobbin' an' a-moanin', an' we hed to hold a hand over her mouf, an' half tote her out ob de room ez fast ez we could. I heard Mars' Thompson say, 'Who's in dar?' An' den Mars' Barksdill he lights de can'le, an' comes an' opens de dinin'-room do'; but, Lor' bress ye! der wan't nobody in dar — nobody at all."

"What did you do then?"

"Nuffin' at all. Jest waited, an' kep' still. Cynthy an' 'Riar an' me we talks it over a little, an' concluded ez we'd better not let on dat we knowed any fing about it. So when Bob Watson come over some time 'fore mornin', an' whistled me out, an' tole me dat Mars' Walters was a-missin', an' dat eberybody ob de colored folks was a-huntin' for him, an' de whole town jest alive an' a-light all night, I didn't say noffin', only, arter a while I turns to Bob an' I says, says I, —

" 'Bob, dey won't never fine him.' An' he sez, sez he, 'Dat's my notion too.' So we passed de time o' day, an' he went home, an' I turned in ter sleep agin."

"Have you ever told any one else of this?" asked the Fool.

"Nary one," was the reply. "A few days arterwards, ole man Barksdill he questioned me some, an' arter dat de gals telled me dat he axed dem some questions 'bout what we know'd or hed heard 'bout Mr. Walters. But he didn't git no satisfaction outer me, dat's shore, an' I don't reckon he did out ob de gals. Howsomever, 'twan't long afore he an' his boys begun ter talk right smart 'bout what would happen ter any nigger ez should testify agin any white man ez havin' any fing to do along o' Mr. Walters. An' finally Mr. Barksdill he tole me — an' I found dat he tole de wimmen too — dat any nigger dat knowed any fing 'bout dat matter would be a heap more likely to die ob ole age ef he lived in anudder State. Dis scart de gals nigh about to deaff, an' I 'llowed dar was a heap o' sense in it myself. So we lit out; an' I never hinted a word about it afore, only to Uncle Jerry h'yer, an' he brought me to you, sah."

Upon further investigation, Servosse learned several facts strongly confirmatory of this strange story, the details of which harmonized with wonderful accuracy with all the known facts of the bloody deed. The men named as the associates of Thompson, it appeared, were all present at the meeting. Some of them had before been suspected of complicity in the act; while others had not been thought of in connection with it. They were all of good families, and of undoubted respectability. The two women, being separately examined, confirmed, with only such variation as rendered their accounts still more convincing, the story which has been given.

CHAPTER XXXI

THE FOLLY OF WISDOM

Uncle Jerry was much excited by the narrative which he had heard. For a long time the outrages which had been perpetrated upon his race and their friends, the daily tale of suffering and horror which came to his ears, had been working on his excitable temperament, until it needed only the horrible recital which Nat had given, to destroy entirely his self-control. During its repetition he had uttered numerous ejaculations expressive of his excitement; and, when he went away with his friend, he was in a sort of semi-unconscious state, his wide-open eyes full of a strange light, and muttering brokenly as he went along the road to his own house, short ejaculatory remarks.

"Lor' God ob Isr'el!" "Lor', Lor', whar is yer gone?" "Don't ye h'yer de cry ob de pore no mo'?" "Whar is de 'venger ob blood?"

These and many similar expressions fell from his lips as he wandered about his garden and lot that evening. To Nat, who had returned with him, and was his guest, he said but little: he seemed absorbed in dreamy thought. Even before this time, Uncle Jerry had been noted for his openly-expressed defiance of the Ku-Klux, his boldness in denouncing them, and the persistency with which he urged the colored men of his vicinity to organize, and resist the aggressions of that body. In this he had been partially successful. A considerable number of the inhabitants of the colored suburb had armed themselves, had appointed a leader and lieutenants, and agreed upon signals, on hearing which all were to rally for defense at certain designated points. He had infused into his duller-minded associates the firm conviction which possessed himself, — that it was better to die in resisting such oppression than to live under it. He had an idea that his race must, in a sense, achieve its own liberty, establish its own manhood, by a stubborn resistance to aggression, — an idea which it is altogether probable would have been the correct and proper one, had not the odds of ignorance and prejudice been so decidedly against them.

As matters stood, however, it was the sheerest folly. When experience, wealth, and intelligence combine against ignorance, poverty, and inexperience, resistance is useless. Then the appeal to arms may be heroic; but it is the heroism of folly, the faith — or hope, rather — of the fool.

Nevertheless, chiefly through Uncle Jerry's persuasions, and because of his prominence and acknowledged leadership, this spirit had gone out among the colored men of the county; and a determination to resist and retaliate such outrages had become general among them. The first effect of this determined stand upon their part seemed to have been to prevent the repetition of these offenses. For several weeks no one had been beaten or scourged in that county, and the impression seemed to gain ground that there would be no more. This was especially strong after two full moons had passed without disturbance, since it was at those seasons that the disguised horsemen were particularly active. This fact had tended strongly to confirm old Jerry in his theory of resistance, and at the same time had relaxed the vigilance of himself and his neighbors. The night of the day on which he had listened to the recital given by Nat was the time for the regular weekly prayer-meeting at the schoolhouse. Of course he attended; and, as it chanced, there were several white men also in attendance, — strangers, it seemed, — who sat in the back part of the audience, and seemed to be making light of the exercises. This was an indignity which always aroused the strongest feeling on the part of Uncle Jerry. To such he was accustomed to say, with a sweet-voiced boldness, —

"We's allers glad ter hab de white folks come to our meetin's, an' allers tinks it may do us good, an' dem tu. It sartin can't hurt nobody tu be prayed fer; an' we prays for 'em, an' hopes dey prays for us, an' hopes de good Lord'll bress us all. But when white folks comes an' laughs at our weak praars, — dat hurts. We knows we ain't larned, nor great, nor perfic; but we tries to do our best. An' when you all laughs at us, we can't help tinkin' dat we mout 'a' done better ef we hadn't been kep' slaves all our lives by you uns."

Few could continue to mock after this reproof. On this occasion, when the meeting had progressed for some time, the conduct of the white visitors became very annoying. Two or three times, it was noticed that Uncle Jerry raised his head, and stretched forward his hands upon his staves, as if he would speak; but each time, upon second thought, it seemed, he abandoned the idea. Finally it could be endured no longer; and he arose, and walked toward them, speaking in an unusually harsh and aggrieved tone as he did so. When he came within two or three steps of them, he took both staves in his left hand, raised the right, with the finger pointing toward them as steady as a rifle-barrel, and became at once rigid and silent. At first the mockers attempted ridicule; but the pale, still face, and fixed, staring eyes, as well as the awe-stricken hush of the colored portion of the congregation, soon reduced them to silence. When at length his tongue was loosed, and he poured forth one of his wonderful rhapsodies, a mortal terror seemed to take hold upon his hearers, and they sat listening to his burning words, while he told the story of the Ku-Klux, and ended his horrible portraiture with a detailed statement of the manner in which John Walters had been killed, giving the names of those engaged, and the part taken by each in the bloody deed. He painted as by magic the scene of the murder, and gave the very tone and manner of each of those engaged in it, though he had never seen them. Before the recital was ended, there was a shriek from one of the white men, as he rose, and staggered toward the door. Then the others followed after him, and silently left the house.

When the "spell" was over, and Uncle Jerry was lying back, panting and moaning, in his seat, Nat came to him, and broke out, — "Fo' God, Uncle Jerry, what ye mean?'

"What's de matter, Brudder Nat? What I done? Hurt your feelin', Brudder? Bress God, I hope not!"

"Hurt my feelin's? No!" said Nat. "You'se not likely to do dat, Bre'r Jerry. But, Lor' bress us! d'you kno' one o' dem ar men waz nobody else but Jim Bradshaw!"

"De Lord's will be done! He's done use his pore sahvent for his glory, wedder he will or no. Bress de Lor'!" said Uncle Jerry, with a look of resignation.

"Dat's all right, Bre'r Jerry; but I feel jes' ez ef I could trust de Lor' a heap better ef I wuz 'cross de line, an' out o' de State: so I bids you good-by, Uncle Jerry! I'se gwine ter cut outen h'yer, shore."

The news of this terrible revelation soon spread far and wide among the colored people, and there was great apprehension on account of it. Uncle Jerry alone did not seem to be disturbed or alarmed. Since this last display of his strange peculiarity, he seemed to have lost all apprehension, and all feeling of annoyance or trouble, as to the future of himself or his race.

"De Lord's will be done," he said, with entire composure, whenever the matter was mentioned to him. "He knows what's best, an' he's made dis pore sahvent see dat he knows. Bress his holy name! He brings de good out ob evil, an' ober-rules de bad. He's been wid de pore culled man in de six troubles, an' he not gwine ter desart him in de sebenth! Uncle Jerry'll jes' try an' wait on de Lor', so dat when he call fer me, I jes' answers, 'H'yer, Lor'!' widdout waitin' ter ax eny questions 'bout his business."

So the days went on until a week from the Saturday night which followed his denunciation of the slayers of Walters at the meeting, and there had been no disturbance. On that night the little suburban village sank to its usual repose, after the labors and cares which Saturday night imposes upon people of low degree. The bacon and meal for the next week had been purchased, the clothes for the morrow put in order, and preparations made for that Sunday dinner which the poorest colored family manages to make a little better than the week-day meal. It was nearly twelve o'clock when all became silent; and the weary workers slept all the more soundly for the six days' labor of the week which was past.

It was a chill, dreary night. A dry, harsh wind blew from the north. The moon was at the full, and shone clear and cold in the blue vault.

There was one shrill whistle, some noise of quietly-moving horses; and those who looked from their windows saw a black-gowned and grimly-masked horseman sitting upon a draped horse at every corner of the streets, and before each house, — grim, silent, threatening. Those who saw dared not move, or give any alarm. Instinctively they knew that the enemy they had feared had come, had them in his clutches, and would work his will of them, whether they resisted or not. So, with the instinct of self-preservation, all were silent — all simulated sleep.

Five, ten, fifteen minutes the silent watch continued. A half-hour passed, and there had been no sound. Each masked sentry sat his horse as if horse and rider were only some magic statuary with which the bleak night cheated the affrighted eye. Then a whistle sounded on the road toward Verdenton. The masked horsemen turned their horses' heads in that direction, and slowly and silently moved away. Gathering in twos, they fell into ranks with the regularity and ease of a practiced soldiery, and, as they filed on towards Verdenton, showed a cavalcade of several hundred strong; and upon one of the foremost horses rode one with a strange figure lashed securely to him.

When the few who were awake in the little village found courage to inquire as to what the silent enemy had done, they rushed from house to house with chattering teeth and trembling limbs, only to find that all were safe within, until they came to the house where old Uncle Jerry Hunt had been dwelling alone since the death of his wife six months before. The door was open.

The house was empty. The straw mattress had been thrown from the bed, and the hempen cord on which it rested had been removed.

The sabbath-morrow was well advanced when the Fool was first apprised of the raid. He at once rode into the town, arriving there just as the morning services closed, and met the people coming along the streets to their homes. Upon the limb of a low-branching oak not more than forty steps from the Temple of Justice, hung the lifeless body of old Jerry. The wind turned it slowly to and fro. The snowy hair and beard contrasted strangely with the dusky pallor of the peaceful face, which seemed even in death to proffer a benison to the people of God who passed to and fro from the house of prayer, unmindful both of the peace which lighted the dead face, and of the rifled temple of the Holy Ghost which appealed to them for sepulture. Over all pulsed the sacred echo of the sabbath bells. The sun shone brightly. The wind rustled the autumn leaves. A few idlers sat upon the steps of the court-house, and gazed carelessly at the ghastly burden on the oak. The brightly-dressed church-goers enlivened the streets. Not a colored man was to be seen. All except the brown *cadaver* on the tree spoke of peace and prayer — a holy day among a godly people, with whom rested the benison of peace.

The Fool asked of some trusty friends the story of the night before. With trembling lips one told it to him,

"I heard the noise of horses — quiet and orderly, but many. Looking from the window in the clear moonlight, I saw horsemen passing down the street, taking their stations here and there, like guards who have been told off for duty, at specific points. Two stopped before my house, two opposite Mr. Haskin's, and two or three upon the corner below. They seemed to have been sent on before as a sort of picket-guard for the main body, which soon came in. I should say there were from a hundred to a hundred and fifty still in line. They were all masked, and wore black robes. The horses were disguised, too, by drapings. There were only a few mules in the whole company. They were good horses, though: one could tell that by their movements. Oh, it was a respectable crowd! No doubt about that, sir. Beggars don't ride in this country. I don't know when I have seen so many good horses together since the Yankee cavalry left here after the surrender. They were well drilled too. Plenty of old soldiers in that crowd. Why, every thing went just like clock work. Not a word was said — just a few whistles given. They came like a dream, and went away like a mist. I thought we should have to fight for our lives; but they did not disturb any one here. They gathered down by the court-house. I could not see precisely what they were at, but, from my back upper window, saw them down about the tree. After a while a signal was given, and just at that time a match was struck, and I saw a dark body swing down under the limb. I knew then they had hung somebody, but had no idea who it was. To tell the truth, I had a notion it was you, Colonel. I saw several citizens go out and speak to these men on the horses. There were lights in some of the offices about the court-house, and in several of the houses about town. Every thing was as still as the grave, — no shouting or loud talking, and no excitement or stir about town. It was evident that a great many of the citizens expected the movement, and were prepared to co-operate with it by manifesting no curiosity, or otherwise endangering its success. I am inclined to think a good many from this town were in it. I never felt so powerless in my life. Here the town was in the hands of two or three hundred armed and disciplined men, hidden from the eye of the law, and having friends and co-workers in almost every house. I knew that resistance was useless."

"But why," asked the Fool, "has not the body been removed?"

"We have been thinking about it," was the reply; "but the truth is, it don't seem like a very safe business. And, after what we saw last night, no one feels like being the first to do what may be held an affront by those men. I tell you, Colonel, I went through the war, and saw as much danger as most men in it; but I would rather charge up the Heights of Gettysburg again than be the object of a raid by that crowd."

After some parley, however, some colored men were found, and a little party made up, who went out and saw the body of Uncle Jerry cut down, and laid upon a box to await the coming of the coroner, who had already been notified. The inquest developed only these facts, and the sworn jurors solemnly and honestly found the cause of death unknown. One of the colored men who had watched the proceedings gave utterance to the prevailing opinion, when he said, —

"It don't do fer niggers to know *too much!* Dat's what ail Uncle Jerry!"

And indeed it did seem as if his case was one in which ignorance might have been bliss.

CHAPTER XXXII

"OUT OF THE ABUNDANCE OF THE HEART"

THE events which have been narrated in the preceding chapters, with others of like character, filled the mind of the Fool with a sort of dull horror. Strangely enough, he was not affected with fear. He knew that he was equally in the power of the strange organization, which was as secret and as fatal in its proscription as the Thugs of India. He knew that he was quite as obnoxious to its leaders, and as likely to feel their vengeance, as any of the men who had suffered at its hands; and yet he was far more moved with consideration of the general results which must flow from the evil than at any personal consequences which might befall himself.

So he wrote to one of the Wise Men, and told them all that he knew, all that he feared. He recounted to them what had already been done, and his apprehensions as to what might be done in the future. He called attention to the fact that these acts sprung from a common motive, and all tended to a subversion of liberty, and a prevention of the exercise of those very rights or privileges which it was the spirit and essence of the war, upon the part of the nation, to confirm and secure in their completeness and universality. He pointed out the mockery of that boast which had so many thousand times already been heralded to the world, — that slavery had been abolished, and liberty established without "distinction as to race, color, or previous condition of servitude," while men were submitted to a persecution not less bitter, and hardly less sanguinary, than that which "Bloody Mary" visited upon the heretics of her day. "What they did unto Walters," he wrote, "and unto Uncle Jerry, might as reasonably have been done to me, or to any other man of like political faith." He

showed that it was not personal hostility or antipathy which
had made them victims, but their public character and affilia-
tions. He declared that these acts of outrage numbered not
less than a thousand in the district in which he resided, and
that not one had been punished, or could be punished, by the
ordinary tribunals, because of the perfection of the disguise
which was worn, from the precautions taken to avoid detec-
tion, and the fact that so large a proportion of those competent to serve as jurors were quite likely to be *particeps
criminis.*

He asked if there was not some manner in which the government could move for the suppression of this evil. The letter
was the spontaneous outpouring of a heart surcharged with
the agony of a hopeless conflict with a hidden and unrelenting
foe. It was without reservation, being sent to a Wise Man with
whom he had maintained such intimacy of relation as folly
may be allowed to hold with wisdom.

This letter, for some reason or other, though it was a private
one to himself, the Wise Man allowed to be published in the
newspapers: so it resulted that the Fool received more than
one answer thereto. The answer received from the Wise Man
to whom he had addressed it, though somewhat petulant, — as
if the glory which he had won by his advocacy of the successful plan of reconstruction had already soured upon his stomach — was at least frank and honest in its sentiments, and no
doubt expressed the writer's views with precision: —

"WASHINGTON, D.C., Nov. 10, 18—.
"MY DEAR COLONEL, — Your letter of recent date is received, and I have duly considered its contents. The state of
affairs which you picture is undoubtedly most distressing and
discouraging; but I can not see how it can be improved by any
action of the General Government. The lately rebellious
States are now fully restored, and are sovereign republics, of

co-ordinate rights and powers with the other States of this Union. The acts of violence described are of course offenses against their laws, and as such are punishable in their courts. It is no doubt a misfortune that those courts are either unable or unwilling to punish such crimes; but it is a misfortune that does not seem to me to be remediable by national legislation.

"It must be evident to you that the government can not always interfere in the internal affairs of those States. They must be allowed to control, direct, and order their own affairs, as other States do. It is, no doubt, very unfortunate; but it is far better than to break down or disregard the fundamental principles of our government, — the sacred barriers of the Constitution. Individual discomforts and evils must give way to the public good. The principle of self-government must be recognized and maintained, even at the sacrifice of individual interests and rights. The States must protect the lives, persons, and property of their own citizens from aggression on the part of others. The National Government can not act, so long as *its* existence or *its* authority is not assailed or interfered with.

"Of course there will always be instances of grievous wrong practiced, both upon individuals and upon classes, in all of the States. I suppose there are classes, in every State, which are liable to injustice and oppression; but the government can not interfere. You say these acts are done to prevent the free exercise of the ballot, and I have no doubt you are right; but I do not see how that affects the question. In fact, my friend [for the Wise Man called all men his friends], it is necessary that the people of the South should learn, what it seems almost impossible that some can apprehend after so many years of military government, — that all these questions of the rights of citizens are relegated, by the fact of reconstruction, to the tribunals of the States, and must be settled and determined there, according to the spirit of the Constitution.

"There is one thing, however, that you will allow me to say. If the colored people and the Union men of the South expect to receive the approval, respect, and moral support of the country, they must show themselves capable of self-government, able to take care of themselves. The government has done all it can be expected to do, — all it had power to do, in fact. It has given the colored man the ballot, armed him with the weapon of the freeman, and now he must show himself worthy to use it. We have prepared him for the battle of freedom, and it is for him to furnish the manhood requisite for the struggle. The same is true of the poor white and of the Union man. Instead of whining over the wrongs they suffer at the hands of the rebels, they should assert themselves, and put down such lawless violence. They should combine to enforce the law, or, if the law can not be enforced, then to protect themselves. The capacity of a people for self-government is proved, first of all, by its inclination and capacity for self-protection. This capacity must exist in order that self-governing communities may exist. The doctrine of government by majorities is based upon the idea that the majority will be sufficiently bold and self-asserting to claim and maintain its rights. It is contemplated, of course, that they will do this in a lawful and peaceable manner; but it is also presumed that they will be capable of such assertion by physical means, should an appeal to force at any time become necessary. If you can not obtain protection through the courts, I do not see why you should not protect yourselves. If people are killed by the Ku-Klux, why do they not kill the Ku-Klux?

"These are the questions that arise in my mind. I would not presume to advise, but think they are the questions which all reasonable men must propound to themselves in regard to this matter.

"Very respectfully,

"_____."

To this letter the Fool answered as follows: —

"MY DEAR SIR, — Your letter in reply to mine of the 5th inst. recalls the recent past very vividly. I am perhaps bound to admit your conclusion that the National Government can not interfere without violating some of the *traditions* of our Federal Republic, but *not* its principles, and especially not its spirit.

"It should be remembered that these States as re-*created* — not re-*constructed* — are mere creatures of the national power. Our legislators and theorizers have been puttering and quibbling upon the idea, that because there can be no secession, or dissolution of the Union, upon any principle of reserved right, therefore there can be no destruction of the States. By a flimsy fiction it is held that Georgia was a *State of the Union* at the very time when a hostile government was organized there, dominated every foot of her territory, exacted allegiance and tribute from every inhabitant of her soil, and furnished her contingent for armed resistance to the United States.

"It is a shallow trick of the sciolist. The act of rebellion, when it is so far successful as to overturn the government of a State of this Union, and establish a hostile one in its stead, *destroys* that State. The fallacy lies in the application of the word 'State,' in its original or international sense, to one of the subordinate commonwealths of our nation. A 'State,' in that sense, is simply (1) a certain specific territory (2) occupied by an organized community (3), united under one government. If that could be applied to any of our States without modification, this conclusion might be true. But, in order to define *our* 'State' correctly, we must add one other element; to wit (4), sustaining certain specific and defined relations to other States, and to the National Government of the *United States* of America.

"It is this last element which rebellion destroyed, and thereby *annihilated the State*. Every element of a State of the American Union remained, except this statal relation to the Union; and this is just the very element which is as necessary to statal existence as breath to life. It is what distinguishes a *State of the Union* from all other organized communities of earth called 'States.' You may have all but this, and there is no *State* in the sense we use it, but only a skeleton, a lifeless body. It is this element which *reconstruction* restored. It is this element which is under the control of the General Government, and *must* be so held and deemed, or reconstruction was a clear and flagrant usurpation.

"You think this a startling doctrine; but, if it be not true, then both the nation and the loyal people of the South are in a most dangerous dilemma. It may not be permissible even to suppose that the plan of reconstruction adopted was not absolutely perfect; but for the argument, allowing it to be found impracticable and ineffective, then, according to the reasoning adduced by you, there is no remedy. As the tree fell when the State was admitted by congressional action, so it must lie to the end of time. It is like marriage, — a contract indissoluble by either or both of the parties, a relation which no antagonism can ever impair or destroy. If that is so, then you are right, and our appeal for aid is worse than futile.

"But, if it be true, how great was the crime of those who thrust upon the poor, ignorant colored people of the South, upon the few inexperienced and usually humble Union men, and the still fewer Northern men who have pitched their tents in this section, the task — the herculean and impossible task — of building up self-regulating States which should assure and protect the rights of all, and submit quietly and cheerfully to the sway of lawful majorities!

"It should be remembered that the pressure for reconstruction came from the North, — not from the *people* of the North, but from its *politicians*. It was reduced to practice, not because society here was ripe for its operation, but to secure political victory and party ascendency. I do not object to this motive: it is the very thing that makes the government of parties generally safe. I allude to it only to show that we of the South, native or foreign-born, are not responsible for the perils which are now threatening the work that has once received the approbative fiat. 'It is finished!' When we prophesied failure, as so many of us did, we were pooh-poohed like silly children; and now, when we announce apparent failure, we are met with petulant impatience, and told to take care of ourselves.

"It is all well for you, sitting safely and cosily in your easy-chair under the shadow of the dome of the Capitol, to talk about asserting ourselves, protecting ourselves, and retaliating upon our persecutors. Either you have not apprehended our condition, or you are inclined to 'mock at our calamity.'

"Resistance, I mean such resistance as would be effective, is very nearly impossible. In the first place an overwhelming force is always concentrated on the single isolated individual. It is not a mob, except in the aggregation of strength and numbers. Every thing is planned and ordered beforehand. The game is stalked. He that resists does so at hopeless odds. He may desperately determine to throw away his life; but he can accomplish no other result than to take one with him as he goes, and the chances are against even that. You must remember that the attack is only made at night, is always a matter of surprise, and put in operation by a force whose numbers strike terror, always enhanced by their fantastic guise, which also greatly increases the chances of a misshot or false blow, should the unfortunate victim try to defend himself.

"Resistance by way of retaliation is still more absurd. Suppose a party of men should whip you to-night, and you should find yourself unable to penetrate their disguise, or discover their identity in any manner, would you start out to-morrow, and run a-muck among your fellow-townsmen? Or would you guess at the aggressors, and destroy without proof? Evidently not. To organize such retaliation would not be difficult. Such is the exasperation of the colored people, that they would readily join to give a smoking house in exchange for every bleeding back: indeed, if they were not restrained by the counsel of cooler and wiser heads, we should soon have a servile insurrection here, which would make the horrors of Santo Domingo pale before its intensity. Should we put your advice into practice, the government would soon find a way to interfere, despite the constitutional provisions, or, more properly, constitutional *scruples*, of some. Leaving out of sight the fact that this is a contest of poverty, ignorance, and inexperience, against intelligence, wealth, and skill, — the struggle of a race yet servile in its characteristics with one which has always excelled in domination, — you will perceive that the idea of retaliation, even among equals in rank and intelligence, would be futile and absurd.

"As to the State authorities: the courts, you have seen, are powerless. In a county in which there have been two hundred such outrages, there has never been a presentment by the grand jury for one of them. The impossibility of identification, the terror which prevents testimony being given, and the fact that the very perpetrators of these midnight assassinations are found on all juries, show this beyond a peradventure: so that is out of the question also. The Executive of the State is bound by constitutional limitations much less fanciful and airy than those which you have adduced in excuse for the national legislation. He can not interfere where the process of the courts is not resisted. The whole theory and policy of our government is to secure this right to the citizen. The denunciations of all our old Declarations of Rights were leveled expressly at such usurpations. The Executive who should dare to organize a military force to protect its citizens, or to aid in apprehending or punishing such men, would do so, not only in peril of his life from assassination, but also at the risk of impeachment, degradation, and ruin.

"So we are remitted to our original petition to the National Government. If that can give us no aid, we have none to hope for. We can only repeat the Petrine cry, 'Save, Lord, or we perish!'

"Respectfully,

"COMFORT SERVOSSE."

To this letter the Wise Man made no answer, but verbally stated to a mutual friend that he considered it very disrespectful to him. The Wise Men of that day looked upon the supporters of reconstruction at the South as mere instruments in their hands, — to be worked as puppets, but to be blamed as men, for the results of their acts. They had not yet arrived at that refinement of cruelty which also made them scapegoats for the results of others' ignorance and folly. That was to come afterward.

CHAPTER XXXIII

"LOVE ME, LOVE MY DOG"

THE Fool's neighbors having read his letter to the Wise
Man, as published in the great journal in which it appeared,
were greatly incensed thereat, and immediately convened a
public meeting for the purpose of taking action in regard to
the same. At this meeting they passed resolutions affirming
the quiet, peaceful, and orderly character of the county, and
denouncing in unmeasured terms all reports or rumors to a
contrary purport as false and slanderous, and especially affirming with peculiar earnestness that the recent act of violence
which had startled and amazed this law-abiding community
was not the work of any of its citizens, but an irruption from
beyond its borders.

It was noticeable that none of the colored people joined in
this demonstration, nor any of those white people, who, on
that night of horror, had stood with bated breath behind their
barred doors, in the midst of weeping and terrified households
momently expecting attack. There were not many of the
latter, it is true, and what was termed "respectable society"
had long ago shut its doors in their faces; and it was by no
means to be expected that the respectable white people of any
county would seek to have their declarations confirmed by the
testimony of an inferior race, whose evidence, at best, would
have to be taken with many grains of allowance. There were
many eloquent and impressive speeches made on this occasion.

The lawyers were, of course, in the lead, as the profession
always is in all matters of public interest in our land. They
descanted largely upon *magna charta*, and the law-abiding and
liberty-loving spirit of the people of the grand old county, on
which the sun of American liberty first arose, and had shone

his very brightest ever since. They told how the people, after
being overwhelmed in the holiest crusade for liberty that the
world had ever known, by the hosts of foreign mercenaries
which the North had hurled against them, after having their
fields and homes ravaged and polluted by Yankee vandals, had
surrendered in good faith, and had endured all the tyranny
and oppression which Yankee cunning and malice could in-
vent, without resistance, almost without murmuring. They
painted the three years of unutterable oppression, when they
were ground under the heel of "military despotism," deprived
of the right of self-government, their laws subverted to the
will of a "military satrap," and their judges debarred from
enforcing them according to their oaths of office. They recalled the fact, that in that very county the sheriff had been
prevented by a file of soldiers from carrying into effect the
sentence of the court, given in strict conformity with the law
of the State, and requiring the offender to be publicly whipped
on his bare back. They called attention to the fact that the
whipping-post, the stocks, and the branding-iron, — the significant emblems of their former civilization, — had been
swept away by the influx of "Yankee ideas," which had cul-
minated in the inexpressible infamy of military reconstruction,
and "nigger supremacy."

Then they turned the torrent of their denunciatory wrath
upon the Fool, and gave free rein to their fancy as they
invented for him a boyhood, youth, and early manhood, sufficiently degraded and infamous to fit him for the career of the
carpet-bagger. With a magnificent disregard both of chro-
nology and geography, he was represented as having been born
"at Nantucket, Cape Cod, and all alongshore;" and by each
successive speaker was credited with a new birth more infamous, if possible, in its surroundings and associations, than
any theretofore conferred upon him. A life of corresponding
depravity was also invented for each new birthplace, every

one culminating in that last act of unparalleled infamy, — the utterance of slanderous reports against the ever-martyred and long-suffering South, which had laid aside the memory of its manifold wrongs, and received with open arms one of its oppressors, — a man whose hands were red with the blood of her sons slain in battle. Nay, more, he was denounced as one of those modern moss-troopers who raided and ravaged, and stole and burned, with the robber-chief, Sherman, on his torch-lit pathway to the sea, — Sherman, whose infamies were so unparalleled as to require the use of a new word to express their enormity, who had made the term "*bummer*" expressive of the quintessence of all ignominy.

Then spoke the grave and reverend divine who had discoursed with unruffled serenity of "the peaceable fruits of righteousness" on that chill sabbath when the body of poor Jerry swung from the adjacent oak, turning here and there the unseeing orbs in unsyllabled prayer for the common charity of Christian burial. He deplored, as his calling required him to do, all violence and harshness. He even deprecated harsh words and violent language. But when he saw his people assailed with false and infamous aspersions by one who had come among them, and had for years been the recipient of their forbearing charity and long-suffering patience, he could not hold his peace. And, after that frank acknowledgment of his fallibility, the good man did not seem to make any further effort to do so, but followed the lead of the gentlemen of the bar with a zeal that showed a determination to excel, until he grew hoarse and sweaty, and red in the face, and had lost his eye-glasses, and shed half a mouthful of false teeth. Then he sat down for repairs, and the sheriff gave *his* testimony.

He was a man of few words; but he avouched the peace and quiet of the county by telling how few warrants he had in his hands; how few presentments had been made by the grand jury; how certain he was that the acts of violence (which all regretted) had been almost entirely committed by lawless bands from other counties; and, in conclusion, he asserted that he had never had a paper which he could not serve without the aid of a *posse*. Indeed, so potent was the law-abiding spirit, that a boy of ten, armed with a lawful warrant, could arrest any man in the county charged with crime.

To the same effect testified all his deputies, and many other most honorable men; and all expressed as much indignation as the imperfection of the language would allow, at the atrocity of the Fool's conduct in reporting any thing derogatory to the honor of the South, and especially of the law-abiding character of the people of that county.

When all who were full enough for utterance had borne their testimony, and the laudatory resolutions had been adopted, one of the young hot-heads of the meeting thought to immortalize himself by offering a resolution denouncing the Fool by name, in the strongest terms he could command. Some of the older and cooler ones were somewhat doubtful about the policy of such a course; and, after some discussion, the resolution was withdrawn, and a committee appointed, with instructions to confer with the Fool, see if he still avowed the authorship of the letter in question, and affirmed its contents, and report the result of such conference to another meeting, to be called by them at such time as they might select. Thereupon the meeting adjourned, and on the next day the Fool received the following letter from the committee: —

"COLONEL COMFORT SERVOSSE. *Sir*, — The people of Verdenton and vicinity have seen, with surprise and regret, a letter purporting to have been written by you, and published in the *New York Age* of the 10th inst., stating, among other things, that there had been 'one thousand outrages committed in this congressional district by armed men in disguise,' in other words, by the Ku-Klux as they are called. The good citizens of this county feel that they would be open to the most just censure, and dereliction of duty to themselves and the country, should they permit such communications to pass without their notice and condemnation. Not wishing to act in haste, or to do any injustice, the undersigned have been appointed a committee, on behalf of the law-abiding people of this vicinity, to inquire of you whether you wrote said letter, and, if so, whether you still affirm its contents.

"An immediate answer is required.

"Respectfully,

"A. B——,
"C. D——, } *Committee.*"
"E. F——,

To this letter the Fool made answer: —

"To A. B. AND OTHERS, COMMITTEE, — Your favor of this morning is at hand, informing me that you have been appointed a committee, by a meeting of the citizens of Verdenton and vicinity, who desire to ascertain whether I am the writer of a certain letter published in a Northern journal, which they wish to notice and condemn.

"In reply, I would state that I have read the article to which you refer; that I did write the letter as published, and most unhesitatingly re-affirm its contents to the best of my knowledge and belief. I do not exactly understand the nature of the demand made upon me; but as I am always willing and anxious to gratify my neighbors with a declaration of faith, and such reasons as I may have, you will, I feel sure, pardon me if I see fit to give something more than a mere categorical answer to your inquiry.

"I am not a little surprised that such a demand should be made, and in the formal manner which characterizes this. I find nothing in the letter which I have not repeated and affirmed over and over again in private conversation, and several times on public occasions. It would seem, however, from the tenor of your letter, that the part of it which especially arouses the objurgation of my good neighbors, and the part which I am informed was especially inveighed against at the meeting last night, is my estimate of one thousand outrages in this congressional district. With regard to this, you will permit me to remark that I am clearly satisfied that it is altogether below the fact. Of course, as I have not access to the secret archives of the Klan, I have no means, at present, of verifying this estimate. You will recollect that this estimate embraces every unlawful act perpetrated by armed and organized bodies in disguise. The entry of the premises, and surrounding the dwelling with threats against the inmates; the seizure and destruction, or appropriation of arms; the dragging of men, women, and children from their homes, or compelling their flight; the binding, gagging, and beating of men and women; shooting at specific individuals, or indiscriminately at inhabited houses; the mutilation of men and women in methods too shocking and barbarous to be recounted here; burning houses; destroying stock; and making the night a terror to peaceful citizens by the ghastly horror of many and deliberate murders, — all these come within the fearful category of 'outrages.' I have reason to believe that the greater proportion of these acts are studiously concealed by the victims, unless of so serious a character as to render concealment impossible, because of the invariable threat of more serious punishment in case complaint is made. I know, in many instances, when parties have come to me from all parts of the district to seek legal redress, that, when advised that it could not be obtained, they have begged me to keep silence in regard to it, lest they should pay with their lives for having revealed it.

"I am aware, gentlemen, that many of those who are classed as 'our best citizens' have heretofore insisted, and perhaps even yet do insist, that these things were unworthy of serious attention; and I will confess that I have always suspected such parties of a peculiar knowledge of these crimes which could only be obtained by privity in regard to their perpetrators. You yourselves, gentlemen, will bear me witness that I have omitted no proper opportunity to denounce these acts, and warn both the perpetrators, and the community at large, that such horrible barbarities, such disregard of human right and human life, must bear some sort of bitter fruit in the near future. That I was right, witness the horrid culmination of deliberate and cowardly barbarity of which your streets were recently the theater! Witness the Temple of Justice in a neighboring county besmeared with the blood of an officer assassinated with cowardly treachery and cold-blooded deliberateness!

"The evidences in support of my estimate are daily accumulating, and convincing the most incredulous that it is even below the horrible truth. And yet you wish to know if I re-affirm that estimate! I am uncertain how to regard this demand. It seems too absurd to be serious, and too polite for a threat. If it was supposed that recent events, or the meeting of last night, had so intimidated or alarmed me as to lead me to retract such statement as the price of immunity, it was a mistake. I stated in the letter to which you have directed attention, my apprehension that I might at any moment meet the fate of John Walters. With that apprehension strengthened by your demand, I still reiterate my belief, and hope I would have fortitude to do so if it were to be my dying declaration, as indeed it may well be, since no man can be considered safe from assassination who has rendered himself obnoxious to this band of Christian Thugs.

"With these views, I have done, and shall continue to do, all in my power to direct the attention and influence of the government to this monster evil.

"And now, gentlemen, as I have answered your questions thus fully, will you permit me to ask one or two for my own enlightenment? If the 'good citizens of this county' are so anxious to play the censor, why have they not found breath to utter, in their collective capacity, a protest against the outrages which bands of disguised villains have perpetrated in this county? For more than a year, at brief intervals, under the very noses of the 'people of Verdenton and vicinity,' every right of the citizen has been violated by gangs of masked villains; and yet they have let them pass without 'notice' or 'condemnation.' Some of the most atrocious outrages which even the annals of this modern barbarity can furnish were perpetrated in this very county; and yet no word of censure has ever come from the 'people of Verdenton and vicinity.' No meeting of sympathy, no expression of indignation, no utterance of horror, is heard from the 'people of Verdenton and vicinity.' They have no 'duty to the country' to perform when men are whipped, women beaten almost to a jelly (white women too), children made imbecile by fright, and other outrages perpetrated upon the persons of citizens dwelling 'in the peace of God and the State,' within the limits of this very county. But no sooner does one utter a cry of warning, a call for help, a protest against these fearful enormities, wrung from his very soul by their frequency and horror, than 'the people of Verdenton and vicinity' have a duty to the country, and must not let this cry escape their 'notice' and 'condemnation.' The scourged and mangled victims had no claim upon your sympathy; but the masked and uniformed desperadoes and assassins who perpetrated these fearful, bloody deeds — ah! —

> 'Take *them* up tenderly,
> Touch *them* with care.'

Whoever speaks of their crimes above a whisper must be 'noticed and condemned.' Ah, 'people of Verdenton and vicinity,' with the highest personal regard for many of your number, I must say, with 'surprise and regret,' that the conduct of many in this matter bears a flavor which I hesitate to name!

"Duty is a good thing, gentlemen. The notice and condemnation of evil, the reprehension of vice, is so noble a virtue that even an excess of zeal in its exercise may be pardoned or admired. *Amor patriæ* is a thing so glorious that poets will hymn its praises for all time. But I have understood, gentlemen, that respected brands are sometimes placed upon spurious articles. Duty is sometimes but the livery of an unworthy purpose; reprehension of evil, only the flurry which wrong stirs up to cover its retreat; and *amor patriæ* — well, it has different faces, 'sometimes the image of good Queen Bess, and anon of a Bloody Mary.' There are near at hand some very ugly facts which it would be well for you to consider at this time.

"Let it not be understood, that, by these remarks, I would reflect upon *all* the 'people of Verdenton and vicinity.' Some of them have stood forth and denounced these acts from the first; but these, however, are rare.

"Regretting both the events which originally called forth my letter, and have made our State a hot-bed of horrors, and the course which the 'people of Verdenton and vicinity' have seen fit to adopt in relation to the same,

"I remain, gentlemen, your obedient servant,

"COMFORT SERVOSSE."

CHAPTER XXXIV

THE HARVEST OF WISDOM

THE cry which the Fool had uttered, however, was but the echo of that which had already come up to the ears of an astonished nation from the mouths of thousands upon thousands of those who had seen and suffered the evils which he portrayed, and of other thousands of dumb mouths which spoke of the voiceless agony of death.

This new Reign of Terror had come so stilly and quietly upon the world, that none realized its fearfulness and extent. At first it had been a thing of careless laughter to the great, free, unsuspecting North, then a matter of contemptuous ridicule, and finally a question of incredulous horror. Two things had contributed to this feeling. Those who had suffered had, in the main, been humble people. The public press did not teem with their wrongs, because there were none to tell them. They were people, too, whose story of wrong had been so long in the ear of the public, that it was tired of the refrain. It had yielded, very slowly and unwillingly, to the conviction that slavery was an evil, and the colored man too near akin to white humanity to be rightfully held in bondage, and subjected to another's will. It had slowly and doubtfully been brought to the point of interference therewith on the ground of military necessity in the suppression of rebellion, and, after a grand struggle of conflicting ideas, had finally settled down to the belief that enfranchisement was all that was required to cure all the ills which hitherto had afflicted, or in the future might assail, the troublesome and pestiferous African. This had been granted. The conscience of the nation was satisfied, and it highly resolved that thereafter it would have peace;

that the negro *could* have no further ground of complaint, and it would hear no further murmurs. So it stopped its ears, and, when the south wind brought the burden of woe, it shook its head blankly, and said, "I hear nothing, nothing! All is peace."

But, when the cries became so clamorous that they could not longer be ignored, the Wise Men appointed a committee who should investigate the matter, and hear all that could be said both *pro* and *con.*

Oh! a strange, sad story is that which fills the thirteen volumes of testimony, documents, and conclusions, reported by that committee; a strange commentary upon Christian civilization; a strange history of peaceful years; — bloody as the reign of Mary, barbarous as the chronicles of the Comanche!

Of the slain there were enough to furnish forth a battle-field, and all from those three classes, the negro, the scalawag, and the carpet-bagger, — all killed with deliberation, over-whelmed by numbers, roused from slumber at the murk midnight, in the hall of public assembly, upon the river-brink, on the lonely woods-road, in simulation of the public execution, — shot, stabbed, hanged, drowned, mutilated beyond description, tortured beyond conception.

And almost always by an unknown hand! Only the terrible, mysterious fact of *death* was certain. Accusation by secret denunciation; sentence without hearing; execution without warning, mercy, or appeal. In the deaths alone, terrible beyond utterance; but in the manner of death — the secret, intangible doom from which fate springs — more terrible still: in the treachery which made the neighbor a disguised assassin, most horrible of all the feuds and hates which history portrays.

And then the wounded, — those who escaped the harder fate, — the whipped, the mangled, the bleeding, the torn! men despoiled of manhood; women gravid with dead children!

bleeding backs! broken limbs! Ah! the wounded in this silent warfare were more thousands than those who groaned upon the slopes of Gettysburg! Dwellings and schools and churches burned! People driven from their homes, and dwelling in the woods and fields! The poor, the weak, the despised, maltreated and persecuted — by whom? Always the same intangible presence, the same invisible power. Well did it name itself "The Invisible Empire." Unseen and unknown! In one State ten thousand, in another twenty thousand, in another forty thousand; in all an army greater than the Rebellion, from the moldering remains of which it sprung, could ever put into the field! An Invisible Empire, with a trained and disciplined army of masked midnight marauders, making war upon the weakling "powers" which the Wise Men had set up in the lately rebellious territory!

And then the defense! — no, not the *defense*, — the excuse, the avoidance set up to rebut the charge, to mitigate the guilt! Ah, me! it is sad, sadder almost than the bloody facts themselves. What is it?

"We were rebels in arms: we surrendered, and by the terms of surrender were promised immunity so long as we obeyed the laws. This meant that we should govern ourselves as of old. Instead of this, they put military officers over us; they imposed disabilities on our best and bravest; they liberated our slaves, and gave them power over us. Men born at the North came among us, and were given place and power by the votes of slaves and renegades. There were incompetent officers. The revenues of the State were squandered. We were taxed to educate the blacks. Enormous debts were contracted. We did not do these acts of violence from political motives, but only because the parties had made themselves obnoxious."

Alas, alas that a people who had inaugurated and carried through a great war should come to regard any thing as an excuse for organized Thuggism!

Yet it was a magnificent sentiment that underlay it all, — an unfaltering determination, an invincible defiance to all that had the seeming of compulsion or tyranny. One can not but regard with pride and sympathy the indomitable men, who, being conquered in war, yet resisted every effort of the conqueror to change their laws, their customs, or even the *personnel* of their ruling class; and this, too, not only with unyielding stubbornness, but with success. One can not but admire the arrogant boldness with which they charged the nation which had overpowered them — even in the teeth of her legislators — with perfidy, malice, and a spirit of unworthy and contemptible revenge. How they laughed to scorn the Reconstruction Acts of which the Wise Men boasted! How boldly they declared the conflict to be irrepressible, and that white and black could not and should not live together as co-ordinate ruling elements! How lightly they told the tales of blood, — of the Masked Night-Riders, of the Invisible Empire of Rifle Clubs and Saber Clubs (all organized for peaceful purposes), of warnings and whippings and slaughters! Ah, it is wonderful!

And then the organization itself, so complete, and yet so portable and elastic! So perfect in disguise, that, of the thousands of victims, scarce a score could identify one of their persecutors! And among the hundreds of thousands of its members, of the few who confessed and revealed its character, hardly one knew any thing more than had already been discovered; *or, if he knew it, did not disclose it!* It is all amazing, but sad and terrible. Would that it might be blotted out, or disappear as a fevered dream before the brightness of a new day!

Yet in it we may recognize the elements which should go to make up a grand and kingly people. They felt themselves insulted and oppressed. No matter whether they were or not, be the fact one way or another, it does not affect their conduct. If the Reconstruction which the Wise Men ordained was unjust; if the North was the aggressor and wrongful assailant of the South in war; if, to humiliate and degrade her enemy, the terms of surrender were falsified, and new and irritating conditions imposed; if the outcasts of Northern life were sent or went thither to encourage and induce the former slave to act against his former master, — if all this *were* true, it would be no more an excuse or justification for the course pursued than would the fact that these things were honestly *believed* to be true by the masses who formed the rank and file of this grotesquely uniformed body of partisan cavalry. In any case, it must be counted but as the desperate effort of a proud, brave, and determined people to secure and hold what they *deemed to be their rights.*

It is sometimes said, by those who do not comprehend its purpose, to have been a base, cowardly, and cruel barbarism. "What!" says the Northern man, — who has stood aloof from it all, and with Pharisaic assumption, or comfortable ignorance of facts, denounced "Ku-Klux," "carpet-baggers," "scalawags," and "niggers" alike, — "was it a brave thing, worthy of a brave and chivalric people, to assail poor, weak, defenseless men and women with overwhelming forces, to terrify, maltreat, and murder? Is this brave and commendable?"

Ah, my friend! you quite mistake. If that were all that was intended and done, no, it was not brave and commendable. But it was not alone the poor colored man whom the daring band of night-riders struck, as the falcon strikes the sparrow; that indeed would have been cowardly: but it was the Nation which had given the victim citizenship and power, on whom their blow fell. It was no brave thing in itself for old John Brown to seize the arsenal at Harper's Ferry; considered as an assault on the almost solitary watchman, it was cowardly in the extreme: but, when we consider what power stood behind that powerless squad, we are amazed at the daring of the Hero of Ossawattomie. So it was with this magnificent organization.

It was not the individual negro, scalawag, or carpet-bagger, against whom the blow was directed, but the power — the Government — the idea which they represented. Not unfrequently, the individual victim was one toward whom the individual members of the Klan who executed its decree upon him had no little of kindly feeling and respect, but whose influence, energy, boldness, or official position, was such as to demand that he should be "visited." In most of its assaults, the Klan was not instigated by cruelty, nor a desire for revenge; but these were simply the most direct, perhaps the only, means to secure the end it had in view. The brain, the wealth, the chivalric spirit of the South, was restive under what it deemed degradation and oppression. This association offered a ready and effective method of overturning the hated organization, and throwing off the rule which had been imposed upon them. From the first, therefore, it spread like wildfire. It is said that the first organization was instituted in May, or perhaps as late as the 1st of June, 1868; yet by August of that year it was firmly established in every State of the South. It was builded upon an ineradicable sentiment of hostility to the negro *as a political integer*, and a fierce determination that the white people of the South, or a majority of that race, should rule, — if not by the power of the ballot, then by force of skill, brain, and the habit of domination. The bravest and strongest and best of the South gave it their recognition and support, — in most cases actively, in some passively. Thousands believed it a necessity to prevent anarchy and the destruction of all valuable civilization; others regarded it as a means of retaliating upon the government, which they conceived to have oppressed them; while still others looked to it as a means of acquiring place and power.

That it outgrew the designs of its originators is more than

probable; but the development was a natural and unavoidable one. It is probable that it was intended, at first, to act solely upon the superstitious fears of the ignorant and timid colored race. The transition from moral to physical compulsion was easy and natural, especially to a people who did not regard the colored man as having any *inherent* right to liberty and self-government, or the personal privileges attendant thereon, but only such right as was conferred by a legislation which was deemed at least questionable. The native whites who had identified themselves with that movement which gave political power to the blacks were regarded not only as mercenaries and renegades who had deserted their section, but also as traitors to their race. The Northern men who did likewise were regarded as intruders and invaders, and believed to be instigated, not only by the basest personal motives, but also by that concentrated hate which the Southern man always attributed to the Northern opponent of slavery. Unaccustomed to immigration as the South was, accustomed, indeed, to regard all strangers with suspicion, until assured of their harmlessness as regarded the main institution of their land, it needed but the conviction of oppression, and the chagrin of defeat, to make them look upon every individual from the hostile section as an active and virulent enemy, whose claim of citizenship there was a false pretense, constituting the owner, in effect, an emissary of the enemy, entitled only to the consideration and treatment of the spy.

All this was natural, and *should have been foreseen and acted upon* by the Wise Men whose task it was to reform the shattered nation. As it was not done, however, and the cry for relief came up from so many thousands, the Congress appointed this committee, and enacted certain laws in regard to the matter for the protection of its citizens. At the same time, the various State governments in the South (which, it will be remembered, had been placed in power by the new political elements) began to move in the same direction. In some, the Executive levied troops, and suspended the writ of *Habeas Corpus*, on the ground that the power of the State was threatened and subverted by this organization. But meantime, and before either power had carried their designs into practical execution, the Klan organization had accomplished its primary object, the majority which had pronounced in favor of the Reconstruction measures had been suppressed in quite a number of the States, and the minority found themselves in legislative control. Instantly, upon this being ascertained, the power of such States was turned upon those who had exerted extraordinary powers to protect their people from the raids and violence of the Klan. The governors of some were impeached and deposed for this cause. Others were threatened with the same fate, and resigned to avoid it.

This new revolution which had begun went on. The Klan increased in numbers and in power, — an *imperium in imperio*, — until its decrees were far more potent, and its power more dreaded, than that of the visible commonwealths which it either dominated or terrorized. This fact, together with the fear of the new laws which had been adopted by the National Government, the authority of which had not then been questioned, tended somewhat to repress actual violence. Having gained what was sought, — to wit, the control of their States, — the leaders now exercised their authority to prevent further raids; and the hostility against the colored man and his allies gradually died out as these suppressed classes ceased to be a political element which need be feared, in the struggle for domination. The national law, moreover, could not extend to the crimes perpetrated before its enactment. They were still only cognizable in the State tribunals, in which it was not supposed that prosecution would ever be possible. So the organization was easily maintained, lying quiet and unnoticed, except when, upon occasions, it was deemed proper to manifest its power to restrain or punish some daring leader who refused to obey the logic of events, and give up the contest for the rule of the majority of *voters* in those States, instead of the majority of the White Leaguers therein.

The revolution had been inaugurated, and its feasibility demonstrated. Henceforth it was only a question of time as to its absolute and universal success. The rule of the majority had been overthrown, the power of the Government boldly defied, and its penalties for crime successfully evaded, that the enfranchisement of the colored man might be rendered a farce; and the obnoxious Amendments and Reconstruction legislation had been shown to be practically nullified. Read by the light of other days, the triumph of the ancient South was incredibly grand; in the then present there was little lacking to give it completeness; in the future — well, that could take care of itself.

CHAPTER XXXV

AN AWAKENING

LILY, the one child of Comfort and Metta Servosse, had developed under the Southern sun, until, almost before her parents had noted the fact, she had the rounded form and softened outlines indicative of womanhood. The atmosphere in which she had lived had also developed her mind not less rapidly. From her infancy almost, owing to the peculiar circumstances which surrounded their life, she had been the constant companion and trusted confidant of her mother.

Shut out from all that may be termed "society" by the unfortunate relations which her husband and she herself sustained to those around them, regarded either as enemies, intruders, or inferiors, by those whose culture rendered their society desirable, Metta had not sought to remove this impression, but, acting upon her husband's advice, had calmly and proudly accepted the isolation thus imposed upon her, only compensating herself by a more intimate and constant association with her husband, sharing his thoughts, entering into his plans and purposes, and interesting herself in all that interested him. It resulted that she took the liveliest interest in all that concerned the present and future of that community in which they dwelt. Side by side with her husband she had digged into the history of the past, studied the development of the present, and earnestly endeavored to find some clew to the clouded and obscure future. In this absorbing question her heart had become weaned from many of those things which constitute so much of the ordinary life of woman; and, in the society of her husband and the care and education of her daughter, she had almost ceased to miss those social enjoyments to which she had been accustomed before their migration.

The exciting events which had occurred around them had drawn this little family into even closer relations with each other than this involuntary isolation would, of itself, have compelled. The difficulties and dangers attending the Fool's life and duties had woven themselves into the daily life of the wife and daughter, until they became the one engrossing theme of their thought and the burden of their conversations. During his absence, anxiety for his safety, and, during his presence, thankfulness for his preservation, filled their hearts. Every act of violence perpetrated by the mysterious enemy which lay hidden all about them was one more evidence of the peril which surrounded him on whom all their hopes were centered. Every call of duty which took him from their sight was another trial of their faith in the great Deliverer. Every absence and every return increased the intensity of their anxiety, and fixed their minds more exclusively upon those events which were passing day by day about them. Each farewell came to have the solemnity of a death-bed, and each return, the solemn joy of an unexpected resurrection.

In this furnace-blast of excitement and apprehension the young girl's heart and mind had matured even more rapidly then her person. A prudence unknown to one of her years who had lived in quiet times and under other conditions of society, had come to be habitual with her. The constant apprehension of attack from the masked marauders had familiarized her with danger, and given her a coolness and decision of character which nothing else could have developed. She had seen the dread cavalcade pass in the dim moonlight, and had stood at her chamber-window, revolver in hand, prepared to take part in the expected defense of their home. She had learned to watch for danger, to see that all precautions were adopted against it, to be cautious what she said, and to whom she said it, to weigh with suspicious doubt the words and acts of all whom she met. Many a time, while yet a mere child, she had been called upon to be her mother's consoler in seasons of doubt and apprehended danger. A thousand times she had seen the dull gray look of agonized foreboding steal into the loved face, and had bravely undertaken the duty of lightening the mother's woe. All this had ripened her mind with wonderful rapidity.

As she had shared the anxieties and perils of her parents, she had participated also in their joys. She had early been trained to the saddle; and, from the very outset of their life in the new home, her pony had been the frequent companion of both Lollard and Jaca in many a long ride. As she grew older, the pony gave way to her own petted mare; and a more easy, graceful, and daring rider it was hard to find, even in that region of unrivaled horsemen and horsewomen. She had also been trained to the use of arms, and handled both rifle and revolver, not only without fear, but with readiness and precision.

In person she was by no means unattractive. She had the lithe, trim figure of her mother, and, united with it, that softness of outline, delicacy of color, and ease and grace of carriage which the free, untrammeled life, and soft, kindly climate of that region, give in such rich measure to those reared under their influences. Her eyes were of that deep blue which evinces fortitude and sincerity; while her luxuriant hair took the character of its hue from the light in which it was viewed, — "golden in the sunshine, in the shadow brown," and, touched by the moonbeam, a spray of tinted silver. It had been the joy and pride of the fond mother. Shears had never marred its glossy sheen; and it had rarely felt the restraint of twist or braid, but had hung naturally about the child's shoulders, until it fell, in rippling cascade, to her waist. To these personal attributes Lily joined a sunniness of temper, a sparkle and vivacity of mind, inherited from far-away French ancestors, which seemed to have been brought out by the sunny brightness of the kindred clime in which she had been reared. These charms combined to render her an exceedingly piquant and charming maiden; so that, as she rode here and there with her parents, or scrambled about the shady bridle-paths of the adjacent country alone, her beauty came to be remarked. The young people of the vicinity began shyly to court her presence, and finally opened their social circles and their hearts to her, only regretting that her parents were not "our people," and kindly exercising more or less forgetfulness of her origin.

Among those who had seen and admired the bright presence which reigned supreme at Warrington was Melville Gurney, the son of General Marion Gurney of Pultowa County, adjoining that in which the Fool resided. Young Gurney was a splendid specimen of the stock of Southern gentlemen from which he sprung, being tall and commanding in person, of that easy grace which is rarely matched in other portions of the country, and admirably adapted to excel in field-sports, in all of which he was an acknowledged proficient. His early youth had covered the period of the war, in which his father had won no little renown, and before his sixteenth birthday he had run away from home, riding his own horse, to take part in the last campaign of Early in the Valley of the Shenandoah, where his father's command was engaged. After the last defeat he found his father lying wounded in a Federal hospital, and by unremitting exertion saved him from fatal prostration, and brought him home to slow but certain recovery. The daring youngster could not, after that, confine himself to the dull routine of the college; but in his father's library, and afterwards in his office, he had received a culture not less complete, although very different from what he would have gathered in the course of a collegiate career. This young man, bold, active, and endowed with a superabundant vitality, had met the little lady of Warrington at a festive gathering near his father's home a few months before the time to which our story has advanced, and, with the frank impetuosity characteristic of his nativity, had forthwith testified his admiration, and asked an invitation to Warrington.

That the young girl should be flattered by the attentions of so charming a cavalier, was but natural. It was the first time, however, that she had been asked to extend the hospitalities of her father's house to any of her associates, and at once the anomalous position in which they stood to those by whom they were surrounded forced itself upon her thought. Her face flushed for an instant, and then, looking up quietly into his, she said, —

"Are you in earnest, Mr. Gurney? Would you really like to visit Warrington?"

The inquiry brought the young man to a serious consideration of his own request. When he had first preferred it, he had thought only of the fair creature by his side: now, he thought of a thousand incidents which might flow from it. Bold almost to recklessness, he was sincere almost to bluntness also, even with himself: therefore, ready as he would have been with the words of a mere outward politeness, he honestly hesitated before answering the question. Instantly the quick perceptions and natural pride of the "carpet-bagger's" daughter were aroused; and she said somewhat haughtily, but with a studied courtesy of tone, —

"I see, Mr. Gurney, that your request was merely intended as an empty compliment, which it is not worth the trouble either to accept or decline. Excuse me," — and, having already removed her hand from his arm, she bowed lightly, and turned with a smile to begin a lively conversation with a friend who stood near.

The incident showed such coolness and self-control, as well as frank sincerity, that the admiration of Melville Gurney was increased rather than diminished thereby. He did not regard it as a rebuff, but as a self-respecting assertion that one who doubted as to the propriety of visiting her father's house had no right to prefer such a request to her. So he did not approach her again during the evening, but watched her attentively. And the next day, when he saw her pass his father's office, mounted upon Lollard (now full of years, but still a horse of magnificent action and unabated fire), her fair hair falling free over her dark habit until it almost touched the glossy coat of her steed, each fiber transformed by the sunlight into a gleaming thread of gold, he began to feel something of regret that he had not answered her question, and pressed for an answer to his request.

General Gurney was as active and prominent a political leader upon the other side as the Fool was upon his, and was looked upon as a partisan of similar intensity of conviction. Both were pronounced and positive men. They were well-matched opponents too, had more than once met upon the stump, and had served together in public bodies. There was that acquaintance between them which such association gives, without further personal relations, and perhaps something of that esteem which is sure to prevail between men often pitted against each other without decisive victory. The general was the representative of an old and honored family, and felt, with the utmost keenness, the degradation resulting from defeat, and the subsequent elevation of the colored man to a position of political co-ordination with the white race. He had married early; Melville was the oldest child, and on him the hopes, aspirations, and love of the father were centered in an unusual degree.

"What do you think of Colonel Servosse, Pa?" asked the son a few moments after Lily had passed.

"Think about him? That he is the worst Radical in the State. He has the most ineradicable hate of every thing Southern that I have ever known," answered the father.

"But aside from his politics, — as a man, Pa, what do you think of him?"

"Oh! as a man he is well enough; in fact, better than I could wish. Personally there seems to be no weak spot in his armor. They did try to make some attack upon his character; but no one really believed it, and I am of the notion that it did us more harm than good. I never did believe it, though I have sometimes hinted at it, just because I saw that I could get under his hide in no other way. He is the coolest and most collected man I have ever met in public life."

"Is he a gentleman?"

"Well — yes, in a Northern sense," answered the father. "I have no doubt that if he had staid at the North, and I had known him as a Northern man, I should have enjoyed him thoroughly. Everybody who is acquainted with him admits that he has fine social qualities. He is somewhat reserved to strangers. He is a man of decided ability and culture, and I count him one of the most dangerous Radicals in the State. But why do you ask?"

"Well, I thought I would like to know all sides of him," replied the son. "I had read so much of him, and had heard you speak of him so often in a semi-public manner, that I thought I would like to know your actual opinion in regard to him."

"That's right. You ought to learn every thing you can of a man of his mark. You will meet his influence in the State as long as you live. He has left an impress upon it that would remain, even if he should die to-morrow.

Soon afterwards Melville Gurney wrote a note to Lily Servosse, which contained only these words: —

"MISS LILY, — Will you allow me, after mature deliberation, to renew the request which I made to you?

"Respectfully,

"MELVILLE GURNEY."

Lily took this to her mother, and told her all that had occurred. For the first time the mother realized that her daughter was growing into womanhood. The blushes which accompanied her narrative told that her heart was awakened. It
seemed but a little while since she was only a prattling child;
but now, as the mother looked on her budding beauty, she
could but admit, with a pang of sorrow, that the days of girl-
hood were over, that the summer of love had come, and that
her pretty bird was but pluming her wings for the inevitable
flight. Like a prudent mother, she determined to do nothing
to hasten this result, and yet to so act as to keep her daughter's
confidence as implicit and spontaneous as it had hitherto
been. So she only kissed the girl's blushing cheek, asking
lightly, —

"And would you like to have him come?"

"I don't know, mamma," answered Lily artlessly. "I *would*
like to be more like — like our neighbors, and have more
young companions."

"And so you shall, my daughter," answered the mother. So
it resulted, that, a few weeks after, a party was given at Warrington, and Mr. Melville Gurney, with several others of
Lily's friends in Pultowa, received an invitation to be present.
Metta did not see fit to confide any thing of this to the Fool,
who only knew that young Gurney came with others to a
party given for his daughter's pleasure. It was the first time
that wife or daughter had ever had a secret which the husband
and father had not shared.

Mr. Denton, the district-attorney, whose letter to Comfort
Servosse has already been given to the reader, had been elected

a judge of the State courts, and had recently, before the period at which we have now arrived, been very active in his efforts to suppress the operation of the Klan, and punish those engaged in its raids. By so doing, he had incurred the hostility of the Klan at large, and especially of that portion with which the suspected parties had been actually connected. There had long been threats and denunciations afloat in regard to him; but he was a brave man, who did not turn aside from the path of his duty for any obstacles, and who, while he did not despise the power of the organization which he had taken by the throat, was yet utterly oblivious to threats of personal violence. He would do his duty, though the heavens fell. This was a fact well known and recognized by all who knew him; and for this very reason, most probably, it was generally believed that he would be put out of the way by the Klan before the time for the trial of its members arrived.

It was under these circumstances that the Fool received a telegram from Judge Denton, requesting him to come to Verdenton on a certain day, and go with him to his home in an adjoining county. It was seven miles from Glenville, the nearest railroad-station, to the plantation of Judge Denton. To reach it, the chief river of that region had to be crossed on a long wooden bridge, four miles from the station. The Fool accepted this invitation, and with Metta drove into Verdenton on the day named.

The railroad which ran nearest to the home of Judge Denton connected at an acute angle with that on which he was to arrive at Verdenton. Between the two was the residence of Colonel Servosse, six miles from Verdenton, and sixteen from Glenville.

The train left Verdenton at eight and a half o'clock in the evening, and ran to the junction, where it awaited the coming of the northward-bound train on the other road; so that they would not arrive at Glenville until ten o'clock, and would reach the river-bridge about eleven, and the judge's mansion perhaps a half-hour later. By previous arrangement, his carriage would meet them at the station. Metta intended to remain until the train reached Verdenton, and bring home a friend who was expected to arrive upon it.

Lily remained at home. She was the "only white person on the lot," to use the familiar phrase of that region, which means that upon her rested all the responsibility of the house. The existence of a servile, or recently servile race, devolves upon the children at a very early age a sort of vice-regal power in the absence of the parents. They are expected to see that "every thing goes on right on the plantation" and about the house in such absence; and their commands are as readily obeyed by the servants and employees as those of their elders. It is this early familiarity with the affairs of the parents, and ready assumption of responsibility, which give to the youth of the South that air of self-control, and readiness to assume command of whatever matter he may be engaged in. It is thus that they are trained to rule. To this training, in large measure, is due the fact, that, during all the *ante bellum* period, the Southern minority dominated and controlled the government, monopolized its honors and emoluments, and dictated its policy, in spite of an overwhelming and hostile majority at the North. The Southrons are the natural rulers, leaders, and dictators of the country, as later events have conclusively proved.

It was just at sundown, and Lily was sitting on the porch at Warrington, watching the sunset glow, when a horseman came in sight, and rode up to the gate. After a moment's scrutiny of the premises, he seemed satisfied, and uttered the usual halloo which it is customary for one to give who desires to communicate with the household in that country. Lily rose, and advanced to the steps.

"Here's a letter," said the horseman, as he held an envelope up to view, and then, as she started down the steps, threw it over the gate into the avenue, and, wheeling his horse, cantered easily away. Lily picked up the letter. It was directed in a coarse, sprawling hand, —

"COLONEL COMFORT SERVOSSE,
"WARRINGTON."

In the lower left hand-corner, in a more compact and business-like hand, were written the words, "Read at once." Lily read the superscription carelessly as she went up the broad avenue. It awakened no curiosity in her mind; but, after she had resumed her seat on the porch, it occurred to her that both the messenger and his horse were unknown to her. The former was a white lad of fourteen or fifteen years of age, whom she might very well fail to recognize. What struck her as peculiar was the fact that he was evidently unacquainted with Warrington, which was a notable place in the country; and a lad of that age could hardly be found in a circuit of many miles who could not have directed the traveler to it. It was evident from the demeanor of this one, that, when he first rode up, he was uncertain whether he had reached his destination, and had only made sure of it by recognizing some specific object which had been described to him. In other words, he had been traveling on what is known in that country as a "way-bill," or a description of a route received from another.

Then she remembered that she had not recognized the horse, which was a circumstance somewhat remarkable; for it was an iron-gray of notable form and action. Her love of horses led her instinctively to notice those which she saw, and her daily rides had made her familiar with every good horse in a circle of many miles. Besides this, she had been accustomed to go almost everywhere with her father, when he had occasion to make journeys not requiring more than a day's absence. So that it was quite safe to say that she knew by sight at least twice as many horses as people.

These reflections caused her to glance again, a little curiously, at the envelope. It occurred to her, as she did so, that the superscription was in a disguised hand. Her father had received so many letters of that character, all of threat or warning, that the bare suspicion of that fact aroused at once the apprehension of evil or danger. While she had been thinking, the short Southern twilight had given place to the light of the full moon rising in the East. She went into the house, and, calling for a light, glanced once more at the envelope, and then broke the seal. It read, —

"COLONEL SERVOSSE, — A raid of K.K. has been ordered to intercept Judge Denton on his way home to-night (the 23d inst.). It is understood that he has telegraphed to you to accompany him home. Do not do it. If you can by any means, give him warning. It is a big raid, and means business. The decree is, that he shall be tied, placed in the middle of the bridge across the river, the planks taken up on each side, so as to prevent a rescue, and the bridge set on fire. I send this warning for your sake. Do not trust the telegraph. I shall try to send this by a safe hand, but tremble lest it should be too late. I dare not sign my name, but subscribe myself your

"UNKNOWN FRIEND."

The young girl stood for a moment paralyzed with horror at the danger which threatened her father. It did not once occur to her to doubt the warning she had received. She glanced at the timepiece upon the mantel. The hands pointed to eight o'clock.

"Too late, too late!" she cried as she clasped her hands, and raised her eyes to heaven in prayerful agony. She saw that she could not reach Verdenton in time to prevent their taking the train, and she knew it would be useless to telegraph afterwards. It was evident that the wires were under the control of the Klan, and there was no probability that a message would be delivered, if sent, in time to prevent the catastrophe.

"O my dear, dear papa!" she cried, as she realized more fully the danger. "O God! can nothing be done to save him!"

Then a new thought flashed upon her mind. She ran to the back porch, and called sharply, but quietly, —

"William! *Oh*, William!"

A voice in the direction of the stables answered, —

"Ma'am?"

"Come here at once."

"*Oh*, Maggie!" she called.

"Ma'am?" from the kitchen.

"Bring me a cup of coffee, some biscuits, and an egg — quick!"

"Law sakes, chile, what makes ye in sech a hurry? Supper 'll be ready direckly Miss Mettie gits home. Can't yer wait?" answered the colored woman querulously.

"Never mind. I'll do without it, if it troubles you," said Lily quietly.

"Bress my soul! No trouble at all, Miss Lily," said the woman, entirely mollified by the soft answer. "On'y I couldn't see what made yer be in sech a powerful hurry. Ye'se hev 'em in a minit, honey."

"William," said Lily, as the stable-boy appeared, "put my saddle on Young Lollard, and bring him round as quick as possible."

"But Miss Lily, you know dat hoss" — the servant began to expostulate.

"I know all about him, William. Don't wait to talk. Bring him out."

"All right, Miss Lily," he replied, with a bow and a scrape.

But, as he went toward the stable, he soliloquized angrily, "Now, what for Miss Lily want to ride dat pertickerler hoss, you s'pose? Never did afore. Nobody but de kunnel ebber on his back, an' *he* hab his hands full wid him sometimes. Dese furrer-bred hosses jes' de debbil anyhow! Dar's dat Young Lollard now, it's jest 'bout all a man's life's wuth ter rub him down, an' saddle him. Why can't she take de ole un! Here you, Lollard, come outen dat!"

He threw open the door of the log-stable where the horse had his quarters, as he spoke, and almost instantly, with a short, vicious whinney, a powerful dark-brown horse leaped into the moonlight, and with ears laid back upon his sinuous neck, white teeth bare, and thin, blood-red nostrils distended, rushed towards the servant, who, with a loud, "Dar now! Look at him! Whoa! See de dam rascal!" retreated quickly behind the door. The horse rushed once or twice around the little stable-yard, and then stopped suddenly beside his keeper, and stretched out his head for the bit, quivering in every limb with that excess of vitality which only the thorough-bred horse ever exhibits. He was anxious for the bit and saddle, because they meant exercise, a race, an opportunity to show his speed, which the thorough-bred recognizes as the one great end of his existence.

Before the horse was saddled, Lily had donned her riding-habit, put a revolver in her belt, as she very frequently did when riding alone, swallowed a hasty supper, scrawled a short note to her mother on the envelope of the letter she had received, — which she charged William at once to carry to her, — and was ready to start on a night-ride to Glenville. She had only been there across the country once; but she thought she knew the way, or was at least so familiar with the "lay" of the country that she could find it.

The brawny groom with difficulty held the restless horse by the bit; but the slight girl, who stood upon the block with pale face and set teeth, gathered the reins in her hand, leaped fearlessly into the saddle, found the stirrup, and said, "Let him go!" without a quaver in her voice. The man loosed his hold. The horse stood upright, and pawed the air for a moment with his feet, gave a few mighty leaps to make sure of his liberty, and then, stretching out his neck, bounded forward in a race which would require all the mettle of his endless line of noble sires. Almost without words, her errand had become known to the household of servants; and as she flew down the road, her bright hair gleaming in the moonlight, old Maggie, sobbing and tearful, was yet so impressed with admiration, that she could only say, —

"De Lor' bress her! 'Pears like dat chile ain't 'fear'd o' noffin'!"

As she was borne like an arrow down the avenue, and turned into the Glenville road, Lily heard the whistle of the train as it left the depot at Verdenton, and knew that upon her coolness and resolution alone depended the life of her father.

CHAPTER XXXVI

A RACE AGAINST TIME

It was, perhaps, well for the accomplishment of her purpose, that, for some time after setting out on her perilous journey, Lily Servosse had enough to do to maintain her seat, and guide and control her horse. Young Lollard, whom the servant had so earnestly remonstrated against her taking, added to the noted pedigree of his sire the special excellences of the Glencoe strain of his dam, from whom he inherited also a darker coat, and that touch of native savageness which characterizes the stock of Emancipator. Upon both sides his blood was as pure as that of the great kings of the turf, and what we have termed his savagery was more excess of spirit than any inclination to do mischief. It was that uncontrollable desire of the thorough-bred horse to be always doing his best, which made him restless of the bit and curb, while the native sagacity of his race had led him to practice somewhat on the fears of his groom. With that care which only the true lover of the horse can appreciate, Colonel Servosse had watched over the growth and training of Young Lollard, hoping to see him rival, if he did not surpass, the excellences of his sire. In every thing but temper, he had been gratified at the result. In build, power, speed, and endurance, the horse offered all that the most fastidious could desire. In order to prevent the one defect of a quick temper from developing into a vice, the colonel had established an inflexible rule that no one should ride him but himself. His great interest in the colt had led Lily, who inherited all her father's love for the noble animal, to look very carefully during his enforced absences after the welfare of his favorite. Once or twice she had summarily discharged grooms who were guilty of disobeying her father's injunctions, and had always made it a rule to visit his stall every day; so that, although she had never ridden him, the horse was familiar with her person and voice.

It was well, for her that this was the case; for, as he dashed away with the speed of the wind, she felt how powerless she was to restrain him by means of the bit. Nor did she attempt it. Merely feeling his mouth, and keeping her eye upon the road before him, in order that no sudden start to right or left should take her by surprise, she coolly kept her seat, and tried to soothe him by her voice.

With head outstretched, and sinewy neck strained to its uttermost, he flew over the ground in a wild, mad race with the evening wind, as it seemed. Without jerk or strain, but easily and steadily as the falcon flies, the highbred horse skimmed along the ground. A mile, two, three miles were made, in time that would have done honor to the staying quality of his sires, and still his pace had not slackened. He was now nearing the river into which fell the creek that ran by Warrington. As he went down the long slope that led to the ford, his rider tried in vain to check his speed. Pressure upon the bit but resulted in an impatient shaking of the head, and laying back of the ears. He kept up his magnificent stride until he had reached the very verge of the river. There he stopped, threw up his head in inquiry, as he gazed upon the fretted waters lighted up by the full moon, glanced back at his rider, and, with a word of encouragement from her, marched proudly into the waters, casting up a silvery spray at every step. Lily did not miss this opportunity to establish more intimate relations with her steed. She patted his neck, praised him lavishly, and took occasion to assume control of him while he was in the deepest part of the channel, turning him this way and that much more than was needful, simply to accustom him to obey her will.

When he came out on the other bank, he would have resumed his gallop almost at once; but she required him to walk to the top of the hill. The night was growing chilly by this time. As the wind struck her at the hill-top, she remembered that she had thrown a hooded waterproof about her before starting. She stopped her horse, and, taking off her hat, gathered her long hair into a mass, and thrust it into the hood, which she drew over her head, and pressed her hat down on it; then she gathered the reins, and they went on in that long, steady stride which marks the highbred horse when he gets thoroughly down to his work. Once or twice she drew rein to examine the landmarks, and determine which road to take. Sometimes her way lay through the forest, and she was startled by the cry of the owl; anon it was through the reedy bottom-land, and the half-wild hogs, starting from their lairs, gave her an instant's fright. The moon cast strange shadows around her; but still she pushed on, with this one only thought in her mind, that her father's life was at stake, and she alone could save him. She had written to her mother to go back to Verdenton, and telegraph to her father; but she put no hope in that. How she trembled, as she passed each fork in the rough and ill-marked country road, lest she should take the right-hand when she ought to turn to the left, and so lose precious, priceless moments! How her heart beat with joy when she came upon any remembered landmark! And all the time her mind was full of tumultuous prayer. Sometimes it bubbled over her lips in tender, disjointed accents.

"Father! Papa, dear, dear Papa!" she cried to the bright still night that lay around; and then the tears burst over the quivering lids, and ran down the fair cheeks in torrents. She pressed her hand to her heart as she fancied that a gleam of redder light shot athwart the northern sky, and she thought of a terrible bonfire that would rage and glow above that horizon if she failed to bring timely warning of the danger.

How her heart throbbed with thankfulness as she galloped through an avenue of giant oaks at a cross-roads where she remembered stopping with her father one day! He had told her that it was half way from Glenville to Warrington. He had watered their horses there; and she remembered every word of pleasant badinage he had addressed to her as they rode home. Had one ever before so dear, so tender a parent? The tears came again; but she drove them back with a half-involuntary laugh. "Not now, not now!" she said. "No; nor at all. They shall not come at all; for I will save him. O God, help me! I am but a weak girl. Why did the letter come so late? But I *will* save him! Help me, Heaven! — guide and help!"

She glanced at her watch as she passed from under the shade of the oaks, and, as she held the dial up to the moonlight, gave a scream of joy. It was just past the stroke of nine. She had still an hour, and half the distance had been accomplished in half that time. She had no fear of her horse. Pressing on now in the swinging fox-walk which he took whenever the character of the road or the mood of his rider demanded, there was no sign of weariness. As he threw his head upon one side and the other, as if asking to be allowed to press on, she saw his dark eye gleam with the fire of the inveterate racer. His thin nostrils were distended; but his breath came regularly and full. She had not forgotten, even in her haste and fright, the lessons her father had taught; but, as soon as she could control her horse, she had spared him, and compelled him to husband his strength. Her spirits rose at the prospect. She even caroled a bit of exultant song as Young Lollard swept on through a forest of towering pines, with a white sand-cushion stretched beneath his feet. The fragrance of the pines came to her nostrils, and with it the thought of frankincense, and that brought up the hymns of her childhood. The Star in the East, the Babe of Bethlehem, the Great Deliverer, — all swept across her wrapt vision; and then came the priceless promise, "I will not leave thee, nor forsake."

Still on and on the brave horse bore her with untiring limb. Half the remaining distance is now consumed, and she comes to a place where the road forks, not once, but into four branches. It is in the midst of a level old field covered with a thick growth of scrubby pines. Through the masses of thick green are white lanes which stretch away in every direction, with no visible difference save in the density or frequency of the shadows which fall across them. She tries to think which of the many intersecting paths lead to her destination. She tries this and then that for a few steps, consults the stars to determine in what direction Glenville lies, and has almost decided upon the first to the right, when she hears a sound which turns her blood to ice in her veins.

A shrill whistle sounds to the left, — once, twice, thrice, — and then it is answered from the road in front. There are two others. O God! if she but knew which road to take! She knows well enough the meaning of those signals. She has heard them before. The masked cavaliers are closing in upon her; and, as if frozen to stone, she sits her horse in the clear moonlight, and can not choose.

She is not thinking of herself. It is not for herself that she fears; but there has come over her a horrible numbing sensation that she is lost, that she does not know which road leads to those she seeks to save; and at the same time there comes the certain conviction that to err would be fatal. There are but two roads now to choose from, since she has heard the fateful signals from the left and front: but how much depends upon that choice! "It must be this," she says to herself; and, as she says it, the sickening conviction comes, "No, no: it is the other!" She hears hoof-strokes upon the road in front, on that to her left, and now, too, on that which turns sheer to the right. From one to the other the whistle sounds, — sharp, short signals. Her heart sinks within her. She has halted at the very rendezvous of the enemy. They are all about her. To attempt to ride down either road now is to invite destruction.

She woke from her stupor when the first horseman came in sight, and thanked God for her dark horse and colorless habit. She urged young Lollard among the dense scrub-pines which grew between the two roads from which she knew that she must choose, turned his head back towards the point of intersection, drew her revolver, leaned over upon his neck, and peered through the overhanging branches. She patted her horse's head, and whispered to him softly to keep him still.

Hardly had she placed herself in hiding before the open space around the intersecting roads was alive with disguised horsemen. She could catch glimpses of their figures as she gazed through the clustering spines. Three men came into the road which ran along to the right of where she stood. They were hardly five steps from where she lay, panting, but determined, on the faithful horse, which moved not a muscle. Once he had neighed before they came so near; but there were so many horses neighing and snuffing, that no one had heeded it. She remembered a little flask which Maggie had put into her pocket. It was whiskey. She put up her revolver, drew out the flask, opened it, poured some in her hand, and, leaning forward, rubbed it on the horse's nose. He did not offer to neigh again.

One of the men who stood near her spoke.

"Gentlemen, I am the East Commander of Camp No. 5 of Pultowa County."

"And I, of Camp No. 8, of Wayne."

"And I, of No. 12, Sevier."

"You are the men I expected to meet," said the first.

"We were ordered to report to you," said the others.

"This is Bentley's Cross, then, I presume."

"The same."

"Four miles from Glenville, I believe?"

"Nigh about that," said one of the others.

"We leave this road about a mile and a half from this place?"

"Yes, and cross by a country way to the river-road."

"What is the distance to the river-road by this route?"

"Not far from five miles."

"It is now about half-past nine; so that there is no haste. How many men have you each?"

"Thirty-two from No. 8."

"Thirty-one from No. 12."

"I have myself *forty*. Are yours informed of the work on hand?"

"Not a word."

"Are we quite secure here?"

"I have had the roads picketed since sundown," answered one. "I myself just came from the south, not ten minutes before you signaled."

"Ah! I thought I heard a horse on that road."

"Has the party we want left Verdenton?"

"A messenger from Glenville says he is on the train with the carpet-bagger Servosse."

"Going home with him?"

"Yes."

"The decree does not cover Servosse?"

"No."

"I don't half like the business, anyhow, and am not inclined to go beyond express orders. What do you say about it?" asked the leader.

"Hadn't we better say the decree covers both?" asked one.

"I can't do it," said the leader with decision.

"You remember our rules," said the third, — "'when a party is made up by details from different camps, it shall constitute a camp so far as to regulate its own action; and all

matters pertaining to such action which the officer in command may see fit to submit to it shall be decided by a majority
vote.' I think this had better be left to the camp?"

"I agree with you," said the leader. "But, before we do so,
let's have a drink."

He produced a flask, and they all partook of its contents.
Then they went back to the intersection of the roads, mounted
their horses, and the leader commanded, "Attention!"

The men gathered closer, and then all was still. Then the
leader said, in words distinctly heard by the trembling girl, —

"Gentlemen, we have met here, under a solemn and duly
authenticated decree of a properly organized camp of the
county of Rockford, to execute for them the extreme penalty
of our order upon Thomas Denton, in the way and manner
therein prescribed. This unpleasant duty of course will be
done as becomes earnest men. We are, however, informed
that there will be with the said Denton at the time we are
dircted to take him another notorious Radical well known
to you all, Colonel Comfort Servosse. He is not included in
the decree; and I now submit for your determination the
question, 'What shall be done with him?' "

There was a moment's buzz in the crowd.

One careless-toned fellow said that he thought it would be
well enough to wait till they caught their hare before cooking it. It was not the first time a squad had thought they had
Servosse in their power; but they had never ruffled a hair of
his head yet.

The leader commanded, "Order!" and one of the associate
Commanders moved that the same decree be made against him
as against the said Denton. Then the vote was taken. All
were in the affirmative, except the loud-voiced young man who
had spoken before, who said with emphasis, —

"No, by Granny! I'm not in favor of killing anybody! I'll
have you know, gentlemen, it's neither a pleasant nor a safe

business. First we know, we'll all be running our necks into hemp. It's what we call murder, gentlemen, in civilized and Christian countries!"

"Order!" cried the commander.

"Oh, you needn't yell at me!" said the young man fearlessly. "I'm not afraid of anybody here, nor all of you. Mel. Gurney and I came just to take some friends' places who couldn't obey the summons, — we're not bound to stay, but I suppose I shall go along. I don't like it, though, and, if I get much sicker, I shall leave. You can count on that!"

"If you stir from your place," said the leader sternly, "I shall put a bullet through you."

"Oh, you go to hell!" retorted the other. "You don't expect to frighten one of the old Louisiana Tigers in that way, do you? Now look here, Jack Carver," he continued, drawing a huge navy revolver, and cocking it coolly, "don't try any such little game on me, 'cause, if ye do, there may be more'n one of us fit for a spy-glass when it's over."

At this, considerable confusion arose; and Lily, with her revolver ready cocked in her hand, turned, and cautiously made her way to the road which had been indicated as the one which led to Glenville. Just as her horse stepped into the path, an overhanging limb caught her hat, and pulled it off, together with the hood of her waterproof, so that her hair fell down again upon her shoulders. She hardly noticed the fact in her excitement, and, if she had, could not have stopped to repair the accident. She kept her horse upon the shady side, walking upon the grass as much as possible to prevent attracting attention, watching on all sides for any scattered members of the Klan. She had proceeded thus about a hundred and fifty yards, when she came to a turn in the road, and saw, sitting before her in the moonlight, one of the disguised horsemen, evidently a sentry who had been stationed there to see that no one came upon the camp unexpectedly. He was facing the

other way, but just at that instant turned, and, seeing her indis-
tinctly in the shadow, cried out at once, —

"Who's there? Halt!"

They were not twenty yards apart. Young Lollard was
trembling with excitement under the tightly-drawn rein.
Lily thought of her father half-prayerfully, half-fiercely,
bowed close over her horse's neck, and braced herself in the
saddle, with every muscle as tense as those of the tiger waiting for his leap. Almost before the words were out of the
sentry's mouth, she had given Young Lollard the spur, and
shot like an arrow into the bright moonlight, straight towards
the black muffled horseman.

"My God!" he cried, amazed at the sudden apparition.

She was close upon him in an instant. There was a shot;
his startled horse sprang aside, and Lily, urging Young Lollard to his utmost speed, was flying down the road toward
Glenville. She heard an uproar behind, — shouts, and one
or two shots. On, on, she sped. She knew now every foot
of the road beyond. She looked back, and saw her pursuers
swarming out of the wood into the moonlight. Just then she
was in shadow. A mile, two miles, were passed. She drew
in her horse to listen. There was the noise of a horse's hoofs
coming down a hill she had just descended, as her gallant
steed bore her, almost with undiminished stride, up the opposite slope. She laughed, even in her terrible excitement, at the
very thought that any one should attempt to overtake her.

> "They'll have fleet steeds that follow, quoth young
> Lochinvar,"

she hummed as she patted Young Lollard's outstretched
neck. She turned when they reached the summit, her long hair
streaming backward in the moonlight like a golden banner,
and saw the solitary horseman on the opposite slope; then
turned back, and passed over the hill. He halted as she dashed
out of sight, and after a moment turned round, and soon met

the entire camp, now in perfect order, galloping forward dark and silent as fate. The Commander halted as they met the returning sentinel.

"What was it?" he asked quickly.

"Nothing," replied the sentinel carelessly. "I was sitting there at the turn examining my revolver, when a rabbit ran across the road, and frightened my mare. She jumped, and the pistol went off. It happened to graze my left arm, so I could not hold the reins; and she like to have taken me into Glenville before I could pull her up."

"I'm glad that's all," said the officer, with a sigh of relief. "Did it hurt you much?"

"Well, it's used that arm up, for the present."

A hasty examination showed this to be true, and the reckless-talking young man was detailed to accompany him to some place for treatment and safety, while the others passed on to perform their horrible task.

The train from Verdenton had reached and left Glenville. The incomers had been divided between the rival hotels, the porters had removed the luggage, and the agent was just entering his office, when a foam-flecked horse with bloody nostrils and fiery eyes, ridden by a young girl with a white, set face, and fair, flowing hair, dashed up to the station.

"Judge Denton!" the rider shrieked.

The agent had but time to motion with his hand, and she had swept on towards a carriage which was being swiftly driven away from the station, and which was just visible at the turn of the village street.

"Papa, Papa!" shrieked the girlish voice as she swept on.

A frightened face glanced backward from the carriage, and in an instant Comfort Servosse was standing in the path of the rushing steed.

"Ho, Lollard!" he shouted, in a voice which rang over the sleepy town like a trumpet-note.

The amazed horse veered quickly to one side, and stopped as if stricken to stone, while Lily fell insensible into her father's arms. When she recovered, he was bending over her with a look in his eyes which she will never forget.

CHAPTER XXXVII

THE "REB" VIEW OF IT

Lily had faltered out her message of horror even in the unconscious moments when she was being carried in her father's arms to the hotel. Indeed, her unexpected appearance, and clamorous haste to prevent her father's departure from the town, would have been sufficient to inform him that she knew of some danger that impended. Her unconscious mutterings had still further advised him of the character of the danger and the fact that she herself had narrowly escaped. This was all he could glean from her. Her over-taxed system had given way with excitement and fatigue, and, fortunately for her, she slept. A physician was called, who, after examination of her condition, directed that she should in no event be aroused. A telegram from Metta, which should have been delivered on the arrival of the train, confirmed the conclusion at which Servosse had arrived. He left the bedside of the daughter who to his eyes had grown to womanhood since the noon of the day before, but once during the night, and that was but to telegraph to Metta, to provide that Young Lollard should be well cared for, and to consult with Judge Denton, who had remained with them in the town. It was by no means certain that the danger had passed by: so these two men concluded to watch until morning.

It was broad daylight when Lily opened her eyes, to find her father holding her hand, and gazing upon her with inexpressible affection. She told him all as soon as her weakness and her sobs would permit, and was more than repaid for all she had dared and suffered by the fervent embrace and the tremulous "God bless you, my daughter!" which followed her recital. Then he ordered some refreshments for her, and recommended further sleep, while he went to recount her story to his friend.

Somehow the story seemed to have leaked out during the night, and every one about the town was aware of its main features. That there had been a raid intended, nay, that it had even been organized, and proceeded to the bridge across the river, for the purpose of intercepting Judge Denton on his way home, was undoubted. That the party had rendezvoused at Bentley's Cross-Roads was also known, as well as the fact that the judge's carriage had been stopped and turned back, just on the outskirts of Glenville, by the arrival of the daughter of Colonel Servosse, bareheaded, and mounted on a foaming steed. That she had come from Warrington was presumed, and that she must have passed Bentley's Cross about the time of the rendezvous was more than probable. Added to this was the fact that a countryman coming to market early had brought in a lady's riding-hat which he had found at the very spot where the Klan had met. He was closely examined as to the appearance of the ground, and the precise point at which he found it. Of course, it was by no means sure that it was Miss Lily's hat; but such was evidently the impression. The loud-voiced young man who had been detailed to take care of the wounded sentinel, and who had come into the same town with his charge, volunteered to ascertain that fact, and took the hat into his possession. Returning to the hotel, and entering the room where a young man lounged upon the bed, with his left arm in a sling, he exclaimed, —

"I thought it was mighty queer that a rabbit had made Melville Gurney shoot himself, and let his horse run away too. I think I understand it now."

He laid the hat upon the bed beside his friend as he spoke. Melville Gurney recognized it in an instant; but he tried to betray no emotion, as he asked, —

"Well, what is it you understand, John Burleson?"

"The whole thing. I see it now from beginning to end. The little Yankee girl had just come to the Cross when our bands began to close in on her. She hid in the pines, — probably right there at the Forks, — and no doubt saw and heard every thing that went on. By Gad! she's a plucky little piece! But how the deuce do you suppose she kept that horse still, with a hundred horses all around her? Gad! it was close quarters! Then, as she is coming out, she stumbles on Mr. Melville Gurney standing sentry over that devil's gang of respectable murderers, shoots him before he has time to say Jack Robinson, and comes sailing in here like a bird, on that magnificent thorough-bred, overhauls Judge Denton's carriage, and saves her father's life like a heroine, and a lady too, as she is. Dang my buttons if I ain't ready to kiss the hem of her garments even! Mel. Gurney, I'll be hanged if I don't envy you the pleasure of being shot by such a splendid plucky little girl! D'ye know her? Ever met her?"

"Yes."

"Of course. They say she knows almost as many people as her father, who, by the way, Mel., is no slouch, either. I know him, and like him too, if he is a carpet-bagger. I'm glad I put in a good word for him last night. No doubt she heard me. Mel. Gurney, I'm in luck for once. Give me that hat! What am I going to do with it? Why, restore it to the owner, make my peace with her pa and Judge Denton, and in the fullness of time offer her my hand and heart."

"Pshaw!" exclaimed Gurney.

"Pshaw? My dear friend, you seem smitten with a big disgust all at once. Perhaps you would like to take my place? Remember you can't have all the good things. It's enough for you to have her sling a lump of cold lead through your carcass. Be thankful for what you enjoy, and don't envy other people their little pleasures."

"I wish you would stop fooling, and talk sense for a moment, Burleson," said Gurney fretfully.

"Hear him now! As if I had been doing any thing else! By Gad! the more sense I talk, the less I am appreciated. Witness Jake Carver last night, and Mel. Gurney this morning. I'm no spring-chicken; and, allowing me to be the judge, I feel free to say that I have never listened to more sound and convincing sense than flowed from these lips on those two occasions," responded Burleson.

"Are you in earnest?" asked Gurney.

"What, about the sense? Entirely so."

"No, about Miss Lily Servosse," said Gurney.

"And the proffer of my heart and hand?" answered Burleson. "No. *Unfortunately*, — don't you blow on me, and tell that I ever used that word; but in earnest truth I never came nearer feeling it, — unfortunately, I say, I am, as you have reason to know, under bonds to confer my precious personality upon another, — a Miss Lily too, (thank Heaven for the name, at least!) — and so must deny myself the distinguished privilege I for a moment dreamed of. No, I'm not in earnest about that part of it."

"Well, I am," said Gurney emphatically.

"The devil you say!" exclaimed Burleson in surprise. "You don't mean it!"

"I will win and wed Lily Servosse, if I can," said Gurney modestly.

"Well, *I* swear!" exclaimed Burleson. "But do you know, old fellow, I don't think you put that in the hypothetical without reason? It's my notion you'll have a hard time of it, even if you manage to pull through at all on that line. Remember, old fellow, your family, position, and all that, won't count a rush for you in this matter. These carpet-baggers don't care a continental cuss how many niggers your ancestors had. Then your father is an especial antagonist of Servosse;

and for yourself — all that *I* can see that you have to put up is, that you went along with a crowd of respectable gentlemen to kill her father, and would have done so, but for her nerve: in fact, you can claim very justly that you would have prevented her saving him, if she had not shot you, and effected her escape."

"That is not so. Her father was not included in the decree, and I had no reason to suppose he would be in company with Denton," interrupted Gurney.

"Well, we will say on your way to roast — yes, by Heaven! to *roast alive* — Judge Denton! Think of that, will you? General Gurney's son, in the middle of the nineteenth century, nay, almost in its last quarter, — in the blaze of American freedom and civilization at all events, — goes out by night to broil a neighbor, without even the cannibal's excuse of hunger! Bah! that's a fine plea for a lover, isn't it?"

"My God, Burleson!" cried Gurney, jumping up. "You don't think she'll look at it in that light, do you?"

"Why not? Oughtn't any decent woman to do so, not to say a carpet-bagger's daughter? I vow I shouldn't blame her if she took another shot at you for your impudence!"

"Nor I either, Burleson, that's a fact!" said Gurney musingly.

"Ha, ha, ha!" laughed Burleson. "I understand that rabbit story now. You recognized Miss Lily?"

"Of course," said Gurney simply.

"'Of course,' it is, indeed!" said Burleson. "I might have known it would have taken more than one broken arm to make Mel. Gurney let a rider run his guard unhurt. You recognized her, and galloped after her to prevent suspicion, and on the way invented that story about the rabbit, and your pistol going off. By Gad! it was a gallant thing, old fellow, if we were on a heathen errand. Give me your hand, my boy! It's not so bad, after all. Perhaps Miss Lily might make a decent man of you in time; though we both ought to be hanged, that's a fact!"

"I never thought of it in that way, Burleson; but it *is* horrible," said Gurney, with a shudder.

"Horrible? — it's hellish, Mel. Gurney! That's what it is! If I were the Yankees, and had the power of the government, I wouldn't see these things go on one hour. By Gad! I'm ashamed of them as Americans! When the war was going on and we met them in battle, there was always one satisfaction, whoever got "fanned out," — it was always our own folks that did it, and one couldn't well help being proud of the job. I tell you what, Mel., there's been many a time when I could hardly tell which I was proudest of, — Yank, or Reb. There was Gettysburg, now! You know I was in the artillery, and had a better chance to see the *ensemble* of a battle than one in the infantry line. We had been pouring a perfect hell of shot upon the cemetery for an hour, when the charge was ordered, and we ceased firing. We were black and grim, and almost deaf with the continuous roar. I remember the sweat poured down the sooty faces of my gun-mates, and I don't suppose there was a dry rag about them. Some leaned on the smoking piece, and some threw themselves on the ground; but every one kept his eyes riveted on that line of bright steel and dirty gray which was sweeping up to the low wall that we had been salting with fire so long. We thought they would go over it as the sea breaches a sand-dike. But we were mistaken. Those men who had hung to their ground through it all, sent their plague of leaden death in our fellows' faces, and met them at the point of the bayonet as coolly and stubbornly as if it were but the opening of the ball, instead of its last *gallopade*. Bad as I felt when our fellows fell back, I could have given three cheers for those Yanks with a will. I thought then, that if the worst came, as I always believed it would, we could have a genuine pride in our conquerors.

"And so I had, until this Ku-Klux business came up. I told our fellows on the start, they would burn their fingers; for I could not forget that the men they were whipping and hanging were the friends of those same Yankees, — the only friends they had here too, — and I had no idea that *such* men would suffer them to be abused at that rate. Some of the boys got the notion, however, that I was afraid; and I went in just to show them I was not. For a time I looked every day for an earthquake, and, when it didn't come, I felt an unutterable contempt for the whole Yankee nation; and damn *me* if I don't feel it yet! I really pity this man, Servosse! He feels ashamed of his people, and knows that even the white Republicans — poor shotes as many of them are — despise the whining, canting sycophancy which makes their Northern allies abandon helpless friends to powerful enemies. I tell you what, Mel. Gurney, if we Southerners had come out ahead, and had such friends as these niggers and Union men, with now and then one of our own kidney, scattered through the North, we would have gone through *hell-fire* before we would have deserted them in this way!"

"That is no justification to us, though," said Gurney, who was now walking back and forth across the room, quite forgetful of the pain of his arm.

"On the contrary, it makes it worse," said Burleson. "We are advancing the power of a party to which we are devoted, it is true; but in so doing we are merely putting power in the hands of its worst elements, against whom we shall have to rebel sooner or later. The leaders in these cowardly raids — such men as Jake Carver and a hundred more whom I could name — will be our representatives, senators, legislators, judges, and so forth, hereafter. It is the simple rule of human nature. Leadership in any public movement is the sure pathway to public honor. It has been so since the war. Look at the men to whom we have given civic honors. How many of them would have been heard of, but for their soldiering? In that case, I don't complain of it. They were all brave men, though some were great fools. But when it comes to preferring midnight murderers and brutal assassins for legislators and governors and judges, and the like, simply *because* they were leaders in crime, I swear, Mel. Gurney, it comes hard! Some time or other we shall be sick and ashamed of it."

"I am that now," said Gurney.

"No doubt; especially since you have thought how Lily Servosse must look at it. Now, I'll tell you what, Mel., I like you, and I like Servosse's little girl too. I believe you can get her, — after a while, you know, — if you've got pluck enough to own up and reform, 'repent and be baptized,' you know. And it *will* be a baptism to you: you can bet on that, — a baptism of fire!"

"You don't suppose I'd 'peach,' do you, John Burleson?" said Gurney, turning indignantly towards his friend.

"Hell! You don't think I've turned fool, do you?" asked Burleson, with equal indignation. "See here, Gurney, you and I were boys together. Did you ever know me to do a mean thing?"

"Never!"

"Well now, listen. I'm going to bolt this whole business. I'm not going to tell on anybody else (you know I'd be drawn and quartered first); but I'm going to own up *my* connection with it, tell as much as I can, without implicating any one else, and do my best to break it up. I never thought of just this way of doing it before, and should not have hit on it now but for your sake."

"For my sake?" asked Gurney in surprise.

"Yes, for your sake. Don't you see you will have to own up in this way, before either father or daughter will look at you?"

"Well?"

"Well? I'll just go ahead and break the way, that's all."

"When will you begin?"

"To-day — now!"

"How?"

"I shall go down upon the street, and publish as much as I well can of this raid, and try to laud the pluck of that young lady about half as highly as it deserves. God bless her! I would like to kiss the place where she has set her foot, just to show my appreciation of her!"

"Do you really think you had better venture upon such a course? It might be a very dangerous business," said Gurney.

"The very reason above all others why John Burleson should undertake the job. Some one must do it, and it would not do for you to be the first. It's not often one has a chance to serve his friend and do a patriotic duty at once. It's all out now, in fact. The guesses and rumors that are afloat are within an ace of the facts. There may as well be some advantage gained by that, as not. I shall take the young lady her hat" —

"Let me do that, if you please," said Gurney anxiously.

"All right, if you think you can face the fire."

So down upon the street went John Burleson. The first man whom he met ascending the steps of the hotel was Judge Denton. Extending his hand cordially, he said in a voice that all could hear, —

"Judge, I am ashamed to say I was in that hellish affair last night. I did not know what it was till we got to the Cross, nor did any of them but the Commanders. That made no difference, though. We were in for it, and I do not doubt would have carried it through, but for Miss Lily Servosse. She deserves a statue, judge. I've no excuse to make. I'm not a child, and was not deceived. Any time you want me, I'm ready to plead guilty to any thing I've done. In any event, this is the last raid I shall join, and the last that will be made, if I can prevent it."

He stalked off, leaving the astonished judge to gaze after him, and wonder if he had heard aright. Burleson repeated the same language, with various *addenda*, to every group of loungers he met on the street, so that in a quarter of an hour the word had gone out that John Burleson had "gone back" on the Ku-Klux. It spread like wildfire. He had occupied a prominent place in the order, and it was known that he knew many fatal secrets connected with it. It was telegraphed in every direction, and went from man to man among the members of the Klan in a dozen counties where he was well known. They knew that he could not be silenced by threats or bribes. A great fear took hold of them when they heard it, and many fled the county without further inquiry. The little town in which they were was almost deserted in an hour. Perceiving this effect, and thoroughly comprehending its cause, John Burleson approached Judge Denton and Colonel Servosse, and said to them, —

"Gentlemen, the train will be here in an hour. I have no right to advise with regard to your movements; but you will allow me to say that I think, after what occurred last night, that the more prudent course would be for Judge Denton to return with us to Verdenton, and then spend a few days at Warrington. It will be only an exchange of hospitalities anyhow.

"On the contrary," said Denton, "I was just trying to persuade Colonel Servosse to send for his wife, and make his visit, despite our *contretemps* last night."

"It is quite impossible," said Servosse. "Lily says she could never endure to cross that bridge; and, in her present condition, I do not think she should be subjected to any unnecessary excitement."

"Certainly not!" said Denton. "After her heroism of last night, she is entitled to the gratification of her every wish."

"That being your feeling," said Servosse, "I am emboldened

to second Mr. Burleson's view by saying that it is my daughter's especial desire that you should come home with us. She is under a terrible apprehension in regard to the future, and especially in reference to you, sir. She thinks, that, if you should go off into the country there, you would be sure to be assassinated. She thinks there is far less danger, if we are together; not only because there would be more hesitation in attacking two, but because, being both men of some prominence, our joint assassination would be more likely to attract the attention, and awaken the resentment, of the government and the people of the North, than our individual destruction. Indeed, she has an idea that the very fact of my Northern birth — my prominence as a 'carpet-bagger,' so to speak — is in itself a sort of protection."

"And in that she is quite correct," said Burleson. "I have wondered that it has not occurred to you gentlemen before, to inquire why it is that so few Northern men of any standing or position have been molested. It's not been from any kindly feeling for them, I assure you; but there has been a notion that if such men as you — Northern men of some prominence — were interfered with, it might stir up a hornet's nest that would make us trouble. This very fact is all that has saved more than one man whom I could name."

"That is her very idea," said Servosse, "and there may be some truth in it. Certainly Mr. Burleson should know" he added, with a meaning glance at Denton; for the judge was too suspicious, and the new fact was too unaccountable to allow him yet to put full confidence in the professed change of that gentleman. His suspicion was increased by the next remark of Burleson.

"By the way," he said, "it never occurred to me before; but how on earth did Miss Lily get information of that raid? I don't reckon she was out riding your pet racing-horse at that time of night just for fun!"

"We do not feel at liberty to speak of that at this time," said Comfort seriously.

"All right!" responded Burleson. "I only hope it is a hole that will let light in upon the thing. I have always supposed it would come, and have known, that, if one ever pipped the shell, a thousand would try to be the first to get their heads out. If the idea once goes out, Judge, that any one has given the thing away, you will have your hands full taking confessions. They will be full of horrors too, — more than you ever dreamed of. You'll think you've tilted off the lid of the bottomless pit, and that the devils are pouring out by brigades."

"Perhaps," said Denton, with a look of keen scrutiny, "you could tell something yourself?"

"Whether I could or not," said Burleson, "is all the same. You know me well enough, Judge, to know that I *will not* tell any thing which would compromise anybody else. I am willing to admit that I belonged to this organization, that I was the chief of a county, because I think it is necessary that I should do so in order to break it up; but I do not intend to confess myself into the penitentiary nor on to the gallows. Yet I would go there sooner than to betray those who have trusted their lives and honor with me. So far as I can go without such betrayal, I am willing to act with you. That is one reason I wish you to return to Verdenton: I want it clearly understood that I have renounced the whole business. It is by no means a safe proceeding, and I may have to turn in with you, gentlemen, and fight for my life. If it comes to that, I propose to make every edge cut, and, if I go down, I mean to have lots of good company. I would like to have you go in order to be convenient if the fight comes!"

Judge Denton yielded to these solicitations, and accompanied his friends, first sending word to his family to follow on the next day.

Before the train left, Melville Gurney sent a servant to

Colonel Servosse, asking a moment's interview. When Servosse came to his room, and, seeing his injury, asked the cause, he betrayed himself by asking, —

"And has not your daughter told you, sir?"

"My God!" said Servosse, sinking into a chair, overwhelmed with amazement. "Was it you, Mr. Gurney? Can it be that the son of one who has known me so long as your father, even though as an opponent, should have engaged in an attempt on my life? I could not have believed it."

He covered his face with his hands, and shuddered as he spoke.

"I assure you, Colonel Servosse," said Gurney, "I had no idea that such was the purpose of the raid, nor, indeed, did I know its purpose. I was well aware that it must be an unlawful one, however, and can not blame you for the horror you manifest. I am horrified myself, and am amazed that I could ever have regarded it otherwise."

"I can not understand it, — I can not understand it," said the carpet-bagger. "I always thought your father was an honest, high-minded man, and a good citizen."

"And so he is, sir," said Gurney hotly. "There is none better nor purer!"

"And you," said Servosse, rising, and looking keenly at him, —"*you* are a *murderer!*"

"I suppose," answered Gurney, with some confusion, "that I should have been, constructively at least, but for your daughter's daring interference."

"Nay, you were already," said Servosse severely. "You had started out on an unlawful errand, and were ready to shed blood, if need were, to accomplish it, — whether it were my blood or another's it is immaterial to consider. That is almost always the mental condition of the murderer. Murder is usually a means, not an end."

"It is a hard word, Colonel Servosse; yet I do not know but

I must submit," said Gurney. "I wish to say, however, that I did not engage in this at the wish or suggestion, nor with the knowledge, of my father. Indeed, my greatest trouble comes from the fact that I must inform him of the fact."

"Gad!" said Burleson, who had entered unperceived by both, "you needn't trouble yourself so much about that. He belongs to it himself."

"John Burleson!" cried Gurney, springing to his feet.

"Oh, you needn't mind!" said Burleson. "Colonel Servosse is too much of a gentleman to take advantage of such a statement made by me at this time." He turned, and bowed toward Servosse as he spoke.

"Certainly," said the latter. "I should not think of using a private conversation."

"It is not that!" exclaimed Gurney, — "not that at all! But it is false!"

"H'st! Steady, my young friend!" said Burleson hotly. "I happen to know whereof I speak. I was present, and helped initiate him. Do you believe me now, Mel. Gurney?"

"Great heavens!" exclaimed Gurney. "I did not know that! I would not have believed it but upon your assurance."

"I declare," said the Fool, "I can not understand, — I can not understand!"

"Well," said Burleson, laughing, and taking Lily's hat from the bed, "here is something you can understand, I reckon."

"My daughter's hat!" said Servosse in surprise, looking from one to the other.

"For that matter," said Burleson bluffly, "I brought it here. You see, when Miss Lily rode out of the pines last night, she lost this; and so, when she charged on Gurney there, he recognized her, — for it was as light as day: our chaplain could have seen to read the burial-service, — and, being a fellow that has his wits about him, Gurney quietly jogged on behind her after she had shot him, with that broken arm flop-

ping up and down at every step, until he was sure she had got
clean off, when he came back with a cock-and-bull story about
a rabbit having scared his horse, and his pistol having gone off,
and busted that arm."

"Is that so?" asked Comfort in surprise.

"Lit-er-ally," said Burleson, with distinct enunciation. "Not
a man in that camp had any idea that a woman had witnessed
its proceedings, until we heard of your daughter having
interrupted your journey. Even then it was a mere surmise,
except with Gurney here."

"Then," said Servosse, extending his hand to Gurney, "it
seems I have to thank you for an intent to save my daughter."

"Indeed, sir," replied Gurney, "with that horse, she had
little need of my aid."

"Young Lollard is not easily matched," said Servosse, with
some pride. "But that does not detract from the merit of
your intention. I suppose," he added, smiling, and touching
the hat, "that you wish me to relieve you of this toy."

"On the contrary," said Gurney earnestly, "my request
for this interview was because I desired to ask your leave to
return it to the owner myself."

"Well, sir," said Servosse thoughtfully, "I do not see but
you have earned the right to do so. I will see if she can receive
you."

A few moments later, Melville Gurney, somewhat weak and
tremulous from the loss of blood and subsequent excitement,
came down stairs, leaning on the arm of his friend Burleson,
and was ushered into the parlor of the hotel, where Lily Servosse leaned upon her father's arm. Pale and trembling, he
presented the hat with a low bow, and withdrew without a
word.

"Well, I swear!" said Burleson a minute after, "if I had
thought you would show the white feather just at the last, I
never would have seconded you!"

Comfort Servosse never once dreamed that the trembling creature clinging to his arm, and dropping tears upon the hat as she brushed and picked at it, was any thing more than a simple child. So he said, with an amused smile, —

"It's not even rumpled, is it, dear?"

CHAPTER XXXVIII

"AND ALL THE WORLD WAS IN A SEA"

T HE train which brought Lily and her father, Judge Denton, Burleson, and Gurney to Verdenton, did not arrive unnoted. The report of Lily's heroic ride, and of Burleson's defection from the Klan, had preceded it; and a great crowd had collected, anxious for a sight of the brave girl who had courage and wit enough to circumvent the Ku-Klux, and of the yet braver man, who, having been one of their number, had yet courage to denounce them.

What he would say, what he would do, there was the utmost anxiety to know. For once no imputation was made upon the motives of one who saw fit to stem the popular current. Men cursed and denounced him; but it was for what he had done, or was supposed to have done, and not on account of the motives which they believed to have animated him.

No one attributed either cowardice, ambition, or avariciousness to John Burleson. He was known to have disapproved from the first, at least of all the violent features of the organization, and to have done not a little to prevent their being carried into execution. He had been advanced to be the Chief of the County, both because of his known and acknowledged capacity for organization and leadership, and also because this very disinclination to promote unlawful acts had met the approval of many of the more conservative members of the order. As he had said, he went upon the raid which we have described simply to accommodate a friend, who, being required to attend, had afterward sickened. He was recognized as bold, generous, and impulsive. He was one of the very few *private* soldiers who survived the surrender of the Confederate armies. Entering the service at the very outset of the war, he had never failed to perform his full duty, and not seldom had done considerably more; yet he had received no promotion, and, since the collapse of the Rebellion, not a sign of any military title had attached itself to his name. The man who should have saluted him as "Captain" would probably have been whipped first, and invited to drink afterwards, for his temerity. The reason of this was twofold. In the first place, young Burleson, a man of unusually broad and catholic feeling, and of varied personal experience and wide observation, was as thoroughly convinced of the hopelessness of the Confederate cause in the field of battle at the outset of the war as at its close. This view he did not hesitate to declare on all occasions; and, when reproved for so doing by an upstart superior, he had the boldness and arrogance to assure the official, that, if he knew half as much as himself, he would desert to the Yankees in two days. Besides this, it suited his humor to boast of his disinclination for a military life. When offered promotion, he curtly declined it, on the ground that he did not wish to do any thing that might remove his dislike for the service.

Of course such a man, though he had been of the ripest culture and most marked capacity, was only fitted for the place of a private soldier; and so a soldier he remained, always scornful of control, and utterly regardless of the Pharisaical distinctions of rank, respected for his unshrinking bluntness, and feared for his terrible directness of thought, and explicitness of statement. He was perhaps the most dangerous man who could have renounced his fealty to the Klan.

As he stepped upon the platform at Verdenton, a man whom he knew to be a very prominent member of the Klan touched him upon the shoulder, and said, with a meaning look towards the rear of the train, —

"Let me see you a moment."

"Oh, go to the devil!" said Burleson, in a loud but good-natured tone of voice. "I know what you want; and I had just as lief tell you here as around the corner, or in the camp. I am neither afraid nor ashamed. I am out of it, and opposed to it root and branch. If any one has any thing he wants to say or do about it, he knows where to find John Burleson.

"Judge Denton!" he cried in the same tone, as that gentleman appeared on the platform, "these people are my Ku-Klux friends and neighbors, who have come to see if John Burleson has the pluck to renounce what he was a fool for engaging in, and knew himself to be such at the time. They don't look like Ku-Klux, do they? But they are — nearly every man you can see. I don't believe there are a dozen white men on this platform whom I don't know to be such, and have not seen in their meetings more than once. They are most of them church-members, and all of them respectable. You ought to see them with their gowns and masks on! they look savage enough then. You know a good many of them, Judge, and will get acquainted with them all if Justice ever gets her dues. There's right smart of men here who to my knowledge deserve a hanging."

Such language as this increased the consternation which already prevailed; and, before it was ended, nearly every white man had left the platform, and only a crowd of wondering colored men remained to grin applause to his concluding remarks. He knew that he had thrown a bomb, but he was not ignorant that its explosion might endanger himself. He knew very thoroughly the temper of the people whom he had been addressing, and did not under-estimate his own danger. So when he had bidden good-by to Gurney, who went on to his home, he went and assisted his other fellow-travelers to enter their carriage. Then he took the Fool aside, and said in a low voice, —

"Colonel Servosse, I dislike to ask a favor of you; but it may be that I shall be able to render you a like service before long. You know what has occurred. If I remain here tonight, the probabilities are that I shall not be troubled about getting up in the morning. I wish you would invite me to Warrington for a day or two. I do not think you will be attacked there. If you should, you would not find me entirely useless in the defense. I think we three would make a bad crowd for any force to attack. In a short time we can tell what will be the result. Either they will cry for mercy, or we must fight. I don't know which it will be as yet."

"Certainly, certainly, Mr. Burleson!" said Servosse heartily. "I have been studying for the last hour, as to whether I ought not to invite both you and your friend."

"Oh, he is all right!" said Burleson lightly. "He is not tainted with my offense. No one regards him now except as the poor fellow who had the good fortune to be shot by your daughter."

"The fact is," said Servosse apologetically, "I have become so suspicious since I have been a 'carpet-bagger,' that I am never quite sure whether it is expected or desired that I should either tender or receive hospitality as a matter of course. Besides that, you will permit me to confess that I was by no means sure that you were in earnest until within the last few minutes. Of course we shall be glad to have you at Warrington, and hope you may find it both safe and agreeable there, though I confess I share your apprehensions."

It was a very thoughtful company which drove to Warrington that evening. Metta, with the overwrought Lily in her arms, listened, with overflowing eyes and irrepressible sobs, to the girl's broken recital of that adventure which had been so perilous to her, and so providential to her father and one of their guests, whose hearts were of course deeply affected at the thought of the barbarous death they had escaped. The other guest, realizing even more clearly than they both what they had escaped and what still impended, was deeply concerned lest he had added to the peril of those with whom he had sought shelter.

A few colored people had collected at the depot, anxious to welcome those in whom they took so deep an interest, after the great peril they had escaped. A few of them had spoken to the Fool; and all had manifested a sense of the utmost satisfaction, both at their arrival and at what had transpired at the station, but made no clamorous demonstrations of joy. Hardly had they started for home, however, than it became evident that the excitement extended to all classes of society. From almost every house along the road they saw white faces peering at them with troubled and apprehensive looks, while the cabin of every colored man gave them looks and words of cheerful greeting; and, long before they reached Warrington, it became evident that the negroes were hastening from all directions to meet Servosse. Arrived in the neighborhood of his home, the Fool found that the news of his coming had gone before, as well as the report in regard to Burleson's defection from the Klan; and a great crowd of colored people, as well as many of their white political associates, had gathered to congratulate them on their escape, and to make inquiry as to the other report.

It was a most cordial welcome which the Fool and his brave daughter received from these neighbors; and the presence of Judge Denton and Mr. Burleson fully confirmed the rumor in regard to the latter. Several parties who seemed ill at ease with the company which had gathered on the lawn were cordially greeted by Burleson in his loud, careless manner; but they were rendered still more uncomfortable by this, and soon slunk away, one by one, and left only the constantly increasing crowd of colored men and friendly neighbors, whose gratulations could not find sufficient words.

As night came on, it became evident that these good friends, apprehensive of an attack from the Klan, had determined to stand guard about the Fool's house. This was deemed unadvisable; and, after thanking them again for their sympathy, he requested them to disperse, saying that ample precautions had been taken to secure the safety of Warrington, and naming a number of their most devoted white friends who would sleep there that night. So with cheers, and overflowing wishes for their peace and happiness, the colored people dispersed, and an eventful night settled down upon Warrington.

It was a little after dark, and while the company at Warrington were seated at supper, that a man rode up to the gate, who, after the customary hail had been answered by a servant, made some cautious inquiries as to who was within, and then asked to see Mr. Eyebright, a prominent Union man of the neighborhood. On being informed that he was at supper, he finally consented, not without considerable hesitation and evident doubt, to enter and take a seat in the Fool's library, enjoining again and again upon the servant that only he whom he had inquired for should be informed of his presence.

Mr. Eyebright was a portly, well-to-do planter, whose bluff and hearty manliness gave everybody the utmost confidence in his sincerity and kindliness. He had been noted for his unsparing denunciations of the Klan at all times and in all places. To hear him lavish curses upon them as he filled his pipe, or puffed at the long reed stem before a glowing fire, a stranger would have imagined that nothing would have afforded him more intense and unadulterated satisfaction than the utter destruction of the Klan, and the incineration of each and every one of its individual members, unless he should note the twinkle in his soft, lazy-rolling brown eye, or mark the lurking smiles that passed over his rotund countenance, or hid away at the corners of his wide, mobile mouth. At home he was known as the gruffest and kindliest of neighbors; abroad he was accounted one of the most sanguinary and revengeful of the degraded Radicals. A noticeable birthmark had given him a ludicrous nickname, which had contributed not a little to confer upon one of the kindliest and most peaceful of men a reputation for blood-thirstiness and savagery almost equal to that of the original Blue-beard. This quaint and humorous giant, with his assumed ferocity, abundance of unmeaning oaths, and real goodness of heart, was a special favorite of the Fool, whose devotedness he heartily returned. He had insisted upon staying as one of the sort of guard of honor that night, upon the ground that he would be of the utmost value in case of an attack, which was very true; but the Fool knew very well that the prospect of a jolly night beside the smoldering fire in the library, with abundance of good company, and now and then a sup of good peach-brandy, made at his own still, and softened with honey, interspersed with pipes and politics, and stories of "the good old time when we *had* a country," had far more attractions for his fat friend than a night of actual guard-duty.

As they filed out of the dining-room, Eyebright laid one ponderous arm on the Fool's shoulder, and, extending the other over his own expansive person, remarked, —

"After such a supper as that, Colonel, one could not help enjoying a smoke."

Servosse merely answered with a low chuckle, to which Eyebright responded, —

"I know what you mean, you rascal! You think I just staid here to-night to have a good time. Suppose I did, now. It's not often we poor devils can get a dozen good fellows together, and I am for making the most of the opportunity. I tell you, you don't know how hungry I get sometimes to hear somebody else talk sense beside myself [with a laugh]! There's Judge Denton, I'm going to pull him out to-night. They say he's just about the best company in the State — that is, they used to say so before he became one of us 'scalawags.' I s'pose that's had a bad effect on him, as well as the rest of us. There's that Burleson: I like him. He'd be a good fellow if he hadn't been a Ku-Klux. Cussed if I can ever get over that! Oh, don't tell me he's out of it now, and all that! It's like sheep-killing in a dog: once they've learned how, they never forget. I wouldn't sleep in the same room with him for the State! I wouldn't, I swear! I should expect to wake up with my throat cut, at the very least."

"Hush! He'll hear you," said Servosse.

"Oh, that's nothing!" responded Eyebright. "I've been trying to devil him all the evening. He asked me at supper — you were serving the meat, and didn't hear it — if I didn't think Judge Denton and himself represented the lion and the lamb very well. I told him I'd never heard before of a lion that took his lamb *roasted*."

Just then the servant who had waited on the door touched him, and whispered in his ear.

"Wants to see me, you say, Jim?" he asked in surprise. "What does the damn Ku-Klux want of me, Jim?"

"Dunno, sah," answered Jim. "Sed he want ter see you mighty pertickeler."

"He didn't say what about?"

"No, sah."

"Well, give me a light," said he, feeling in one pocket after another for his pipe, "and let me go and see what 'tis, and send him off. We don't want no such cattle around here to-night, Jim. Heh? Where is he?"

"In de libery, sah."

So, puffing his long reed pipe, Eyebright rolled down the steps of the porch, and across the intervening space to the detached wooden building which served as the Fool's office and library. Pushing the door open with his stick, he ascended the steps and entered, exclaiming, as the door swung together behind him, —

"Hello, Kirkwood, is this you? What the devil are you doing here?"

The rest of the company drifted into the spacious sitting-room, and for half an hour Eyebright and his visitor were forgotten. At the end of that time his rotund face appeared at the door, and he hastily motioned to the Fool to come out into the hall. As soon as he came, and the sitting-room door was shut, Eyebright caught his hand, and said, in tones trembling with excitement, —

"Colonel, I'll be damned if the bottom hasn't fallen out at last! Don't ask me any questions. Bring Judge Denton over to the office. Quick! Don't let on that any thing is up! I daren't show my head in there: everybody would know something was wrong. But you Yankees — you could keep your faces straight if the world was coming to an end!"

The Fool did as requested; and, upon their entering the office, was surprised to find there a young man of good family in the neighborhood, whom Mr. Eyebright introduced to the judge as Ralph Kirkwood.

"He says he's got something to say to you, Mr. Denton, which, judging from what he's told me, will be of interest to a good many."

Eyebright spoke with a great effort at self-restraint.

"Yes," said Kirkwood absently: "there's a thing on my mind I've wanted to get off it for a long time."

"I will hear any thing you have to say, Mr. Kirkwood," said the judge with some formality; "but I must warn you that any thing you say must be purely voluntary, and is given without threat or promise. I can not hear it otherwise."

"So Mr. Eyebright said," responded Kirkwood, without looking up.

"And I must further advise you," remarked the judge, "that any thing you may say here may be used against you upon trial for any crime."

"It makes no difference," said Kirkwood after a moment. "I can not keep still any longer. I haven't had a good night's rest since it occurred. I went to Texas, and it followed me there. I came home, and it came with me. It's been with me all the time, and given me no rest, night nor day. I can see him now just as plain as I saw him that night!"

"See who?" asked the judge in surprise.

"Jerry Hunt," responded Kirkwood, in the same matter-of-fact, even tone, and without looking up from the smoldering fire in the grate on which his gaze had all the time rested.

If he could have seen the look of horror and amazement which his auditors exchanged, it would perhaps have surprised him almost as much as his declaration did them. Surrounded year after year by this terrible organization, whose secret blows had fallen upon every side, with no tangible clew to their source, there had grown up in the minds of these men a conviction that there would some time come a day when confidence would be lost between the perpetrators of these crimes, and they would turn upon each other, and confess their evil deeds. They thought, that, when that time did come, there would be a race to be among the first to confess. It is true there had been before some defections from this body, who had disclosed something, in a general way, of its workings, but nothing of any importance. Indeed, their disclosures had been regarded with more of ridicule than respect, because of the conspicuous ignorance which they manifested of what they pretended to disclose. They were usually attended, too, with some circumstance of suspicion antecedently or subsequently occurring, which had destroyed almost all confidence in their verity, or the good faith of the parties making them. That they should at this peculiar moment be confronted with the prospect of a revelation of one of the most noted of its crimes may well have startled them from their composure. Servosse remembered Eyebright's declaration, "The bottom has fallen out at last!"

"What do you know about Jerry Hunt?" asked the judge, as soon as he could master his emotion.

"I know a heap about his death," said Kirkwood, with a sigh, — "a heap more'n I wish I did."

"Is it that you wish to tell me about?"

"Yes, — that for one thing."

"Well," said the judge, "this thing must be done deliberately and in order. You remember my caution. — Colonel Servosse, will you take a pen, and write down what Mr. Kirkwood says. — Please lock the door, Mr. Eyebright, so that we may not be interrupted."

Eyebright did as directed. Servosse placed himself at a table with writing-materials before him; and the judge continued, —

"Now, Mr. Kirkwood, we will hear any thing you have to say. Speak slowly, so that it may be written down. Take your own course and your own time."

"Well," said Kirkwood, "I suppose you want to know it all. I was a student here at Verdenton in the year 18—. I belonged to the Klan, — almost all the boys in the school did. I belonged to Camp No. 4, which met at Martin's most of the time. The sheriff, Colonel Abert, was a member, and was one of the officers. I think he was what they call a South Commander. My uncle was one of the officers too. We were all sworn to obey orders. The oath was very strong; and we were all sworn to kill anybody who did not obey, or who revealed any of the secrets of the order. I was at Mr. Hoyt's school — had been there better than a year: I was preparing for the ministry then. I had been on two or three raids when people were whipped, and never thought much about it: in fact, it seemed right good fun, riding round in disguise at night, frightening niggers, and white folks too sometimes. I didn't think much about whether it was right or not. There were plenty of old men in it who decided all such things, and men that I had always been accustomed to think well of: so I supposed it was all right.

"One day my uncle came in and brought my horse. He put

him in Mr. Crather's barn. Then he came to me, and told me that Camp No. 4 had got a decree from a Rockford camp to make a raid in Verdenton. You know that is the way they do. A camp hardly ever executes its own decree. They send it to another camp, or two or three others; and the camps that get it have to detail men to execute it. He said our camp would send a squad which would meet another squad from Camp No. 9, at the forks of the road near the Widow Foster's; and I was ordered to meet them, and act as guide for them, as I was well acquainted about Verdenton. He asked me if I knew where about half a dozen white men and about as many of the leading niggers lived. I told him I did. He said my disguise was in my saddle-bags on the colt. I was to meet the raid just above the Widow Foster's at nine o'clock.

"I thought it was all right; and, when the hour came, I rode out to the Widow Foster's, and met our folks. Pretty soon afterward the party came from No. 9. The East Commander of that camp was among them, and he took charge. His name is Watson. He's here in the county yet. We went into an old pine field opposite the Widow Foster's, and put on our disguises. We had just been in our own clothes before.

"Then Watson took command, and organized the raid very strictly. He asked me if I knew Jerry Hunt's house. I told him I did. He said that was the man they wanted. Then he said that they had a decree from the Rockford Camp to visit the extreme penalty (that meant kill, always) on Jerry Hunt, but nothing was said as to how: so he left that to the camp then. It was voted that it should be by hanging. I don't reckon anybody voted against it.

"Then we started on. I rode beside Mr. Watson, in the lead. When we came near the colored village west of the town, he ordered out pickets to stop on every corner, and some patrollers to ride up and down the streets, and prevent any interruption. They had orders to shoot anybody that gave the alarm, or interfered with them at all. Then we went to Jerry Hunt's house; and Mr. Watson tried the door, and it wasn't even locked. He opened it, and thought at first there was nobody there. Then we went in; and Watson struck a match, and there was Uncle Jerry, laying there on the bed, sleeping as quiet and peaceful as a child. We waked him up, took the bed-cord out of the bed, and tied him on to the horse next to the one I rode. He never said nothing after we waked him up, only, 'Lord Jesus, have mercy!' 'Father, forgive 'em!' and 'Come, Lord Jesus, come quickly!' At least, I didn't understand any thing more. He was praying all the way in, and never offered any resistance at all.

"When we got in there, they rode down by the trees nigh the Court-House. I had been feeling mighty bad all the way; and when they halted, and began to make preparations, I rode out towards the Court-House, so as not to see any thing more."

He stopped abruptly.

"Well, did you see any thing more?"

"Yes," he responded with a sigh. "I couldn't help looking around after a while; and, just as I did so, some one drew a match, and held it up, and I saw the face of Uncle Jerry as he hung there on the limb. I've been seeing it ever since, gentlemen."

"Did you recognize any of the men?" said the judge.

"Must I answer that?" asked Kirkwood.

"Just as you choose," said the judge coolly. "You have already confessed enough for your own conviction."

"Of course," said Kirkwood thoughtfully. "And they got me into this trouble, and thousands of other good young men too. I'm going to make a clean breast of it, gentlemen, and tell all I know. My conscience would not be any easier, if I screened these men, than it is now. Yes, I recognized a good many."

Then he named some forty men whom he could remember

having seen, and said he had nothing more to say about it. What he had said was read over to him, and signed by him.

"I shall have to hold you to answer a charge of murder, Mr. Kirkwood," said the judge, with a choked voice.

"I suppose so," said Kirkwood. "And I'm guilty: I don't deny the fact. But I shall sleep quiet to-night, which is what I haven't done before since that night. I've only one request to make, Judge."

"What is that?"

"Don't send me to the jail in Verdenton. I don't want to dodge or run, — 'twouldn't do any good to do so now, — but, *you* know, if I were put in that jail now, I'd be hanging on the same limb they hung Jerry Hunt on, before two days were over."

It was arranged that he should be held in custody without being sent to jail at that time. And then the three overwrought men turned to each other, and clasped hands solemnly, with the full conviction that "the bottom had indeed fallen out," and that thereafter it might be said of that section, that "the nights are wholesome."

There had been many knocks at the door in the mean time. It was now opened, and their friends who crowded in were briefly informed of the facts. Servosse slipped away into the house, and informed his wife and daughter.

But the night was not yet ended. By some strange intuition, these facts seemed to have transpired almost before they had taken place. Others came to confess other crimes, and to confirm the confession of young Kirkwood. Hour by hour evidence accumulated, until, that very night, all the ramifications of the Klan in that county, and much in adjacent ones, were laid bare before the magistrate. It was a strange scene indeed; and the party who had assembled at Warrington in expectation of a night of vigil were kept awake by excitement, surprise, and gratitude at the marvelous turn of affairs.

Thomas Denton was one of those men who believed that crime should be punished, not from resentment toward the offenders, but for what he deemed the safety of others, and especially the well-being of future generations. He therefore began the next day to issue the proper processes of law, and pushed with vigor the prosecutions, sitting day by day as a committing magistrate, taking the confessions of hundreds whose awakened fears laid bare the hidden mechanism of thousands of acts of violence. Those whose confessions related to the most trivial and unimportant of the personal outrages were released upon their own recognizances merely, or were dismissed with a sharp rebuke. Those guilty of more serious crimes were bound as witnesses. Many arrests were made, and a universal reign of terror of the law seemed impending among those who had so recently terrorized others. Already the line of examination was threatening hundreds who had been unsuspected, and had involved other hundreds who were deemed equally immaculate.

No one was more astounded or distressed at the revelations made than the Fool. He could not understand how men of the highest Christian character, of the most exalted probity, and of the keenest sense of honor, could be the perpetrators, encouragers, or excusers of such acts. He thought that the churches ought to be hung in black, that the pulpit should resound with warning, and the press teem with angry denunciation. He could not understand how the one should be silent, and the other should palliate or excuse. Of excuse or palliation he did not deem that there could be any thing worthy of consideration. The suggestion that it was personal hostility, or a semi-public animosity against individuals, which animated these acts of violence, he deemed unworthy of a moment's thought, for three reasons, — because it was negatived by the purpose and scope of the organization, because it was denied by all the confessions of repentant members, and because the

victims were uniformly of one mode of political thought, or
had specific relations which placed them in antagonism with
the purposes of the organization. Yet the pulpit kept silent, and the press excused. The Fool
knew not what to think. There were hundreds of these men
whom he knew well, and esteemed highly. Were they deliberately savage and vicious, or was he in error? Was there any
absolute standard of right, or were religion and morality
merely relative and incidental terms? Was that right in
Georgia which was wrong in Maine? Were those ideas of
liberty and of universal right, in which he had been reared,
eternal principles, or merely convictions, — impulses of the
moment? He could not tell. He began to doubt even his own
experience and reason.

Never was the horror which attended this secret organization so fully realized. Even those who had suffered most were
moved to pity. Now that the law, stern and inexorable, was
about to lay its hand upon them, the cry for charity and mercy
came up from every corner. The beauty of peace and reconciliation was heralded throughout the land.

Fortunately, the Legislatures of the several States were in
session, and most of them passed immediately an act of amnesty
and pardon for all who had committed acts of violence in disguise, or at the instigation of any secret organization; and in
the excess of their zeal, and lest it should be supposed that they
desired to screen only their friends, they extended their
mantle of forgiveness so as to cover apparently the innocent as
well as the guilty; those who sought no pardon, as well as the
kneeling suppliants. In short they pardoned not only the perpetrators of these outrages, but, in a reckless determination to
forgive, *they even pardoned the victims!* In this act of wholesale forgiveness they included not only the members of the
"Ku-Klux Klan," the "Invisible Empire," the "Constitutional
Union Guards," and other organizations which had consti-

tuted orders or degrees of the Klan, but also the members of
the "Union Leagues," "Red Strings," and other secret societies,
for all acts done in pursuance of the counsels of such societies.
Strangely enough these societies were not known to have
counseled any unlawful acts; but these legislators were bound
to show that "the quality of mercy is not strained."

They took care, however, not to pardon any, even the least,
infraction of the law, or assumption of power, committed by
the Executive, or any one in authority, for the purpose and
with the intent of repressing and punishing such acts, or protecting the helpless victims thereof. There are some things
which can not be forgiven, even in an era of "reconciliation"!

So the Ku-Klux was buried; and such is the influence of
peace and good-will, when united with amnesty and pardon,
that in a twelvemonth it was forgotten, and he who chanced
to refer to so old and exploded a joke was greeted with the
laughter-provoking cry of the "bloody shirt."

CHAPTER XXXIX

"LIGHT SHINETH IN DARKNESS"

WELL, time went on; and, twelve years from the day when Lee surrendered under the apple-tree at Appomattox, there was another surrender, and the last of the governments organized under the policy of reconstruction fell into the hands of those who had inaugurated and carried on war against the Nation; who had openly opposed the theory of reconstruction, had persistently denied its legality or the binding nature of its promises, and had finally, with secret, organized violence, suppressed and neutralized the element on which it had depended for support. It was true, that, in form and letter, the laws of that period remained: in spirit and in substance they were abrogated. Yet the Nation looked on without wonder or alarm, and by its executive head testified a somewhat more than tacit approval of the result.

That those governments should fail was no matter of surprise to the Fool. He had anticipated and foretold failure from the first. He had always believed that they were prenatally infected with the seeds of fatal disease. He had looked for them to disappear. Their dissolution, and the resumption of some other relation to the government, would hardly have surprised him. He was ready to acknowledge that the rule of majorities, when majorities are composed of the weak, illiterate, and poor, is not likely to be successful. All that was involved in the failure of practical reconstruction he was ready to admit, and willing to see the steps taken in error retraced. For a time, however, he was staggered to note what an utter reversal of the decision made upon the field of battle had been effected.

Then he began to study the matter more in the aggregate,

and found that he had hitherto been blinded by details. The object-plate on which he gazed had been too near the retina to be clearly pictured thereon. He reviewed the course of events from *ante bellum* times; and what he now saw was this: —

First, A people proud, brave, and fond of self-laudation, who had been joined in formal union with a people less showy, but more thrifty; less boastful, but more resolute; less self-assertive, but more industrious. In this union the former had ruled, until the right to dominate had seemed almost inherent; and finally, when their will was thwarted by an aroused majority, earnestly believing themselves to be oppressed beyond endurance, they flew to arms, and contested with marvelous courage and tenacity for the right to sever the compact which bound them to the other. Failing in this, they were at the will of the conqueror; to which they submitted sullenly, but silently, not deeming it a matter of right, not enforced by any sense of duty or obligation of honor, but simply yielding because they had been conquered, and were compelled to submit.

Second, Among the terms prescribed for this subjugated people was one condition which required that a lately servile race dwelling among them — which was of necessity not only servile, but poor and ignorant — should be admitted to an equal share and voice in the government with themselves. This race, as it chanced, was earnestly and devoutly regarded by them as inherently and unutterably inferior and degraded, so that even its generic name had become an epithet of scorn and contempt. Until the hour of their subjugation, this inferior race had not been regarded by them or the nation as worthy of possessing any inherent rights. The law had regarded them as mere chattels; and it had passed into a proverb in the nation, that they had "no rights which white men were bound to respect." To buy, to sell, to task, to whip, to mayhem this race at will, had been from immemorial days a right which the now subjugated people had claimed and exercised, and which had been conceded and admitted in their previous union with their conquerors. It had also been a part of their religious belief, and had been taught from their pulpits, together with other truths which they deemed sacred, that this inferior race was divinely created and ordained to be subject and subordinate to their white fellow-creatures, so that any attempt to change their relations was looked upon as a subversion of the divine will.

Third, This elevation of a race regarded as such inferiors, marked by a distinctive color which of itself had become a badge of shame and infamy, to be co-ordinate in power with that people who had but lately dominated the nation, and had then given four years of inconceivable suffering and blood and toil for the right to keep them in slavery, which they deemed to have been imperiled by their confederates in the government, was, very naturally, most exasperating and humiliating to the conquered people. They deemed it a blow in the face, given in the mere wantonness of power, and for the sole purpose of revenge. To them it was an act intended and designed to humiliate and degrade them, simply because, in the conflict of arms to which they had appealed, they had been unsuccessful. They thought it a gratuitous and needless affront to a brave and unfortunate foe, and their resentment burned hotly against an enemy who could do an act of such dastardly malice.

Yet, after it was imposed, they seemed without remedy. They were subject, broken, scattered. An appeal to arms was hopeless. The power which had but recently forced them to submission was still more potent and compact than when the battle was joined before. Its armies in considerable force were scattered over the subject territory, and those which had been disbanded needed but one blast of the trumpet to fall again into line; while those of the subject people were hopelessly shattered and disheartened, their armaments gone, and the power and opportunity to organize and concentrate impossible to be obtained.

However, such was the indomitable spirit of this people, that they scorned to yield or submit to what they deemed oppression. They denounced with unparalleled temerity these terms of restoration as unjust and infamous, and openly declared that they would obey and regard the laws and acts passed and done in pursuance thereof, in so far as it was absolutely impossible for them to avoid doing otherwise — and no farther. They gave full and fair notice that they would resist, evade, nullify, and destroy these laws and the work done under them, as soon as opportunity should occur so to do, in any manner that might offer. It was a defiance openly and fairly given; and to the redemption of this challenge was plighted the honor of a people even more scrupulous of their collective than of their individual rights, exasperated by defeat, and aroused by a sense of unparalleled and unpardonable wrong and oppression.

The Fool saw them resisting bravely every step leading to the adoption of this plan, protesting with indignation, denouncing with rage, and finally submitting almost with tears. No conquered foe ever passed under the yoke which they conceived to mean servitude and infamy to them, with more unwilling step, or with more deeply muttered curses. He saw men and women afflicted with the keenest sense of personal humiliation because of their enforced submission to the power of a people they had always deemed their inferiors, — the traditional foe of the South, the "groveling and greedy Yankee," — and then still further degraded by being placed on a level, in legal and political power and privilege, with a race despised beyond the power of language to express, whom they had always accounted too low and mean even for contempt, — mere ethnological ciphers, who had no power, except when

acting in conjunction with some significant figure in the nota-
tion of human races.

Moreover, — and this is the vital point, — he saw them,
while thus bowing beneath the scourge of shame, early apprehending the weak point in their enemy's coat of mail, and
steadily addressing themselves to planting therein a fatal
stroke. They could not fight, and thus avenge the affront that
had been put upon them; but by infinite patience, matchless
organization, unremitting and universal zeal, they could surely
foil the design of their foe. Nay, more, they could turn against
that enemy the weapon by which he had sought to secure
their degradation, and by means of it, perhaps, accomplish a
like degradation of their oppressor. It was a daring conception
for a conquered people. Only a race of warlike instincts and
regal pride could have conceived or executed it.

To accomplish this end, the most unshrinking and universal
courage, united with a sleepless caution, was required on the
part of every individual member of this class, besides the most
unswerving confidence in each and every one of his fellows.
Men, women, and children must have and be worthy of implicit mutual trust. Having eyes, they must see not; and, having ears, they must hear not. They must be trusted with the
secrets of life and death without reserve and without distrust.
The whole South must be fused and welded into one homogeneous mass, having one common thought, one imperial
purpose, one relentless will. It was a magnificent conception,
and, in a sense, deserved success!

It differed from all other attempts at revolution — for revolution it was in effect — in the caution and skill with which
it required to be conducted. It was a movement made in the
face of the enemy, and an enemy, too, of overwhelming
strength. It must be concealed and disguised from that enemy,
or its success would not only be imperiled, but absolutely and
irretrievably destroyed. If the North had seen and realized in

any thing of the true nature of this movement at the outset the power of the nation would have crushed it in its incipiency. To overawe and suppress the Union, Federal, or Reconstructionary element of the South, was of itself an undertaking of no difficulty whatever to the trained leaders of that section, with an exasperated soldiery and an unconquerable people at their backs, whose confidence in their wisdom and loyal devotion to their rights was yet unshaken, and to whom they were all the dearer by reason of the misfortunes they had already endured; but to do this without awakening the suspicions and fears of the North until the result was an accomplished fact, was a task requiring infinite skill, patience, and courage for its accomplishment. Should it succeed, it would be the most brilliant revolution ever accomplished. Should it fail — well, those who engaged in it felt that they had nothing more to lose. When the war ended, they had proudly said, "All is lost but honor;" but, when the reconstruction measures came, they felt themselves covered with shame, degraded in the eyes of the world; not by their own acts, — of them, indeed, they were proud, — but by what had been done unto them. They felt like one who has been assaulted by a scavenger.

The Fool deemed it likely that actual violence was not at first intended. It was probably believed that mere intimidation, the appeal to superstitious fears and the threat of corporeal punishment, would have the effect thoroughly to demoralize and disintegrate the colored vote, and leave the white minority powerless. When, from the unexpected manhood of the recent slaves and the long-suffering "Unioners," it was found that this result would not follow a mere display of force and the assumption of ghostly habiliments, some degree of violence followed as an almost necessary consequence. The pride of a haughty people, the resentment of one that deemed itself bitterly wronged, and the ambition of those greedy for power, were all staked on the issue of the struggle. The battle had already been joined; and it would have been not only fatal, but ignominious, to have turned back.

After this review, the Fool could well see how slight a thing in comparison was the mere question of the political rights of those whom the Southerners considered as legally without political right, and morally and intellectually incapable of exercising such rights. He could see, too, that the maltreatment of these men over whom they had been accustomed to exercise the right of castigation, and, indirectly at least, of life and limb, at pleasure, should not produce in their minds the same feeling of repulsion and horror that it would evoke from the "exaggerated" humanitarianism of the North, as well as that which may still be considered genuine and wholesome. He could perceive, too, that an especial resentment very naturally existed in the minds of this people against all those persons of the white race who aided, abetted, encouraged, organized, and directed the colored voters in the assertion of political right and the exercise of political power.

The means which had been instituted and pursued for the protection of slavery, and which had approved themselves as effective for that purpose, had especially cultivated that spirit which countenances the forcible suppression of unpopular ideas, which at the North was called "intolerance," and at the South "self-preservation." So that he could well understand how it should be considered a very slight and venial offense to beat, wound, and ill-treat one of the recently servile race, and by no means a serious thing, from a moral standpoint, to kill them if necessary to attain their purpose. He could understand, too, how they should consider it only a "species of wild justice" to suppress or destroy those who were active in rendering this newly created political power effective as against its former owners. He began to see that the hostility against men of Northern birth was not entirely because of their nativity, but because they were regarded as, in a sense, public enemies; and he could understand why the

hostility and antipathy against himself, and others of prominence and activity in organizing reconstruction, had greatly
moderated, and acts of violence against all these classes almost
entirely ceased, as soon as they became innocuous, or incapable
of organizing a successful opposition to the will of a majority
of the white race, in whom alone they most sincerely believed
there resided the inherent right to rule, not only themselves,
but also that lately servile population which dwelt among
them.

He believed that this solution answered every condition of
the problem, was a key which opened every mystery attending the existence of the Ku-Klux Order, both during the reign
of terror which attended its establishment, and that peace
(which otherwise "passeth all understanding") that followed
its accession to unquestioned supremacy. The *Policy of Suppression*, in every form, he believed to be the fruit of these
complex motives; and its completeness and success commanded his unbounded admiration. It then became apparent
to him that the pride, resentment, and sense of ignominious
oppression, in the hearts of the Southern people, had swallowed up all other thought, had rendered all other considerations trivial and unimportant to their minds, when compared
with the one "great and holy aim" of redeeming the land to
which they were attached with such unalterable devotion,
from the oppression of foes whom they regarded with hereditary contempt and hate. All else was lost in this one thought.
All else could be forgiven and forgotten; all other sins might
be condoned, but the one sin against this all-pervading purpose.
It gave tone and color to the whole intellectual and moral life
of this people, and made that appear venial and insignificant
which would otherwise have been counted horrible and atrocious.

Lest it be thought that the Fool judged harshly in this
matter, an illustrative incident is given in the next chapter.

CHAPTER XL

PRO BONO PUBLICO

THERE was turmoil in the county of Rockford. The repressive policy in all its various phases had been successfully made effective there. Though everybody knew that the county — when that policy was not applied, and every voter exercised the privilege of casting his ballot as he pleased — was opposed to the party of repression by several hundred majority, yet it had been so skillfully manipulated since the death of John Walters, that the majority upon the other side had been maintained at a steady and reliable figure, which, strangely enough, had been just about as large as the majority had formerly been against it.

Yet Rockford was entirely peaceful; in fact, a very paradise of harmonious unity. There were 1143 more colored men than white in the county, according to the census report; and, during the first years in which these colored voters exercised the prerogatives of citizenship, they had been accustomed — very foolishly, it is true, but perhaps naturally, and at all events very clamorously — to demand that a portion of the offices should be filled by men of their own race. After the policy of repression became fully established, and John Walters was so mysteriously but effectually disposed of, the hearts of these innocent and misguided Africans underwent a marvelous change. They still continued to vote, as appeared from the poll-books and returns of election, with the most persistent regularity; but they ceased to vote for those to whom they had once been so warmly attached, and ceased to demand and elect persons of their own color or formerly universal sentiment for places of trust and emolument. It was a very strange coincidence; and there were not wanting those who

pointed to it as undeniable evidence of fraud, or, as it was
sometimes termed, "intimidation." Some of the Wise Men who
dwelt at a distance tried to raise a clamor over it; but they
were easily put to rout by silver-tongued orators who painted
wonderful pictures of the millennial life and Edenic peace
which had prevailed in Rockford since the hour when the
pestiferous Walters departed from its coasts.

It is strange what metamorphoses the unaccountable African
has undergone. In the good old times before the war for the
right of Southern States to secede, it was established by the
concurrent testimony of all the most intelligent, wealthy, refined, honorable, and high-toned among the Southern people,
— those who owned slaves, and worked and whipped, and
bought and sold, and married and unmarried, as the exigencies
of the race and the taste of the breeder demanded, — it was
established beyond question by these (and certainly they
must have known more about the negro than any one else,
since they had better opportunity), that the colored man was
not only divinely created and designed for a state of bondage,
but that he had a keen and subtle appreciation of his own
needs, requisites, and capabilities, and recognized with tran-
scendent delight the prevision of Providence which had kindly
left him not unprovided with a master. In short, it was established, beyond all doubt or controversy, that the African
was not only created for a state of slavery, but so conscious
of the object of his creation, and so anxious to fulfill the
purpose thereof, that he was both contented with a lot of
servitude, and actually clamorous for its delights, and unable
to express his sympathy and commiseration for the few individuals of his race who were without the crowning blessing
of a master. It is true, that, even in those days, there were a
few insane individuals of this race (poor misguided creatures!)
who were always running away from the peace, plenty,
happiness, and divine beatitude of the plantation, and making

towards poverty and want, and labor and disease, and frost and the north pole and — liberty! But they were erring creatures, who only served to disturb the peace of the Eden they were not wise enough nor good enough to enjoy.

There were some, too, who would not believe the testimony in regard to the unalloyed happiness of the slave, but persisted in maintaining that the sanest, bravest, wisest, and noblest of the African race, were those who ran away to freedom. But these people were not many, and they were also insane, — and not only insane, but envious, wicked, and bloody-minded. They were called "fanatics" and "abolitionists."

As soon as the war came on, and they were offered their liberty, the nature of the perverse African seemed at once to change. Every one of them accepted it, and that, too, with a readiness and an eagerness which went very far to induce the belief that they had wanted it all the time. Of course, we know this was not so, by the testimony of those who knew more about them than anybody else could; but it did *seem* so when they swarmed in the rear of the Federal armies, and forsook home, friends, relatives, and patriarchal masters, for privation, danger, and liberty.

And ever since, they have been manifesting a like contrariness and contradictoriness of character. Up to the very time when the Ku-Klux Klan became well established in the South, the negro manifested a most inveterate and invincible repugnance and disinclination towards allowing his former masters to define, regulate, and control his liberties, *unless* such person had formally renounced the ideas of slavery and rebellion, had openly and unmistakably declared himself in favor of the equal legal and political rights and power of the colored race, and had shown a disposition to concede them.

As soon as this beneficent institution, the Klan, and its more subtle and complete successors, under various and sundry names, "Rifle-Clubs," "Sabre-Clubs," "Bull-dozers," and so forth, had fully established themselves throughout the country, and it became apparent that the paternal and patriarchal spirit of the nominally defunct system of Chattelism was still alive, and was watching with assiduous care over the welfare and happiness of its former childlike subjects, their hearts turned again with the old-time affection to the former masters, who they now again saw were not only their best, but their sole friends, not only the chief and best guardians of their liberty, but absolutely its primal authors. So they despised and es-chewed "nigger-politicians," and Radicals, and turned in scorn and contempt away from those whose teachings disagreed with the tenets of the Ku-Klux Klan, the Rifle-Clubs, and the Bull-dozers, and clung again to their first loves, — their natural and divinely-ordained friends and protectors!

At least that is what these natural friends and protectors said; and we must allow that they know more about the negroes than anybody else, just as a groom knows more about the horse he drives and controls than anybody else, and, of course, is best informed as to the horse's opinion of him, the said groom.

So there was peace in Rockford. But in an evil hour the serpent of Ambition entered this Eden, and left his trail among its flowers. Two of the party of peace, reform, and conserva-tism, cast a yearning eye upon the same office. The authority of a convention was set at defiance; and one reckless and am-bitious man declared that he would appeal to Cæsar, and not only to Cæsar, but to Tony also, and, in fact, to all the chil-dren of Ham in said county resident, to decide betwixt him and his fellow. In the party of peace and order the thing seemed to be pretty evenly divided; and the recalcitrant bolter and his friends promised to the unaccountable Africans, that all who should vote for him should be protected in so doing, and that the regular organization of that party should not molest them, or make them afraid. And, in proof of that, they showed their revolvers and Winchesters, and used many "cuss-words," and imbided courage by the quart.

And to them inclined the Africans.

This absurd perversity on the part of the dusky voters greatly disturbed the party of law and order. If one was allowed thus to appeal to this ebon vote, and ride into power thereby, what would become of the party of peace and law and order? Something must be done, — something which would destroy this presumptuous man's hold on his deluded followers. It would not do to apply the usual tactics of the party, because it was doubtful how such application would result. So it was determined to destroy the hopes of the bolters, and detach from them their new supporters by means of their tender devotion to the memory of their *quondam* leader, the infamous Walters. It was believed, that, if they could be convinced that this man who asked their support was one of the band who had dipped their hands in his blood, the silly Africans would at least refrain from voting for him, out of a foolish veneration for the memory of the dead leader. So the following card was published, and scattered broadcast throughout the county, as well as being given a prominent place in the columns of *The Moccason Gap Rattler:* —

"WHO IS COLONEL MARCUS THOMPSON?

"The colored voters of Rockford, who are so anxious to elevate this notorious desperado, infidel, and renegade, to the position of sheriff of that county, are probably not aware of all the infamy which surrounds his character. It is well known that he was for several years the chief of the Ku-Klux and head of the Bull-dozers of that county, and was of course responsible, as such, for the acts committed by them. It is not, however, so generally known that it was he who planned and executed the murder of JOHN WALTERS, being himself the leader of the band who first inveigled him to the place of his death, and afterwards not only killed him, but took from his person a considerable sum of money, which Colonel Marcus Thompson appropriated to his own use. Yet such is the fact. It is susceptible of abundant proof that he not only devised the killing, but was the very first one who imbrued his hands in the blood of Walters. He expected to be rewarded for this act, by his then political associates, with the office to which he now aspires. Failing in this, he now appeals to the followers of Walters for support. Whether they will indorse this red-handed murderer and robber of the widow and the fatherless remains to be seen."

In reply to this, Thompson published the following: —

"TO THE VOTERS OF ROCKFORD COUNTY.[1]

"It has been industriously circulated by the opposition, for the purpose of inducing parties to withhold their support from me, that I took, and appropriated to my own use, *two thousand dollars* found on the person of John Walters at the time of his death. I did not wish to refer to such old matters, since to do so *must necessarily involve many of our best citizens*. Those were times of great excitement, and no doubt many things were done which it were better to have left undone. I was at that time the Chairman of the Executive Committee of my party for this county; and I hereby pronounce the charge that I used or appropriated a solitary cent of the money found on the person of Walters *for my personal* benefit or advantage, to be an *infamous, unfounded, and malicious lie*. On the contrary, I affirm that every cent of this money

[1] There is a remarkable similarity between these circulars and the open letters recently published by the chairman of the executive committee of Yazoo County, Mississippi, and the late Mr. Dixon, then an independent candidate for sheriff of that county.

was used to defray the current expenses of the party in that campaign, to stuff ballot-boxes, and to purchase certificates of election for persons now holding office in the county. I have in my hands the documents necessary to prove these facts, and will exhibit them whenever called upon so to do.

"Respectfully,
"MARCUS THOMPSON."

The Fool read these cards, and smiled, even in the sadness of the memory they evoked, at the sweet and peaceable fruits of that spirit of conciliation which had swept over the land when punishment impended over the heads of these knights of law and order, — the masked Uhlans who had ridden at midnight. As before stated, under the impulse of a divine compassion, it had been enacted in the several States, that all crimes perpetrated by Ku-Klux, Bull-dozers, and other political societies or orders, or by individuals under their authority, direction, or instigation, should be absolutely and entirely amnestied and forgiven. By reason of this enactment, it had become a matter of little or no moment who killed John Walters. That was a charge not even worthy of denial. But the charge that Colonel Thompson had appropriated the money taken from the body of the murdered man was an imputation under which no honorable man would rest.

It would seem, in some states of society, that the open confession that he had used the money thus obtained for the purpose of bribing and corrupting officers of election, would of itself be counted scarcely less nefarious. However that may be, Mr. Thompson evidently felt called upon, in vindication of his personal character, to deny the one, and assert the other. As to the mere killing of the Radical John Walters, he considered it unnecessary for him to make any admission or denial. That was an act of no more consequence than the infantile query, "Who killed Cock Robin?"

The Fool pondered this matter sadly and earnestly. He thought it indicative of a distorted and blunted moral sense; yet he could not but pity the suffering, and admire the resolution, which had wrought such insensibility of soul. He remembered the story of the Spartan youth who stood smiling and indifferent while the stolen fox gnawed at his vitals.

CHAPTER XLI

"PEACE IN WARSAW"

As time wore on, the personal relations which the Fool sustained to his neighbors continued to improve. It seemed as if there had been a mutual discovery of agreeable attributes. Men who had kept aloof from him during all the years of his sojourn, or had greeted him but coolly, and had been accustomed to speak of him to others with any thing but kindliness, came gradually to manifest, first tolerance, and then something of kindly partiality for him. This was especially true of the more cultivated and active-minded men of the vicinage. They seemed to recognize, with a kind of surprise, the fact that the man they had been accustomed to denounce so bitterly was yet not entirely uncompanionable. So, among these, his companionship increased in a way that reminded him of the forbearance sometimes extended to a not altogether unpleasing and quite harmless lunatic.

This state of things not unfrequently caused the Fool to smile, though he had now become wise enough to prize aright the honest effort which many of these men made to overcome an hereditary prejudice, and accord to him that personal recognition which they believed him to have merited. He no longer wondered that the welcome which the ever-ready West extends to the ceaseless tide which crowds its gates was not given to him on his arrival; but he did wonder that these men could so overcome the force of a prejudice which had become instinctive, an exclusiveness which had been for some generations almost as complete as that of the Celestial Kingdom, and a pride which had been so deeply wounded by the ruthless outcome of recent events, as even to recognize his *personal* right and merit when the same was entirely disassociated from any recognition of political privilege. He did not deceive himself in regard to these appearances. He knew that they did not portend any cessation of what was termed political intolerance; that there was no relaxation of that feeling which would not allow practical opposition to its mandates. He knew that he was not tolerated because his political convictions were conscientiously entertained, nor because of any feeling, on the part of those with whom he was surrounded, that every man was entitled to entertain and advocate such political views as he might prefer, or that such freedom was an essential element of republican government, — but rather in spite of his conscientiousness, and because his views could have no chance of practical application in the future. The lauguage which they held of him in their hearts, he correctly believed to be "He's a terrible Radical; but he is not so *bad* a man, after all. His political views can do no harm now. No doubt he is honest in them: it is natural that a Northern man should hold such views. But, otherwise, he is not so disagreeable." So his daily life became far more endurable.

A conviction of the utter powerlessness of those elements with which the Fool had politically co-operated no doubt had a certain effect upon his mind and conduct. His views had not been changed by the great counter-revolution which had swept on around him. His belief in the equality and inherency of human right, whether it be termed a principle or a prejudice, was equally strong as upon that day when it first flashed upon his mind that those around him excepted from the operation of this democratic formula all individuals of the African race. He could not bring himself to see that race, color, or previous condition of servitude, had any thing to do with the doctrine of *inherent* right. Neither could he adopt that belief with which the judicial philosophers of our American bench had reconciled themselves to neutrality in the more recent conflict for liberty, which is more usually formulated in the

expression, "Suffrage is not a right, but a privilege." So he
could not reconcile himself with any line of thought or policy
which depended for its success upon silencing and negativing
— either by fraud, misrepresentation, or violence — the voice
of the majority. The fact that a man had been born a slave
did not, in his eyes, affect the question of his inherent right;
because he regarded slavery simply as an unnatural and wrongful accident, — a state of society which had been superim-
posed on the rightful and natural one, suspending the operation of the latter, and taking from certain parties the rights
which they had. On account of which, when such false and
anomalous relations ceased, all parties affected by it were
relegated to those rights they would have been entitled to,
if it had never existed; and these rights, he thought, must
relate back to, and take effect from, the first, precisely as if
this unnatural state of servitude had not intervened.

It is by no means improbable, however, that he found fewer
occasions to utter such opinions, and took less trouble to incul-
cate such views, from the fact that it might cause suffering to
those who should accept and believe the doctrine. For himself, he could not see that a man's race or condition, wealth or
poverty, ignorance or intelligence, should affect his civic
right: he was sure they should not, if the theory of republican and democratic governments be true, — that the majority
should rule. He felt that ignorance, poverty, and an ebon skin,
were each of them terrible afflictions, and acknowledged that
they might all of them be classed as public evils in our American democracy; but he could not admit that either or all of
them constituted true or just limitations of political power or
inherent right. He despised that lack of manhood which seeks
to avoid responsibility by silence, or which submits to wrong
to avoid the trouble of resistance.

Yet he admitted to himself that if he were one of the unfortunate and despised race, if he shared its poverty, inex-

perience, and helplessness, in short, if he were even as one of his colored fellow-citizens in these respects, he would not think of such a thing as exercising or asserting his political rights, but, on the contrary, would submit, with such patience as he could command, to whatever might impend, hoping and waiting for one of two things to occur; viz., either an improvement in the temper and inclination of the ruling class, or an opportunity to get away to some region beyond their power. He really thought it an amazing piece of heroism that the colored man should so long have taken, not merely his own life, but the lives of his little ones, in his hand, and have gone to the ballot-box to deposit his ballot against such fearful odds of power. He thought that those who had died of one form of intolerance and another, since the time when a great nation falsely guaranteed to them safety, liberty, and the rights of citizenship; the thousands who fell victims to the violence of Ku-Klux and Rifle Clubs, the natural sad barbarity which inaugurated and sustained the Repressive policy, — these thousands he deemed to have constituted an army of martyrs for those very principles which he still believed, and of which he was once so proud.

Yet he did not feel that it would be right for him to induce or encourage other thousands to tempt the same fate, or to seek to exercise the same rights. He could not encourage them to do what he would not do under like circumstances. So he did not feel like urging them to make any further stand for what were termed their rights, nor to seek to gain any thing by the exercise or assertion of them.

While, therefore, he was not silenced by personal fear or violence, while he even boasted with no little stubborn pride that he could declare his opinions there as freely as on the hills of New England or in his native Western home, he could not but smile at the fallacy which lay hid in his own words. The Repressive policy had as effectually eradicated his desire for self-assertion as if it had consummated the design which was instituted at Bentley's Cross. He might not be in any danger from declaring his opinions; but he well knew that those who listened to him would invite danger and suffering, should they resolutely seek to carry his views into effect. He was, in a sense, at liberty to act as he chose; but the consequences of his action to others were so terrific that he must have been either more or less than man to have invited them. So, without abandoning his principles, as he called them, — for he had come almost to believe that what are termed "principles" are only ingrained habits of thought, and hereditary systems of belief, — he submitted quietly to having them rendered inoperative and nugatory by the suppression of the will of the majority, or, rather, by excluding from the estimate those who were opposed to the white majority. By this course he found himself enjoying a personal peace and toleration which was very grateful, after what had gone before. Where he had been hated without stint, and maligned without scruple, he was now tolerated with an "if," or commended but a "but."

The Fool felt that he was learning wisdom in thus submitting himself to the inevitable, and gradually came to regard himself and his neighbors with far more of reasonable complacency than he had hitherto done. He saw that he had expected too much, that he had been simple enough to believe that the leopard *might* change his spots, while yet the Ethiopian retained his dusky skin. He was even grateful for the toleration which was extended to him, and looked with a sort of wonder on the men who so far forgot, or put aside, the past, as to do this. He even advanced to the point where he looked back with no inconsiderable surprise at the state of mind which had once possessed him. He was inclined to ridicule many of the exalted notions of manhood and independence which he had once entertained, and to wonder that he could have ever been so idiotically stupid as to have expected aught except what had in fact occurred. So there arose a spirit of mutual forbearance; they forbore to take offense at his views, and he forbore to express them; they excused his views because of his Northern birth and education, and he excused their acts because of their Southern nativity and training; they disregarded his political convictions because a method had been discovered to prevent their crystallizing into results, and he refrained from urging them because to do so was a useless travail.

In fact, by this change of heart, the Fool gradually ceased to interest himself in those things which had formerly been of such engrossing moment to him. Realizing his own folly, and the foolishness of that struggle with the spirit and civilization of a great people which had been so rashly inaugurated, he sought only to enjoy what was pleasant in his surroundings, and to put behind him the conflicts of the past. He had learned that the spirit, the mode of thought, the life of the North, can not be imposed upon the South in an instant; that if the two divergent civilizations are ever to meet, and harmonize with each other, it must be when time and circumstance are more propitious than the present, or when some great convulsion has so swerved the currents, that they meet in one overwhelming flood.

So there was peace at Warrington. Without forgetting old friends, the Fool made new ones, blessed the sunshine and the shade, thought less of the welfare of his fellows and more of his own comfort, and rejoiced that the struggle which the Wise Men had cast upon his fellow-workers and himself was at an end. He had fought stubbornly and well. All admitted that. Until he felt that he was betrayed, renounced, discredited, and condemned by the very element which had thrust this burden on him, he had never thought of surrender. Having given in his adhesion to the plan of reconstruction, even though it were under protest, he felt that he could not honor-

ably abandon the contest until discharged by the act or permission of those allies in the contest. This had been done, and
he was relieved from further duty. When the power of the
Nation was withdrawn, the struggle was at an end. Failure
was written above the grave of the pet idea of the Wise Men.
It was with a feeling of relief, if not of satisfaction, that the
Fool recognized this result. He was like the battered soldier,
who, though not victorious, sits in his old age, crowned with
the glory of many wounds, peaceful and contented despite
the undesired outcome of his warfare.

He still believed in the cause for which he had struggled,
and believed in the capacity of those with whom he had
worked to achieve for themselves, at some time in the future,
a substantial freedom; but in that struggle he could do but
little. He believed that it would be long and tedious; that the
wavering balance would hang in doubt for generations; and
that, in the mean time, that haughty, self-reliant, and instinctively dominant element which had already challenged
the Nation to a struggle of strength, had been defeated, and
*out of disaster had already wrested the substantial fruits of
victory*, would achieve still greater triumphs, and would for
an indefinite period dominate and control the national power.
He saw this without envy; for it was apparent to him that
a people who could perform such wonders of political legerdemain without awakening the fears, or hardly the distrust,
of those whose power they had felt, but whose prestige they
had overthrown — whose glory they had already trailed in the
dust until it was accounted far more honorable to have struck
at the Nation's life than to have interposed a life to avert the
blow — had, in a peculiar degree, those characteristics which
are necessary to secure and hold dominion.

While it was not without chagrin that he noted these facts,
and while his cheek flushed with something like shame as he
remembered the halting, shuffling indecision of his own peo-

ple, and how they had pandered to a sickly sentimentalism, relinquishing therefor the substance of power, betraying and abandoning their allies, and heaping upon them the contempt and shame of the failure which resulted thereby, he could but admit, with something of pride in the conviction, that those who had thus thwarted and overthrown their conquerors were born rulers of men, whose empire was not likely to fail from any lack of vigor. He looked forward to see them regaining the proud supremacy of *ante bellum* days, — not indeed with satisfaction; for what he had so long called his "principles" stood stubbornly in the way, and he was sure that they would fall some time, — but at least with admiring pride in the capabilities of that branch of the American stock.

So the days flew on, and the sun shone, and Warrington grew brighter, and Lily grew fairer and riper, and Metta looked more matronly and grave, and the Fool sat in the sunshine. The tie between Lily and her father, unusually strong before, had been redoubled in strength and intensity by her heroic act. Before, she had been his companion and his pupil; since then, she had been his companion even more frequently, but the idea of pupilage seemed to have been absorbed in the self-abnegation of parental hope and pride. To her improvement he now devoted the ripest powers of the life she had saved. Comprehending fully the defects of her somewhat desultory education, when he came to examine the results he was surprised at what had been accomplished. The basis which Metta had laid with untiring devotion had been strongly built upon by that confiding freedom which had been exercised toward her by both her parents, and especially by her father's custom of conversing with her upon all those subjects which had especially engaged his attention. The desire to converse with him intelligently upon these themes had induced her, partly by means of questions directed to such subjects, and partly by consulting the books and periodicals which he read, to familiarize herself with them, until there were few subjects of current thought upon which she was not able to converse, not only intelligibly, but readily, and with a clearness and originality which had surprised the few strangers with whom she had opportunity to exchange thought. Seeing this foundation laid, Servosse decided to continue her education in pretty much the same manner, directing it now towards specific objects, and making what are termed accomplishments the fringe of her education, rather than its web, it being his impression that about the same relation should be maintained between them as should exist in real life. Being of the opinion that true education consisted more in a power to master a subject, to perceive, discover, and marshal facts in relation thereto, than in the mere acquisition of those facts, he did not confine her to dry details, nor occupy her mind with the probing of specific systems. For her sake, he turned again to those fields of thought which had been the delight of his youth and early manhood, and with a gentle hand led her feet through the fair fields of literature, — the history of the world's thought. Side by side with this, he unfolded before her that other book which we *call* history, — the story of the world's outward happenings, the deeds of her heroes, the wrongs of her martyrs, and the sins of her great criminals, together with the little which we know of the sufferings, burdens, and misfortunes of her great masses. She had never known any other school than her home, and no masters but her devoted parents. For her sake they had banished from the home-circle the language of their childhood, and had confined themselves to dialects which had grown unfamiliar to their tongues from long disuse. She had learned three things which Servosse accounted all important; *first*, that education was a life-work, and not a matter to be crowded into a few early years; *second*, that the learner must in most matters be also the teacher, or, in other words, that the province of the

teacher is rather to test the attainments of the learner than to
direct his acquirements; and, *third*, that to know is to observe,
to understand, and to delineate.

As a relief from the absorbing thought which he had given
to public matters, this duty was most delightful to Servosse,
and it seemed as if the fruition of their early hope had been
vouchsafed to himself and his wife, when he begun to realize
that the relations and feelings of this period must necessarily
soon take from him this crowning pleasure of his life. Metta,
ever anxious for the interests of her daughter, began to urge
the necessity of travel, and desired that the well-prepared
mind should be finished and rounded by the experiences of
varied life. This question had already been one of anxious
consideration, when one day Servosse was amazed at an occurrence which his wiser-hearted wife had foreseen.

For over them both watched the tender and careful Metta,
proud and happy in her fair daughter's present, and hopeful of
her future, but, with strange inconsistency, exulting more in
what her husband had been during his *accès de la folie* than in
what he now was when following the paths of wisdom. But
such is ever the contradictoriness of woman's nature.

CHAPTER XLII

A FRIENDLY MEDIATION

It will be remembered that John Burleson had not failed to acquaint Colonel Servosse with the device which Melville Gurney had adopted to favor the escape of Lily, after he had recognized her on the night of her perilous ride. Servosse had such confidence in the qualities of his favorite horse that he was not at first inclined to attribute so much importance to the act.

"After Young Lollard had once passed him, there was little chance of Mr. Gurney's stopping her, even had he desired. There is not a horse in the State that can cover four miles in the time that colt makes light of," he said to Burleson.

"That may be," responded that worthy, in his usual brusque and defiant manner, "though the mare Mel. Gurney rode that night was no slouch, either. But suppose he had used his pistol, which he handles with one hand as well as with the other. I don't believe Mel. Gurney could be induced, under any circumstances, to shoot at a lady; and no one could ever mistake Miss Lily for any thing else, in any sort of light. Her very seat on horseback shows that. But suppose he had, — suppose he had not been the gallant, chivalric Mel. Gurney that he is: what then?"

"A man with a shot through his left arm, and a high-blooded horse to manage, is not very dangerous with a revolver, to one who has Young Lollard under him, and an open road before him," replied the Fool, with an amused smile. "Really, Mr. Burleson, I am half inclined to think the favor was on the other side. In the first place, Mr. Gurney should be grateful that her shot struck his arm. Of course that was accident; but I would not like to trust to such accidents, with Lily pointing a revolver at me less than ten steps away. She has a wonderfully steady hand. Besides that, I am not sure that Mr. Gurney should not count among the mercies of that night the fact that his mare could not overtake Young Lollard. I am not at all sure that Lily, wrought up as she was to desperation, would not have proved the more dangerous adversary."

"I see you are bound not to give my friend Gurney credit for any thing except a cunningly-invented tale to cover his own discomfiture," said Burleson.

"I confess," replied Servosse coolly, "that I can see little further merit in it. It seems to me that the young man did about all he could to prevent her escape, and, when this proved unavailing, invented the story about the rabbit, and the accidental shooting, to avoid ridicule for allowing a woman to pass his guard. I suppose he would rather have died than confess that fact. I believe I would have preferred almost any thing short of that, in his place. Of course, I mean no offense to you in speaking thus of your friend. At first I was so astounded at the fact that one whom I had accounted such a fine, manly fellow, who had been at my house, and for whose father I had such a sincere regard, should have been with that crowd, and upon that errand, that I could not think coolly in regard to it. Indeed, I was so grateful for my daughter's escape from deadly peril, to say nothing of our rescue from the horrible fate, I think I could have hugged with gratitude any of that crowd of cut-throats, simply because of their failure to do what they intended."

"Including among them your humble servant, I suppose," said Burleson good-naturedly.

"Of course," replied Servosse. "I had then no reason to except you from my general estimate. Indeed, from what I had previously known and heard of you, I was not at all surprised at finding you in such company."

"You are like me in one thing, at least," said Burleson,

flushing as he spoke. "Your speech is not hurt by a lack of frankness."

"There is more than one point of resemblance between us, Mr. Burleson," said the Fool thoughtfully, and taking no note of his embarrassment. "I have thought of it several times since that night. Considering all the circumstances of your connection with the Klan and the raid (and the same is true of young Gurney), it seems to me that I should have done the same in your place; except, I am afraid I should not have had the courage to renounce my error, and especially not to protest so manfully as you did at Bentley's Cross, which Lily told me about."

"Don't, if you please, Colonel!" said Burleson, as the blushes chased each other over his manly face. "I am thoroughly ashamed of having been betrayed by any sort of foolish fear of ridicule into any connection with the thing whatever. Do you know, I never once thought about the right or wrong of the matter, the view which instinctively presents itself to your mind. I only thought of the impolicy and danger of it — I mean danger to our people, to the South. I did not think particularly of myself; for I had made up my mind to take what came, with the rest. I wanted to see our party succeed, and gave no consideration to the rights of yours. Indeed, I never regarded you as having any rights, — any legal or moral right to political power, I mean. I considered the enfranchisement of the negro as an act of legal usurpation and moral turpitude, and considered all you carpet-baggers and scalawags as parties to the offense. I thought this outrage was enough to excuse any sort of irregular warfare short of the actual taking of life, which, in fact, was not at first dreamed of. To tell the truth, I thought it would be a good thing if about half the niggers in the country were taken out and whipped about once a fortnight; and I am not sure but it would be a good thing now.

"The killing of old Jerry first woke me up. I was away at the time, and never knew a word of it. If I had been here, it should not have been done, except over my dead body. I knew him from my boyhood; and if there ever was an honest, Christian nigger on earth, his name was Jerry Hunt. Gad! sir, it made my hair stand on end, when I heard of it! and, to save my soul, Colonel, I have not been able to get over the idea that I have his blood on my hands, yet. Damned if I don't feel just so!

"They were hot for you after that, Colonel. Men are just like dogs, anyhow. Just let them get a taste of blood, and they are as savage as wolves. As soon as Jerry was killed, it seemed as if the whole Klan was wild for blood. Only a few opposed it, — just enough, and of the right sort. As it happened, too, most of these were young hot-heads, like Mel. Gurney and myself. The old men generally take the credit for all the conservatism in the world: but it's a mighty bad mistake. The old man's conservatism means only to keep out of danger, — keep his own skirts clear; but a young man backs just as hard as he pulls. If he opposes a thing in such a body, he fights it — tooth and toe-nail. If he is beaten, just as likely as not he goes with the crowd, shares the danger, and takes the blame. But when a man passes a certain age, he becomes smart of a sneak. These old fellows who were opposed to such things simply said they would have nothing to do with them, and kept aloof. That was the way with Melville Gurney's father, the General. He joined it before it got to doing more than just go about and scare the niggers, which he had no objection to being done, especially as he was a candidate for something about that time. When these worse things begun, he quietly let it alone; so much so, that his son never knew of his having been a member until that day at Glenville. I reckon if it had come to that, he would have stood up for *you*. I've heard him speak very highly of you. But he never had a chance. I suppose really I stood between you and danger some three or four times when you knew nothing of it."

"And no doubt saved me at Bentley's Cross, by your altercation with Jake Carver, which enabled my daughter to slip away unperceived," said Servosse warmly.

"Well, perhaps that is so," said Burleson with surprise. "I had never thought of that; but I am not entitled to any credit for it, since it was unintentional. Melville Gurney's chivalry and presence of mind is what saved you — next, of course, to Miss Lily's heroism."

"I can not see," said Servosse impatiently, "why you will give so much credit to Gurney. Your friendly partiality blinds you to the probable motive which animated him."

"No," replied Burleson, "it is you that are blind, — blinder than a bat, as you will find out some day."

"I have no disposition to do the young man any injustice," said Servosse.

"Oh! I do not suppose so, — not at all," said Burleson; "but you don't know Melville Gurney as I do. He is as true as steel, and as straight as an arrow, both literally and figuratively. I only wonder that he came to be in the thing at all. I *know* the motive that influenced his action that night, from his own mouth; and Melville Gurney would not lie for a kingdom. See here, Colonel!" he added impetuously, "I am surprised that you can not see this thing in its true light. Suppose Melville Gurney had not wished your daughter's safety and success in her errand: what would he have done? Given notice to the camp of what had occurred on his post, wouldn't he?"

"Yes, I suppose so," said Servosse.

"And what would have been the result?"

"I'm sure I don't know."

"You don't? Do you know Jake Carver?"

"Yes."

"A bold and resolute man, relentless in his purpose, and ruthless in his antipathies."

"I have heard so."

"And that man was in command of a hundred well-mounted and reckless men."

"Well?"

"Well? My God, man! how long would it have taken him to decide to follow your daughter's track, and seize you and Judge Denton in the town, instead of at the bridge?"

"Heavens!" cried Servosse, springing to his feet. "I had never thought of that."

"I should think not," said Burleson in a tone of triumph. "But if Melville Gurney had not put him off the scent you would have thought of it! In less than fifteen minutes, — before you got Miss Lily back to the hotel, — you would have had Jake Carver and the rest on you, and you would have been roasted to a turn on Denton's Bridge. Miss Lily, too" —

"My God!" said Servosse, "you are right! I had never thought of it in that way. I have done the young man injustice. I will write to him, and render our thanks."

John Burleson was in high glee, thinking he had served his friend not only effectually but skillfully; for Servosse had no idea of the real motive which animated Melville Gurney in inventing the fiction which he had used to account for his wounded arm.

At the earnest solicitation of Lily, all knowledge of the shooting had been confined to Judge Denton and her mother, so that Melville's excuse was still regarded by all others as the true explanation of his misfortune. It was well known that she had ridden to Glenville to warn her father of his danger, and there was an indefinite idea that she had had a wonderful escape from the Klan on the way; but even those who composed the party had no distinct idea of the manner of her

escape. If it occurred to any one of them to suspect the fidelity of Melville Gurney, that suspicion was put at rest by the
fact that he had ever since seemed utterly oblivious of her
presence.

So Servosse repeated to his daughter the story which Burleson had given, and at its conclusion said, "I think that we
have done him injustice, and that I ought to write, and acknowledge his considerateness; don't you, my dear?"

The blushes had deepened on her cheeks as he thus spoke,
and she looked up shyly with a tender light in her eyes, at the
question he asked. If he had looked at her, she would have
opened her heart, and shown him a tender secret which lay
hidden there even from the watchful eyes of her mother, who
for a while after her adventure had half-suspected the truth,
and had laid many innocent little plans to surprise her secret,
but without success. The Man did not look up, however, so
she only answered him demurely, —

"As you choose, Papa. I am sure you know best."

And so, he wrote his letter of acknowledgment, had the
satisfaction of having done his duty, and thought no more of
the matter.

CHAPTER XLIII

UNCONDITIONAL SURRENDER

I HAVE come, Colonel Servosse," said Melville Gurney, sitting in the other's office a few days after the events narrated in the preceding chapter, "to ask your permission to pay my addresses to your daughter."

"What!" exclaimed Servosse, starting from his easy attitude, and gazing at the flushed and embarrassed young man, with a look of consternation which the latter mistook for anger.

"I know, Colonel Servosse," he began in a stammering, apologetic voice —

"Stop, stop!" said Servosse, springing to his feet, and beginning to pace up and down the room. "Do not say any thing now, if you please. I wish to think."

The young man looked with amazement on the evident agitation of the man whose coolness and self-possession he had so often heard his father mention with admiration and surprise. He had expected to be embarrassed himself; and, during the half-hour's conversation which had preceded his avowal, he had fully realized his premonition. The reiterated thanks of the other for the service rendered himself and daughter had been received with confusing blushes; and his replies had been disjointed and irrelevant. As is always the case, his embarrassment kept adding to his confusion of ideas, until at length he had blurted out the words which had produced such a surprising effect on his auditor. For a time, the younger man was by far the more composed of the twain. The elder walked back and forth across the room until his face settled into those calm, rigid lines which betoken a fixed purpose. Then he sat down opposite the young man, and, looking at him quietly but not unkindly, said, —

"Well?"

"I have loved Miss Lily," said Melville, thus inquiringly addressed, "ever since I first saw her."

"On the night of"—asked Servosse, with an expressive tone and gesture.

"No," returned the other: "I had met her before, while she was visiting some friends in Pultowa. She was little more than a child then; but I was so impressed with her that I asked leave to visit her at home, and was shortly after invited to a party here."

"Ah, I recollect!" interposed the listener.

"Soon after that time occurred the incident of which we have been speaking. I should have spoken immediately after that: but I inferred, from her silence and your seeming coolness, that she had lost all regard, or, rather, entertained a positive dislike, for me. I was too proud to take any indirect method to satisfy myself upon this point. Your letter seemed to open the way for me, and I came as soon as I thought would appear seemly."

"And Lily, have you spoken to her?" asked Servosse, with some sternness.

"I have not seen her since the day after her adventure, save at a distance, and have never spoken a word to her in regard to such a matter."

"And your parents, young man, what do they say?" asked the Fool sharply.

The brown-bearded face before him flushed hotly, and the young man drew himself up somewhat haughtily, as he replied, —

"I am twenty-eight years old, have a fair estate in my own right, and chiefly of my own acquisition. I am not under the control of my parents."

"I did not ask with regard to your estate, sir," said Servosse quietly: "I asked as to your parents' wishes."

"I beg pardon," said the lover. "I should have answered before; but I hardly see why my happiness should be made to depend on my parents' wishes. If I were a minor, it would be natural."

"Yet I suppose I may ask, whether the answer be material or immaterial to your proposal," said the Fool with the utmost composure.

"Oh, certainly!" said the young man, with considerable confusion. "Well, to tell you the truth, Colonel, they are very strongly averse to it. I considered it my duty to let them know what I intended doing."

"I am very glad you did so," interposed Servosse.

"I told them, and was met with remonstrances and reproaches by my mother, and with more of anger than my father had ever shown towards me before."

"Their objection was what?" sharply.

"I don't know exactly. In the first place, they had made up their minds that I should do otherwise. I knew that before, had known it for years. They had looked forward, and mapped out my life for me, — all in kindness and love I know, — and I am sorry I can not comply with their wishes. I told them that I could not, and that I must be the judge of my own happiness."

"And then?" as the young man paused.

"Well," said he apologetically, "there was as much of a scene as there ever is in my father's house. He told me that if I persisted in ruining my prospects I might take the responsibility. And my mother, — well, sir, you must excuse her: she was much disappointed, but it will not last, — she said that if I must marry a Yankee girl I need not bring her there."

"In other words, your parents object to an alliance with my family because we are of Northern birth," said the Fool.

"Not exactly: not so much because you are Northerners, as because you are *not* Southerners, — are strangers so to speak; not of *us*, nor imbued with our feelings; speaking our language, but not thinking our thoughts. Then, too, you know, Colonel, there has been much political bitterness, and very harsh things have been said; and there is among the people — I mean those who constitute our best society — a strange sort of prejudice against you, which naturally extends, in some measure, to your family."

"Was there any other objection urged?"

"None."

"And what did you say to this?"

"Only what I said years ago, when I first realized the strength of my attachment: 'I will woo and win Lily Servosse for my wife if I can.'"

"And you are still so disposed?"

"Most assuredly."

There was silence between them for a time, and then Servosse said, —

"Your conduct in this whole matter has been most honorable, Mr. Gurney; and, so far as you are personally concerned, you are entirely unobjectionable to me. What may be my daughter's opinion, I have no means of knowing. I have hardly yet accustomed myself to recognize the possibility of such an event as her marriage. She is lively and sociable, and for a few years past has had considerable society of a general sort, but, so far as I am aware, has never before been thought of as marriageable, nor do I think the idea has once entered her own mind.

"I will not conceal from you, Mr. Gurney, that I wish it had not occurred to you. I think your parents' objections are wise and weighty. I do not put it upon the ground of restraint or duty; but I think they correctly estimate the difference of surroundings, habits of thought, and all those things which enter so largely into the make-up of human life, and which youth and passion often fail to consider. I think it would be better for you to wed a daughter of your own people, and better for her to take a husband whose ideas are more in harmony with those to which she has been accustomed. I know these also to be, even more decidedly, the views of my wife. I suppose she would feel almost as badly at her daughter's marrying a Southern man as your mother does at the prospect of a Northern daughter-in-law, or perhaps worse.

"Notwithstanding these views, I admit that it is entirely a question of your mutual happiness, which no one can determine but yourselves. I have the utmost confidence in Lily's judgment and sincerity. I would not have her accept or reject your proposal hastily. It is not the case of two young people who have grown up together, each knowing the other's faults, understanding their mental and moral natures. You are almost strangers.

"Oh, I know!" he continued, responsively to a shake of the young man's head, "Love has wings, and makes swift journeys and instant discoveries; but it will do no harm to have his reports confirmed by reason and quiet observation. I shall do nothing to influence her decision, unless she asks my advice; in which case I shall tell her, as near as may be, what I have told you.

"You have my leave to pay your addresses; and, if I can not wish you success in your wooing, I hope you understand that I will throw no obstacle in your way, and, should you succeed, will do all in my power to render happy the result. I hope that my frankness will induce a like candor upon your part with my daughter. I need hardly tell you that you will find her more ripened and developed in mind and character than her years would lead a stranger to expect."

The two men shook hands, and Melville inquired if he could see Miss Lily. Upon inquiry, it was found that she had just started to ride upon "the three-o'clock road" towards Verdenton, — a road so denominated because it lay through the woods, and, even at that most oppressive hour of the day, the sun did not once beat upon the traveler in the five miles which it extended.

"She has Young Lollard," the father said, as he returned from the house; "but she is too good a horsewoman to ride fast at the beginning, and in this heat. You will probably overtake her before she reaches the town, and you can take your own time on the return. By the way," he added, "I spoke briefly to my wife of your errand, and she fully approves what I have said to you."

The young man thanked him again, sprang on his horse, and dashed off in the direction indicated.

Half way to the town, Lily was passing through a shady bottom, when the clatter of a horse's hoofs behind her attracted her attention, and, turning, she saw a man approaching at full speed, mounted on a powerful gray horse. At the first glance she recognized the horse as that ridden by the messenger who had brought the warning of her father's peril. During all the time that had since elapsed, she had never forgotten the horse or the rider, and had always been on the watch for them, in order that she might testify her gratitude. The memory this discovery evoked so startled and overwhelmed her, that she quite forgot to notice the rider, until Melville Gurney drew up at her side, and, doffing his hat, said cheerily, —

"Good-evening, Miss Lily!" And then, noticing her pallor and confusion, he added, "Pardon me: I hope I did not startle you. It was very thoughtless in me to ride up at that gait; and, indeed, I would not have done so, had I not known your skill as a horsewoman."

"Oh!" she said confusedly, "it was not you, but your horse."

"Of course," he replied, laughing heartily. "That is what I supposed; and it was for my horse I was apologizing."

"But I did not mean that," she said, blushing prettily, and laughing too. "I thought I recognized your horse; and it startled me to see him again."

"Ah! you are a close observer of horses," he said pleasantly. "When and where did you think you had seen him? He is a somewhat notable horse."

"Very! One could hardly fail to remember him. Does he belong to you, Mr. Gurney?"

"What, Reveillé?" he asked, with an amused smile. "No, indeed! He is my father's favorite saddle-horse. Never had a harness on; and I don't suppose any one ever backed him but Pa, myself, and Brother Jimmie."

"A younger brother?" she asked innocently.

"Yes, ten years younger."

"Is he like you?"

"No, lighter. Almost as blonde as you."

"How long has your father owned Reveillé?"

"Raised him from a foal. He is almost as fond of horses as your father, Miss Lily."

"Indeed!" And she thought with a strange pleasure, "And your father saved my father's life." Then it occurred to her that possibly it might have been the act of the man who rode beside her: she would find out. So she said, with burning cheeks and an arch emphasis, —

"You were not so well mounted when we rode together last, Mr. Gurney."

"No, indeed. Pa had Reveillé with him in another county when I left home the day before."

"For which fact it behooves me to be duly grateful, I do not doubt, Mr. Gurney," she said lightly.

"Reveillé *could* have pushed Young Lollard closer than the black mare *did*," he answered, with significant emphasis.

Something in his tone made her heart beat with strange apprehension. To change the subject, she said desperately, eying the horse critically as she spoke, —

"I think I have seen that horse at Warrington."

"I am sure he was never there until to-day," he answered.

"You came by there, then?" she asked, because she could think of nothing else to say. The strange prescience of her woman's heart told her that her hour had come; and, like a moth about a candle, it seemed that she but fluttered nearer to her doom with every weak attempt to avoid it.

"My business was with your father," he replied.

She looked up quickly, as if surprised, and met his eyes flaming down into her own the question which his tremulous lips were trying to syllable forth. The terror of maiden love in its last effort at concealment took hold upon her. She would have given worlds to avert the utterance of words which she knew would come, which her bounding heart was clamorous to reward. The horses were walking slowly, side by side, in the cool shadows. He reached across, and took her bridle-hand in his, and stopped them both. She did not resist. She wished she had not submitted. She could not lift her eyes from her horse's mane. Then came one last struggle of maidenly reserve. As is always the case, it was one of those stupid blunders which throw down the last defense, and leave the fluttering, tender heart at the mercy of the relentless assailant.

"O Mr. Gurney," she cried, in feverish desperation, "I have never had a chance before to beg your forgiveness for what I did that night! I am sure I am very sorry."

"And I am very glad to hear you say so," he said exultantly.

"Why?" She looked up in wonder at his apparent rudeness; but her eyes fell again, as he replied, —

"Because your sorrow for the past will incline you to be merciful in the future. If you are sorry for having broken my arm, how would you feel if you should break my heart?"

Her head sank lower. The two thorough-breds were amicably making acquaintance, regardless of the little drama which was being enacted by their riders.

"Lily," — his head was bent very low, and the word thrilled her heart like the low music of an unseen waterfall, — "Lily, I asked your father to allow me to seek your love; and he sent me to learn my fate from your lips. What shall it be, Lily? Will you be mine?"

"O Melville! I mean, Mr." — she stammered hastily.

His arm was about her waist. She was half drawn from her saddle, and bearded lips took tribute of her trembling mouth, and eyes glowing with impassioned lovelight looked down into hers, before she could protest. One instant she yielded herself to the intoxication of young love. Then there came a chilling fear, and she asked, with shuddering premonition, —

"But your father, your parents, Mr. Gurney, — do they know what you are — what you wish?"

"Yes."

"And do they — do they — approve?" hesitatingly.

"What matters that, darling? *Your* father does not object, and I am of age," he answered, with something of defiance.

She freed herself at once from his embrace, and sat erect and queenly in her saddle. He regarded her changed demeanor with something of apprehension; but he said lightly, —

"You have not given me my answer yet, Lily. What shall it be? Will you break my heart as well as my arm?"

She looked frankly and unflinchingly into his eyes, and laid her hand softly but firmly on his arm, as she replied in a calm, even tone, —

"Melville — Mr. Gurney, there can be no thought of — of what you wish, between us, so long as your father is opposed to the course you have taken."

"But, Lily — Miss Servosse, you surely *do* not, you *can*

not, mean what you have said!" he cried, in an agony of surprise and pain.

She merely turned, and looked into his eyes again, and made no more reply. He knew then that she would adhere to her resolution until death, if there were any need to do so. An icy chill went through his frame. The joy seemed frozen out of his countenance, and only a sad, hopeless hunger remained. After a moment, he said huskily, —

"Will you tell me why, Lily?"

"I can not, Melville," she answered. A little hope shot up in his heart.

"I have waited a long time, Lily. I have tried in vain to remove my father's objection. Is my duty alone to him, and for ever?"

"It is not *your* duty, Mr. Gurney, it is *mine*, that impels me to say what I have."

"*Your* duty? How can that be? What duty do you owe *my* father?"

"I can not tell you."

"Is it your duty, as you say, because you think I have failed in mine?"

"Not at all."

The horses had become impatient, and began to walk on.

"And you mean this to be final?" he asked half querulously.

She drew rein, and looked him full in the eye again.

"Melville Gurney," she said, "you know what I dared for my father. I would dare even more for your sake; but I can not yield to your request, because your father objects, and because — *because I love my father!*"

"Because you love your father? I can not understand. He has not objected."

"So I am aware."

"You are pleased to deal in riddles."

"I am sorry."

They rode on a little way in silence. Then he stopped his horse, and, raising his hat, said coolly, —

"I will bid you good-evening, Miss Lily."

Tears stood in her eyes as she leaned towards him, and laid her hand upon his arm, and said, —

"Do not, Melville. You must not be angry with me. I am sure I am doing right, but I can not explain. Let us go back to Warrington. Be patient. All will be well; and some time, I am sure, you will approve my course."

How beautiful she looked as she pleaded for kindness! But her beauty only inflamed his anger. He seized her fiercely by the arm. She did not shrink, though his grip was like steel, and he knew that the slender arm would bear the marks of his violence for many a day.

"Lily Servosse," he said passionately, "listen to me! You must — you shall be mine! I swear that I will never wed any one but you!"

"I will take *that* oath with you, Melville Gurney," she replied seriously, "and seal it with a kiss."

She lifted up her face, and he pressed a kiss upon her proffered lips.

"And now," she said gayly, as she wheeled her horse, "for a gallop back to Warrington!"

When they came in sight of her home she drew rein, and he asked anxiously, —

"When shall I see you again?"

"When your father sends you to me," she answered gayly.

They said "good-evening" at the gate, and she watched him through her tears as he rode away. She saw her father standing at his library-door as she turned, and dashing up to him she leaped into his arms, and was borne into the library. With her head hidden in his breast she told him all, and more than she had told her lover.

"Did I not do right, dear Papa?" she asked, when the story was completed.

"God knows, my daughter!" he replied solemnly; and his tears fell upon her blushing, upturned face as he kissed her, but his own was lighted up with a rapturous joy, which was an abundant answer.

Then he took her in his arms, and carried her up the steps of the great house (thinking the meanwhile of the romping girl whom he had first borne thither a dozen years before), to the room where the still fair mother sat, and, placing one upon either knee, repeated the story to her.

The setting sun looked in, and kissed their mingling tears with golden light.

"Well," said General Gurney, with a tinge of sarcasm, when he met his son the next morning, "I suppose you accomplished your errand?"

"I saw Miss Lily Servosse," was the terse reply.

"And offered her your heart and hand?" mockingly.

"I certainly did," was the emphatic answer.

"And was accepted *with thanks*, no doubt." The sneer was intense by this time. "Really I" —

"Stop!" said the son, turning on him a brow as haughty as his own, and black with suppressed thunder. "You little know whom you are deriding! Do I look like an accepted lover?"

His father looked after him in open-mouthed wonder as he strode away. He felt for the first time, as he did so, that he had fallen back from the foremost place. He was a part of that ever-shrinking Old which the ever-increasing New is perpetually overshadowing. His sight was not dimmed, his arm was unshrunken; but the life which had sprung from his loins was stronger than he. He might be an equal for a time, by the grace of filial love, but no more the guide and helper. All at once he awoke to the fact that the world had moved while he had been sleeping. For the first time he began to doubt his own wisdom.

"Fanny," he said to his wife later in the day, in an incredulous, querulous tone, "can it be that that — that — minx has refused our Melville?"

"So it seems," answered the good lady, about equally astounded at her husband's tone and the fact she announced.

"Confound their Yankee impudence! Just think of a Gurney jilted by a Yankee! It's like them, though, and I am glad of it. It will teach the young fool to look at some of our home girls."

"Don't think that," said the wife, with truer forecast. "Melville will never marry any one else. He told me so himself."

"Oh! he'll get over that."

"Some might; but he will not. I'm almost sorry we opposed him. It seems that, when she found that out, my lady was on her dignity, and would not hear a word more."

"You don't say so!" he exclaimed in surprise. "I declare, I admire her pluck. There must be good blood about her. It will teach the young rascal to despise his parents' wishes. I never expected to think as well of her. She must be a rough, coarse hoyden, from what I learn about her, though, — any thing but a fit wife for Melville!"

"I suppose so," assented the mother, with a sigh.

CHAPTER XLIV

PRIDE OVERMATCHING PRIDE

F ROM the night of her perilous ride, Young Lollard had become the sole and separate property of Lily Servosse. In acknowledgment and remembrance of that act, a decree had gone forth at Warrington that none else should ride the carefully nurtured horse but his young mistress, or such as she might give express permission so to do. As the public interests and duties of the father lessened, the old routine of rambling rides about the country roads was resumed, — the father and daughter becoming almost inseparable companions, the mother, by reason of her added household cares, seldom accompanying them. Sometimes, however, the daughter went alone.

It was on such an occasion, not long after the events of the last chapter, that Lily one day came upon a pack of hounds running on a hot trail in the low woods upon the left of the road she was pursuing. Such a circumstance was by no means uncommon in that region; and, though she had herself never joined in a chase, yet she had so often listened to accounts of them, and had so observed her father's keen relish of their excitement the few times she had known him to engage in them, that her pulses beat faster as the chase turned toward the road, and grew faster and hotter, and the clamor wilder and fiercer, every moment.

Young Lollard had been ridden to hounds a few times, and had not forgotten the wonderful excitement of the chase. As he heard it now sweeping towards him, he stopped and stood like a statue, save for the tremor of delight which swept through his frame at each new outburst of the clamorous music, and the quivering ears, distended nostrils, and long deep suspirations. Lily knew that he would not long remain so; and with all her fearlessness as a horsewoman she did not quite relish the idea of his bursting away through the low-branching second-growth to follow the pack. She was very doubtful of her power to restrain him. Half laughing, she thought of the tattered plight she would soon be in should she fail to do so. She saw her jaunty hat snatched by overhanging limbs, her flowing habit hooked by thorn and brier, and perchance some of her flowing locks caught like Absalom's. Yet she did not once think of abandoning her seat. She braced herself for whatever might come, determined, if not well satisfied of her power to hold him back, to let him take his course rather than allow him to suppose that he was able to do otherwise than as she desired. Perhaps she was not entirely averse to trying one of those dashes through the brush which she had so often heard described when the trained horse needs no guidance; indeed, none can be attempted, as he leaps with instinctive certainty through the most available openings of the wood. She patted the arched neck, and spoke in her most soothing tones, as the chase drew nearer and nearer. All at once, and just as she expected to see the pack come bursting from the copse upon the roadside, their course changed sharply to the left, and they swept down a little ridge almost parallel with the road. Then she gave her horse the rein, and he bounded forward with his magnificent stride, almost abreast of the hunt, his eye and ear alert for every indication of their presence.

The ridge which the chase was following ran about midway between the road on which Lily was, and another into which this led about half a mile from where she had stopped. Just before reaching this road, the land sloped sharply towards it, the ground was more open, and, beyond the road, fell away to a wide bottom, stretching down to a creek with thick willow margins and occasional patches of dense reeds. It was this shelter that the chase was evidently striving to reach.

Lily felt all the surging frenzy of the huntsman as Young Lollard tore along the slightly undulating road, and once or twice found herself even urging him on, as she fancied the hunt was gaining upon him. As she neared the intersection, she heard a loud view-halloo upon the other road, and an instant after, seeing the chase as he glided swiftly across an open space in the copse, she returned it in her shrill treble as she had been taught to do by her father. Hardly fifty yards behind him came the pack; and, as he dashed across the road into the open ground leading down to the creek, they burst into a louder and wilder chorus, and then, neck to neck, with short, impatient yelps, the sinewy undulating backs rising and falling together, one a length in advance, and one unfortunate fellow struggling along in the rear, they swept across the smooth expanse of old corn-rows down upon their prey.

So absorbed was Lily in the sight and in the exhilarating motion of her horse, that she hardly noticed the horseman whose view-halloo she had heard, but swept on unconscious of all but the hunt, of which she had now become a part. She did dimly notice a horseman who reached the intersection almost at the same time, on a powerful gray, from whose long strides even Young Lollard was able to draw away but little in the few hundred yards over which they flew before the race was ended. The huntsman leaped down at once, and, dashing among the hounds, rescued the chase before they had time to mutilate it, and came towards Lily, holding up a magnificent specimen of the red fox. He smoothed its rumpled coat, and displayed its splendid brush, with the keen appreciation of the veteran hunter, as he came forward, and held it up for her inspection, exclaiming, —

"A fine fellow, Madam, and a splendid chase — at least, a splendid burst at the end! And gallantly ridden, Madam, allow me to say, gallantly ridden!" He raised his hat as he spoke, smiled pleasantly, and continued, "Allow me to present this trophy, Madam, which few ladies have ever as fairly earned. You were easily the first in at the death, though I must confess that I most ungallantly pressed my horse when I saw yours drawing away from him. We had about an even start at the road, and I was greatly chagrined at not being able to keep neck and neck with you. That is a splendid animal you have," he added after he had hung the fox to her saddle. "I did not think there was a horse in this region that could distance mine."

He motioned towards his horse; and Lily knew at a glance that it was the same gray which was indelibly photographed upon her memory, which had brought the messenger who gave warning of her father's peril, and the lover who sought her hand in vain, although he had borne away her heart.

"This, then, is Melville's father, the man who stands between us and happiness," she said to herself, as she turned her gaze upon him, conscious that her cheeks were flushed even beyond what the excitement of the chase would justify.

She saw a tall, haughty-faced man, in whose eye there was no indecision, and whose firm-shut lips confirmed the judgment instinctively made up from eye and brow. The close-clipped beard and slightly-curling hair were of the same rich brown as his son's, but streaked here and there with gray. In form and feature his son closely resembled him, softened in outline, and perhaps somewhat less formal and austere in manner. Despite the feeling of injustice which had rankled in her bosom toward this man since she knew of the objection which he had interposed to her union with his favorite son, she could not avoid a feeling of pride in the father of her lover. While she made these observations, he had been scanning, with the eye of a connoisseur, the proportions of Young Lollard, and remarking upon his excellences. The hounds were stretched about, lolling in utter exhaustion, or wallowing and drinking in the creek near by.

"A splendid horse, Madam, and finely bred. He has a look which I ought to remember, though I can not recall where I have seen it. Not a stock often met with here. Somewhat more of bone than our thorough-breds usually show. You know his stock, of course, Madam. No one could ride such a horse, and ride him as you do, without appreciating his qualities. Let me see," he continued, without waiting for reply, and stepping back a pace or two, so as to get the *ensemble* of the horse more readily, "he is like — no — yes, he is *very* like — Colonel Servosse's Lollard."

"And he is Young Lollard," said Lily.

The man raised his eyes quickly to her face, and let them fall, with careful scrutiny of her dress and figure, to the horse again, as he said musingly, —

"Ah, yes! I remember his telling me about the colt. By a Glencoe dam, I think he said."

"Yes," assented Lily.

"And you?" he asked, looking her full in the face.

"I am Lily Servosse," she answered, in tones as calm as his own.

"So I inferred," he responded. "The Colonel has reason to be proud, both of his daughter and his horse," he added, with quiet approval in his voice. "And I am General Gurney. Allow me to introduce myself, Miss Lily, and wish for our better acquaintance." He doffed his hat again, and watched her keenly, as he extended his hand. Her countenance did not change, and she said, with the utmost composure, —

"Thank you. I had inferred as much."

He smiled at this echo of his own words, and said, looking at his own horse, "Indeed! You have seen him before, I suppose?"

"Twice."

"Yes. That reminds me, Miss Lily, that I am your debtor for refusing the offer of my son's hand, not long since. It seems a queer thing to thank one for; and, now that I have seen you," he added pleasantly, "I can not wonder that he made the tender. At his age, I am almost certain I should have risked a like fate."

"Not unless the horse were to be my dowry, I am afraid," she retorted mischievously.

"Well," said he, laughing, "the pair should not be separated. But seriously," he added, "I am thankful for your rejection of his suit, and hope I may express it without offense. I am not surprised that he should become enamoured of one having such charms, nor surprised at his chagrin; but you must know, Miss Lily, parents will form plans for their children, and we had especially fixed our hearts upon another wife for Melville. I am afraid he may take your refusal so much to heart, that we shall miss having a daughter at all; though it may help him to overcome his attachment."

"But I did not refuse him, General Gurney," she said, with quiet candor.

"You did not refuse him? I understood him to say that he had been refused; or at least his mother so informed me," he responded with surprise.

"I told him," Lily replied to his questioning tone and surprised look, "that, so long as his father was opposed to it, there could be nothing looking towards marriage between us."

"And why did you make that condition?" he asked in surprise. "Such regard for the filial duty of a lover is not usual with our American ladies."

"I refused to explain to Melville," she replied, "but you have a right to inquire. There was little or no thought of his filial duty in it. I simply felt it a duty which I owed to you *myself*."

"How, to me? I do not understand," he said, with a puzzled look.

"Because you sent the warning which saved my father's life," she answered steadily.

He started, and flushed to his temples.

"You infer that also!" he said sharply. "From what, may I ask?"

"Your younger son brought it, riding upon that horse," she said, pointing to Reveillé.

"And that warning caused you to try a perilous ride," said he.

"Which I was only too happy to undertake," she responded quickly.

"And did you not think it was cowardly and mean for me to leave it for you to thwart that horrible scheme?" he asked.

"I had never thought of it in that light," she answered musingly.

"I have often, since; and have thoroughly despised my weakness. I even tried to conceal the fact that I had given the warning. I have never told any one, not even the boy who bore the message."

"I have only told my father," she said simply.

"And you refused my son's addresses solely on account of that fact?" he asked musingly.

"The question is hardly a fair one," she answered, for the first time somewhat confused.

"I beg pardon," he said quickly. "You are right. I have no right to ask that question. I withdraw it."

"No, General Gurney," said Lily, looking at him earnestly, "I will conceal nothing from you. I refused to accede to his request that we should be engaged, for that reason alone."

"And your father — does he know?"

"I have been as frank with him as with you."

"And he approves?"

"Most heartily."

"Miss Lily" —

There was the blast of a horn, and a half-dozen horsemen dashed into sight upon the road by which the general had come.

"Yo-ho-o-o!" he shouted quickly, in reply, adding briefly to her, "There is my friend Morrow. I thought these were his dogs. I stumbled on the hunt, as well as you."

The horsemen were at hand by the time he had finished this remark. Introductions and explanations followed. Morrow gave a history of the run. The general gave a vivid recital of the capture. Compliments were showered profusely upon Lily; and Morrow accepted her invitation to "go by" her father's house, and dine with them, as it was upon his way home. Greetings were exchanged; and, under the escort of the fresh-hearted fox-hunter, Lily returned to Warrington.

"I declare, Colonel," was his final comment as he rode away after dinner, "some of our fine young fellows must make a run for that gal of yours. Ding my buttons if she ain't more Southern than any of our own gals! It won't do for such a gal as that to go North for a husband. It would be a pity, I swear, to let her marry a Yankee! It mustn't be, Colonel. I shall send some one to prevent such a calamity."

"Too late, Morrow," said Servosse briskly. "She leaves for the North on Monday, and takes Young Lollard with her."

"You don't say!" exclaimed the old man ruefully. "Well, they'll never let her come back, that's certain: they've too much sense for that. Gal and hoss both! Well, I swear it's a shame."

After much consideration, it had been decided that Warrington should be closed for a year; that Lily should go to a Northern city to pursue certain studies for which she had developed a peculiar aptitude; and that her mother should accompany her. Colonel Servosse proposed to pass a portion of the time with them, and to devote the rest to certain business matters which would necessarily require his absence during a considerable portion of the year. The next summer it was proposed to spend a couple of months at Warrington, and then leave it, — perhaps for good, at least for a prolonged absence.

It was at Lily's special request that this return to Warrington had been made a part of the family programme. While she had not once faltered in the resolution she had formed, she looked confidently for the time to come when General Gurney should relent. She did not for a moment distrust the constancy of her banished lover, and hardly repined at the fate which separated them, so confident was she that he would return. In the mean time she applied herself with still greater zest to study, counting every acquisition which she made as one more attraction which she would be able to offer Melville Gurney in compensation for his long probation. The autumn leaves were falling when the Fool and his family bade adieu to their Southern home.

A week afterwards Marion Gurney rode up to the gate, and, hailing the deserted house, was told by the faithful Andy, who with his wife had been left in charge of the house and grounds, that "de Kunnel an' all de folks had done gone Norf."

"When will they return?" asked Gurney.

"Wal, sah, I don't 'llow as ever," said Andy. "Dey talks 'bout comin' back h'yer fer a little time nex summer; but I specs dey'll be habbin' sech good times dar, an' fine so many frens in de Norf, dey'll quite forgit dis pore, mean country whar dey's hed so much to contend wid, an' jes' keep on stayin' dar. What makes me tink so more'n all de res' is, dat Miss Lily's tuk Young Lollard. Ef dat hoss hed only staid, I'd felt sure she was comin' back."

"Well," soliloquized General Gurney as he rode homeward, "I reckon it's just as well. I liked the girl mightily, that's a fact; but she's a Yankee, after all. I wish Melville never had seen her. I had made up my mind, though, to eat humble pie, and tell her I withdrew my opposition. I can't bear to see him going round so moody and solemn, when he used to be so bright and cheery. Perhaps, now that she's gone, he'll think better of it, and give her up. I hope so, anyhow.

"Servosse, too, wasn't a bad sort of a man. I used to wish I was better acquainted with him, and really suppose I ought to have exerted myself to make it homelike for him here. He *must* have had a dull life of it. But then he was so awfully radical in his Northern notions! He ought never to have come here, that's the truth of the matter. Nobody can force Northern ideas on the South. The soil and climate don't take to them kindly. It's like Northern farming in a piney old-field, — looks well enough, but don't pay. I'm sure I wish him well, and Miss Lily too. She's just the girl I'd like Melville to marry, if she wasn't a Yankee, and her daddy wasn't a Radical. I reckon he'll forget her now. I hope so, at least."

He sighed as he rode on; but his wish proved abortive. Melville Gurney was seized with a passion for travel as soon as he heard of the hegira from Warrington; and, strangely enough, his footsteps led him to the same city where Lily was studying, with her heart full of dreams of his coming. More than once, as the months flew by, she turned hastily in the crowded thoroughfares with the feeling that his eye was upon her. A few times she thought she saw a familiar figure in the crowd; and her heart would beat fast while her eye sought to catch the loved outlines again. Then she would go on with a light laugh, well pleased that her heart attested its faithfulness by a fond self-deception.

Melville soon became conscious of the true state of affairs, and determined not to be outdone in steadfastness. So he made no sign, but studied the great city that opened its myriad-paged book of life before him, and learned many a rare lesson which the insular exclusiveness of the South could never teach.

Thus the lovers waited; but the father, irritated at his son's course, said, "If he wants to make a fool of himself over that little Yankee, let him go."

CHAPTER XLV

WISDOM AND FOLLY MEET TOGETHER

I⊤ was shortly after the rupture of his home-life and his departure from Warrington, that Servosse visited, by special invitation, Doctor Enos Martin, the ancient friend who had been at first his instructor, and afterward his revered and trusted counselor. In the years which had elapsed since the Fool had seen him, he had passed from a ripe manhood of surpassing vigor into that riper age which comes without weakness, but which, nevertheless, brings not a little of philosophic calm, — that true "sunset of life which gives mystical lore." It is in those calm years which come before the end, when ambition is dead, and aspiration ceases; when the restless clamor of busy life sweeps by unheeded as the turmoil of the crowded thoroughfare by the busy worker; when the judgment acts calmly, unbiased by hope or fear, — it is in these declining years that the best work of the best lives is usually done. The self which makes the balance waver is dead; but the heart, the intellect, the keen sympathy with that world which is fast slipping away, remain, and the ripened energies act without the wastefulness of passion. It was in this calm brightness which precedes the twilight, that Enos Martin sat down to converse with the man, now rugged and mature, whom he had watched while he grew from youth into manhood, and from early manhood to its maturity. A score of years had passed since they had met. To the one, these years had been full of action. He had been in the current, had breasted its buffetings, and been carried away out of the course which he had marked out for himself on life's great chart, by its cross-currents and counter-eddies. He had a scar to show for every struggle. His heart had throbbed in harmony

with the great world-pulse in every one of the grand purposes with which it had swelled during those years. The other
had watched with keenest apprehension those movements
which had veered and whirled about in their turbid currents
the life of the other, himself but little moved, but ever seeking
to draw what lessons of value he might from such observation, for the instruction and guidance of other young souls
who were yet but skirting the shore of the great sea of life.

This constant and observant interest in the great social
movements of the world which he overlooked from so serene
a height had led him to note with peculiar care the relations
of the nation to the recently subjugated portion of the South,
and more especially the conditions of the blacks. In so doing,
he had been led to consider especially that transition period
which comes between Chattelism, or some form of individual
subordination and dependence, and absolute individual autonomy. This is known by different names in different lands and
ages, — villenage in England, serfdom in Russia. In regard to
this, his inquiries had been most profound, and his interest
in all those national questions had accordingly been of the
liveliest character: hence his keen desire to see his old pupil,
and to talk with one in whom he had confidence as an observer, in regard to the phenomena he had witnessed and the
conclusions at which he had arrived, and to compare the same,
not only with his own more remote observations, but also with
the facts of history. They sat together for a long time in the
library where the elder had gathered the intellectual wealth
of the world and the ages, and renewed the personal knowledge of each other which a score of years had interrupted.
The happenings of the tumultuous life, the growth of the
quiet one, were both recounted; and then their conversation
drifted to that topic which had engrossed so much of the
thought of both, — that great world-current of which both
lives were but unimportant incidents.

"And so," said the elder gravely, "you think, Colonel Servosse, that what has been termed Reconstruction is a magnificent failure?"

"Undoubtedly," was the reply, "so far as concerns the attainment of the result intended by its projectors, expected by the world, and to be looked for as a logical sequence of the war."

"I do not know that I fully understand your limitation," said Martin doubtfully.

"I mean," said the younger man, "that Reconstruction was a failure so far as it attempted to unify the nation, to make one people in fact of what had been one only in name before the convulsion of civil war. It was a failure, too, so far as it attempted to fix and secure the position and rights of the colored race. They were fixed, it is true, on paper, and security of a certain sort taken to prevent the abrogation of that formal declaration. No guaranty whatever was provided against their practical subversion, which was accomplished with an ease and impunity that amazed those who instituted the movement."

"You must at least admit that the dogma of 'State Rights' was settled by the war and by that system of summary and complete national control over the erring commonwealths which we call Reconstruction," said Martin.

"On the contrary," answered Servosse, "the doctrine of 'State Rights' is altogether unimpaired and untouched by what has occurred, except in one particular; to wit, *the right of peaceable secession*. The war settled that. The Nation asserted its right to defend itself against disruption."

"Did it not also assert its right to re-create, to make over, to reconstruct?" asked the elder man.

"Not at all," was the reply. "Reconstruction was never asserted *as a right*, at least not formally and authoritatively. Some did so affirm; but they were accounted visionaries. The act of reconstruction was *excused* as a necessary sequence of the failure of attempted secession: it was never defended or promulgated as a *right of the nation*, even to *secure its own safety*."

"Why, then, do you qualify the declaration of failure?" asked Martin. "It seems to me to have been absolute and complete."

"Not at all," answered Servosse with some vehemence. "A great deal was gained by it. Suppose a child does wrong a hundred times, is reproved for it each time, and only at the last reproof expresses sorrow, and professes a desire to do better, and the very next day repeats the offense. The parent does not despair, nor count the repentance as nothing gained. On the contrary, a great step has been made: the wrong has been admitted, and is thereafter without excuse. Thenceforward, Nathan-like, the parent can point the offender to his own judgment on his own act. So Reconstruction was a great step in advance, in that it formulated a confession of error. It gave us a construction of 'we the people' in the preamble of our Federal Constitution which gave the lie to that which had formerly prevailed. It recognized and formulated the universality of manhood in governmental power, and, in one phase or another of its development, compelled the formal assent of all sections and parties."

"And is this all that has been gained by all these years of toil and struggle and blood?" asked the old man with a sigh.

"Is it not enough, my friend?" replied the Fool, with a reproachful tone. "Is not almost a century of falsehood and hypocrisy cheaply atoned by a decade of chastisement? The confession of error is the hardest part of repentance, whether in a man or in a nation. It is there the Devil always makes his strongest fight. After that, he has to come down out of the mountain, and fight in the valley. He is wounded, crippled, and easily put to rout."

"You do not regard the struggle between the North and the South as ended, then," said Martin.

"Ended?" ejaculated the Fool sharply. "It is just begun! I do not mean the physical tug of war between definitely defined sections. That is a mere incident of a great underlying struggle, — a conflict which is ever going on between two antagonistic ideas. It was like a stream with here and there an angry rapid, before the war; then, for a time, it was like a foaming cascade; and since then it has been the sullen, dark, but deep and quiet whirlpool, which lies below the fall, full of driftwood and shadows, and angry mutterings, and unseen currents, and hidden forces, whose farther course no one can foretell, only that it must go on.

'The deepest ice that ever froze
Can only o'er the river close:
The living stream lies quick below,
And flows — and can not cease to flow!' "

"Do you mean to say that the old battle between freedom and slavery was not ended by the extinction of slavery?" asked the doctor in surpise.

"I suppose it would be," answered the Fool, with a hint of laughter in his tones, "if slavery *were* extinct. I do not mean to combat the old adage that 'it takes two to make a quarrel;' but that is just where our mistake — the mistake of the North, for the South has not made one in this matter — has been. We have *assumed* that slavery was dead, because we had a Proclamation of Emancipation, a Constitutional Amendment, and 'laws passed in pursuance thereof,' all reciting the fact that involuntary servitude, except for crime, should no more exist. Thereupon, we have thrown up our hats, and crowed lustily for what we had achieved, as we had a good right to do. The Antislavery Society met, and congratulated itself on the accomplishment of its mission, on having no more worlds to conquer, no more oppression to resist, and no more victims to succor. And thereupon, in the odor of its self-laudation, it dissolved its own existence, dying full of good works, and simply for the want of more good works to be done. It was an end that smacks of the millennium; but, unfortunately, it was farcical in the extreme. I don't blame Garrison and Phillips and yourself, and all the others of the old guard of abolitionists. It was natural that you should at least wish to try on your laurels while alive."

"Really, Colonel," said the old doctor laughingly, "you must not think that was our motive."

"Not confessedly, nor consciously of course," said the Fool. "Real motives are rarely formulated. I don't wonder, though, that men who had been in what our modern slang denominates the 'racket' of the antislavery reform should be tired. I fully realize that a life-time of struggle takes away a man's relish for a fight. Old men never become missionaries. Being in a conflict of ideas, they may keep up the fight till the last minute and the last breath. Old men have made good martyrs ever since Polycarp's day; but they don't long for martyrdom, nor advertise for it. If it is just as convenient to avoid it, they prefer to do so; and in this case they certainly deserved a rest, and more honor and glory than they will ever get, alive or dead.

"It was our fault, — the then youngsters who had just come out of the furnace-fire in which the shackles were fused and melted away from the cramped and shriveled limbs. We ought to have seen and known that only the shell was gone. Slavery as a formal state of society was at an end: as a force, a power, a moral element, it was just as active as before. Its conscious evils were obliterated: its unconscious ones existed in the dwarfed and twisted natures which had been subjected for generations to its influences, — master and slave alike. As a form of society, it could be abolished by proclamation and enactment: as a moral entity, it is as indestructible as the souls on which it has left its mark."

"You think the 'irrepressible conflict' is yet confronting us, then?" said Martin.

"Undoubtedly. The North and the South are simply convenient names for two distinct, hostile, and irreconcilable ideas, — two civilizations they are sometimes called, especially at the South. At the North there is somewhat more of intellectual arrogance; and we are apt to speak of the one as civilization, and of the other as a species of barbarism. These two must always be in conflict until the one prevails, and the other falls. To uproot the one, and plant the other in its stead, is not the work of a moment or a day. That was our mistake. We tried to superimpose the civilization, the idea of the North, upon the South at a moment's warning. We presumed, that, by the suppression of rebellion, the Southern white man had become identical with the Caucasian of the North in thought and sentiment; and that the slave, by emancipation, had become a saint and a Solomon at once. So we tried to build up communities there which should be identical in thought, sentiment, growth, and development, with those of the North. It was A FOOL'S ERRAND."

"On which we all ran, eh?" laughed the doctor.

"Precisely," answered Servosse sententiously.

"I am not sure but you are right," said the elder. "It looks like it now, and every thing which has happened is certainly consistent with your view. But, leaving the past, what have you to say of the future?"

"Well," answered Servosse thoughtfully, "the battle must be fought out. If there is to remain one nation on the territory we now occupy, it must be either a nation unified in sentiment and civilization, or the one civilization must dominate and control the other. As it stands now, that of the South is the most intense, vigorous, and aggressive. The power of the recent slave has been absolutely neutralized. The power of the Southern whites has been increased by exactly two-fifths of the colored adults, who were not counted in representation before the war. Upon all questions touching the nation and its future they are practically a unit, and are daily growing more and more united as those who once stood with us succumb to age or the force of their surroundings."

"But will not that change with immigration? Will not the two sections gradually mix and modify?" asked the doctor anxiously.

"Immigration to the South will in the future, as in the past, be very scattering and trivial, hardly an element worth considering. There are many reasons for this. In the first place, the South does not welcome immigration. Not that it is absolutely hostile, nor intolerant beyond endurance, except upon political subjects; but it has been exclusive until it has lost the power of assimilation; and the immigrant never becomes part and parcel of the people with whom he dwells. His children may do so sometimes, but not always. The West takes a stranger by the hand, and in a day makes him feel at home, — that he is *of* the people with whom he dwells. The South may greet him as cordially as the Orient welcomes the Caucasian trader, but, like the Orient, still makes him feel that he is an 'outside barbarian.' Besides that, the South has no need for mere labor, and the material success of those who have gone there since the war has not been such as to induce many others to follow."

"But why do you think the South more likely to rule than the more populous and more enterprising North?"

"Because they are thoroughly united, and are instinctive, natural rulers. They are not troubled with scruples, nor do they waste their energies upon frivolous and immaterial issues. They are monarchical and kinglike in their characteristics. Each one thinks more of the South than of himself, and any thing which adds to her prestige or glory is dearer to him than any personal advantage. The North thinks the Southern people are especially angry because of the loss of slave-property: in truth, they are a thousand times more exasperated by the elevation of the freed negro to equal political power. The North is disunited: a part will adhere to the South for the sake of power; and, just as before the civil war, the South will again dominate and control the nation."

"And when will this end?" asked the elder man, with a sigh of weariness.

"When the North learns to consider facts, and not to sentimentalize; or when the South shall have worked out the problem of race-conflict in her own borders, by the expiration or explosion of a system of unauthorized and illegal serfdom. The lords of the soil are the lords of the labor still, and will so remain until the laborers have grown, through the lapse of generations, either intelligent or desperate."

"Ah! my young friend," said the old man, with a glow of pride in his countenance, "there you are coming upon my ground, and, I must say, striking at my fears for the future too. The state of the newly-enfranchised freedmen at the South is most anomalous and remarkable. I can not help regarding it with apprehension. There are but few cases in history of an enslaved race leaping at once from absolute chattelism to complete self-rule. Perhaps the case of the ancient Israelites affords the closest analogy. Yet in their case, under divine guidance, two things were found necessary: First, an exodus which took them out from among the race which had been their masters, away from the scenes and surroundings of slavery; and, second, the growth of a new generation who had never known the lash of the task-master, nor felt in their own persons the degradation of servitude. The flight from Egypt, the hardships of the wilderness, the forty years of death and growth away from and beyond the ken of the Egyptian, all were necessary to fit the children of Israel for self-government and the exercise of national power, even without the direct and immediate interposition of divine aid and the daily recurrence of miraculous signs and wonders. Can the African slave of America develop into the self-governing citizen, the co-ordinate of his white brother in power, with less of preparation?"

"The analogy of the Israelitish people is so striking, that it seems to recur to almost every mind," said Servosse. "It is a favorite one with the colored people themselves. The only important difference which I can see is the lack of a religious element, — the want of a prophet."

"That is the very thing!" said the old Doctor, with animation. "Do you know that I doubt very much whether there was any special religious element in the minds of the Jewish people at that time? They did not leave Egypt, nor venture into the wilderness, because of religious persecution, or attachment to their faith. Those were things which came afterwards, both in point of time and in the sequence of their growth and development. It was to the feeling of servitude, the idea of oppression, that the twin-founders of the Judaic empire, Moses and Aaron, appealed, in order to carry *their* religious idea into effect. The Israelites followed them, not because they were their religious leaders, but because they promised relief from Egyptian bondage. The instinct of the slave is to flee from the scene of servitude when his soul begins to expand with the aspirations of independent manhood. That this spirit has not manifested itself before, in our case, I think a matter of surprise: that it will come hereafter, I fear is a certainty. I can not see how a race can become prepared for absolute autonomy, real freedom, except by the gradual process of serfdom or villenage, or by the scath and tribulation of the sojourn in the wilderness, or its equivalent of isolated self-support, by which individual self-reliance, and collective hardihood and daring, may be nourished and confirmed."

"They are likely to have their forty years," said Servosse, "and to leave more than one generation in the wilderness, before they regain the rights which were promised them, and which they for a little time enjoyed."

"Yes," said the elder, "there is another dangerous element. They have tasted liberty, full and complete; and the loss of that, even by indirection, will add to the natural antipathy of the freedman for the associations and surroundings of his servitude. I very greatly fear that this unrest is inseparable from the state of suddenly-acquired freedom; and that, animated by both these feelings, the race may attempt an exodus which will yet upset all our finely-spun theories, and test, at our very doors, the humanitarianism of which we boast. What do you think of it, Colonel?"

"Honestly, Doctor, I can not tell you," answered Servosse. "That such a feeling exists is beyond question. There is something marvelous and mysterious in the history of the African race in America, too, which appeals most powerfully to the superstitious mysticism which prevails among them. Brought here against their will; forced to undergo the harsh tutelage of slavery in sight and sound of the ceaseless service our nation offers up to liberty; mastering in two hundred years of slavery the rudiments of civilization, the alphabet of religion, of law, of mechanic art, the secrets of husbandry, and the necessity and reward of labor; freed almost without exertion upon their part, and entirely without their independent and intelligent co-operation, — with all this of history before their eyes, it is not strange they should consider themselves the special pets of Providence, — a sort of chosen people. This chapter of miracles, as they account these wonderful happenings, is always present to the fervid fancies of the race; and, while it has hitherto inclined them to inaction, would be a powerful motive, should it once come, to act in concert with a conviction that their future must be laid in a region remote from the scene of their past. If they were of the same stock as the dominant race, there might be a chance for the line of separation to disappear with the lapse of time. Marked as they are by a different complexion, and one which has long been accounted menial and debased, there is no little of truth in the sad refrain of their universal story, 'Niggers never can have a white man's chance here.' "

"But what can be done for their elevation and relief, or to prevent the establishment of a mediæval barbarism in our midst?" asked the doctor anxiously.

"Well, Doctor," said the Fool jocosely, "that question is for some one else to answer, and it must be answered in deeds, too, and not in words. I have given the years of my manhood to the consideration of these questions, and am accounted a fool in consequence. It seems to me that the cure for these evils is in a nutshell. The remedy, however, is one that must be applied from the outside. The sick man can not cure himself. The South will never purge itself of the evils which affect it. Its intellect, its pride, its wealth, in short, its power, is all arrayed against even the slow and tedious development which time and semi-barbarism would bring. Hour by hour, the chains will be riveted closer. Look at the history of slavery in our land! See how the law-makers, the courts, public sentiment, and all the power of the land, grew year by year more harsh and oppressive on the slave and his congener, the 'free person of color,' in all the slave States! I see you remember it, old friend. In direct conflict with all the predictions of statesmen, the thumb-screws of oppression were given a new and sharper turn with every passing year. The vestiges of liberty and right were shred away by legislative enactment, and the loop-holes of mercy closed by judicial construction, until only the black gulf of hopeless servitude remained."

"I see the prospect, and admit the truth of your prevision; but I do not get your idea of a remedy," said the elder man doubtfully.

"Well, you see that the remedy is not from within," said the Fool. "The minority knows its power, and the majority realizes its weakness so keenly as to render that impossible. That which has made bulldozing possible renders progress impossible. Then it seems to me that the question is already answered, — *It must be from without!*"

"But how?" queried the old man impatiently.

"How?" said the Fool. "I am amazed that you do not see; that the country will not see; or rather, that, seeing, they will let the ghost of a dogma, which rivers of blood have been shed to lay, frighten them from adopting the course which lies before us, broad and plain as the king's highway: *The remedy for darkness is light; for ignorance, knowledge; for wrong, righteousness.*"

"True enough as an abstraction, my friend; but how shall it be reduced to practice?" queried his listener.

"The Nation nourished and protected slavery. The fruitage of slavery has been the ignorant freedman, the ignorant poor-white man, and the arrogant master. The impotence of the freedman, the ignorance of the poor-white, the arrogance of the late master, are all the result of national power exercised in restraint of free thought, free labor, and free speech. Now, let the Nation undo the evil it has permitted and encouraged. Let it educate those whom it made ignorant, and protect those whom it made weak. It is not a matter of favor to the black, but of safety to the Nation. Make the spelling-book the scepter of national power. Let the Nation educate the colored man and the poor-white man *because* the Nation held them in bondage, and is responsible for their education; educate the voter *because* the Nation can not afford that he should be ignorant. Do not try to shuffle off the responsibility, nor cloak the danger. Honest ignorance in the masses is more to be dreaded than malevolent intelligence in the few. It furnished the rank and file of rebellion and the prejudice-blinded multitudes who made the Policy of Repression effectual. Poor-Whites, Freedmen, Ku-Klux, and Bulldozers are all alike the harvest of ignorance. The Nation can not afford to grow such a crop."

"But how," asked the doctor, "shall these citizens of the States be educated by the Government without infringement of the rights of the States?"

"Ah, my good old friend!" said Servosse, rising, and placing a hand upon the other's shoulder, "I will leave you, now that you have brought out for me to worship that Juggernaut of American politics by which so many hecatombs have been crushed and mangled. This demon required a million lives before he would permit slavery to be abolished: perhaps as many more would induce him to let the fettered souls be unbound and made free."

"You are bitter, my son," said the old man, rising also, and looking into his companion's eyes with a glance of calm reproof. "Do not indulge that spirit. Be patient, and remember that you would have felt just as we of your native North now feel, but for the glare of slumbering revolution in which you have lived. The man who has been in the crater ought not to wonder at his calmness who has only seen the smoke. I have often thought that St. Paul would have been more forbearing with his Jewish brethren if he had always kept in mind the miracle required for his own conversion."

"Perhaps you are right, Doctor," said the Fool; "but ought not something also be allowed to the zeal of the poor old Jonah who disturbed the slumbers of Nineveh? At any rate, I leave your question for the Wise Men to answer. I will only say two words about it. The South — that *pseudo* South which has the power — does not wish this thing to be done to her people, and will oppose it with might and main. If done at all, it must be done by the North — by the Nation moved, instigated, and controlled by the North, I mean — in its own self-defense. It must be an act of sovereignty, an exercise of power. The Nation expected the liberated slave to be an ally of freedom. It was altogether right and proper that it should desire and expect this. But it made the fatal mistake of expecting the freedman to do successful battle on his part of the line, without training or knowledge. This mistake must be remedied. As to the means, I feel sure that when the Nation has smarted enough for its folly, it will find a way to undo the evil, whether the State-Rights Moloch stand in the way, or not."

CHAPTER XLVI

HOME AT LAST

The year had nearly passed; and Comfort Servosse returned to Warrington a little in advance of the time set for his family to come, in order to see that the place was duly prepared for their reception.

He had been engaged by a company of capitalists to take charge of their interests in one of the republics of Central America. The work was of the most important character, not only to the parties having a pecuniary interest therein, but also as having a weighty bearing upon that strange contest between civilization and semi-barbarism which is constantly being waged in that wonderfully strange region, where Nature seems to have set her subtlest forces in battle-array against what, in these modern times, is denominated "progress." While the earth produces in an abundance unknown to other regions, the mind seems stricken with irresistible lassitude, and only the monitions of sense seem able to awaken the body from lethargic slumber.

The struggle suited his adventurous nature, and the enterprise afforded scope for his powers of projection and organization. He had returned only to fulfill the family compact, and meant, when the months of respite were over, to take back his household to a mountain villa in that land of the sun where the delights of nature are so sweetly blended, and incessantly varied, and its extremes so tempered by the concurring influences of wind and wave and mountain-heights, that the traveler wonders if the Fountain of Youth and the Aiden of sinless bliss are not yet to be found amid its enchantments.

On his return, he had to pass through that belt in the Southern States, where science is periodically called upon to wage unsuccessful warfare with that most inscrutable form of disease, that plague, which mocks at human skill. Two or three, upon whose brows the fell destroyer had already set his brazen seal, had been taken from the very train which brought him northward towards Warrington. He had wondered at the mystery before which science is as powerless as superstition, as he saw them borne from the train, which sped on its hurried way as if fleeing from the pestilence. He had seen, wondered, and swept on, thinking no more of the strange, sad fact of inexplicable doom.

It was the second morning after his return to Warrington. The day before, oppressed with the lassitude which always follows a long journey, he had wandered aimlessly about the familiar grounds. The colored people had gathered to welcome him, asking and answering a thousand interrogatories. In little groups of four and five they had dropped in on the way to church (for it was the Sabbath) and on their return. All day long he had been repeatedly called on to rack his memory in order to recognize some once familiar face. Andy and his good wife were in a seventh heaven of delight. Old Lollard had recognized his master's whistle, and stiff with age, and almost blind, had followed him with sad pertinacity from place to place in the grounds. The house, the library, the lawn, were alive with pleasant memories of the loved ones whom he was soon to meet. His old neighbors dropped in: Eyebright and Nelson; John Burleson, still clamorous and insubordinate; the irrepressible Vaughn, still vaporing and effusive, but kindly flavored at the core; Durfee and Dawson, and a hundred more, — came to shake his hand, and chat of that past which was full of the shades of others whom they would greet no more, and waken memories of those days when his heart-strings were bound so close around a grand idea, which had yielded, as it seemed, only a Sodom-like fruitage of ashen words.

The night had found him sad and weary, his heart full of

grateful tears for the pleasant greetings he had received, and fuller yet of tenderer tears for those whose greetings he had missed. He longed more than ever for the coming of his loved ones, and for the lapse of the brief period allotted for his stay amid the old familiar scenes. It was no longer home, but only the sepulcher of a dead past, whose joys had flitted with its sorrows, and brought but the sadness of the grave into his heart as they swept by in the funereal ghastliness of shadowy unreality.

When he woke in the morning, he felt a lethargic sensation, which he tried in vain to throw off. There were dull, heavy pains about the head, too, and sharp, shooting ones here and there in chest and limb. His feet dragged wearily. There was a burning sensation somewhere, he could not tell exactly where. He thought he would try a bath, and Andy prepared him one, — a great tub of the sparkling spring-water which used to be so grateful to his weary limbs, — ages ago, it seemed. He only dabbled in it with his hands and feet: the sun-burnished wavelets seemed full of barbed arrows to his strangely fevered flesh. When he dozed a little, the air seemed full of bright scintillating sparks.

Andy called in Dr. Gates, who happened to be passing.

"Good-morning, Colonel! Glad to see you," said the cheer-ful-minded physician, whose hair and beard Time had suc-ceeded in bleaching, but whose rotund form, keen eye, and bounding heart seemed to bid him an unceasing defiance. "Got you down at last, eh?" he continued jocularly. "I was afraid I should never get a chance at you. That constitution of yours is magnificent. Used to think you were made of whip-cord. Been to Central America, eh? Going back there? And Miss Lily and the Madam — where are they?"

Servosse answered dully and wearily. The doctor watched him keenly.

"Let me feel your pulse, please."

"Ah! a little feverish — considerably so. Bilious? No? Let me see your tongue. That will do. Where's that boy?"

The doctor went out upon the porch, and called, "Andy! O Andy! come here!" When the boy came, he asked him a great many questions. Then he went back, and examined his patient again very carefully. Then he recalled Andy, and said to him, —

"Andy, you think a good deal of the Colonel, don't you?"

"I should think I did, sir! More'n ub anybody else I ebber seed."

"Enough to stand by him, even at the risk of your life?"

Andy looked around at the bright sunshine, and thought of the wife, and three ebon-hued children who were sprawling about the kitchen.

"Because, if you don't," said the doctor, who had watched him keenly, "I must get some one else."

That settled it.

"Nobody else ain't gwine ter nuss de kunnel, dat's shore!" he said with emphasis. "I'll do it."

"The Colonel is going to be mighty sick, Andy, and the disease may be contagious, — catching, you know. I don't think there's very much danger; but he's got to have some one to stay right by him all the time."

"All right, Doctor, I'll do it," said the colored man promptly.

"Very well, Andy," said the Doctor. "I'll get some one to help you: but you must always be here; you mustn't leave the house. A heap depends on the nursing he gets, and you know there's none of his own folks here to take care of him."

"Nebber you mind, Doctor," said Andy. "Kunnel Servosse won't have no lack ub 'tention while dar's a colored man lives dat ebber seed his face. I can git plenty ub 'em to help me."

"But you must not leave the house."

"Don't want to. They'll come here."

"All right. I shall be out two or three times a day till it's over. Go and tell your wife; bid her not to trouble you, nor be alarmed."

"Don't you be afraid fer her, Doctor," said Andy stoutly: "she'd go jes' as fur ez I would ter sarve de Kunnel."

The colored man did as directed, and, returning to the room where Servosse lay, received minute directions as to his care. While the doctor was engaged in giving these, Servosse roused himself from the stupor into which he had fallen, and listened to the conversation between his physician and his nurse.

"You think me pretty sick, Doctor?" he asked presently.

"Pretty sick," answered the doctor sententiously, as he went on putting up his prescription.

"Very sick, perhaps, Doctor?"

"Well, yes, *very* sick, Colonel."

"What is the matter?"

"Well, you have some fever, you know."

"You are trying to deceive me, Doctor," said the patient. "Don't do it. I have heard and noted enough of what you have done and said since you have been here, to know that you consider the case a very serious one. Let me know now just how serious."

"I do not wish to alarm you needlessly, and the disease has not yet developed so that I can speak with certainty," replied the doctor.

"You are still evasive, Doctor," said Servosse. "Well, then, let me tell you what I think is your opinion. You think I have the *yellow-fever*."

"I can not deny, Colonel, that I have such a suspicion. You have just come through the infected belt, and your symptoms certainly do point that way. But then we are very often mistaken in those things. The symptoms of yellow-fever are not at first sufficiently distinctive to enable a physician who has not recently met it to pronounce with certainty in regard to it. Now, I haven't seen a case of yellow-fever in — let me

see — twenty years and better. And, for that matter, I hoped I
never should see another. But your case does look very like
what I remember of that. So far as concerns the technical
symptoms, those we find in the books, they are at first about
the same as other fevers of its class."

"I have no doubt your surmise is correct," answered Servosse calmly. "I remember now that two cases of the fever, or
what was said to be the fever, were taken off the train at
Meridien when I came through."

"Well," said the physician, "the best way is to treat it for
that, anyhow. There is a fair chance, even with Yellow Jack,
when one has your courage and constitutional stamina. We'll
do the best we can, Colonel, and I trust you may pull
through."

The doctor had completed his directions, and was about to
leave, when his patient said earnestly, —

"Doctor, you said just now that it was wise to treat this as
if you were sure of the worst. I think that is true for me too.
I ought to do as I would if I were sure of the worst. I have
not much to do, but I must do that now. How long before this
thing will be over — if — if you are correct?"

"Well," said the doctor, "in that case — well, the worst
ought to be over by, say, Saturday."

"Thank you, Doctor," said the patient solemnly. "Now, if
you will wait on the porch a little while? I am sorry to detain
you; but I must do a little writing, and wish you would stay
until it is done. Andy will wait on me," he added in reply to
a questioning look.

"Certainly, Colonel," answered the doctor; "and you had
better make all your arrangements for — well, for a long sickness, anyhow."

"I understand," said the patient quietly.

Nearly an hour passed by before the doctor was called in
again.

"My head is a little confused, Doctor," said the sick man;

"and I wish you would glance over this codicil which I have added to my will, just to see that it is properly expressed."

The doctor read it aloud.

"That will do," said Servosse: "I merely wished to leave some directions as to my burial, and so forth. I thought of it yesterday. I don't know why; but there came over me a sort of impression that I should not live long, and I thought, that, if I should die here, I would like to select my burial place, and prescribe the inscription on my tomb."

"But this — you are quite sure this is what you wish?" asked the doctor. "Your head is not" —

"Oh, yes! my head is all right," said the sick man with an amused smile. "You need not have any fear about that. I have said what I mean, and mean what I say. Then there is the little legacy to Andy and his heirs; that is, on condition that he nurse me through my last sickness. That is all right. Now, Doctor, I wish you and Andy to witness this will. I had always intended to leave it as a holograph; but it is perhaps as well to have it attested, under the circumstances."

The will was signed and witnessed; and then Servosse handed to the doctor a letter and a telegram, both directed to his wife.

"You will please send the telegram as soon as you return," he said. "Metta will start back in a day or two if you do not."

"You have not forbidden her coming?" asked the doctor in surprise.

"I tell her I shall not be ready to receive her before Saturday or Sunday," was the reply.

"But, Colonel, there is but little danger — very little."

"And they must not incur even that," said Servosse with decision.

"Really, Colonel," pleaded the physician, "I can not consent to doing as you wish. You know well enough that both your wife and daughter would be very willing to face any infection to serve you."

"And for that very reason must not be allowed to come here. Insensibility will come before they could arrive, and I am sure I shall be well taken care of. You and Andy will look out for that. I know it will seem cruel to them, but it is real mercy. You must promise me that you will send that, and nothing more."

"If you fully desire it, I can do nothing less," responded the doctor with hesitation.

"Thank you, Doctor. And this letter, please keep it, until — until you know the result, and then send or deliver it to — to Metta." His voice choked, and he seemed about to lose his self-control. "You will tell them, Doctor, that it was my love which was unkind. It's hard — hard. If I could only see their faces once more! Tell them how I loved them in this — this" —

"Oh, you must not give way!" cried the doctor, with a professional endeavor at encouragement. "We shall have you all right soon."

"Tell them — what I can not say, Doctor — if I should never see them again."

"All right," said the doctor, wringing his hand. "I will do all you say."

"And, Doctor," — detaining him still, — "my old friends and — and acquaintances. I would like you to say I have no ill-will. I was no doubt mistaken; perhaps I was too — too intense in my notions: but I hated no man, Doctor, and injured no man knowingly. If any feel that I have wronged them — in any manner, perhaps they will forgive me: I hope so, at least. I wish that you would say so to — to — any who may ask for me."

"I am sure, Colonel," said the doctor with emotion, "there is no one who harbors any resentment towards you. You were counted a hard hitter and a hot opponent; but no one ever thought you held spite, or harbored malice against you personally."

"I hope not — I hope not," — said the Fool. "I would have been glad to see more of those I knew; but I hope they will think kindly of me — as kindly as I do of them. That's all I ask."

With these words in his ears, the doctor rode back to Verdenton, and made report of his condition. The little town had its share of those modern Athenians whose only business was to hear and to tell some new thing; so that in an hour it was reported all over its streets that the owner of Warrington had returned, and was prostrate with the dreaded disease. Little fear was then entertained of isolated cases occurring in regions not subject to the ravages of the plague, which was then thought to be comparatively innocuous beyond certain limits of latitude, elevation, and temperature.

It was wonderful to note, however, how quickly the thought of disease or death eradicated all thought of hostility from the minds of those who had been the most avowed enemies. That most beautiful phase of the Southern character was never more nobly displayed. All were ready and anxious to do something for the relief of the lonely sufferer.

"Colonel Servosse sick!" cried Vaughn, riding up to where the doctor stood talking with others. "I declare, it's too bad! Just come back from Mexico, too, or somewhere down that way. Was out to see him yesterday. Hasn't seen his wife and daughter in six months, and now has got the fever! Too bad, I swear! Look here, men, we must go out and see him, and take care of him! Just think of it! He's there sick, and all alone 'cept for the niggers! He was a good fellow, Servosse was, after all, a good fellow! I don't believe he ever had any spite. He was full of notions and ideas, and was always making everybody a present of them, whether they agreed with him or not. Some of 'em wa'n't so bad notions, either, come to

look back at 'em! We must organize a committee and take
care of him, gentlemen. 'Twon't do to leave him in that condition — not a minute. I'm going right out as soon as I can
get a buggy now. Who'll go along with me, and take the
first watch?"

"I will," said a voice behind him.

Vaughn turned, and exclaimed in surprise, —

"What, is it you, General Gurney? Well, I declare, you
surprised me! I'm sure I shall be honored with your company.
I'm glad you're going too. 'Twill do Servosse good. — Don't
you think it will, Doctor?"

In reply, the doctor told what Servosse had said about his
old acquaintances, and how he would not let him send for
his wife and daughter, though he had assured him that the
danger would not be great.

"So he was going to tough it out alone, was he?" said
Vaughn. "He can't do that around Verdenton, if he *is* a
carpet-bagger. Confound him! if he hadn't been so radical,
he would have known that. — Here, you boy!" calling to a
colored man who was listening to the conversation with great
interest, — "take my horse home, and put him on the buggy,
so that General Gurney and I can go out and see after Colonel
Servosse. D'ye know he'd got the yellow-fever? Hurry up,
you rascal, or the damned Radical will die before we get there.
We oughtn't to go near him at all, just to pay him for taking
up with you niggers; but we ain't that kind of folks. We'll
see him through it, or give him a fair send off, if he did try to
put you all over the white folks' heads."

As usual, Vaughn but echoed the general voice, — in a
rough, loud manner, it is true, but with a sincerity of kindness
to those suffering affliction which is a most noticeable characteristic of the Southern people. Scarcely one of those who had
so bitterly denounced and recklessly defamed the Fool in
former days, perhaps not one of those who had voted to

take his life by unlawful and barbarous violence, would have
hesitated to watch over him with the tenderest care in sickness, to have shown every favor to his family in consequent
bereavement, or to have attended his interment with decorous
and sympathizing solemnity and punctiliousness. No words
can overdraw the beautiful kindness and tenderness of the
Southern people in this respect.

While they waited, General Gurney, who seemed to be
affected by some unusual emotion, after some further conversation with the physician, said, half to himself as he stepped
into the telegraph-office, —

"I will do it. It may be too late but I will do it."

Then he wrote a telegram which read thus: —

"MELVILLE GURNEY, — Bring Mrs. Servosse and Lily without delay. Tell Lily it is my request.

"MARION GURNEY."

When they arrived at Warrington, they found the ever
ready Burleson already installed at the bedside; but it was
already too late for the Fool to realize and appreciate the kindness that flowed in upon him from all sides. The neighbors
who came and went received from him but dull, vacant
glances, and heard only the rambling, half-incoherent words
of love and longing which his fevered lips uttered to the dear
ones whom he imagined at his bedside. The flowers which
fair hands culled and arranged to charm his eye, the delicacies
which were sent in lavish abundance to coax his palate, were
unheeded by the sufferer, who was alone with his pain and
his doom. The faithful Andy was the only one he recognized;
for only that was true to him which had been before the full
light of reason was obscured by the clouds of disease. Once
or twice, it was true, General Gurney, who was unremitting
in his attention, heard his name muttered, and thought himself recognized; but, instead, he always found, when he lis-

tened more closely, that the wandering intellect was running upon Lily and his son.

On Wednesday appeared the *Verdenton Gazette*, and in it was the following: —

"We are pained to announce that Colonel Servosse, who returned to his home on Saturday last for a brief sojourn, is prostrated with the fever which is now making fearful ravages in the adjoining States. Notwithstanding the infectious character of the disease, scores of our best citizens have volunteered to attend upon him; and hundreds have called, and otherwise testified their sympathy and kindness. His family have been telegraphed for, but little hope is entertained of their arrival before his death. He has been delirious almost from the first, and his physicians consider it barely possible that he should recover.

"Colonel Servosse removed to this county from the State of Michigan immediately after the war, and has resided here constantly until about a year since. He was an active and able political leader, and was instrumental in molding and shaping legislation under the Reconstruction measures to a very great extent. Naturally, he was the mark for very bitter political attack, and was for a time, no doubt, greatly misrepresented. That he was a man of marked ability is now universally admitted, and it is generally conceded that he was thoroughly honest in the views which he entertained. Personally, he was a man of fine qualities, who made many and fast friends. He is not thought to have been capable of deliberate and persistent malice; but his audacious and unsparing ridicule of the men and measures he opposed prevented many of his opponents from appreciating the other valuable and attractive elements of his character. Whatever may have been their past relations, however, our citizens will be sincerely sorry to learn of his death."

The wife and daughter read this, copied into a Northern

journal, as they hurried southward, the day after its publication.

On the evening of that day a vast concourse gathered beneath the oaks of Warrington to do the last honors to its master. There were grave, solemn-faced men who had been his friends, and others who had been enemies, who stood side by side around the open grave under the noblest of the trees which he had loved. Beyond these there was a dark, sobbing circle, — men, women, and children, — who wept and groaned as the clods fell upon the coffin of one whom they had so long trusted and revered.

Yet bitterer tears fell on the fresh, red mound upon the morrow; and then the sun shone, the birds sang, the bright creek babbled by, and the dead slept in peace. Time smiled grimly as he traced anew the unsolved problem which had mocked the Fool's heart.

CHAPTER XLVII

MONUMENTUM

GRASS had grown above the grave. A covered wagon stopped before the grounds, and a jean-clad countryman, descending therefrom, led a little boy seriously and reverently to the railed inclosure.

"There, son," said David Nelson, as he pointed through the railing at the tombstone, "is where they laid away our Carpet-Bagger. You remember him, I reckon: he staid at our house one night, two or three years ago, — Colonel Servosse. He was too earnest a man to have much comfort here, though. I want you should remember his grave; for he was a powerful good friend to your father, and the common people like him. He come from the North right after the war, an' went in with us Union men and the niggers to try and make this a free country accordin' to Northern notions. It was a grand idee; but there wa'n't material enough to build of, on hand here at that time. There was a good foundation laid, and some time it may be finished off; but not in my day, son, — not in my day. Colonel Servosse always felt as if somebody had made a mess of it, and said the fault wasn't half of it with them it was laid on, here at the South, but was mainly with the master workmen at the North, who would insist on the tale of bricks without furnishin' any straw. The failure of what we called Reconstruction hurt him mighty bad, an', to my mind, hed more ter du with takin' him off than the fever. That's why he hed that line put on his tombstone. What is it? Let me git out my glasses, child, and I'll read it for ye: —

'He followed the counsel of the Wise,
And became a Fool thereby.'

What does it mean? I'm not jest sure that I rightly know, son; but it was one of his notions that he'd been fooled, along with the rest of us, by tryin' to work up to the marks of men that only half-knew what sort of a job they were layin' out. He was a good man, according to my notion, and an earnest one; but — somehow it seemed as if his ideas wa'n't calkilated for this meridian. It mout hev been better for us, in the end, if they hed been."